STRESS AND SATISFACTION
ON THE JOB

STRESS AND SATISFACTION ON THE JOB

Work Meanings and
Coping of
Mid-Career Men

Patricia E. Benner

PRAEGER

PRAEGER SPECIAL STUDIES • PRAEGER SCIENTIFIC

New York • Philadelphia • Eastbourne, UK
Toronto • Hong Kong • Tokyo • Sydney

Library of Congress Cataloging in Publication Data

Benner, Patricia E.
    Stress and satisfaction on the job.

        Bibliography: p. 187
        Includes index.
        1. Job stress--Case studies. 2. Job staisfaction--
Case studies. 3. Employment of men--Case studies.
4. Adjustment (Psychology)--Case studies. I. Title.
HF5548.85.B46 1984   158.7   84-3252
ISBN 0-03-063839-9 (alk. paper)

Support for this book was provided in part by
a grant from the National Institute on Aging,
Grant #AG 00002.

Published in 1984 by Praeger Publishers
CBS Educational and Professional Publishing
a Division of CBS Inc.
521 Fifth Avenue, New York, NY 10175 USA

© 1984 by Praeger Publishers

456789 052 987654321

Printed in the United States of America
on acid-free paper

To Richard, John, and Lindsay

FOREWORD

Dr. Benner's insightful and useful book on work stress grew out of a quest to study the person in the situation. It was part of a larger research project under my direction begun in 1977 on stress and coping and aging supported by the National Institute on Aging. The project also represents my debut in field research after a long career as an experimenter.

It was my great fortune to have collected around me in this effort a diverse and talented group of which Patricia Benner was then a doctoral student. This conclave of people, which changed in size and personnel over the years as people left for professional positions, became the Berkeley Stress and Coping Project. We had been seeking new methods to overcome the difficulties of studying person variables and situation variables separately and then trying to bring the two back together into their context by statistical interactional procedures. We wanted to put methodological vigor behind the notion that the person both changes and is changed by the situation and to study the dynamic relationship between the person and the situation.

From the start, the work on this field study was divided into two general approaches. On the one hand, we examined quantified measures and scales leading to a number of publications on stress measures such as daily hassles and health outcomes, the assessment of coping, and the conceptual issues involved in them. On the other hand, we performed in-depth assessments and analyses of senistructured, open-ended interview data.

Dr. Benner was active in the project from the start, and along with a few other advanced students gave much of her attention to the interview material. This reflected her strong interest in finding a way to account for the role of taken-for-granted meanings in stress and coping. In this work she pursues the methods of interpretive social science and seeks understanding rather than prediction and control. What emerges is a stunning example of how intelligent and creative handling of such material—with all of its inherent hazards—can reveal what other, more objective measurement procedures cannot about the psychodynamics of stress and coping.

Dr. Benner's concerns in this book center on the meanings and experience of work in middle-aged subjects, more particularly among the males for whom work is so central in their lives. Although there is growing interest in work as a source of stress and satisfaction, little attention has been given to the diverse meanings given to work by different persons and how these mesh with stress and coping processes. These meanings vary from viewing work as a basis of one's worth, as a coping resource, as demeaning, as a rut from which one must escape to find new horizons, as a condition of life that one must control and make predictable, as a meaningful and satisfying experience, and as life itself.

The study of meaning-centered definitions of work flows easily from the theoretical perspective of the larger Stress and Coping Project in which people are said to construe, interpret, or appraise the impact of life encounters on their well-being. To the extent that what people want and how they view themselves varies, their emotional life also will vary predictably. Therefore, to understand work stress in any individual depends on the meanings inherent in work for that individual and how problems stemming from personal agendas and conditions at work are managed. Dr. Benner provides a revealing look at the work experiences of 23 men from this perspective. The men range in age from 45 to 54. They were interviewed once a month for one year to explore stressful experiences at work and patterns of coping.

What is unique in this study is the grouping of subjects on the basis of common ways in which they interpret the place of work in their lives. This corrects the narrow view that work is necessarily alienating and inherently threatening, and therefore stressful. Some people thrive on work and work can serve as a positive coping resource. In the accounts of the coping and emotion episodes of these participants, Dr. Benner reveals that work can become easier over time and that a "cushion of experience" can sometimes be gained as a coping resource or be blocked by personal or situational characteristics.

Dr. Benner's research also has important implications for stress management programs and particularly for cardiac rehabilitation programs. For example, it is questionable whether people who have suffered heart attacks should automatically change jobs, since their work, though stressful, may serve as a major coping resource that is not easily replaced. Changing jobs without a change in work meanings may only increase work stress. Dr. Benner's analyses point to promising possibilities for changing work meanings that are inherently stressful. Different work meanings breed different work stresses. Thus, distancing and strategies for increasing a sense of personal control—often recommended for the overextended, overinvolved worker—will not benefit the depressed person whose work is meaningless and who is bereft of coping resources.

This book is innovative in its attempt to capture the processes of stress and coping and in its interpretation of work meanings embedded in actual coping and work episodes over the course of a year in a sample of adequately functioning middle-aged men living in the community. It offers a fresh perspective to the field of work stress and coping that will be of great interest to researchers, clinicians, organizational psychologists, and managers. Unlike more statistically focused survey studies, it provides rich descriptive accounts of stressful work experiences that are engaging to read and relate to.

Richard S. Lazarus, Ph.D.
Professor, Department of Psychology
University of California, Berkeley

ACKNOWLEDGMENTS

This project spans six years and I am indebted to many who have contributed to this work on many different levels. I cannot acknowledge nor adequately repay everyone who has contributed so generously during this time, but a few words of acknowledgment and gratitude are in order.

Richard Lazarus opened the way to do a descriptive, phenomenological study of stress and coping. For his direction, encouragement, and scholarliness I am most grateful. Hubert L. Dreyfus contributed much to the methodology and theoretical base through his critique and through his masterful teaching of Heidegger, Kierkegaard, and hermeneutical strategies for human science. Jane Rubin, colleague and Kierkegaard scholar, provided the background for understanding the relationship between coping and personal meanings. Judith Wrubel provided expert tutoring in interpretive methodology and many productive dialogues on the case studies and early drafts. I am also grateful to Judith Wrubel, Gloria Golden, and Catherine Schaefer for their expert validation of selected case studies. Dr. Shirley Chater and Dr. James Stone provided thoughtful reading and comments.

My husband and colleague, Dr. Richard Benner, provided intellectual, social, emotional, and tangible support throughout this endeavor. Other major sources of support came from my parents and from Harry and Irene Duke. They all provided just the right amount of friendly prodding and questioning. I especially appreciate all the hours Harry Duke gave to the proofreading of the final draft. Finally, I am grateful for Abigail Shaw's intelligent and cheerful editorial help.

To all these and many more who remain unnamed, I say thank you.

CONTENTS

1

THE RELATIONSHIP BETWEEN WORK STRESS, COPING, AND HEALTH

This book examines patterns of work-related stress. The study is especially interested in how a person's perception of the meaning of his work affects his reaction to stress. The study seeks to show that these meanings determine a person's perception of a stressful episode and his subsequent response or coping options.

This study's methods and instruments were framed according to the Lazarus Stress and Coping Paradigm (1981; Lazarus and Launier, 1978), which defines stress as any event that taxes or exceeds normal adaptive resources. A potentially stressful incident causes a physiological response when the person perceives the event as threatening or harmful. The physiological response to stress reflects a person's emotional and intellectual response as well. Thus these perceptions and interpretations mediate the person's response to stressful incidents. Stressful incidents may originate in the psychological, physiological, or social realms, but stress responses are triggered through the person's perceptions and interpretation of the event. For example, sales meetings are extremely stressful for one of the participants even though he is a top salesman and has been attending sales meetings for over 20 years. Prior to the meetings he spends sleepless nights and worries about how his superiors will judge him. Sales meetings mean that he may be judged and found wanting.

The particular notion of meanings used in this study comes from the work of Heidegger (1962). His view of the person departs from other Western thinkers by asserting that the background of cultural practices and meanings can never be made completely explicit. A person participates in meanings through his cultural practices without being able to verbalize those meanings clearly or completely. There-

1

fore, participating in certain skills and activities can evoke emotional responses that are based on unarticulated meanings inherent in the activity itself. A person may take up cultural meanings that are embedded in the particular skills and practices of his work without ever being aware of those meanings. Because meanings are inherent in work skills and practices, they are best studied by examining actual events at work.

According to Heidegger, the meaning of an event refers to its significance. Its meaning is already present in the person's practices, emotions, skills, expectations, commitments, and beliefs. People inherit meanings through their culture, their language, and practices. Meanings are not freely chosen. They are given. Meanings reside in skills and practices and not solely in concepts. Thus a person can have an emotional response to an event without being able to conceptualize or even explain the meanings responsible for his emotion. Individuals can never stand outside their cultural heritage and personal history and choose what is meaningful. Events are meaningful because an individual's cultural heritage and personal history acts like a perceptual lens. Background meanings are invisible to the person because they are deeply held and pervasive, not because they are esoteric. They determine what is experienced as stressful, and what coping options are available to the person.

If people did not have a background of meaning to support their action, they would not be able to make decisions and act in an uncomplicated, smooth fashion. Even their smallest actions would require effort. Background meanings show up in daily activities, practices, skills, choices, and, thus, in stress and coping episodes. Cross-cultural experiences show that when a person's background meanings are changed or lost, he perceives more and different events as stressful and his coping options are changed. For example, when people try to conduct social interactions and achieve goals in a foreign culture they make errors, experience anger, surprise, and disappointment because things do not go according to their expectation. The errors and surprises display some of the usually taken-for-granted background meanings. They experience "culture shock" (Oberg, 1960). If they remain in a foreign culture for a long time, they experience culture fatigue, which comes from having constantly to make decisions about how to act or respond in situations that are ordinarily taken for granted or automatic. College graduates face a similar cultural disorientation when they switch from the subculture of school to that of work. The new graduate's school-bred assumptions and expectations do not match those of the workplace and they consequently experience surprise and conflict (Kramer, 1974; Hall, 1976).

The consciousness raising of the 1970s provides a less extreme example of changes in background meanings and practices. Consciousness raising is possible only when there is a shift in taken-for-granted background meanings so that a portion of background meaning is challenged. What was once invisible to the person engaged in consciousness raising now becomes visible, challenged, and open to change. The process can go forward because a large body of unchallenged assumptions and practices remain as they were. These unchallenged assumptions and background meanings allow the areas of one's life unaffected by the consciousness-raising efforts to continue to function smoothly. Yankelovich (1981, p. 97) provides an example of changes in background meaning in survey and interview responses. He notes that some women in the 1950s found questions about why they wanted to get married and have children meaningless and unanswerable. One young woman answered sarcastically: "Why do you put your pants on in the morning? Why do you walk on two feet instead of one?"

Some changes in background meaning are pervasive, such as those experienced by survivors of the Nazi holocaust or in rapid cultural disruption, as in the case of war, famine, or the displacement of an entire cultural group. These changes are irrevocable and have long-term stress and coping consequences that appear in higher morbidity and mortality rates in these populations (Benner, Roskies, and Lazarus, 1980; Antonovsky, 1980).

Other examples of the relationship between background meanings and stress and coping are more common and less extreme. People who suffer from "meaninglessness" temporarily are said to be "burned out." Their meanings have gone "flat" on them. Tasks that once seemed important no longer seem worth doing. The person who has lost deeply held commitments (that is, personal meanings) feels depressed (Klinger, 1975; Wrubel, Benner, and Lazarus, 1981). The person who has lost many of his culturally shared meanings suffers from nihilism and anomie (see H. L. Dreyfus, 1980). Nihilism, in turn, inhibits personal commitments (that is, personally held meanings).

THE LAZARUS STRESS AND COPING PARADIGM

Thus, background meanings determine whether an event is perceived as stressful. Under the Lazarus Stress and Coping Paradigm the perception and interpretation of potentially stressful events are called cognitive appraisal processes (Lazarus, 1981; Lazarus and Launier, 1978). Though this appraisal has been called "cognitive appraisal," it is not the cognitive appraisal of the information-processing model (Folkman, Schaefer, and Lazarus, 1979). The information-processing model views the mind as a computer and assumes that meanings can be built up from context-free, isolated bits of information (see H. L. Dreyfus, 1979, for a critique of this model). As noted above, this present study views meaning as a preexistent whole that is greater and different than the sum of the parts. Thus, cognitive appraisals are not necessarily deliberative because they are always somewhat based on a background of personally and culturally held meanings that cannot be made explicit.

In keeping with this contextual nature of meanings, Lazarus (1981) views stress and coping as transactional variables so that stress and coping appraisals neither reside solely within the person nor the situation. The terms "stress" and "coping" as transactional variables refer to the dynamic relationship between the person and his situation. Three tenets of transactionalism, originally proposed by Dewey and Bentley (1949) and outlined by Pervir and Lewis (1978), central to this position are:

1. No part of the system is independent of the other parts of the system or of the system as a whole.

2. All parts of the system have a constant reciprocal relationship; one part does not simply act on another part.

3. Action in any part of the system has consequences for other parts of the system.

Whether considered when they are isolated, or considered separately when they are together, neither the person nor the situation is the same entity as when each is considered relative to the other, as in a transactional relationship. This was exemplified by the Kohn and Schooler (1978) study of the reciprocal relationship between work complexity and intelligence (see pp. 36-37). A particularly stressful relationship is itself laden with meanings and intentions that alter the way both the situation and the person are influenced. Coping cannot be studied statistically as an isolated response generated by a specific stimulus situation. Such stimulus-response units can be isolated for observation and analysis; but to accept such small units of analysis as anything more than a convenient methodological technique ignores the practices, meanings, and commitments that the individual brings from previous experience to any new event. An excessively narrow scope of analysis also ignores the way coping is continuously modified by demands, resources, and constraints in the situation. Thus, in order to consider the dynamic relationship of the person in the situation, stress and coping must be considered from a transactional standpoint. This means that efforts to increase the effectiveness with which people cope, or to build coping competence, cannot act exclusively on the person or on the environment, but must consider both as interdependent factors.

This study interprets personal and cultural meanings of work shown in specific coping and emotion episodes related to work. This

synthetic, interpretive approach best captures the transactional relationship between the person and the situation because it depends upon
and maintains the context of the episode. Interpretation is synthetic
instead of analytical. An analytical approach isolates and "decontex-
tualizes" elements in a situation, while an interpretive strategy
synthesizes as many aspects as possible into a meaningful whole.
The interpreter seeks the best interpretation based upon the available
information about the person and the situation. In this study, the interviewers were trained to solicit full descriptions of coping and emotion
episodes selected by the participants so that the context and content
of the episodes were available to the interpreter. Participants were
encouraged to tell their story as naturally and as fully as possible.

This study's naturalistic focus follows Lazarus's (1981; Lazarus
and Cohen, 1976) recent shift from an experimental approach to a
field approach. This shift, at its heart, emphasizes naturalism instead of experimentalism. The questions are descriptive and ecolog-
ical, but also interpretive. Lazarus (1981) points out that "we still
do not know the stressors ordinary people or special subgroups face,
their daily hassles, sources of positive feeling or their patterns of
daily emotional response."

Clearly Lazarus is not calling for superficial description, or
a simple catalog of behaviors. His question about the potential importance of a broken shoe lace evidences his interest in a person's interpretation of an event that is described in the following poem by
Charles Bukowski:

> It's not the large things that
> send a man to the madhouse . . .
> No, it's the continuing series of
> small tragedies that send a man
> to the madhouse . . .
> not the death of his love
> but a shoelace that snaps
> with no time left . . .

Lazarus (1981, p. 184) points out the symbolic nature of the
episode described above:

> Although I believe it is true that people can be distressed
> over what seem at the moment to be trivialities, they are
> not really trivial at all in meaning, since they symbolize
> things that are very important to the person. The shoelace
> might break, but a major part of the psychological stress
> created thereby is the implication that one cannot control
> one's life in the face of the most stupid of trivialities, or

even worse, that one's own inadequacies have made the obstacle occur in the first place. This is what brings the powerful and pathogenic message that breaks one's morale. In any case, how is one to evaluate such a momentous issue in the traditional style of laboratory stress research? No way.

Thus, Lazarus's paradigm of stress and coping includes the symbolic nature of stressful events and seeks to interpret that symbolism. Lazarus calls the interpetive process in which the person engages "cognitive appraisal." This appraisal is always transactional because it is fused with the situation and with the situation's meaning for the person. Typically the appraisal is "hot" and does not involve conceptual clarity or even awareness (Lazarus and McCleary, 1951). As noted earlier, this is not the cognitive appraisal of information-processing theory.

As an interpretive process, appraisal constantly fluctuates, so its study must be process-oriented. For study purposes, Lazarus (1981; Lazarus and Launier, 1978) divides appraisal processes into primary and secondary appraisals. Primary appraisal refers to whether the event is perceived as irrelevant, benign-positive, or stressful. If the event is perceived as irrelevant or benign-positive, then normal adaptive functioning or understanding continues and coping efforts are not required. If the event is perceived as stressful, then its meaning can be categorized into harm/loss, threat, or challenge.

The secondary appraisal is the person's sense of resources, possibilities, and constraints. It represents the way a person copes with a stressful event and includes the person's decisions, actions, interpretations, and search for help. Lazarus (1981) identifies four major modes of coping. The first mode, information seeking, may bring about some action or reappraisal of the harm, threat, or challenge. In the second mode, direct action, one may change the environment or oneself in order to undo the injury, prevent the harm, or meet the challenge. In the third mode, inhibition of action, the person resists action because it is poorly grounded, dangerous, embarrassing, or morally reprehensible. Finally, there is a complex class of intrapsychic forms of coping, called cognitive coping. When people engage in cognitive coping, they manipulate their own attention or interpret events differently so that the original sense of injury or threat is reduced.

In earlier studies, Lazarus and his colleagues referred to cognitive coping as "palliation" because such self-generated cognitive coping makes the person feel better about things even though the objective situation may not have changed. Cognitive coping includes denial, avoidance, intellectualized detachment, as well as interpretive efforts. The modes of coping provide the broad classification of coping strategies that will be used in this study. They provide a more balanced view of a broad range of coping activity. In the past, psychologists have attended to cognitive coping to the exclusion of information search, direct action, and inhibition of action.

These structural distinctions are useful for study purposes but they do not represent the lived experience of stressful transactions. Because stress and coping are dynamic and open to change, a reappraisal of the stuation may occur at any point in the coping process, which would cause the sense of threat or challenge to change. The lived experience occurs rapidly and changes quickly. Typically the person does not make clear conceptual distinctions about the event as it unfolds. However, these distinctions allow the interpreter to consider stress and coping processes over time and to examine the relationship between stress and coping.

MEANINGS OF WORK AND WORK INVOLVEMENT

Appraisal processes determine whether the person experiences stress, and appraisal processes are shaped by the person's cultural and personal meanings, their commitments and their beliefs (Lazarus, 1978; Wrubel, Benner, and Lazarus, 1981; Lazarus, 1966). Thus appraisal processes cannot be understood outside the event's context and the person's particular history. The appraisal process cannot be studied by listing relevant situation or personality variables out of context. A transactional variable is not merely additive; it does not represent personality characteristics plus situation characteristics. Nor is a transactional variable even an independent interaction whose effects can be independently measured (see Pervin and Lewis, 1978). Thus, instead of analyzing situation characteristics and person characteristics separately and then recombining them, this study examined two relevant transactional variables: the meanings of work and involvement with work.

Work meanings and work involvement were studied over the course of a year. The participants' past work meanings and work involvement were assessed through the Cantril Ladder of Concerns (Cantril and Roll, 1971) and the Work, Life Review, and Aging Interview. Work involvement refers to how much time work consumes and how important work is when compared to other concerns. This study expected to find patterns of meanings shared among participants because they share a common cultural heritage. Personal meanings based on personal commitments and particular life histories will show up in the interviews because relevant past experiences and commitments were systematically sought in the interviews.

The Lazarus Stress and Coping Paradigm provided a framework for designing the research interviews and for interpreting them. This interpretive framework made it possible to study the actual content and nature of stressful events and strong emotions described by participants without unduly predetermining or prescribing the response categories. This paradigm neither predicted specific content of stressful episodes nor made predictions about the relative merits of various coping strategies. It permits the identification of effective and ineffective coping efforts. Unlike other theories this paradigm does not assume that the worker is alienated, though this paradigm does not overlook the possibility of alienation from work. Thus, this paradigm could consider a full range of positive and negative emotions and a full range of coping episodes described by the participants. The paradigm predicts that the context of events can be as important as the specific content or the nature of the event.

In sum, the Lazarus Stress and Coping Paradigm, when used as an interpretive framework, overcomes the problem of "mentalism." Mentalism causes the researcher to overlook the demands, resources, and constraints of the actual situation by locating all causal forces within the person. This paradigm also overcomes the behaviorist problem that ignores the volition of the person and locates all influence externally. An interpretive approach such as this one permits the investigator to identify meanings without decontextualizing them or transforming them into theory-laden variables that would destroy the meanings of the situation for the person. For example, theoretical variables such as dependence/independence needs may be relevant but may actually cloud the meanings inherent in a particular situation. Once an event is described in terms of psychological needs, it is difficult to recapture the meanings of the situation.

Thus, the method used is interpretive and the Lazarus Stress and Coping Paradigm is the interpretive framework. Coping and emotion episodes from work provide the text analog. The particular interpretive strategy used is based upon the work of Heidegger (1962) and Taylor (1971) and is described further in Chapter 2.

STRESS AND COPING PROCESSES

Although stress is increasingly understood as a complex process, few studies systematically describe the relationship between stress and coping processes. Typically stress and coping are conceptualized as separate, distinct processes. Most research ignores the context of stress and coping. Consequently popular writers recommend conflicting techniques for coping with work stress because they fail to match the advice with appropriate person and situation characteristics (Burke and Weir, 1980). When the context of stress and coping is ignored, the relationship between stress and coping is also lost. This study attends to the context of examining the meaning of specific stress and coping episodes for the person in the situation. A better understanding of the context of stress and coping is needed to improve stress prevention and management programs. To this end, a number of recent studies have called attention to this need for descriptive studies of coping processes (Roskies and Lazarus, 1980; Dewe, Guest, and Williams, 1978; Kobasa, 1979; Folkman, 1979). In this study, a phenomenological method of inquiry is used to study stress and coping processes related to work over the period of a year based upon 12 monthly in-depth interviews. The participants are 23 men from the ages of 45 to 54. All are employed full time or are seeking full-time employment. The study focused on discovery rather than verification and was guided by the following question: What is the relationship between work meanings and involvement and stress and coping at work?

THE NATURE OF STRESS AND COPING: THE EFFECTS ON HEALTH

A growing body of research links health and longevity with the absence of work stress and the presence of work satisfaction. For example, in a 15-year longitudinal study of aging, the strongest predictor of longevity was work satisfaction (Palmore, 1969). Increasingly social scientists cite the workplace as a point of health promotion (Task Force Report, 1973; Brennan, 1981). Employers are beginning to see merit in health promotion programs, partly for humanitarian, altruistic reasons and partly because the costs associated with disability, death, and rehabilitation are so high (Brennan, 1981). Adults spend about 40 percent of their waking life at work, therefore work is a prime target for health promotion (see also Ashord, 1976; House and Jackman, 1981). The estimates of the costs of work stress are extremely high. For example, Greenwood (1977) estimated that the annual cost of executive stress is between $10 and $20 billion annually. This is a conservative estimate based upon lost work days, hospitalization, outpatient care, and mortality of executives. Regardless of the costs, most researchers agree that lack of stress management leads to a poor quality of life and to poor health.

Occupational stress research is necessarily multidisciplinary. It is studied by epidemiologists (see review by Kasl, 1978), organizational sociologists, social psychologists, psychologists, occupational health workers, and by those interested in adult development and aging. The largest body of systematic research in stress and coping at work has come from social psychologists and has been based upon role theory (Kahn et al., 1964; French and Caplan, 1972; Beehr, Walsh, and Taber, 1976). Recently researchers have recommended that this perspective be broadened (Cooper and Marshall 1976; David-son and Cooper, 1981; Love and Beehr, 1981).

Cooper and Marshall (1976) call for a multidisciplinary approach to the study of stress in the work environment and acknowledge that stressors in the home and social environment can affect the individual in the work environment and vice versa. Davidson and Cooper (1981, p. 64) list potential stressors in three major life arenas: "1. The home environment, (e.g.) marital satisfaction, financial concerns; 2. The social environment, (e.g.) social activities and relationships, urban versus rural living; and 3. Individual differences and determinants, (e.g.) personality, life history and events, Type A coronary-prone behavior patterns." These researchers' (Copper and Marshall, 1976; Davidson and Cooper, 1981) analyses of sources and consequences of stress drawn from the current research on work stress and coping emphasize the interdependent nature of stress in that stress in one arena affects others.

A number of researchers including Lazarus (1966, 1981; Pearlin et al., 1981) view stress as a process. They too agree that the stress process is highly interactive and cannot be studied adequately when work is compartmentalized or limited to the work arena alone. Stress experienced at work affects one's homelife and influences other areas of life outside of work (Sarason, 1977; Feather, 1975).

Epidemiological studies linking differential morbidity and mortal-ity rates with different occupations and with different work stresses (Kasl, 1978) provide an impetus for descriptive and interpretive studies that explain why this is so. The fact that different occupations and different roles within occupations have differential morbidity and mortality rates lends credence to the causal link between work charac-teristics and health. For example, Guralnick (1963, as cited by Kasl, 1978) found that the mortality rates due to arteriosclerotic heart disease among different occupations is much lower for certain occu-pation groups (for example, college presidents, professors, instruc-tors, teachers) and much higher than expected for others (for example, lawyers and judges; physicians and surgeons; pharmacists; insurance agents and brokers; real estate agents and brokers). Kasl (1978) rea-sons that since the differences in Guralnick's study were quite large (about two to one), and since they involve groups with comparable social status, level of physical activity, and physical hazards in the workplace, differential job "stresses" may be involved. However, these correlational studies do not explain why lawyers and judges should suffer more from occupational stress than college presidents and professors.

The differences in morbidity and mortality indicate that the content and characteristics of the job are significant in health and ill-ness patterns. But equally interesting is the fact that within the same

occupation, persons are affected differently. This observation has
led to a search for different person and situation characteristics that
could explain the differences. Typically the search has consisted of
looking for causal stressors, for example, role conflict, role overload,
noise, poor pacing, and so on; strains or outcomes, both in terms of
mental and physical health characteristics; protective resources, for
example, social supports, coping; and stressful and protective personality characteristics.

THE INFLUENCE OF SOCIAL SUPPORT

Social support is typically viewed as a resouce that protects the
person from the negative impact of stress. This study views the use
or nonuse of social support as a part of the coping process. Empirical
evidence is mounting that integration in a social network is healthy
(Cassel, 1976; Cobb, 1976). However, research findings are contradictory. Some studies have found that social support promotes health
even in the face of stressful life circumstances (Nuckolls et al., 1972;
Myers et al., 1972, 1975; Pearlin et al., 1981). Other studies support
the notion that life events (or stress) have a direct negative effect on
health and that social support has a direct positive effect but they have
failed to find support for the buffering hypothesis (that is, that social
support promotes health by protecting one from stress) (Williams,
Ware, and Donald, 1981; Lin et al., 1979; Schaefer, Coyne, and
Lazarus, 1982).

Pearlin et al. (1981) noted the contradictory findings within the
social support research and attributed the contradictions to the complexity of the stress process. They separate the use of social support
from the coping process and suggest that social supports and coping
can prevent, mediate, and intervene in the stress process:

> There are several junctures at which the mediators can
> conceivably intervene: prior to an event, between an event
> and the life strains that it stimulates, between the strain
> and the diminishment of self-concept, or prior to the
> stress outcome (p. 341).

To understand how social support affects the experience of stress
and the coping options available, specific transactions in specific
contexts must be studied in a way that leaves the context and meaning
of the events intact. Such an approach offers an avenue for increased
understanding of the possible influence of social support on health
(see Wrubel, Benner, and Lazarus, 1981). In this study, relationships
between stress and social support will be pursued as they occur in the

case studies. The uses of social support and/or social influence in actual coping and emotion episodes are viewed as specific coping strategies. The goal will be to understand how the person's use of social support alters specific stress and coping episodes.

STUDIES ON COPING WITH WORK STRESS

One of the earliest studies to examine coping with stress in the work environment is the classic contribution of Kahn et al., (1964). They identified coping behaviors of 53 workers responding to the open-ended question: "when you get into a situation of stress or exceptional pressure, what do you usually do to handle the situation?" They present their results in the form of six case studies that they consider representative of the whole. The coping strategies they outline are: work addiction, cynicism, idealization of others, dependent behaviors, and contrived interpersonal conflict. However, their stem question did not ask for coping strategies used in specific episodes but instead asked what the person usually did.

Dewe, Guest, and Williams (1978) found that questions about what one usually does as opposed to questions about specific episodes elicit more frequent reporting of palliative or emotion-focused coping strategies and fewer reports of problem-focused or direct-action strategies. Also, the theoretical assumption behind the Kahn et al. (1964) study may also have inhibited their exploration of a full range of coping behaviors. They viewed coping as hierarchical and concep-tualized problem-focused coping as adaptive and emotion-focused coping as a deterioration of coping behavior that occurred usually only after problem-focused attempts had been abandoned. This conceptual-ization has been demonstrated to be inadequate by Folkman's disser-tation research on the total study population of this study (1979). Folkman found in a sample of 1,332 specific coping episodes that both problem-focused coping (direct action or behavior focused on the solution of the problem) and emotion-focused coping (coping devoted to to the decrease of distress) were used 98 percent of the time. In other words, in an adequately functioning population, most people used both problem-focused and emotion-focused coping most of the time. There-fore, earlier conceptualizations that have relegated emotion-focused coping to defensive maneuvers used in place of problem-focused coping have missed the complexity and full range of coping strategies used by most people most of the time.

The study of middle managers in the transport industry by Dewe, Guest, and Williams (1978) points to the importance of the particular stem question used to elicit coping behavior. They noted the limited number of empirical studies that actually describe coping behaviors and constructed specific and general open-ended questions to evoke descriptions of coping behaviors from 34 middle managers. The specific questions, asking for a specific stressful episode and how the managers coped with it, elicited 33 coping behaviors with 78 percent of the responses taking the form of direct-action and 22 percent taking the form of palliation (managing the distressful emotions related to the event). The general question did not ask for a specific episode but rather asked what the person usually did when they "were particularly fed up with their job or felt tense." With the general question, 77 percent of the 42 coping behaviors elicited were palliative and only 33 percent were direct-action or problem-focused.

Pearlin and Schooler's (1978) study on the structure of coping also used stem questions that called for generalizations. They asked people what they usually did in relation to work. For example: "How often do you: 1. Take some action to get rid of the difficulties in your work stuation? 2. Talk to others to find a solution to difficulties?"

The coping strategies generated by these questions are necessarily out of context and cannot be related to specific incidents. Therefore, the Pearlin and Schooler (1978) conclusion that coping strategies used in the work context are less efficacious than those used in other role domains, such as parenting and marriage, is open to question. They reasoned that larger social systems such as work would be more intractable to personal influence and therefore less amenable to coping efforts. But given the structure of their study it would be difficult to conclude that coping strategies at work are less efficacious than is possible in more intimate domains. Also, since their study focused on persistent role strains, successful resolutions or successful prevention of problems were not explored. Finally, what one reports that one usually does, and what one actually does, often has little correspondence with what one actually does in a specific encounter (see Folkman and Lazarus, 1980, for a fuller critique of the Pearlin and Schooler study).

In the more recent study by Pearlin et al., (1981) cited earlier, coping responses related to control of the meaning of the problematic situations were examined. Specifically they studied the use of comparative frames of reference and decreasing the importance or value of economic achievements as two coping responses used to alter the meaning of job loss and thus alter the strain of job loss. As noted above, they found that positively comparing one's economic fate with others and devaluing economic gain does decrease the impact of job loss on self-esteem and on strain. However, despite these coping efforts the person still loses the sense of mastery with job loss. Once again, it is not possible to determine the range of coping behaviors outside those in the two response categories available on the questionnaire.

The coping and emotion episodes examined in this research are self-reported accounts of specific episodes. The episodes were selected by participants from any area of their life about which they chose to talk. Positive as well as negative episodes were solicited. Interviewers sought episodes where coping efforts were effective as well as those where they were not. These strategies overcome the problem of underestimating the "direct action" coping behaviors by asking a general question. They encourage the reporting of actual responses to the situation. They allow a full range of coping efforts to be reported.

Burke and Belcourt's study (1974) is notable for its description of specific coping behaviors. They identified 19 types of coping behavior related to specific sources of stress in a study of 137 managers and managerial trainees. The following five coping behaviors accounted for 65 percent of the variance: talking to others, working harder and longer, changing to an engrossing nonwork or play activity, changing the strategy and approach, and withdrawing from the situation. However, the listing of coping behaviors out of context offers little understanding of the effectiveness of specific coping behaviors in specific situations. Context-free lists of coping behavior offer very little understanding and frequently resemble a catalog of trivial advice once they are considered outside the situations where they arise. Also to study coping behaviors outside the context of the specific stressful events at work is to conceptualize coping as an antidote to stress rather than a response to stress that may or may not be effective. To overcome this difficulty this study examines coping in relation to specific stressful episodes. The efficacy of the person's coping for altering the situation are examined in light of what is at stake or what is at issue for the person in the particular situation.

PERSON CHARACTERISTICS AND STRESS

Kobasa (1979) and her associates (Kobasa, Maddi, and Currington, 1981) found that the personality style that they label as "hardy" to be more resistant to the strains of life events as measured by the Holmes and Rahe Schedule of Recent Life Events (1967). The Kobasa (1979) and Kobasa et al. (1981) studies are particularly relevant to this study since they conclude that meaningfulness and a particular personality style related to meaningfulness, which they term hardiness, allows for transformational coping. Transformational coping, as they define it, allows for adjustment and growth as a result of change, instead of illness or even stability. By contrast, protective or conservative coping allows the person to protect, minimize, or ward off danger or disappointment. Stability and absence of illness are the most for which the person can hope. In transformational coping, the person gains or grows, or reappraises the situation in such a way that it is no longer damaging or threatening, and therefore no longer calls for coping effort.

Kobasa (1979, p. 3) defines hardiness as a composite of three interrelated personal characteristics: "(a) the belief that they can control or ingluence the events of their experience, (b) an ability to feel deeply involved in or committed to the activities of their lives, and (c) the anticipation of change as an exciting challenge to further development." Kobasa et al. (1981, p. 369) illustrate the interrelatedness on these components in the following example:

Thus a hardy person's attempt to influence the course of some event (control) includes curiosity about how it happened and interest in what it is (commitment), plus an attempt to learn from it whatever will enhance personal growth (challenge). For example, faced with being fired from work, the hardy person might not only try to have the decision reversed or look for another job (control), but also interview peers and supervisors in an attempt to get more information about what happened (commitment), and consider how the decision might actually be an important occasion to reconsider career plans (challenge).

In a retrospective study, Kobasa (1979) located two groups of middle- to upper-level executives who had comparable levels of stress within the past three years. One group had high stress and high illness and one group had high stress and low illness. The high stress, low illness group shared "hardiness" personality characteristics. Kobasa did not explore specific coping strategies or social supports; however, the condition of experiencing meaningfulness and challenge during changing circumstances apparently facilitated the appropriation and use of social supports and effective coping strategies.

In a prospective study, Kobasa et al. (1981) found that the personality disposition toward commitment, control, and challenge, (that is, the hardy personality) functions as a resistance resource. They conclude that hardiness protects the individual from illness in the face of high stress life events and even in spite of consitiutional predisposition to illness. It is noteworthy that their subjects were predominantly Protestant white men, married, and without close ethnic ties. From the perspective of this study the personality traits described by Kobasa (1979) can be understood as meaningful participation in the Protestant Work Ethic. From Antonovsky's (1980) perspective this would represent a sense of coherence.

The study of personality characteristics unrelated to person-environment fit creates the same problems as identifying context-free coping strategies. For example, general studies of personality traits conclude that extroverted, rigid, internally oriented individuals who have a high tolerance for ambiguity suffer less from job stress than their opposites (Brief, Sculer, and Van Sell, 1981). But these personality characteristics are not necessarily less prone to stress in all environments.

THE PERSON-ENVIRONMENT FIT MODEL

Recently researchers have used the Person-Environment (P-E) Fit Model of stress and coping in order to relate the person to the environment. It is generally acknowledged that the study of any one set of variables related to work stress and coping and health is not an effective strategy for understanding the complex interactions between people and their environment. Thus, integrative theories with transactional variables are sought to capture the complex relationships between particular personality traits and particular environments. One of the most frequently cited integrative theories of stress and coping related to work is that of the Person-Environment Fit Model developed by various members of the Institute for Social Research at the University of Michigan (Campbell, 1973; Caplan, 1972; French and Caplan, 1972; French and Kahn, 1962; French, et al., 1974; House, 1972; Pinneau, 1976; and Harrison, 1976, 1978; see Figure 1.1). Since the P-E Fit Model shares many of the same concerns taken up in the Lazarus paradigm of stress and coping used in this study, important distinctions between these two models will be drawn.

The P-E Fit Model can be traced to descriptions of motivational processes by Lewin (1951) and to Murray's (1938) analysis of person-environment interaction of needs and environmental press. The P-E Fit Model is a mechanical process theory that looks for law-like relationships or causal links between person and environment fit and strain. It is more predictive than single measures of environment or person characteristics and has utility for job screening and selection. The P-E Fit Model is structural and can account only for static or frozen relationships in time. The P-E Fit Model identifies person characteristics, environment characteristics, and strain, and searches for determinates among the components of the model. However, it does not focus on the transactions between the person and environment across time and is less useful in explaining or guiding personal change.

The P-E Fit Model is useful in explaining differences in stress and coping responses in the same environment. For example, Chesney et al. (1981) found that Type B persons are particularly sensitive to their environment and that Type A persons are particularly insensitive to theirs. When Type As were in work settings that they perceived as encouraging workers to make their own decisions and to take initiative and responsibility, they had lower blood pressure. This "fits" with the Type A personality style, which is autonomous, dominant, and self-

FIGURE 1.1

A Model Describing the Effects of Psychosocial Stress
in Terms of Fit between the Person and the Environment

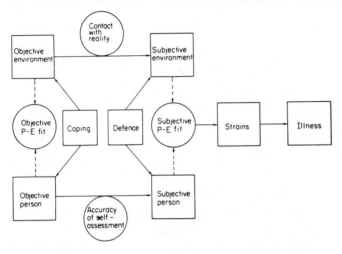

Notes:Concepts within circles are discrepancies between the
two aduoining concepts. Solid lines indicate causal effects. Broken
lines indicate contributions to interaction effects.

Source: From R. Van Harrison in Cooper and Payne (1978,
p. 176). Reprinted with permission.

confident. This parallels Glass's (1977) laboratory findings that Type
A subjects experience higher blood pressures when confronted with
situations that they cannot control. However, unlike Type As, Type Bs
had higher blood pressures in job environments that foster autonomy
and lower blood pressures in work settings that promote dependence on
others and dependence on established routines. Thus, a Type B person
could be at risk for coronary artery disease in a setting that fosters
autonomy. Another example of different person-environment fit between
these two personality styles is that Type As showed higher blood pressures in settings where peer cohesion was low, whereas Type Bs
showed higher blood pressures in settings where peer cohesion was
high. Chesney et al. (1981, p. 554) conclude:

> This differential respones may be related to another
> difference reported in the literature between these two
> groups. That is, consistent with their relative scores on
> measures of autonomy, Type As score higher than Type
> Bs on measures of extroversion. Thus, when the extro-

verted Type A is in an environment high in peer cohesion, there is person-environment fit. On the other hand, when the more introverted Type B individual is in an interpersonally cohesive environment, there is a lack of fit.

Fit, the relational variable in the P-E Fit Model, is a summation of the match of the parts. Three questions can be addressed within the model: What are the components that contribute to the fit? How great is the fit? How small is the fit? The probability of accurately predicting the fit of the person and the work situation is enhanced if many work situations are tapped along with many salient work and person qualities. However, once the fit is summarized, there is no way to account for person or situation change. For example, one can determine whether or not the person has personal and social resources, but one would not be able to identify the processes involved in the person's decision to use those resources nor to describe how the use of those resources transform the person-situation fit.

Summation of fit, even when applying a "weighting" factor to the various components, can be misleading since one's perceptions in one sphere of activity colors the perception of another. Feather (1975, p. 80) has pointed out this problem with the P-E Fit Model:

> Indeed, an individual's ratings of satisfaction with a particular environment might be influenced by sources of satisfaction or dissatisfaction elsewhere. Thus, the discontent engendered by one badly fitting environment (the family situation) might spread to other environments (the school situation), and the happiness that comes from one well fitting situation (the work environment) might also spread elsewhere—both generalization effects adding to those particular effects of structural discrepancies that are specific to defined environments.

Thus, if one is overwhelmed by either the quantitative or qualitative difficulty of the job, the status prestige, or financial reward may not compensate or make the perceived difficulty less stressful for the individual. On the other hand, a stable and happy home situation can change one's perceptions of work (Burke and Weir, 1980). The influence of other life contexts on work will be systematically explored in this study.

This study uses a transactional perspective to study the person in the environment. A transactional perspective focuses on the relationship between the person and the environment and anticipates that each will be changed by the other. Since the focus is on the ways in which the person and environment are mutually changed, summaries of the relationship, as in a structural relationship such as "fit," are not the focus of this inquiry. Rather, the focus is on the meanings inherent in the situation for the person, and how those meanings alter and are altered by the situation. Specific episodes are important in themselves, and the point of the inquiry is to capture the process of change over time.

STRESS MANAGEMENT

The study of the meanings of work for the person offers new avenues for the development of stress management programs. Currently stress management strategies proven to be beneficial include exercise programs, meditation and relaxation programs, behavior modification therapies, and planning (Brief, Schuler, and Van Sell, 1981; Burke and Weir, 1980; Yates, 1979). Insight therapies have been less effective (Brief, Schuler, and Van Sell, 1981). However, insight therapies have been limited to psychodynamic therapies (Freudian psychoanalysis; Carl Rogers Client-Centered Therapy; Ellis's rational-emotional therapy; Gestalt therapy; and encounter groups). In psychodynamic therapies the person looks for insight within their early development and personality style. These approaches are based on theories of the personality rather than on the meanings of work for the adult. This study can augment current insight therapies by demonstrating the link between work meanings and stress and coping at work.

Roskies (1983) points out that the major conceptual problem for the therapist who would develop an early preventive intervention program for the Type A individual is that it is not clear which type A behavior is coronary-prone behavior, and not all coronary-risk behavior, even in Type A individuals, is necessarily coronary-prone behavior. For example, you might teach a person to modify their rapid implosive speech without actually changing any of their preappraisal meanings that keep the individual chronically agitated and from gaining a sense of ease in the situation. This study offers one more clue to understanding this complex puzzle and offers a hypothesis that the way the individual draws on or appropriates past experience may have a significant impact on whether or not they continue to appraise events as threatening or merely challenging or interesting.

Furthermore, if this relationship is borne out in future studies it offers a new strategy for preventive and rehabilitative interventions. Intervention programs similar to cross-cultural training programs can be developed to have workers clarify their own taken-for-granted background meanings that prevent them from drawing on past experience as a coping resource. This would have appeal to the highly work-involved success-oriented Type A individual because it would also offer the possibilty of enhancing their effectiveness through increasing their flexibility. Instead of offering them the alternative of increasing their self-control (internal control), this strategy would help them get beyond the "control" paradigm or conceptual system, which is probably inherently stressful (see Chapter 6).

To view the environment as a place that offers raw material that must be dominated, mastered, and controlled is inherently demanding on the individual. The added emphases on time as linear raw material and the person as an autonomous source of influence, which must be able to stand outside the situation and create options on the spot, ignore the social reality that people actually have a shared background of common meanings and skills that they bring to each situation. Perfect prediction and perfect control limit possibility. One need not give up the <u>content</u> of one's work in order to relinquish the meanings of work that are inherently stressful and create repeated stressful appraisals.

Current stress intervention and prevention programs that are based upon an equilibrium model typically work toward having the person increase their sense of personal control, or their sense of control over the situation. This position reinforces the cultural press that the individual can and should control their circumstances. It ignores the human capacity to participate in shared meanings, and to take over work meanings handed down in skills and through mentors. Equilibrium models necessarily focus on control and presentism. They ignore personal and group history and shared experience. Shils (1981, pp. 7-8) points this out in his discussion of the social sciences to tradition:

> The temporal dimension is obscured by the concept of equilibrium, stressing as it does the immediately present function of each of the variables in the system. Whatever history each of these variables possesses has been deposited in its present state; the mechanism of recurrent self-reproduction is not sought. Having no significant history, there is no need to refer to it in accounting for one's own or another's conduct. The ends and rules of action, the grounds and motives of the acceptance of those ends and rules and the recurrence to the "giveness" of those beliefs, practices, and institutions, which we call "traditional" all tend to be viewed as unproblematic. The more theoretically sophisticated the branch of social science, the less attentive it is to the traditional element in society.

Models that fail to account for history and context fail to capture the coping resources available to the person who is necessarily historical. Furthermore, equilibrium models cannot account for the person's particular relationship to their history. This study presents evidence that people draw on their history in different ways. The historical nature of the individual is captured better in developmental models than in equilibrium models. In the remainder of this chapter, the developmental sources of work meanings, and the meanings embedded in work practices and cultural traditions, are considered.

ADULT IDENTITY, DEVELOPMENT, AND WORK MEANINGS

According to adult development theorists, work meanings change across the career span. As these meanings change, so does the person's self-definition. In answer to the question "Who are you?" most Americans respond by first giving their name, and then by telling what kind of work they do. In less industrialized societies the answer might as easily be related to geographical location or to kinship ties. A number of theorists have linked adult identity with work and career stages (Erikson, 1963; Friedman and Havighurst, 1954; Super, 1957; Super and Bohn, 1970; Holland, 1973; Tausky and Piedmont, 1967-68).

Increasing attention is being paid to the stages of the adult life cycle that are characterized by changing patterns of developmental tasks, career concerns, activities, and situational pulls (Hall, 1976; Levinson et al., 1974; Kroll et al., 1970). The adjustment demands of work during the first stages of one's career are theorized to be different than those experienced in later stages. Thus, a lawyer or a business school graduate with a new degree and entering a new field are both in their first career stage and are apt to be concerned with proving themselves and getting ahead whether they are in their twenties or their forties.

Career entrants have been found to be actively pursuing their identity as workers through testing themselves, actively seeking feedback on their performance, and by being preoccupied with the question of what kind of worker they are and want to be (Schein, 1964; Benner, 1974; Benner and Benner, 1979). Testing is a part of acquiring a new identity in our culture. Festinger (1954) and Schachter (1959) have theorized that there is a drive for self-evaluation and that individuals engage in social comparison as a means of evaluating themselves. Informal testing performs important functions developing an identity with and membership in a group. Most career-stage theories are based on Erick Erikson's eight stages of the life cycle (1963). Erikson theorizes that each stage has a developmental task that must be worked through before the person can advance fully to the next stage. The task of the adolescent is to establish identity and that task is achieved in part through matching one's skills and talents with available occupational roles.

Daniel Levinson and his colleagues (1974) outline four major career stages. They refer to the early career exploration period as "Getting into the Adult World," to a second growth stage as "Settling Down," and to a mid-career stage as "Becoming One's Own Man." The final career stage is most often depicted by theorists as a period of decline rather than maintenance or continued promotion; however, the possibility of growth, maintenance or stagnation are acknowledged by most theorists (Brim and Wheeler, 1966; Hall, 1976). The participants in this study were selected because their age range (ages 45-54) falls within the mid-career stage of career development.

Becker's (1964) theory of adult development through situational adjustment is a plausible explanation of the link between work adjustment and adult development. Work presents the adult with major situational challenges for adjustment, many of which call for personal change and growth. How one copes with the situational demands influences the course of adult development. Thus, the career entrant who never finds a career that suits his or her talents and inclinations might stay in a permanent exploratory stage of career development. The career entrant who fails to adjust his practices and expectations that are based upon his idealized version of his work role will experience extreme role conflict and moral outrage when confronted repeatedly with the exigencies and less-than-ideal circumstances of the work situation (Schein, 1964; Benner, 1974; Kramer, 1974). If the career entrant's commitment to their ideal is rigid, they may embark upon an elaborate exploration looking for the ideal context in which to live out their ideal.

The mid-career employee is faced with the possible situational adjustment of reconciling their anticipated career trajectory with their actual career. This issue is particularly salient in terms of promotion within an organization during the mid-career years. How this adjustment works out may determine whether or not the person experiences a mid-life crisis. Bray, Campbell, and Grant's (1974) longitudinal study of American Telephone and Telegraph workers found that men who were passed over for promotion did adjust by changing their commitment pattern. Those who were promoted became even more focused on work, while those who were passed over became more committed to their families or to other outside interests.

Super's (1957) theory of career stages predicts that the mid-career stage (ages 40-45) is one of maintenance, but the empirical evidence is mixed (Borland, 1978). Though recent writings intimate that the mid-career period can be one of crisis, searching, reappraisal, depression, and redirection (Brim and Wheeler, 1966; Hall, 1976; Sheehy, 1976; Levinson, 1978), few large-scale empirical studies confirm this description. Throughout the case studies, attention is given to the relationship of personal identity in relationship to work and to possible influences of the career stage on work meanings.

This study was conducted with the presupposition that there is a transactional relationship between the nature and content of the individual's work and the stress and coping and general functioning of the worker. In other words, it was assumed that personality and capability both shape and are shaped by specific work experiences. This assumption is supported by the theories of adult development described above. An empirical longitudinal study of the substantive complexity of work and intellectual flexibility conducted by Kohn and Schooler (1978) has documented a change in intellectual flexibility as a result of work complexity. In the past, theorists assumed that personality was based primarily on childhood experiences and that the personality was well-formed prior to occupational careers. However, based upon the more recent work in adult development (Brim and Wheeler, 1966; Levinson, 1978), the old stability view has been replaced by a more dynamic developmental view of adulthood.

Becker (1964, p. 52) theorized that change and stability in adult life are brought about by the processes of situational adjustment and commitment:

> Situational adjustment produces change; the person shifts his behavior with each shift in the situation. Commitment produces stability; the person subordinates immediate situational interests to goals that lie outside the situation. But a stable situation can evoke a well-adjusted pattern of behavior which itself becomes valuable to the person, one of the counters that has meaning in the game he is playing. He can become committed to preserving the adjustment.

Kohn and Schooler's (1978) 10-year longitudinal study on the relationship of personal change based upon the characteristics of work also supports a transactional view of the mutual influence of work and worker. The worker both changes the work and is changed by it. Their study was conducted on men who were at least 26 years of age and who had been in their occupational careers at least ten years. They conclude:

> The longitudinal analysis thus demonstrates something that no cross-sectional analysis could show—that over time the relationship between substantive complexity and intellectual flexibility is truly reciprocal. The effect of substantive complexity on intellectual flexibility is more rapid: current job demands affect current thinking processes. Intellectual flexibility, in contrast, has a delayed effect on substantive complexity: current intellectual flexibility has scant effect on current job demands, but it will have a sizable effect on the further course of one's career. The cross-sectional

> analysis portrayed only part of this process, making it
> seem as if the relationship between substantive complex-
> ity of work and psychological functioning were mainly
> unidirectional, with work affecting psychological function-
> ing but not the reverse. The longitudinal analysis portrays
> a more intricate and more interesting, truly reciprocal
> process (p. 43).

This view does not negate the fact that childhood and family experience do strongly influence aspiration, vocational choice, and even career options as demonstrated in a number of sociological stud-ies (Kohn, 1969; Blau and Duncan, 1967; and Elder, 1974). Nor does it negate the fact that work meanings are handed down by parents and school experiences. The point is that in addition to the background meanings and skills one learns from birth, personality and adult de-velopment are also shaped by the specific work demands, resources, and constraints of their particular lines of work.

WORK MEANINGS EMBEDDED IN PRACTICES AND TRADITIONS

This discussion of the literature on work meanings is bounded by the work experiences and work meanings discovered in the 23 case studies as a means of limiting the review. This discussion is grounded in the actual concrete work experiences described by the participants. Work was defined as paid employment. The content of the work is thus taken seriously. This follows Fromm's (1941, pp. 17-18) observation:

> To put this in a simple formula: man must eat, drink,
> sleep, protect himself against enemies and so forth. In
> order to do all this he must work and produce. "Work,"
> however is nothing general or abstract. Work is always
> concrete work, that is, a specific kind of work in a spe-
> cific kind of economic system. A person may work as a
> vassal in a feudal system, as a peasant in an Indian pueblo,
> as an independent businessman in capitalistic society, as
> a salesgirl in a modern department store, as a worker on
> the endless belt of a big factory. These different kinds of
> work require entirely different personality traits and make
> for different kinds of relatedness to others.

The truck driver in this study does not have the same possibil-ities or same social definition and status as the doctor in this sample.

The content of the work calls for different talents and different responses. However, the cases were not approached with a definition of particular ideal meanings, talents, or attitudes toward work, nor were the jobs parsed in advance along any predefined work characteristics such as "highly significant," "complex," or "autonomous." The strategy was to allow whatever meanings that the work held for the participant to show up in what was discussed as satisfying or stressful. For example, the architect states that his work has caused him to be more isolated because he works alone at his drawing board. In addition, he thinks that he has a different understanding of people than a physician might because he sees people when they are creating, when their life is working, whereas a physician sees people when they are down and ill. He thinks his exposure to people when they are creating has made him more optimistic. So the cases were approached with the idea that the content of work <u>does</u> make a difference, not only in the participants' understanding and approach to their work but also in their personality.

The participants in this study understand work as paid employment, and it is their definition that is used. Thus, working on a planter box is considered enjoyable and as leisure by one participant even though the activity might qualify as work. To define work as paid employment is to view it as it is viewed by society in general. It is not the most accurate or most equitable, or even most socially enlightened, definition, since there is little doubt that a mother or father working at home for "no pay" is engaged in serious work.

Theoretical definitions of work were avoided because they limit what can be uncovered in the particular work practices of the participants. Rohrlich's work (1980) points to the problem of predefining work theoretically because his theoretical definition limits the meanings of work that can be discovered. Rohrlich separates the "activity of work" and the "state of mind" of work. The activity of work he defines as "any activity designed primarily for the realization and achievement of a goal, no matter what that goal may be." He defines the "mental state of work" as "the skillful organization, manipulation, and control of the external and internal environments, to achieve a desired goal most efficiently and effectively" (Rohrlich, 1980, p. 38).

He prefers the mental state of work definition and explains that it applies whether the person is doing the work of a bus driver, a corporate attorney, a mother, a tennis professional, or whatever. He goes on to elaborate on the central core of the definition as "the skillful organization, manipulation and control of the external and internal environments" in a way that illustrates a dominant Western view of work and what it means to work:

"Organization, manipulation, and control" refer to the operation of the analytic attitude and the aggressive instinct in all forms of working. No matter what the task, the worker must approach it by "breaking it down" into manageable blocks. The first step in the analytic approach to a problem, once the goal is established, is a naming or labeling of tools and materials. We screen out the extraneous and identify that which will lead to our goal. . . . The aggressive nature of this entire process should be clear. We react to our materials as if they were adversaries to be subdued and dominated—not destroyed, but mastered. That is the essence of creative work. . . . Mental concentration, or the aggressive harnessing of all cerebral activity on the goal of a task, gives rise to what C. Wright Mills has called the ulterior quality of work. When we are concentrating on our goal and on the methods designed to take us there, we cannot permit ourselves to be distracted by fascination with or enjoyment of the materials immediately at hand. We must always be "getting on with it" or "getting to the point.". . . Because work is productive activity, it is always linear. . . . A zigzag course to a stated goal, full of side trips to take in scenery, is inefficient and undermines effectiveness. Aggressive pruning of peripheral activity strengthens the linear growth of the central trunk. In the definition of work, achievement of a desired result is accomplished "efficiently." Efficiency implies linearity, a situation in which extraneous, non-goal-directed experience must be repudiated (pp. 39-43).

The view of the self in Rohrlich's definition of work is that of an isolate who gives all meanings to external events. Activity in this view comes to the person as undefined raw material that the individual must shape and make sense of. As such, work is effortful and created from the ground up by the individual. In the real world, the worker participates in a subculture of work where the tools, procedures, and practices are "given" to him, already imbued with meaning. The successful worker does not aggressively shape and conquer the work goal but must also be avilable to listen and draw on what is already there. Rohrlich's description of work provides a good example of a Western technological view of work. As such it is compatible with the understanding of work found in many of the case studies with one notable difference: No one actually goes about work in such a linear fashion. One may hold the ideal that plans will go as they are planned and that goals will be achieved in a linear manner; however, life seldom accommodates this ideal. The work product and even efficiency are often better for it, because expert human decisionmaking in actual stuations allows for multiple options and possibility in a situation that perfect forecasting and control would necessarily exclude (see Dreyfus and Dreyfus, 1980, S. E. Dreyfus, 1982, Dreyfus and Dreyfus, in press). Linearity, domination, and breaking the tasks down into parts are not essential attributes of a mental state of work. A task may be goal-directed without being linear. Rohrlich's view confuses outcomes with means. However, the person who rigidly clings to the goal of perfect planning and control finds the inevitable deviations and changes stressful, as illustrated in Chapter 6.

Despite the technological view of work dominant in this culture, the actual work functions and practices discovered in the cases are broader. This study uncovers a broad range of meanings inherent in the functions and work practices of the participants.

THE PROTESTANT WORK ETHIC

The meanings handed down in the thoroughly secularized practices of the Protestant Work Ethic and Utilitarian Individualism were pervasive in the case studies. This is not surprising since the tenets of these traditions show up in the empirical studies describing the coronary-prone personality (Friedman and Rosenman, 1974; Jenkins, 1976; Cohen, 1978; Marmot and Syme, 1976). Chesney and Rosenman (1980, p. 202) summarized the characteristics of the coronary-prone personality drawn from empirical studies as follows:

(1) Experience time pressures because they underestimate the time required to do tasks.

(2) Tend to work quickly and to show impatience and decreased work performance if forced to work slowly.

(3) Ignore, suppress, or deny physical or psychological symptoms while working under pressure, and report symptoms only when the work is finished.

(4) Work harder and experience physiological arousal when a task is perceived as challenging.

(5) Along with hard-driving and competitive behaviours, express hostility and irritation in response to challenge or threat.

(6) Need to be in control of the immediate environment to such an exent that a lack of control may elicit a hostile, competitive Type A Response.

Because of the above characteristics, the Type A workers tend to work hard and long under constant deadline pressures and extreme work overload. Time is experienced as an adversary. They find leisure and relaxation stressful, and tend to work during their "time off" from work. They constantly compete with the high standards that they have set for themselves. Finally, control, domination, and linearity are preferred work characteristics (compare Rohrlich's definition of the mental activity of work on the preceding pages). These characteristics fit the constructs Weber (1958) extracted from the Protestant tradition and those of Utilitarian Individualism outlined by Gouldner (1971).

Utilitarianism views the individual as an agent who seeks to satisfy his own desires. Acts are judged according to how much satisfaction or pleasure they yield. A person is judged by what they do, not by what or who they are. Tipton (1982, p. 8) points out the similarities between the individual's social status in the Utilitarian and Protestant traditions:

> Like radical Protestantism, the utilitarian viewpoint dismissed feudal social identities and exposed every individual to the same standard of judgment. . . . All men are equal in both ethics. However, for Luther all men are equal by virtue of their relation to the highest authority, God. For [Utilitarianism] all men are equal by virtue of their relation to the most basic drive, self-preservation.

Both of these traditions promote the estimation of self-worth based upon work and individual achievement. It is taken for granted that being a good person just means that one works hard, uses time wisely, and acquires wealth. Success is viewed as a sign of election, of salvation in the Protestant Work Ethic. Success is a sign of self-worth for the Utilitarian. Thus, inactivity, unemployment, or lack of money are signs that one is not worthy in both traditions. Doing is synonymous with being.

For the person living in these traditions, it is no longer possible to reduce the personal and cultural meanings of work to economic gain, though economic gain is important. Work is so linked to a sense of self-worth and identity that even when work is experienced as drudgery, it is still preferable to unemployment (see section in Chapter 3 of this volume entitled "Work as a Source of Structure, Authority, and Boundaries"). Retirement works in this set of practices and beliefs as the promised payoff for all the hard work. It is earned. But retirement can produce a crisis in meaning for this tradition of a goal-oriented structure of meaning. The person whose meanings are structure around goals and a future reward cannot afford to reach goals without finding or setting new ones. In fact, an extreme version of a goal-oriented structure of meaning precludes the enjoyment of leisure, which is nonstructured and nongoal oriented.

The cultural practices of the Work Ethic and Utilitarianism shape the experience of work for this group of middle-aged participants. The individual variations among participants demonstrate that everyday practices are more flexible and varied than formal tenets and concepts of a tradition can capture. No one embraces all the tenets in the same ways. The content of the work itself also shapes which precepts are emphasized. For example, the structure of work for a salesman in the sample promotes his emphasis on future achievements and his relatively impoverished sense of past or present achievements by an ever-increasing quota system and constant evaluations.

Recent large-scale surveys indicate that the Protestant Work Ethic, particulary the aspects of endowing work with moral worth in its own right and believing that everyone should do their best regardless of financial rewards, is strong (Yankelovich, 1982). However there may be a shift in the aspect of doing one's duty regardless of whether the work is self-fulfilling.

Yankelovich (1981), who has surveyed attitudes surrounding work and family life in America since the 1950s, has charted a changing in cultural patterns. He has noted a shift to an ethic of self-fulfillment that he calls an ethic of self-duty. The particular notions of self-fulfillment he describes stem from Utilitarianism. It is the work ethic turned inward. The self that is to be fulfilled is viewed as a collection of wants, needs, and desires and it is the obligation of the self to be true to these desires, to express them fully.

The clash between the work ethic and the self-fulfillment ethic was evident in this study (see Chapter 6).

[The] shift in the shared meaning of profit making—from immoral to ethically worthy—took several centuries to complete. But the shift from self-denial to duty to self has taken place within our lifetime. . . . Since [the 1950s] we have been engaged in a cultural tug-of-war between the part of the American public that continues to adhere to the old rules, and the part that embraces its free-to-be-me opposite, with the majority in the middle, picking and choosing from both sides (Yankelovich, 1981, p. 247).

A number of social observers have prematurely predicted the fading of the Work Ethic. Its passing has been foretold and celebrated in the book by Charles Reich (1970) entitled The Greening of America, which was written in the 1960s. However, its celebrated replacement, the duty to self-fulfillment, has been received less enthusiastically by other social observers in the 1970s—a decade that has been labeled by various social observers as the "me decade" and the "culture of narcissism" by Christopher Lasch (1978) This tug-of-war between the duty to self and the duty to duty, while not universal, was evident in this study and will be commented on as it presents itself in the interview material.

SUMMARY

Descriptive studies that attend to the context of work stress and coping are needed in order to understand how stress and coping are related in actual episodes of work stress and coping. Interpretive studies are also needed to explain why people within the same occupational groups have different responses to work stress. Insight approaches to stress management based on psychodynamic personality theories have not been successful. This study offers new alternatives to psychoanalytically based insight work stress intervention by describing the relationships between work meanings and stress and coping at work.

Research strategies that decontextualize person and situation characteristics lead to conflicting findings because stress and coping are context dependent. This study overcomes the limitations of structural studies that ignore context by using an interpretive approach. The meanings of stressful work situations are interpreted within and across cases.

Work meanings change across the career span. Therefore, the influence of career stage on work meanings was examined with an emphasis on the mid-career stage. Work meanings stemming from the Protestant Work Ethic and Utilitarian Individualism were reviewed in light of their pervasive influence on the work meanings of the participants in this study. However, work meanings embedded in actual work practices are broader and more varied than any formal statement of a tradition can capture. Therefore, work meanings were not predefined. Instead they were discovered in coping and emotion episodes described by the participants.

Chapter 2 describes the methodology used in the study.

2

METHODOLOGY

Following the dictum that the problem should determine the method, this study is phenomenological in its approach and focuses on discovery and understanding rather than verification. This study seeks to discover relationships between work meanings and stress and coping processes. It uses a particular qualitative strategy called "hermeneutics," an interpretive social science patterned on the work of Heidegger (1962) and Taylor (1971). The interview notes from 12 monthly interviews of 23 working men are viewed as a text, and the actual coping and emotion episodes are viewed as a text analog.

DESCRIPTION OF SAMPLE CHARACTERISTICS

This study was preplanned and nested in a larger study of stress and coping and health of a community-dwelling middle-aged population (see Folkman and Lazarus, 1980; Schaefer, Coyne, and Lazarus, 1982; Kanner, 1981). This larger study had multiple purposes, but they were all related to the description and study of stress and coping and health. Lazarus (1978b, p. 1) describes four main general objectives for the larger research:

(a) The systematic description and measurement in a naturalistic setting of stress, coping, and emotional patterns in daily life in a "normally functioning" population.

(b) An examination of age and sex variations in sources of stress and mediating psychological and social processes related to emotion and coping.

(c) The relating of these sources of stress, patterns of

31

emotion and coping processes to adaptational outcomes such as morale, social functioning and somatic health.

(d) The evaluation of an innovative ipsative-normative research paradigm using both in-depth and survey methods of assessment whose value as predictors could be compared, and developing a set of assessment tools relevant to stress and coping.

Because this study of work was nested in the larger study of stress and coping, neither participants nor interviewers viewed the study as singularly about "work stress." This has distinct advantages and disadvantages. The advantages are several. The participants did not artificially focus on work events and thereby exclude other important concerns. They could select episodes of strong emotion or coping from any area of their life that they chose. Therefore, when participants talked about their work stress, they did so because it was more salient than other sources of stress. Thus it was possible to assess the relative importance of work in comparison to other domains and interests. On the other hand, because work stress was not the only line of inquiry, the interviewers did not pursue questions related to work stress as thoroughly as they might have if the whole study had focused solely on work stress. This disadvantage is slight when compared with the advantage of being able to weigh the relative importance of work to other life domains and of not overestimating the relative importance of work. Also, the demands of the larger study precluded a more in-depth study of the work environment. Even so, an adequate amount of information was obtained through the Work, Life Review, and Aging Interview, and the Social Environment Questionnaire.

This study is somewhat unique in the field of work stress and coping because it focuses on the meanings of work in diverse occupations instead of focusing on one particular occupational group. This approach allows comparisons of work demands and practices in different lines of work. It also permits the description of meanings inherent in different occupations. For example, the meanings of work for a heavy equipment operator, truck driver, physician, and so on, are different because of the particular meanings of work inherent in the content and structure of the work itself. However, factory workers or workers who have highly automated jobs are missnig from this sample. This study includes a range of occupations from highly trained to semiskilled workers. Although the study of diverse occupations allows different meanings to show up through contrast, the study findings for any particular occupation cannot be generalized because the size is small.

The sample of 23 working men between the ages of 45 and 54 was selected from the larger study of stress and coping and health in 100 Alameda County, California, residents. Participants in this study were assigned case numbers 01-23 to protect their anonymity. "Assumed" names were not used in order to guard against mistaken allusions to people. The Stress and Coping in Aging sample was drawn from a representative sample of the county population surveyed by the Human Population Laboratory (HPL) of the California State Health Department. HPL surveyed 6,928 adults in 1965 and 4,864 members of the 1965 cohort again in 1974. The research objectives of the HPL study were to assess the general level of health in the county and to determine which personal habits, familial characteristics, and demographic and cultural variables most strongly related to health (Hochstim, 1970).

Of those who participated in the 1974 HPL study, 216 were asked to participate in the stress and coping study. Of those who were asked to participate, 109 agreed. Subjects were selected to be between the ages of 45 and 54, be Caucasian, Protestant, or Catholic, to have at least an eighth-grade education, a yearly income of $7,000 or more in 1974, and to be without incapacitating disabilities. The amount of education was the only selection variable that distinguished those who refused from those who agreed to participate in the study. Study participants were better educated (Chi Square = 11.21, df = 3, p .02). During the course of the interview year, nine participants withdrew, leaving the final sample of 100 participants, 27 of whom were between the ages of 45 and 54 and 23 of whom were employed full time or were seeking full-time employment. All but two of the 23 participants were married and all of the participants had been living in the same county for at least 12 years.

INTERVIEW METHODS

Twelve monthly interviews were conducted, with the first interviews beginning in May through August 1977, and the twelfth interviews being completed in May through August 1978. Seven interviewers were selected and trained to conduct the 12 monthly interviews for each participant. Each interviewer was selected based upon prior experience and an actual demonstration of interviewing skills. Group training sessions were held weekly, six weeks prior to the beginning of the study. Practice interviews were videotaped in order to clarify the type of questioning required by the unstructured interviews. The unstructured interviews were designed to elicit an in-depth description of specific coping and emotion episodes. Interviewers were taught to discriminate between description and inference.

Considerable attention was given to the interviewer-interviewee relationship as it developed over the year. The interview strategies were similar to those described by Levinson (1978, p. 15):

A biographical interview combines aspects of a research

interview, a clinical interview and a conversation between friends. It is like a structured research interview in that certain topics must be covered, and the main purpose is research. As in a clinical interview, the interviewer is sensitive to the feelings expressed and follows the threads of meaning as they lead through diverse topics. Finally, as in a conversation between friends, the relationship is equal and the interviewer is free to respond in terms of his own experiences. Yet each party has a defined role as a sustained work task, which imposes its own constraints. What is involved is not simply an interviewing technique or procedure, but a relationship of some intimacy, intensity, and duration. Significant work is involved in forming, maintaining, and terminating the relationship. The recruiting of participants, the negotiation of a research contract, and the course of the interviewing relationship are phases within a single complex process.

Interviewers were supervised by the research staff. Each interviewer's data were reviewed frequently. Each interviewer had at least two people on the research staff who were familiar enough with their participants and their latest interview protocols to discuss them. As supervisors read the interviews, any questions about interpretation and meaning were pointed out and clarified in subsequent interviews.

Group training and supervision, as well as individualized supervision throughout the year, allowed for successful maintenance of this complex research interview relationship. Because the interviews were conducted over a period of a year, there was little problem with impression management. The interviewers soon became friendly and candid with their interviewees so that an atmosphere of confidential friendly conversation was maintained. Most of the interviews were conducted in the home, but some participants chose to be interviewed at work, at a restaurant, or at the research center. Two of the participants in this sample of 23 chose to be interviewed at work frequently. Despite this intensive interviewer training and supervision, variability between the interviewers still exists. However, interviewer variability is not a major problem for this study since the quality of each set of interviews is more than adequate. Each case is studied for itself as a text rather than as a comparison of variables between cases where interviewer variability would have been particularly troublesome.

INTERPRETIVE METHODS

The goals of this research are description, interpretation, and hypotheses generation. Hermeneutical strategies are used since the investigator takes a phenomenological stance that there are no deep structures traits or needs that are free from interpretation. Bias control for the interpretation is achieved by using multiple stages of interpretation, multiple instruments, and consensual validation.

STAGES OF INTERPRETATION

First Stage

The cases of the 23 male participants, who were working or seeking work and who were between the ages of 45 and 54, were read and studied as a whole in order to describe the person's interests, problems and conflicts, and life satisfactions as they emerged throughout the year. Field notes were made with questions and beginning interpretations. The purpose of the first stage of interpretation was to examine the entire year's events and issues without dissecting any of the episodes. By this method the relative importance of work to other life interests was assessed and summarized month by month.

Second Stage

In the second stage, all interview excerpts relating to work and the interface of work and other life domains were extracted verbatim from the interview notes. An in-depth study of these excerpts was made and themes were identified. All 12 interviews were used in addition to the Cantril Ladder of Concerns (see Appendix for the schedule of interviews).

Third Stage

In an independent analysis of each work-related coping and emotion episode, the following aspects of the episode were identified: specific stress appraisals, stakes, coping resources, coping strategies, the emotions experienced in the episode, the effect of the coping on the emotion, and the effect of the coping on the situation. These categories were derived from the cases themselves. This process of interpreting the coping and emotion episodes was developed in a Stress and Coping Project seminar under the direction of Judith Wrubel and Richard Lazarus, this investigator, and other doctoral and postdoctoral researchers. The material in the interviews was organized in advance by the way questions were asked, but actual codes were derived from the material itself. The coding document served as an interpretive guideline for the episodes.

Fourth Stage

The fourth stage consisted of rereading and studying the case material generated in the previous stages for similarities and differences to see if the cases could be grouped by similar meanings. This final stage yielded the findings of the study that are presented in the subsequent chapters. Two strategies for reporting the findings are used: thematic analysis (see Chapters 4 and 7) and case studies (see Chapters 5, 6, 8, and 9). The thematic analysis yielded themes that were evident in all the cases. These themes are presented through interview excerpts. The thematic analysis provides a grouped case study and allows for comparison of similarities and differences between cases.

The case studies illustrate a particular meaning or work involvement pattern so that the pattern can be recognized in other people whose "objective" circumstances might be quite different. It is in this sense that the case is considered a "paradigm" case. A paradigm case stands out for its clarity and descriptive character. It is a "marker" so that once a paradigm case is recognized because of its particular clarity or vividness, other more subtle cases with similar global characteristics can be recognized. The paradigm case allows the consideration of a whole pattern (see Benner, 1984). In the case studies it is possible to illustrate how work meanings shape coping nad emotion episodes. In the thematic analyses and case studies extensive documentation is provided so that the reader can participate in the validation.

Multiple stages of interpretation allow for bias control by confronting the interpreter with contradictions, conflicts, or surprises that cannot be accounted for by an earlier or later interpretation. This is based on the assumption that actions and practices, while not necessarily rational, are constituted by meaningful patterns and practices.

The intent is to go systematically from the whole to the parts and back to the whole. A constant shifting between the whole case and discrete coping and emotion episodes and self-reported characteristics provide the confirming and/or disconfirming evidence for the study's interpretations. The multiple interviews and multiple instruments allow patterns to emerge and prevent the interpreter from putting too much weight on a nonrecurring, idiosyncratic episode, statement, or behavior. Thus a personal meaning (that is, a commitment) or a shared cultural meaning will not be reported unless it can be demonstrated in more than one participant document or text.

Finally, expert consensual validation of the interpretation was obtained on three cases with two colleagues who were familiar with the cases in their own terms, and prior to reading the investigator's interpretation. The assumption underlying this bias control strategy is that the meanings discovered and the interpretations offered are

shared cultural meanings and therefore recognizable by others who
share the same culture and who read the cases. This follows the work
of Dilthey (1976) and Heidegger (1962), who assume that the meaning
and organization of a culture is prior to individual meaning-giving
activity. As H. L. Dreyfus (1977, p. 2) states,

> Heidegger rejects the methodological individualism which
> extends from Descartes to Husserl . . . In this emphasis
> on the social context as the ultimate foundation of intelligi-
> bility, Heidegger is similar to that other twentieth-century
> critic of the philosophical tradition, Ludwig Wittgenstein.
> Both share the view that philosophical problems can only
> be (dis)solved by a return to the study of every day social
> practices.

For Heidegger, human beings are self-interpreting, but their interpretations are not isolated from the tradition and culture in which they
are raised.

The bias controls will not remove the coping and emotion episodes
from their contexts. The premise is that emotions spring from meanings and not from preexisting hidden traits, drives, mechanisms, or
basic needs. Nor does the study treat meanings demonstrated in the
participant's lives as values they freely chose, regardless of their
particular background and history. The cultural meanings to be discovered are considered intersubjective, or shared, and therefore they
are recognizable to anyone who shares the same cultural meanings.
The personal meanings are interpretable to the extent that the participant is able to describe personal history and events that have led to
their commitments. The interpretations will be presented with as much
evidence as possible to allow the reader to participate in the consensual
validation process. "Expert" judges offer further the insurance that the
interpretations offered are compatible with the whole case and thus are
not distorted by the way the evidence is extracted from the case.

The goal was to make the commonplace visible and understood.
In this quest, the interpreter shares the same problems that the
ethnographer has in doing field work at home. Ethnography at home
runs the risk of overlooking key meanings, not because they are so
esoteric or uncommon but, rather, because they are so pervasive (see
Heidegger, 1962).

The five criteria of internal validity outlined by Cherniss (1980,
pp. 278-79) guided this effort to produce reliable and valid results:

> First, they should help us to understand the lives of the
> subjects; we should better comprehend the complex
> pattern of human experience as a result of these. Second,

the themes should maintain the integrity of the original "data." Third, the interpretations should be internally consistent. Fourth, data that support the findings should be presented. Usually, these data will take the form of excerpts from interviews. Finally, the reported conclusions should be consistent with the reader's own experience. In qualitative research, the readers must critically scrutinize the results of the thematic analysis, playing a more active role in the process of "validation" than they normally would.

Cherniss's third point on internal consistency should not be misconstrued to mean that the interpreter expects people to have internally consistent practices and commitments. Conflicting, incongruent practices and commitments are common, and are often the source of stressful transactions. In this research, interpretations are considered internally consistent if the episodes cited match the interpretations given.

The researcher seeks to avoid private subjective interpretations and interpretations imported from theoretical constructs unrelated to the meanings inherent in the events being studied. For example, coping and emotion episodes were not interpreted in terms of "basic drives or needs." The researcher used consensual validation to curtail private subjective interpretations.

THE PROBLEM OF CANDOR

The threat of uncontrolled bias that leads to spurious findings is not limited to investigator bias alone, but can also stem from lack of candor on the part of the participant (Sarason, 1977, p. 103):

> Work or career satisfaction is no easy matter for professionals to talk candidly about, especially if the profession is seen by others as an endlessly fascinating and rewarding line of endeavor. To proclaim one's dissatisfactions or doubts is tantamount to questioning the significance of one's life and future, to appear to others as "deviant," and to raise questions in their minds about one's personal stability. How can you say you are frequently bored in, or feel inadequate about, or unchallenged by your work when the rest of the world sees you as meeting and overcoming one challenge after another, as a fount of ever-increasing knowledge and wisdom, as a person obviously entranced with his career?

In this study the problem of candor is managed by the multiple contacts with participants since they may describe strong emotional or coping episodes during seven different interviews. Participants also discussed any ongoing conflict at work in the introductory, "How have things been going?" questions that were posed monthly so that an ongoing problem could be followed by the interviewers. The investigator can also compare the participant's interpretations of his work with the actual concrete episodes presented.

Since the larger study was neither designed nor presented as a study of work stress per se, but as a study of positive and negative emotions and stress and coping and health in general, participants were probably less self-conscious about presenting a particular description or image of work. The participant did not think of being compared with other people in his own line of work, nor even think about his relationship with his work being the focus of the investigation. Thus, it is doubtful that a deliberate lack of candor was a major problem in this study.

Incidents where the participant's formal descriptions about their work did not match the coping and emotion episodes related to work were not problems of candor. These incongruities reflect the multiple meanings and lived experience of work in comparison to the person's formal description of work. The formal statements about work, and the concrete episodes from work, were compared to aid in the interpretation. The formal statements about the nature of work are not taken to be more or less true than the concrete episodes. Both are considered as valid perceptions and interpretations of work. For example, the physician values the sense of freedom and control he has over his work, and he clearly believes that he is in control and has a great deal of freedom related to his work. However, in actuality he is frequently overloaded, often has to take an unexpected or unplanned duty on weekends, and must always come to grips with the fact that he has no control over when people get sick or will need his services. Nevertheless he does feel that he has a great deal of freedom and control. This is not a problem of candor; he enjoys his work and does think that he can control his schedule and, in fact, does arrange to have an afternoon off during the week and at least every other weekend off. His sense of control illustrates the way his meanings of work serve him in the midst of heavy demands (see Section in Chapter 7 entitled "Beliefs about the Self That Limit a Cushion of Experience."

Honesty and candor cannot exceed the participant's own clarity and self-understanding. Appraisals of work can change even within the course of a week. Thus, a "true" picture of work is not necessarily an unchanging one. There is every evidence that the participants presented their episodes of positive and negative emotions and coping episodes candidly. But they too are caught in the web of their meanings

TABLE 2.1

Description of Participants

Participant	Age	Employment	Family Status
1. Mr. Adams	54	Carpenter	Married, no children at hom
2. Mr. Baker	51	Manufacturing Engineer, Aircraft Industry	Married, no children at hom
3. Mr. Collins	49	Architect	Married, children at home
4. Mr. Davis	52	Salesman	Married, no children at hom
5. Mr. Evans	51	Multiple jobs, Sales, Photography Unemployed	Single, lives alone
6. Mr. Franks	56	Self Employed Salesman	Married, no children
7. Mr. Gough	54	Electrician	Married, no children at hom
8. Mr. Harris	50	Elementary School Teacher	Married, children at home
9. Mr. Ingolls	50	Corporate Advertising Executive	Married, children at home
10. Mr. Jarvis	45	Freight Manager	Married, children at home
11. Mr. Kemp	53	Scientific Research	Single, no children at home
12. Mr. Lewis	52	Store Manager	Married, children at home
13. Mr. Morris	50	Truck Driver	Married, children at home
14. Mr. Narring	50	Purchaser	Married, child at home
15. Mr. Overton	46	Industrial Chemist	Married, children at home
16. Mr. Paul	47	Bus Driver	Married, children at home
17. Mr. Quest	53	Accountant	Married, children at home
18. Mr. Roberts	49	Heavy Equipment Operator	Married, children at home
19. Mr. Smith	49	Self Employed Contractor	Married, children at home
20. Mr. Thomas	50	Technical Writer	Married, children at home
21. Dr. Ursell	46	Physician	Married, no children at hom
22. Mr. Verdent	52	Supervisor	Married, no children at hom
23. Mr. West	46	Carpenter, Supervisor	Married, child at home

Note: Pseudonyms have been used, and the original participant numbers are not used in order to ensure anonymity.

and perspectives and cannot get beyond their own formal and lived interpretations of work. It is not a problem of candor, but is the nature of both the participant and investigator as self-interpreting agents. The role of the interpreter is to examine and study the various interpretations and meanings as they unfold over time and in different circumstances. The interpretive process and distance make the lived interpretations visible. There is no privileged or assumption-free position for the interpreter or for the participant; however, this does not mean that agreement or understanding is impossible.

In summary, the researcher sought to understand how the everyday meanings of work influence stress and coping. The interpreter used the following bias control strategies to ensure validity: compared the interpretations of particular coping and emotion episodes with the reading of the whole case; used multiple sources of information over time so that patterns were interpreted rather than single episodes out of context; relied on "expert," (that is, others who know the text independently); and finally presented extensive documentation so that the reader could participate in consensual validation. Taken together, these bias control strategies ensure that the presented meanings are truly the common meanings of the culture and are evident in the participant's lives as they presented concrete daily episodes of emotion (both positive and negative) and coping episodes. Table 2.1 lists the participants by pseudonym, type of employment, age, and family status.

3

WORK AS A COPING RESOURCE

The way stress and coping related to work is often studied can preclude seeing work as a vital coping resource for the individual because many work stress paradigms carry with them the underlying, untested assumptions that work is stressful or that the worker is alienated from his work. Yet it is a common undersanding that work can be soothing or distracting or a source of reassurance during difficult times. Participants usually did not talk about work as a coping resource, though it is possible to make the case that work functioned as a coping resource for all of the participants at various times. For example, Mr. Smith (see "Work As Life," Chapter 5) frequently uses his work to distract his attention from troubling home situations. However, for three participants the story of work was told in terms of presenting some background reassurance or sense of boundaries and self-definition that enabled them to function in the other areas of their lives that were more in the forefront of their attention.

The first paradigm case is that of a research worker who enjoys his work and who has had an interest in his field since high school. Stress and coping episodes do not arise at work for him during the entire year. Even when he is overloaded, he enjoys his work because he knows he can do the job, and the overload is quantitative rather than qualitative. He knows that he can do well. His stress and coping and emotion episodes stem from his troubled love relationship.

The second paradigm case illustrates the function of work as a coping resource dramatically because the participant is out of work most of the year. The process or activity of work is vital to Mr. Roberts's self esteem. He feels best after a hard day's work. He becomes depressed and immobilized when he is unemployed. He is very involved in his work, but states that he is less involved now than when he was younger. He is a heavy equipment operator. The content or process of work does not create stressful episodes for him until he is forced to go into business for himself where he meets risks and unknowns that are new to him. He would have preferred to continue as an employee, working steadily and hard on a regular schedule.

The third paradigm case is strikingly different than the first two in that the participant claims to hate his work, seems alienated from it, but nevertheless experiences depression and restlessness when he is laid off. He is a carpenter who experiences little internal or external authority in his life in terms of structuring his time. Work serves as the means of structuring his time and functions as a domain where he does not rail against the established order. Work shows up as a coping resource only when he is laid off from work. He is unable to structure his time and resorts to heavy drinking and napping and experiences great restlessness and irritability. This is somewhat puzzling to both the participant and his wife because it is difficult to account for his depression over being laid off from work since he hates his work and is only working to get in his hours for retirement.

WORK AS A STABLE BACKGROUND PROVIDES A SENSE OF MASTERY

Mr. Kemp is a research worker who has had an interest in his field since high school. He has a career position and does well in his work. He gets praise from his coworkers and from his supervisors. Work serves as a coping resource in that it offers him a sense of fulfillment and mastery in the midst of difficulties in his love relationship and in his parenting role. It is a stable background that offers him challenge but little distress. There are no coping or emotion episodes related to work throughout the entire year.

Mr. Kemp lives alone. He was divorced after being married for 23 years. He has two grown sons whom he sees once a week. His positive and negative coping and emotion episodes pertain to his love relationship. In the fifth month, when the woman he loves breaks off their relationship, he feels feelings of "deep sadness." He states that work served as a distraction. He might have added that it also served as a source of comfort:

> I just put it out of my mind by thinking about work.
> I felt good knowing also that I had the resources and
> friends to set up things [entertainment plans on short notice].
> [I: Woke up feeling?] I think that I was in good shape.
> I went into work, cut the lawn, did things. I had folk
> dancing to look forward to the next night. I didn't think
> about it.

It turns out that his friend breaks off their relationship every four to six months; it is broken off twice during the interview year. Both times work serves as a positive source of distraction. He can manage his distress by becoming very involved in his work. This has been going on for 17 months. The interviewer asks, "What if it happens during the work week?" "I'm able to function and always able to do my work, no real problems."

He states in the eleventh interview that his job is more than a means of livelihood. He enjoys it and it's challenging. He has quantitative work overload three times a year lasting for about two weeks. He states in the twelfth interview:

> A person who is under stress means he is ill at ease, not at ease, under pressure. Some stress is positive in my work because I tend to do well. It's a challenge. I feel alert, invigorated, alive. It's the kind of stress I can do something about. Some stress is negative, I feel trapped, frustrated, blocked. I don't know what to do.

Work offers Mr. Kemp an island of mastery. He can feel good about his work when other parts of his life are not working well. He resorts to work as a distraction. Thinking of work offers him a sense of self efficacy and comfort. He has been in the same position for 22 years. He has well-defined responsibilities and authority. He feels fortunate to have his work. He lives alone but wants to get married.

PARADIGM CASE: THE VALUE OF ACTIVITY

Mr. Roberts is a 49-year-old heavy equipment operator who is unemployed for most of the year. Prior to this unemployment he had worked for the same man for 23 years until two years ago when this employer sold his large equipment and paid off his heavy equipment operators. Prior to being a heavy equipment operator, he was a truck driver. When he was 38 he had a heart attack and was advised to choose a less strenuous line of work. He switched from truck driving to operating heavy equipment against his doctor's advice because he could not give up construction—the only thing he had known. With the switch he lost out on his retirement pension with the union. Now that he is unemployed, he fears that he will once again lose his retirement pension. He describes his marriage of 27 years as comfortable and calm with a decrease in passion. He is now quite family-centered. His home is a social center for family who drop in frequently. He says he enjoys his grandchildren more than he did his own children. He was too busy working when his children were growing up to enjoy them.

Work has always been central to Mr. Roberts. When he had his heart attack he had been working for 11 years without a vacation. He averaged 70 to 90 hours a week. He was having marital difficulties at the time and blames the heart attack on the stress of the marital difficulties, overwork, and the fact that his family die young. Few of his family live beyond age 50.

Of the emotions Mr. Roberts discussed in the six emotion interviews, five had to do with unemployment, financial uncertainty, and the the future, and the others had to do with jobs and the future. Two other episodes, one of anger at home and another of irritation with traffic, were the only ones unrelated to his unemployment. Participants were offered the option of telling positive emotional episodes as well as negative ones, but he did not talk about any positive episodes. The themes of Mr. Roberts's coping episodes are markedly similar, and this fits his own description of his coping style. He says he sticks with a problem. He goes over it repeatedly in his mind until it is solved.

All five of the coping episodes he describes in the first interview have to do with hassles around unemployment: frustration over unemployment; disappointment with a person (people who told him to look them up haven't come through with a job); dealing with a difficult person on a short-term job; conscience bothering him: wouldn't take just any position, turned down some jobs; preparing for a big change: he is contemplating moving to another state if things don't work out.

Mr. Roberts describes himself as "a man of habits and routine. I live with it and just do it. I'm always up at 5:00 A.M. or 6:00 A.M. I like being home. I also like work . . . when I can get it, it's satisfying. Sometimes it becomes too important. I feel best when I'm dog tired after a good day's work."

The process of work defines his self-worth. He says in the eleventh interview (I: How do you feel about your work?): "I think a person should have responsibility, something to do to make his existence worthwhile—to produce to become a—a way to develop character, a part of life where you make your mark."

Work is a tool for the process of self-improvement, or as Mr. Roberts says, "a way to develop character." In Weber's terms (1958), this is the ascetic role of work. Weber might have chosen the above quote as an illustration of the sense of worth and election gained by hard work.

Mr. Roberts talks in the eleventh interview about the balance of frustration versus challenge in his work:

Work is challenging more than frustrating. I never did say it was too demanding—when it's too rough for anyone else it's just right for me. I've always been very competent in my work. I hope that my new job will be hectic [he is talking about his self-employment as a heavy equipment operator]. I'm going to work seven days a week.

Mr. Roberts is lost without his work. The interviewer notes in the second month that all the participant seems to talk about is his work, or lack thereof, his nephew and his family. In the fourth month, as unemployment continues to plague him, he states: "I only feel really good after a hard day's work." (Interviewer's note: He gets few these days. Sundays for him are truly depressing. He says that they go downhill from noon. This pattern has been around for two years now. He states that he gets bored, restless, and eats. He claims to have had many projects around the house before, but now he cannot get into them.) He says: "I don't have the motivation." The activity of work serves as a coping resource for the rest of his endeavors and concerns. Work structures his time and is central to his self-esteem.

Being off from work on Sundays is even difficult for him when he is steadily employed:

When I am not working, I'm extremely bored. I think it takes work to make me happy. I always pace the floor and my wife yells at me. I'm thinking really strongly now of buying a back-hoe. It [his unemployment] will be brought to a head when this job down here comes up in 35-40 days. They'll let me know, the job is being redesigned now. [I: What are you like when you are in one of those moods?] I'm edgy—even when I am working. It's the reason Sunday afternoons are so bad. That's a lot of it. It's not having anything to do. The cleanup is done on Saturday and on Sunday. I just have time on my hands that I don't utilize the way I should. When I am unemployed, it [this behavior] is just general [he refers to the restlessness and boredom].

Doing a good job is important to Mr. Roberts, and he is apparently competent in his work. He turns down jobs he does not feel qualified for, and then feels guilty for "turning down work." Despite the guilt over turning down work, however, he will not sign up for equipment that he does not know how to operate. On one job he stopped the work because the soil condition was not right even though the work stoppage brought him more unemployment. If he had continued the work, it would have had to be redone. Thus, integrity and competence are important to Mr. Roberts. Since his self-esteem is so closely tied to his work, it is not surprising that a slovenly job, cutting corners, or even taking risks by operating new equipment are not options for him even during a time of prolonged unemployment.

An emotion episode of anxiety over waiting for work and over taking a loan out for his business typifies many of his concerns and stress and coping patterns:

> Being worried has continued since the process started
> [of going into business for himself]. The heck of it is
> there is nothing to do right now. It's just a matter of
> watching it rain now. I sit and watch T.V. until I think
> the chair is part of my rear end. One of these days
> I'm going to get up and walk and the chair will be part
> of me [laughs].

He explains in another interview that he is more nervous when the weather is good because at least he could be working if he had a job. With the rain, he cannot work regardless of being unemployed:

> Actually the lack of activity makes me restless. I can't
> sit still for two minutes. I'm into the ice-box so much my
> wife says I'm going to wear the door off. I don't get
> anything to eat, I just open the door and look, just to do
> something. The lack of activity drives me up the wall.
> [I: Do you get short?] No, they say I'm grumpy, a little.
> To me I'm not! I've got plans laid; it's just a matter of
> waiting. I'll put the loan in in ten days. . . . [talks about
> the high interest rates]. It makes me nervous. [I: What
> does?] Getting established, getting a following. You
> really need a good year. I need a good year ahead
> of me which I probably won't get. It takes three years
> to establish enough business to keep busy.

Mr. Roberts's coping strategies run the gamut from feeling hopeless, stating that there is nothing he can do—"just go ahead and suffer"— to direct actions to change the situation by going to the union hall frequently and proceeding with his efforts to get a loan. His most stressful state is that of inactivity. He feels better and, from his perspective, functions best when he works. Work is a coping resource for him. Later, after he goes into business for himself, he is overworked and worried about his finances, but he prefers these problems to the helplessness he felt during the "waiting" and unemployment period. His coping on a short-term basis allows him to trade one negative emotion for another. For example, he trades boredom and fear for a anger. In the long term his coping strategies are effective in changing his circumstances. By the end of the year he manages to get out of his unemployment and feeling trapped by becoming self-employed. Throughout the year he restores his morale by planning to move near his bother in another state. This "escape" route, or alternative, prevented him from feeling completely hopeless and helpless.

Mr. Roberts appears to draw from other domains in his life, though they cannot sustain him or sufficiently comfort him during unemployment. In his younger days, Mr. Roberts says, his work was too important to him, he was consumed by it. He states that he admires younger men who do not put so much emphasis on chasing the dollar. He says that he has mellowed some and that work is no longer as important to him. Probably what he means is that other areas, such as family relationships, now are more important than they were in the past when work was his total life, but even so, work is still central to his sense of self-worth. It is a coping resource. Work provides a sense of boundaries and structure. The activity of work distracts him from other worries.

WORK AS A SOURCE OF STRUCTURE, AUTHORITY, AND BOUNDARIES

Mr. Adams is a 54-year-old carpenter. He is happily married to his second wife. His first marriage was unhappy, and his first wife died of a coronary at age 32. He describes himself as just a kid at the time. He has a long-standing drinking problem that may have contributed to the fact that at some point his children were placed in foster homes before his current marriage. He has little sense of continuity to his life in terms of growth and development. He describes the death of his father (when Mr. Adams was seven years old) as being a major significant event in his life. It changed his development. He went wild, his mother could not control him, and he went into the Navy at an early age. He recalls the Navy as a happy time, and a time where he learned that he could not beat the system. He uses this statement to indicate that it was the Navy where he learned to comply and do his duty. He learned carpentry in the Navy.

He describes four distinct periods to his life that seem to have little connection or continuity: his early childhood, before his father's death, which he idealizes as a good time; his uncontrollable period when he was learning the ways of the street; his time in the Navy, which provided both fun and an ability to comply with work demands; and his first marriage, which was unhappy. This was his dark period, when he was working and drinking, and his children were in foster homes. Then there is his current period, which is happy because of the turning point his wife created in his life. The interviewer asks: "Has there been a turning point in your life?"

Yes, I've had one. It was me marrying Jane. She doesn't create any problems compared to what I had before. The changes as I see them were: (1) being in the Navy,

(2) the first marriage, and that was awful, and (3)
marrying Jane. She straightened out my life again.
My life was good while I was in the service, then I
got married and it went rock bottom. And then I married
Jane and that created a new, good life. We don't
create any problems for one another.

At first glance Mr. Adams's relation to work is somewhat confusing. He is a carpenter who feels alienated from his work. He prides
himself in knowing how to slack off on the job without being caught or
found out. Even so he loses many jobs, which might indicate that he
is not as skillful at covering up his lack of industry as he thinks or else
his temper tantrums are very costly. He has little sense of security
about his job. While carpentry is seasonal, and never by its nature
secure, his insecurity is like that of one who has not mastered the
ins and outs of the trade. For example, he says in the third interview:
"I've lost at least 15 jobs [wife interjects laughingly: "He tells them
where to get off"). But construction is that way. If they don't like the
way you part your hair they give you your walking papers. Construction
is very 'iffy.'"

He does not have a sense of security based upon his skill and
experience. This is different from a second carpenter in the sample
who knows if there is work to be had, he will be employed. The other
carpenter knows he is valued for his skill and ability, whereas Mr.
Adams has little sense of being valued for his abilities. He states in
the Work and Life Review Interview that he cannot predict when things
will be pressured: "You just don't know. Every day, every hour is a
new thing." His one strategy offered for altering work pressure is to
slack off a little. He states that there is nothing about work that he
will miss upon retirement. In talking about his death he relates his
distaste for the difficulty and dirtyness of his work:

What bothers me the most is the thought of being
stuck in some goddamn dirty hole when I die. I've worked
in goddamn dirty holes all my life. I want them to throw
me to the sharks or anything else but just don't put me
in no goddamn hole. I've been in dirt all my life. Stick
me in a bag and dump me in the ocean. Let the sharks
eat me. Of course once I go I won't have much choice.
See, I've worked putting foundations in all my life and I
want to be stuck in a vault or anywhere but no goddamn
dirty hole. Christ, I've had to dig so much crap out
all my life, I don't want any part of holes. But it's [death]
not one of my worries for the most part.

Earlier, in this same interview, he stated that if his father had lived he would have seen to it that he did not become a capenter: "He would have seen to it that I was more than that." Thus, the picture is drawn rather clearly and explicitly by Mr. Adams that he does not like his work. It has become physically difficult for him. The injuries he sustains, such as splinters, sprains, and sore muscles, have become a real problem. So a job he has never really liked has become even more difficult with his aging.

In the context of this distaste for his work, it is at first difficult to understand why he finds it hard to cope with being laid off. He says that the only difficulty he experiences is the anger over competing for jobs with affirmative action applicants, and his sense that the union is not doing its fair share for him after all these years. His only concern is getting back on the job so that he can get his hours in for retirement. In fact, he finds being at home unemployed very difficult to cope with. He gets into a pattern of heavier drinking (his normal week includes quite heavy drinking) and napping. This bothers him. He says that he gets irritable and lazy when he is out of work. There are things that he could do, he says, but he does not want to do them when he is not working. This restlessness can be understood in the context of Mr. Adams's need for the authority, structure, and boundaries that work provides for him. While structure and a sense of boundaries are an underlying function and meaning of work for everyone, this meaning of work stands out in bold relief in Mr. Adams's life.

In no other context of his life does he accept authority and boundaries in the unquestioned way he does at work. For example, in the third interview he describes compliance with the boss as the only real solution. He rails against any other authority, and against any demands placed upon him. This seems to be a long-standing pattern that he says was established when he was a boy of seven. He says in the eleventh interview:

> I think my father's death really made a change.
> [Wife interjects: He really loved his father. His whole
> life crumbled when his father died.] No, it didn't
> crumble. It just went in another direction. I just started
> galavanting and I didn't stay studious. I wasn't a bum,
> but I learned all the ins and outs. My mother couldn't
> control me. . . . My whole outlook changed when my
> father died. My mom had no control. I respected her
> but she lost all control of me.

However, a major source of agitation and depression during the year occurs with his being out of work temporarily. At first he denies that being laid off bothers him, but in the twelfth interview, Mr. Adams notes that being laid off from work fits his notion of stress.

> Trying to find work. Being out of work. That way
> I don't make any money, and I don't get my hours in
> for retirement. I get a little crabby. [Wife interjects:
> "Bull, he gets impossible," and she goes on about how
> he is impossible.] Respondent: O.K., I get impossible.
> [I: What is that for you?] Oh, I get nervous sitting
> around doing nothing. I sit around here and there's lots
> to do but I can't do it because I'm feeling stress. Does
> that make sense to you?

For this participant few rewards are expressed in relation to work. Work provides a way to structure one's time. It provides a plan, a structure, where goals are accomplished in regularized ways with established skills, established methods, and timetables. These aspects of work are accepted and generally unquestioned. In most of the participants other meanings of work were more prevalent so that the function of structure and boundaries or work does not become apparent. But for Mr. Adams, work meanings, other than the structure and boundaries work provides, are not apparent. Thus, when he is out of work he gets restless, depressed. Though there are things to be done, he gets "lazy" and drinks and naps away his time. He feels irritable. When he is asked about his plans for retirement, what he looks forward to the most, he says: "Not having to get up early in the morning and go to work. There are no hard things about it. I'm just looking forward to not getting up in the morning. That's it."

He has little sense that he will miss the structure and boundaries that work provides for him in retirement, much like he currently misses them when he is laid off. He is a dependent person who looks to his wife for nurturance and care. His social contacts are limited, and the ones he has are initiated by his wife. He has no hobbies, belongs to no clubs. His free time is spent with his wife, who constitutes his world. He describes their relationship in terms of her care for him. The third interview he is asked, "What is most satisfying about your relationship with your wife?"

> Just being with her. She's company. She's lots of
> fun. She's a real hell raiser. I'm babied to death and
> sure, I like that. . . . I still get breakfast in bed—on
> weekends. She furnishes everything I need without any
> problems. I mean, I don't have to chase anything down.
> She goes out and buys the cigs, the booze, and the beer.
> I just don't have any problems. I don't have to worry
> about her coming home. She always does. And there are
> no outside problems.

Except for periods of time when he is laid off, his time is structured by work, and his "time off" is structured by his wife who takes care of him. He spends much of his time watching T.V. He drinks heavily, at least two bottles of brandy per week, in addition to an undisclosed amount (but apparently a daily after-work drink) of vodka and beer. He does not seek promotion or more responsibility at work, and he looks to his supervisor and bosses to find any errors, so that he does bear that responsibility. For example, one of the coping episodes he describes, in the second interview, in relation to work has to do with a misreading of the architect's plans. Instead of feeling pleased with himself for catching the error, and thus being important to the outcome of the project, he only feels irritated that someone else did not discover the error:

> I was building with a wrong set of plans. The super-
> visor didn't know that there was a revised set of draw-
> ings. . . . When I found out I brought it to the attention
> of the supervisor and then after arguing he checked into
> it. [I: What happened then?] Now we have all sorts of
> undo work. . . . It frustrates me to do something wrong.
> It should have been looked into before starting. One of
> the "great Kahunas" should have brought it to the boss's
> attention. I couldn't really blame the supervisor and
> he couldn't blame me but we were both confused.

While the undoing of the work is understandably frustrating, it is of note that Mr. Adams does not take pride in his responsible role in correcting the error. He neither seeks additional responsibility at work nor does he require that he should feel as if his skill or ability make the job better, or correct. There are no concrete episodes at work that fill him with pride, though he does mention in the Work Interview that his work offers a sense of accomplishment. Thus, one can conclude that work for Mr. Adams offers a predictable set of boundaries that he accepts. It provides a structure that shows up only as an important background for his functioning when he is laid off from work. He does not seem to be able to structure his time in a meaning-ful way on his own while his wife is at work during the day, and it does not occur to him that he misses the structure offered by work. He concludes that he is only hassled by the problems of finding a new job, and by the worry of not getting in his hours for retirement. In fact, his main problem is not being solicited by any tasks, entertainment, or goals when work and his wife are not available. This is a good example of a background meaning of work—one that would not show up on a written questionnaire. It is a meaning that a participant can demonstrate more easily than he can describe explicitly.

SUMMARY AND CONCLUSIONS

These three cases are unique for the way work functions as a coping resource. For Mr. Kemp, work provides a sense of mastery and control that comforts him when other aspects of his life are not going well. He has a great deal of continuity in his work and has not sought discontinuity through job changes or promotion. He is contented with work as stable background the rest of his life. He enjoys what he does and is good at it.

Work shows up as a coping resource for Mr. Roberts because his coping and general level of functioning deteriorate when he is unemployed. He mourns the loss of his work, and states that the routine and hard work make him feel worthwhile. Inactivity is distressing to him even when he is employed. When he is unemployed, inactivity is unbearable. He has no suitable substitute.

Mr. Adams provides a stark contrast in that he hates his work, but it nevertheless plays a background role and serves as a coping resource in that it provides a way of structuring his time. Work serves as a source of boundaries and means of structuring time for most people. What makes this function stand out for this participant is that the sense of authority and boundaries seems to be the primary function and meaning of work for Mr. Adams. For other participants there are many more meanings that show up as more important than those related to structuring time and establishing boundaries, but for Mr. Adams these are the primary meanings and functions of work. Currently, he and his wife plan to retire at the same time. If this works out, it would seem that the wife will take over the role of structuring time and establishing activities for Mr. Adams, although it is not clear whether this will work for Mr. Adams if the activities do not have the sanction and meanings that work holds for him.

These cases, along with the cases presented in the following chapters, demonstrate that work is a coping resource. Since work is an integral part of the person's identity and life, it serves as a coping resource not only as a means of financial survival and comfort but also in providing boundaries, as a way to structure time, and as a way to act in the world and demonstrate one's abilities. Work is more amenable than other life domains to mastery through education and acquired skill. Work operates more explicitly and with clearer contracts than the other more relational aspects of life, therefore one's work can offer a sense of reassurance and confidence in the midst of uncertain, risky ventures. Of course, as will be demonstrated in Chapters 4 and 5, work itself can be a great source of distress but work is also a significant coping resource.

4

THEMES FROM THE UTILITARIAN AND PROTESTANT WORK ETHIC PRACTICES

This chapter presents recurring meanings of work and time use found in the Cantril Ladder of Concerns and the 12 interviews. Recurring themes that can be traced to the Utilitarian and Protestant Work Ethic traditions were identified in all 23 cases. The goal is to present the themes as they showed up in the actual practices of these participants. No effort was made to present a comprehensive description of the tenets of these two traditions. That has been done elsewhere (Weber, 1958; Gouldner, 1971; Glock and Bellah, 1976; Berger, Berger, and Kellner, 1974; Tipton, 1982). Instead, Chapters 4 and 5 examine how these meanings influence stress and coping at work.

The themes in this chapter illustrate the tensions between the duty to duty from the Work Ethic tradition and the duty to self-fulfillment, which is the more recent variation of the Utilitarian Tradition (see discussion in Chapter 1, section entitled "The Protestant Work Ethic"; and Yankelovich, 1981). As might be expected in a sample of participants who range in age from 45 to 54, the duty to work is more prevalent than is a duty to self-fulfillment. However, the cultural pressure for a shift from a duty to work to a duty to self-fulfillment was particularly evident in two cases (see Chapter 6, case studies on Mr. Thomas and Mr. Collins).

In both of these traditions, the person demonstrates worth through acquisition, gain, and winning. Success in the Protestant Work Ethic is a sign of God's election. For the Utilitarian, success demonstrates personal worth and fosters self-esteem. A goal-oriented structure of meaning was pervasive in the cases and forms the background for the four recurring themes: work for a future reward: the progress or promotion theme; the call to be diligent; the value of activity; and time as an adversary.

A GOAL-ORIENTED
STRUCTURE OF MEANING

A goal-oriented structure of meaning supports working for a future reward. It also supports being diligent and doing one's duty regardless of the current rewards, because striving toward a goal is more important than goal achievement. The major source of meaning stems from the journey, not from the destination. Action and speed are necessary tools for goal achievement. Retirement is the ultimate reward for a life of hard work. A future-oriented structure of meaning is the basis for all the themes presented in this chapter and is illustrated in the analysis of the Cantril Ladder of Concerns (Cantril and Roll, 1971).

The Cantril Ladder of Concerns, administered in the first interview, asks the participant to indicate where on a ladder of 1 to 10 they stand presently, where they stood in the distant past (ten years ago), near past (five years ago), where they think they will stand in the near future (five years from now), and in the distant future (ten years from now). In general, the participants indicated a progress theme with the future being the highest number on their present anchored, self-directed range from 1 to 10. All but five (22 percent) of the participants place the future higher than the present. One of these five who gave all periods a "9" noted that it would be a "10" if he were to retire. Of the remaining four who did not select a higher future rating, two had had serious heart attacks, one was dissatisfied with his current work and home life situation, and one was keenly aware of the importance of his work for his sense of well-being. He states that his future would not change unless he took some definite steps to make it change (See Figure 4.1).

Retirement is seen as the promised payoff for all the years of hard work. For those who had health problems or were aware of how dependent they were on work, the progress theme did not hold. For example, Mr. Roberts (heavy equipment operator, see chapter 3), was out of work much of the year and this was a major stress for him. He placed himself as being at a "7" currently, at an "8" ten years ago when he was steadily employed. He notes that a kind of lowering of expectations has set in: "My expectations were better ten years ago than now. I accomplish less now, or just not as fast as I think I should. My expectations lowered when I lost my job recently."

This participant goes on to comment on the future. Five years from now he hopes to be an "8" on the ladder. "I hope I have a steady job. The future always looks better than the immediate past. [And about ten years from now] Same, 8 is the top I can come up with. As you get older, you lower your expectations a bit."

FIGURE 4.1

Cantril Ladder of Concerns

Future Placed Higher Than The Present		Future Placed Same or Lower Than Present	
Number	Percent	Number	Percent
18	78	5	22

Sample Explanations:

"We will both retire then; living where we want to and doing what we want."

"The best will be when we are retired and we can travel."

"I'll be an optimist. My son will find himself and the problems with my daughter will straighten out."

"Unless I take definite action and do things that bother me, nothing will change."

"I'll be semiretired. I feel best when I am working. It was depressing when I was out of work."

"It can't be a "10" ever. I may not be alive; I may have another heart attack."

Thus, a future-oriented structure of meaning was depicted by the responses to the Cantril Ladder of Concerns (Cantril and Roll, 1971). For example, one participant (Mr. Davis, salesman) who hedged on his future rating because of his heart attacks noted that he could never put a "10" down. He explained that there must always be something to look forward to. For this participant, reaching the top meant that there was nothing left to look forward to. Thus, a sense of progress and improvement seems to be taken for granted except where a major illness has intervened to shake the person's confidence in the future. Retirement is the reward for the hard work associated with goal-achievement except in an extreme version of this structure of meaning where the person cannot afford to reach goals.

THE PROGRESS AND PROMOTION THEME

At the mid-career point, progress and promotion take on a new self-definitional role because by mid-career, a person's promotional opportunities begin to become much clearer and usually much more limited. Thus, it is not surprising that a number of participants describe their work against the taken-for-granted background meaning that their success and worth are measured by their past and future promotions. In fact, for some participants, the meaning of work can be summarized in terms of their promotions.

Progress and promotion as major meanings of work rely on a future-oriented structure of meaning. One is expected to progress, to continue to get ahead. In order to have a horizon, a future, one must have a goal to strive toward. Thus, promotions are unquestioned for many of the participants. For example, Mr. Ingolls, an advertising executive, states: "I see advances for me before I retire and with that will come added money and more responsibility in terms of more people under me. I'll retire in 10-12-15 years or so depending on affordability financially."

When advances were not in the picture, the participant frequently saw this as an adaptive, or coping, failure on their part. Mr. Lewis, a store manager, notes in his tenth interview that the turning point of his life occurred eight years ago when he decided not to accept a transfer:

> I'd say it happened about, let's say eight years ago. I was
> very ambitious to move up in my job and to grow and then
> I decided, myself, not to . . . to do my job the best I
> can, but to remain at the status quo. The opportunity
> came up to move up, to move someplace else and I thought
> I really didn't want to do it [move]. And I just accepted
> what I was doing and it changed my attitude. I didn't
> want any more advances, no more challenges except what
> I already had.

In the eleventh interview this same participant sheds light on this decision when he describes his work history in terms of progressing and not progressing:

> Interviewer: Have there been any surprise turns in your
> work?
>
> Yes, 25 years ago I was going to quit X Store, but I got
> a promotion and decided to stay and I started going up
> rather than out.
>
> Interviewer: Have there been any disappointments?
>
> Not being asked to go into district manager training ten to
> twelve years ago.

He decided not to make a lateral transfer even though he would have been managing a larger store. This decision was made in the context of his disappointment ten years earlier at not being moved up to district manager level. He broke away from the unquestioned promotion and progress theme when he did not receive this expected promotion. Somehow dealing with that disappointment made it possible for him to question and turn down a lateral promotion eight years later. It would seem that his turning point—stepping off the promotion ladder—began with the first missed promotion. After that he was able to weigh promotion and not take a bigger store. This participant has difficulty coping with his current level of responsibility (see case study on Mr. Lewis in Chapter 5), so his earlier missed promotion and his later decision not to accept a transfer to a bigger store probably suited his abilities better than a promotion with increased responsibilities. His explanations indicate that his decision not to accept a promotion had to be made against the taken-for-granted assumption that promotion is always best.

Mr. West, a carpenter, explains that he decided not to move up to self-employment as a contractor because he wouldn't be able to take the pressure. He states:

> If I were a contractor, myself, I could make twice as much as I make now, but I would worry too much. I worry too much as it is. I worry about things my boss should worry about but doesn't. My boss is always telling me to forget about it but I can't. I guess I'm a perfectionist.

These participants consider that a decision to not progress or earn more is negative, indicating personal failure or at least personal limitation. They do not believe that their own decisions indicate they are taking positive steps to manage their lives or to choose a path that fits them better personally.

A future goal-oriented structure of meaning works best during the earlier years of one's career when promotions are more plentiful and the alternatives are greater. With advancement, careers must stabilize even for those who reach the top of the promotion ladder. New meaning structures must be found once goals are reached and future promotions or goals no longer dictate daily activities. The architect describes a vacuum in meaning because he has achieved his major goals. He believes that his twenties and thirties are the best years of one's life, the time when the person has everything to look forward to.

A person who is work absorbed to the point that he postpones relaxation and leisure views retirement as the time when he will make up for his hardships. For example, one work-absorbed carpenter imagines that his future retirement will bring all the rewards he has worked so hard for. In response to a question about his thoughts about the future he states: "Less responsibilities, less tension and pressure—in the future things should improve. I look forward to it in the future. We work hard for the future. Our future is when we will make it up."

Thus, retirement is the ultimate payoff for all the hard work and goals achieved. Unfortunately, retirement is also the ultimate form of "arriving." After retirement, promotion and the usual work-related means of measuring progress no longer make sense. If leisure has always served work and has always been interpreted as "time off" to refurbish one for more work, then leisure for leisure's sake may not come easily, or may not come at all.

THE CALL TO BE DILIGENT

As quaint as it might sound in the context of a more self-fulfillment-oriented younger generation, the theme generated by Kant and espoused by Benjamin Franklin, of doing one's duty regardless of the content of the duty, or any connection of duty to personal fulfillment, was expressed explicitly by several participants (see Weber, 1958, pp. 53-54). In contrast with the more current concerns with self-fulfillment, self-expression, and self-actualization through work, the goal is to do a good job regardless of the content of the job or its relationship to one's sense of meaning and fulfillment. As Weber((1958, p. 4) puts it, "It is an obligation which the individual is supposed to feel and does feel towards the content of his professional activity, no matter whether it appears on the surface as a utilization of his personal powers, or only of his material possessions [as capital]."

For example, in answer to the question: "In general, how would you describe the way you think and feel about your work?" Mr. Baker, a manufacturing engineer, responded:

It's a way of earning a living. [I: No other rewards?]
Well, yeah, but they are the same you could get out of
any job if you look for them. What it's all about is
doing a job well regardless of what it is, dishwashing
or brain surgery. You can do it well or make it
drudgery. It's up to the individual.

Mr. Quest (an accountant) says in the eleventh interview that he does not put much importance on his job. His outside life is more important than his job. In this same interview he notes that he would like to retire in about five more years. "After so many years, I'm about to retire and do something else . . . not that I'm tired. But some of it is pure boredom . . . the same thing day in and day out." In the second interview he notes that he is concerned about being criticized for doing things the "right" way. Others at work do it the wrong way. Things are done haphazardly and they shouldn't be. He feels that others criticize him behind his back. However, the form of work—doing it right—is satisfying and he describes his satisfaction with doing a job right in the third interview: "Accomplishing a job well, like at work; work is always satisfying."

Both Mr. Baker and Mr. Quest take a strong stand for a duty ethic and both feel alienated from their coworkers. They also believe that they have higher standards than their coworkers. Doing a job right or well, regardless of how rewarding that work might be, implies that one is disciplined and does one's duty. There is little or no intrinsic reward or satisfaction in the actual output, thus the satisfaction comes from conforming to the ethic of doing a job well. If the social group does not go along with this ethic, a sense of judgment and resentment, and even moral outrage at the violation of this code of ethics, follows. Participant Mr. Thomas has a similar stance. As the interviewer notes after the first interview:

> He is bothered by the attitudes of the people he works with who do not seem to care about the quality of the work they turn out. He considers himself an efficient and conscientious worker who takes a great deal of pride in his work. He made a choice to not take a supervisory position because he knows that he does not work well with people. He also told me that he could not work with the public. He notes in this interview that he has trouble getting along with his coworkers.

In the second interview he describes his diligence:

> I psychologically prepare myself to mentally build a wall around myself. I only wish I could physically isolate myself. [Interviewer note: Respondent's desk is in a crowded room and he is bothered by the noise and lack of privacy.] I take my breaks at my desk and sometimes eat lunch there too. If I'm working and it's "hot" I just go with it. I figure I can mentally relax and goof off when things are slower. I know that I am damn good at my work (you'll excuse me), and I take pride in the work I produce.

Mr. Thomas's attitude toward diligence and achievement come through in his goals for his son:

> I worry that if Son does not develop a better attitude now,
> he will turn out to be like the men at work for whom I
> have no respect. He [son] frustrates me. I have a short
> fuse and I admit I tend to overreact sometimes. I ride
> him. If I back off and don't say anything, I'm afraid
> he'll never get anywhere. The issue is his willingness
> to be second best, to do whatever's easiest. I see
> signposts of an underachiever.

Elsewhere he describes his efforts to teach diligence to his children: "I've always tried to teach punctuality and good work habits. You have an assignment, it's to be done."

Diligence and perfectionism go hand in hand for Mr. Thomas: "I admire perfection. Maybe that is what I am striving for . . . I am my own worst critic. And when I see someone with a sloppy attitude I explode."

For all three of these participants—Mr. Baker, Mr. Quest, and Mr. Thomas—the quest for high standards and diligence regardless of their level of personal involvement makes work a duty. Duty works best when everyone responds similarly, consequently these participants become watchdogs not only for their own perfection but for their coworkers' too. This estranges them from their coworkers and prevents them from drawing support from them. It makes them prone to anger and moral outrage when their coworkers do not subscribe to the duty ethic. As Mr. Thomas says, a slovenly coworker can create a bad day: "One out of 1,000 things could trigger a bad day; for example, Joe, the clown, who is supposed to start work at 7:20, is still talking and still has not removed the cover on his calculator at 8:00 A.M."

The worker who adheres to a sense of duty encounters increasing frustration as coworkers and society in general shift away from duty for duty's sake to the ethic of self-fulfillment. Increasingly the worker is estranged from coworkers because he no longer participates in common meanings related to work. The confict on a cultural level is heightened when the person's own personal meanings center on proving his worth by doing his duty with the expectation that he will be rewarded and feel worthy. When others who do not subscribe to the duty ethic are rewarded or are successful, he feels cheated, angry, and alienated.

This has implications for work stress and coping . These work meanings increase the number of stressful appraisals because duty for duty's sake is no longer culturally supported. Therefore persons who hold to a duty ethic are constantly surprised and experience cultural conflict when their coworkers do not live up to their expectations.

What seems to be an <u>obvious</u> source of irritation to them is not at all apparent to their coworkers. The problem of increased stressful appraisals is compounded by the fact that these persons have almost no coping options related to social support at work.

THE VALUE OF ACTIVITY

The activity of work draws strong cultural sanction from the Utilitarian tradition, which posits that the only valuable activity is "useful" activity. Since useful is defined in terms of commodities and consequences, work <u>activity</u> is considered the most useful activity in this tradition. The Puritan and Calvinistic traditions also valued hard physical and mental labor as an ascetic technique to ward off temptations and also as a sign of worthiness. It is doubtful that the preference for activity has been passed down in explicit beliefs (such as a form of asceticism to control sexual desires) for the participants. But the practices and symbolic power of activity as a sign of worth are evident in many of the participants' interviews. For example, inactivity is frequently cited as more stressful than overwork. Being inactive directly threatens self-esteem. The worker worries about "earning his pay": whereas overwork is a sign of success and an indication that one is needed and is indeed "earning his pay."

Mr. Narring, a buyer, talks about his distress when other people do his job without consulting him; he gets all their paper work and frequently must redo some of the work. Being busy keeps his mind off this problem and his insecurities about his work:

> When I'm busy, I'm not thinking about it [others doing his work], the days go by very rapidly. Those are the days I'm proud of. I know that a lot has been done. [I: What is good about a lot being done?] I know I'm valuable. Someone sent the work to me—they are counting on me. I an a vital cog in the wheel and the wheels continue to turn as long as I'm doing it. [I: Do you ever have thoughts in the other direction?] At times, when my authority is bypassed I have fleeting thoughts —like "What am I here for?" I am too far along to consider quitting. So these are the thoughts that I try to avoid. If I dwell on them, then I am in trouble. Changing jobs is absolutely out of the question. The other thought that creeps in is: "Why am I here?" [I: Where does that come from?] It comes when I am not terribly busy. My mind wanders. It is an inward insecurity, inferiority. Everyone has a little. When I am looking for something to do, the thought comes.

Thus, being busy is reassuring. It confirms his worth and importance. This seems to be the case with Mr. Roberts, Mr. Collins, and Mr. Morris as well. For example, when talking about work stress in the eleventh interview, Mr. Collins says: "Sometimes everything falls at once and you get hammered. Right now it's pretty good. What bothers me most is completely running out of things to do. Then I panic. [I: But you are salaried, aren't you?] Yes."

As described in Chapter 4, Mr. Roberts is unemployed much of the year, and the inactivity is very distressing. He sees a direct link between his self-worth and being busy. He talks about his unemployment in the eighth interview:

> The lack of activity drives me up the wall. [In the ninth interview he states] I wasn't as restless when I had my normal job. I had something to do the next day. But even then Sundays were a problem. [I: How do you feel about your work?] I think a person should have responsibility, something to do to make his existence worthwhile . . . to produce to become a way to develop character, a part of life where you make your mark. . . . Work is more challenging than frustrating. I like the challenge. I never did say it was too demanding. When it is too rough for anyone else it's just right for me. . . . I've always been very competent in my work. [Interviewer notes: he states that he hopes that his new job will be very hectic. He plans to work seven days a week.]

Mr. Roberts believes that work produces character. Thus, when he is out of work he lacks the opportunity to develop his character and make his mark. Had Mr. Roberts been interviewed during a time of employment, it is doubtful that he would have been so aware of how important "feeling tired" at the end of the day was to his self-esteem.

The importance of activity as a sign of worth and security is also repeated in Mr. Morris's interviews. Mr. Morris is a truck driver; his most stressful days are connected with not enough work to do. He associates inactivity with laziness.

> Today was one of the bad days and I know it. [I: Why?] Not enough work for me to do. It happens three-four times a month. There is not enough to keep me going. [I: What do you do?] Nothing. That bothers me. I get lazy. Today I knew that I had just so much to do and that I would run out. I called when I was done. [I: When was that?] 1:15 PM. . . . [I: Is it the feeling of not being

productive that is the main factor?] I'm not sure.
[I: Is the main factor that they might not need you?]
The main factor is not being productive for the day.
Or the fact that they'll wake up and say one day that
they don't need me.

Inactivity for this participant is a real threat in terms of possible
layoff, or even losing his job. But it is also a threat to his self-esteem
as further illustrated in the next interview excerpt about feeling good
when he is busy:

[I: What did you do today?] . . . It was a good day.
More freight to deliver tomorrow. [I: What did you do
yesterday?] Almost the same thing. Good day, got
a lot done [tells route]. It was a lovely day. [I: What
did you do on Monday?] Another good day. Lot of work
done. . . . I feel like I am doing something. . . . [I:
You feel good when you are busy?] Yeah. [I: What
makes you feel good?] The fact that I have done something. It makes you feel good.

Shame and embarrassment are connected to inactivity for Mr.
Morris. He states in the fourth interview:

[I: Did you let your wife know that you weren't busy?]
Only the dispatcher knows. [Do you tell anyone what
kind of day it is?] I might comment to a driver that I
know. [I: Do you tell your family?] No. [I: Your wife
doesn't know?] No. [I: Why?] I really don't know. I
probably think that I would like her to think that when
I go to work, I am working.

Mr. Morris, in this same interview section, talks about feeling
like he is not doing his fair share when he is not busy; he feels like he
is "cheating"; "like the company is getting gypped." There is a strong
element of shame and loss of face when Mr. Morris is not busy at work,
even though he cannot control the workload. He feels worthy only when
he is actually working. While the realistic threat of losing his job is
there, not being busy is a more immediate threat to his sense of
integrity and self-worth.

From the descriptions of these participants, inactivity is more
stressful than work overload. Mr. Smith (a self-employed manufacturer)
illustrates this stance in the next interview excerpt:

> There's been an upswing in work to where things are
> looking good. Of course, that creates a pressure which
> is there . . . the pressure of all the additional work.
> [I: How does that make you feel?] Overall, it's a good
> feeling. You get hemmed in and you might figure that's
> what it is. The increased pressures are creating it.
> [He then goes into concrete examples of the current
> demands of work, but these are described with more
> relish than distaste. He goes on to state:] This is an
> example of getting busy and in a way that I don't mind
> it. But it does cause tension. [I: What does that feel
> like to you?] That we're busy again. [I: Is there any
> emotion connected to it?] Do you know, if you are busy,
> you think you are successful. Emotions would tie into
> that . . . if everything is going well with it. Then you
> have a feeling of the thing being accomplished and well
> organized. When the problems are resolved, it gives
> the satisfaction of a job well done. But if you sit here
> with no work, it really upsets you.

The background meanings inherent in the preference for activity shape the work lives of these participants. They prefer overload to inactivity, because of cultural and personal meanings attached to inactivity. Inactivity can signal job threat, lack of success, a sense of of not being needed, and a feeling of being unworthy. The person may use the busyness of work to distract him from other personal problems or losses. During periods of inactivity, the distraction value of work is lost and the person may be confronted with issues that he normally avoids. Therefore, many participants create work overload for themselves as an insurance against inactivity that they find more difficult to cope with than overload. With overload, there are concrete strategies for coping, and self-esteem is not attacked. With inactivity, the direct options for altering the situation are fewer and one's ability to engage in direct action may be diminished by depression and lowered self-esteem. Inactivity as a source of work stress indicates that work is a coping resource. This becomes particularly noticeable when it is missing (see Chapter 3).

TIME AS AN ADVERSARY

The value for ceaseless activity is often linked to a sense of urgency. A sense of time pressure was as pervasive in the interviews as the preference for activity. Thus, activity is not only valued, but an adversarial, quantitative stance is taken in relation to use of time.

Time is to be redeemed. It is not to be wasted. Activity is conducted in the context of accomplishing as much as possible in the shortest amount of time. Thus, delays, waiting, and loss of productivity become major sources of stress. This is an important point, since with another cultural heritage, focused activity could have been the goal, much like the concentration found in the practices of Zen Buddhism where a much different sense of time prevails. Activity as an ascetic discipline fits well with an adversarial sense of time in the Protestant Work Ethic tradition. As Weber (1958, pp. 157-58) astutely notes,

> waste of time is thus the first and, in principle, the
> deadliest of sins. The span of human life is infinitely
> short and precious to make sure of one's own election.
> Loss of time through sociability, idle talk, luxury, even
> more sleep than is necessary for health, six to at most
> eight hours, is worthy of absolute moral condemnation.
> It does not yet hold with Franklin, that time is money,
> but the proposition is true in a certain spiritual sense.

In addition to the time pressure evident in the practices of those of the Work Ethic tradition, many jobs increase time pressure by promoting the equation: "time is money" (see section with that title in Chapter 5).

Mr. Franks, a self-employed salesman, reasons that he has to schedule as many calls on the customers as he can. He perceives a direct connection between his schedule and his income. Extreme time pressure for this salesman can be partly attributed to the structure of sales. A linear relationship exists between the number of contacts and the volume of sales. Yet this explanation does not entirely justify his perception of time pressure because another salesman (Mr. Davis) talks about learning to work smarter as he has gained experience. He does not go in as many directions at once and focuses on contacts with the highest sales. He also recognizes when he is not up to par, and when his sales will be damaged by his own lack of interest and enthusiasm, and on those days he goes home and takes a nap. Thus with experience he has added qualitative dimensions to his performance, whereas Mr. Franks limits his sense of effectiveness to a strictly time-bounded dimension (that is, number of contacts made).

Mr. Franks is entirely concerned with making each call as fast as possible, because time is money. Wherever he is, he is missing the opportunity to make sales elsewhere. Nothing seems to be of value for itself, or in itself. He has a straightforward quantitative, linear formula. Time is money, and time is his adversary. He seldom "loses himself" in the task at hand, and seldom experiences a leisurely pace at work because he is always striving to make as many contacts as he can, as fast as he can. Any delay or interruption creates a stress appraisal. His coping efforts are limited to working harder and faster. Thus he has frequent stressful appraisals and his coping efforts exacerbate his stress. He is caught in two incompatible guilts described by Kerr (1962, p. 41):

> It is probable that our very awareness of the existence of pleasures that we are either postponing or denying ourselves adds to the tensions induced by unrelieved labor. We feel guilty when we take our pleasure, because there is so much work we might do. We feel guilty when we work so hard, because our lives may depend upon pausing for pleasure. The two guilts are incompatible. . . .

Roskies's (1980) stress-management program designed to modify Type A behavior offers hope for those caught in this dilemma because participants who learn to diminish their sense of time pressure also increase their productivity. Cross-cultural training may also provide an effective way to experientially teach alternative ways of structuring time use.

SUMMARY AND CONCLUSIONS

The duty to duty, the penchant for activity, the future-oriented structure of meaning, and the experience of time as an adversary are background meanings that go hand in hand in the Utilitarian and Protestant Work Ethic traditions. When any of these meanings become the ascendent meaning of work, a means-end displacement occurs (see Merton, 1968). The individual substitutes a commitment to a certain way of going about their work for a commitment to the work itself. While a commitment to the means or way of getting one's work done can supply the motivation and perseverance needed to get the job done, it cannot supply the joy or sense of reward in the actual concrete content of the work itself.

The person who does his duty for duty's sake can feel morally upright but is denied the fulfillment of having his particular talents, interests, and abilities solicited by work. When others do not sanction or value duty for duty's sake, he loses out on his feeling of being upright and exemplary. The person who blindly follows a duty ethic can miss the larger implications of their work as was demonstrated by the bureaucrats in Hitler's regime. On the positive side, the meanings attached to one's duty for duty's sake do enable the person to tolerate and even feel good about doing work that has little intrinsic value to the person. The person caught in time urgency cannot be solicited by any particular task or any particular moment because his time pressure causes his mind to race to the next task. The meaning of the work becomes subordinate to getting the work done fast.

The person who has an adversarial relation to time use can feel trapped in excessive demands on himself. The salesman in the sample, who states that he must kill himself in order to build up the business so that he can hire someone else to take the pressure off, is similar to the trapped friend that Walter Kerr (1962) describes. Kerr's friend states that he feels that he must slow down or else he will get a heart attack, and at the same time he feels he must get as much done as possible before he has his heart attack. Someone who chronically experiences such urgency almost inevitably comes to experience work and life as a rat race.

A future-oriented structure of meaning proves troublesome for the person who has reached his major goals. It creates stress when the cultural press for promotion causes people to seek promotions that go against their talents and interests. In this structure of meaning, retirement can be a time of disappointment and crisis. Persons who always interpret leisure as a means of refurbishing themselves for work may not be able to enjoy leisure for its own sake now or upon retirement.

The stress and coping implications of these meanings for health outcomes have been demonstrated by the research on the coronary-prone personality (Friedman and Rosenman, 1974). These meanings (Work for a Future Reward; The Progress and Promotion Theme; The Call To Be Diligent; The Value of Activity; Time as an Adversary) contribute to coronary artery disease. They determine what is experienced as stressful for the individual and what coping options they have available. In some cases the person is more solicited by their own work meanings (for example, keeping busy, hurrying, doing their duty) than by the particular demands of the situation. His bias or pre-set prevents him from reading the situation in a flexible manner. For example, he may not recognize when a task is not amenable to hurrying, or when doing one's duty is no longer relevant to the task at hand.

These meanings affect appraisals so that some inevitable situations cause inevitably stressful appraisals. Furthermore the coping strategies that are congruent with these meanings can become a source of stress in themselves. Individual variations of these work meanings are presented in Chapter 5 to further illustrate the relationship between these meanings and work stress and coping.

5

PARADIGM CASES:
INDIVIDUAL VARIATIONS OF THE
WORK ETHIC AND UTILITARIANISM
THAT ARE INHERENTLY STRESSFUL

The four cases presented in this chapter illustrate individual variations of the work themes presented in Chapter 4. The way these participants take up these themes creates recurring stressful episodes. Some aspects of the themes have become ascendent so that the recurring stressful episodes have similar stakes. Thus the coping and emotion episodes at work form a predictable pattern.

In each case, the work meanings are embedded in the particular work structure and practices. Thus, the participants' work meanings are congruent with their current work structure and practices. For example, an extreme form of goal-oriented meaning is supported by an ever increasing quota system for one salesman; "time as an adversary" is supported by a relationship between number of contacts made and the volume of sales for another. This illustrates that meaning is transactional. That is, these participants' meanings both shape and are shaped by their work structure and practices.

These four participants mention work stresses monthly; but they are highly involved in their work. All four like their work. They find it exciting and rewarding despite their recurrent stressful episodes. They represent four versions of workaholism, since all four devote most of their energies to work.

Although they are all frequently irritated and frustrated at work, none want to change their type of work or the way they go about it. And they all plan to do some variation of their current type of work when they "retire."

Some aspect of the Work Ethic and/or Utilitarianism dominates other aspects. Thus, the cases are titled by the dominant aspect of these two traditions represented in their case, although all exhibit most of the themes presented in Chapter 4. The four cases are entitled:

Work As a Perennial Proving Ground, The Efficacy of Worry in Achieving Goals, Time Is Money, Work As Life. In each case the relationship between these meanings and stress and coping are examined.

"WORK AS A PERENNIAL PROVING GROUND"

The first career stage, a person's first few jobs, has been viewed as a proving ground (Schein, 1964, 1968; Benner, 1974; Benner and Benner, 1979; and see discussion in Chapter 1, section entitled "Adult Identity . . ."). Proving oneself as a worker is crucial to gaining identity as a worker. Most researchers speculate that once this identity is achieved, the person can and will move on to the other career stages such as Becoming One's Own Person (Levinson et al., 1974; see also Hall, 1976). According to this view of adult development and work, one would not expect to find mid- and late-career persons caught up with proving themselves unless their work identity was unsettled.

The developmental view of work as a proving ground stems from the Work Ethic and Utilitarian bases of proving one's worth through work. However, participants caught in a perennial proving ground do not "intentionally" set out to "prove" their worth. Instead they have a taken-for-granted assumption that work is an arena where they prove their worth. A goal-oriented structure of meaning (see Chapter 4, section entitled "A Goal-Oriented Structure of Meaning") makes it possible for them to focus on future "tests" and never attend to success.

Paradigm Case: Work As a Perennial
Proving Ground

Mr. Lewis is a 52-year-old store manager. He said that he was interested in participating in the study because he has a very stressful job. As he puts it: "Many have fallen by the wayside. But I've been around for 22 years." He feels that his difficulty at work qualifies him for special considerations and attentiveness at home. For example, in the ninth interview he relates an argument he has had with his wife who works on her statistics problems instead of helping with a hobby activity: "I couldn't understand why she doesn't want to help me. God damn it, I've had all these work problems and I don't understand why she doesn't understand and I was really angry."

In the third interview he indicates the kind of work sponsorship his wife usually offers. "I get upset easily and often about work. She is a good listener and is sympathetic, offers considerate advice. It is useful just to let it all out like a boiler with a safety valve."

His marriage of 29 years is going through a transition because his wife has returned to school and is "growing more independent." He is the father of seven children. Two teenage children still live at home.

After 22 years working with the same store, Mr. Lewis has not arrived; he does not indicate during the entire year that he feels masterful in his work. Because he lacks self-confidence and repeatedly describes work stress, one might get the impression that he does not manage his store well. Yet he runs an exemplary store. For example, he is chosen to present a panel discussion on an aspect of store management in a district meeting, and he is given a personal letter of commendation from his supervisor. In the eleventh interview he states: "I am number one in my division in profits and losses. I get a bonus." He also states that he feels adequately rewarded because he has the respect of his superiors. He was offered the managerial position of yet a larger store, which he turned down because he did not want to move his family. His store has its first major cash shortage in 22 years during the interview year. So there is every indication that he performs well, but no indication that he has any sense of mastery or of having arrived. He presents his work as a difficult, risky duty. In the midst of frequent stressful episodes, he wishes he had become a professional baseball player, as he dreamed in his youth.

Mr. Lewis behaves as if every incident on the job has great consequences. He cannot afford to make errors, nor can he afford to have his employees make errors. Making an error is the same as being a certain kind of person—one who is unreliable or unworthy. His ability, performance, and, therefore, his worth are always in question. Consequently, he is overly cautious at work and his days are effortful. His description of an unusually happy day shows just how strained his typical day of work is. He says about a benefit breakfast at church: "I didn't have that on-guard feeling that I usually have of watching what I'm saying." But even in this relaxed setting, he took his resoinsibility for counting the money very seriously and wanted to be sure that he did not make an error, This is striking because counting a relatively small amount of money at a church benefit would appear to be relatively simple for someone as experienced as Mr. Lewis. It seems strange that "doing it right" or worrying about making a mistake could be an issue for a person who has been responsible for counting large sums of money for 22 years. This careful, effortful approach is stylistic for someone who strives for perfection in order to feel worth, approval, and, perhaps, even that he is loved.

This episode is typical of other episodes of frustration at work for Mr. Lewis. He is told that he will get new managers at a holiday time. He becomes very upset and goes into work on Monday with a "negative" attitude. He gives the following description of the event:

The new managers started on [his day off] and there were problems. I'd say it was the most frustrating day of the month. I still haven't accepted the timing of my bosses, preparing for the upcoming holiday. It is a very difficult time for this frustration, and there was a lot of pressure. I hadn't accepted the change and went into work with a negative attitude, negative thoughts and ideas. I seemed to find all the problems, almost saying, I hate to go to work today. [I: What were your emotions going to work?] Not fearful; the emotion would be tense, anxious: "Is the money going to be right? Did they lock up the store correctly? Did they make the right deposits?"

(See Chart 5.1 for interpretation of the coping episode.)

CHART 5.1

Mr. Lewis: Interpretation of Coping Episode

STAKES

Proving his point that his bosses had used poor judgment in changing managers at holiday time. Fear of subordinate's errors reflecting on his performance. Training and learning to trust new employees. "I had to do it because I haven't got anybody capable of doing it [laughs through clenched teeth. I: What were you feeling then?] I was still angry at having to do all this and then at making mistakes because I was not concentrating."

APPRAISAL

Threat.

RESOURCES

Unable to use resources because the point is to dissipate anger and sense of disagreement with upper management and to prove his point that they use poor judgment.

COPING STRATEGIES

● Direct Action
● Information Search
● Planning

- Social Support—<u>Uses unsolicited help that is offered:</u> "My night foreman asked me what was wrong. Telling him took the steam off."
- Social Influence—<u>Complaining to self and others about the situation:</u> "Then I mumbled under my breath for the next hour. . . . I got to the store and was kind of critical."
- Inhibition of Action—<u>Deliberately delays direct action or saying something until a certain time; a kind of inhibition of action:</u> "I had found out the Wednesday before. [What were you feeling then?] I was kind of anxious but put it out of my mind. I thought of things that were positive about it. I talked to the people in the store, put my emotions to the side to face it Monday. I was very nonchalant and didn't get into the feeling until that Monday."
  <u>Manages expression of emotion in order to be effective in the situation:</u> "My boss called me [on Monday] and I told him that everything was fine."
- Cognitive Coping or Palliation—<u>Blames self:</u> [After the anger petered out then what did you feel?] "I feel kind of [frowns] like it was a waste of [hand to brow, pauses] self-downing, and I think, 'What a waste of time to be angry knowing that you'd work it out.' I was unhappy with myself for letting myself lose control. I thought over what I had said and also had done. I felt sad, not feeling like I wanted to smile."
  <u>Temper tantrum:</u> "The thing that kicked me off was the money. Actually it wasn't bad, but I came in with negative thoughts."
  <u>Punishes self:</u> "What I did was to let the office girl wait on the customers and did all the work myself [gestures to self]. I punished myself. I had to do it all because I haven't got anybody capable of doing it [laughs with clenched teeth]."
  <u>Blames others:</u> "I still haven't accepted the timing of my bosses, preparing for [holiday]. [Referring to employees] I used words like 'stupid' and 'dumb' [laughs], 'bad habit,' and belittled the people around,"
  <u>Uses physical activity to dissipate tension:</u> "I tend to do a lot of physical things, it seems to relieve some of the tension inside me."
  <u>Fantasy Revenge:</u> "I was mad, and I wished I could have taken the job and shoved it."
  <u>Try to put it out of mind:</u> "I forgot the feelings; I had to be alert on the job."
  <u>Continues with normal routine:</u> "Then I got involved in telephone calls and put myself into another frame by working."
  <u>Comforting cognition:</u> "Why let this bother you? You know better, it'll work out; you know it will. These are the thoughts that wound me down."

EMOTIONS EXPERIENCED IN EPISODE

"Frustration at not being able to accomplish the things I wanted to at the job."

Tense; anxious: "I get hyper; like I get full of adrenalin."
Anger: "I was mad."
Shame: "How asinine, why let this bother you; . . . I was unhappy with myself for letting myself lose control. I thought over what I had said and done, and felt sad. I had the feeling of not wanting to smile."
Sadness and depression: "I felt sad . . . kind of a depressed feeling; kind of down feeling."

PHYSICAL EXPERIENCE OF EMOTION

"I get hyper [clenching his fist]. I find myself . . . like I get full of adrenalin [rotates hands around like a windmill and furrows brow]. [I: What did you feel like physically during this intense frustration?] I got a feeling inside like I was going to burst [brings fist down hard on the table top]. [I: What were you feeling after the anger petered out?] I feel down, kind of a depressed feeling. [I: Physically?] It doesn't stop me from moving . . . you wouldn't know any difference from my body."

EFFECT OF COPING ON EMOTION

Changed frustration to anger, and anger into shame and depression. Eventually, the emotion dissipated; he was distracted by work. His coping actually exacerbated his negative emotions. According to his own report, his anger was out of proportion to the seriousness of the situation. His anger escalates during the temper tantrum, and then his coping strategies cause him to feel shame and depression.

EFFECT OF COPING ON SITUATION

May have alienated some of his employees. Did nothing to present the problem to management so that things could be different in the future. He probably impressed upon his new managers how important procedural details are to him.

Relationship between Work Meanings
and Stress and Coping

Mr. Lewis is prevented from feeling a sense of mastery, and from having the benefit of his 22 years of experience to cushion his conflicts and difficulties. This is because he believes that he cannot afford to make a mistake, or to have his employees make mistakes.

His excessive fear of mistakes prevents him from learning from them. Instead of being a source of learning, mistakes are a source of shame. Consequently, he spends his efforts coping with the shame and worrying that the problem will happen again; he does less direct problem solving or analyzing the sources of the breakdown. He is caught up with proving his worth, and to do so he believes that he must be error free.

It is difficult to recogize that this person has been on the job for 22 years; he sounds like someone who has just started to work. For the beginning employee, this level of fear about errors is common because a beginner doesn't know the consequences of errors. Beginners do not understand the work subculture. Therefore they are ignorant of back-up systems or the idea of a margin for error. But as people gain experience, they usually learn a tolerance for errors in their work. Experienced workers usually learn what errors are predictable and how tolerable they are. They can usually talk about how frequently certain kinds of errors occur and ways they can or cannot be avoided and corrected. But Mr. Lewis displays neither language nor coping strategies tolerating and planning for errors. Errors are extremely threatening personally and are to be avoided at all costs. He is caught in a perennial proving ground that requires that he continually demonstrate his worth. He can never arrive since he can never drop his guard against errors. He is always on the way to perfection.

His quest for perfection limits the kind of social support he can receive because he typically cannot admit that he is having a problem either to his employees or to his bosses, therefore he cannot ask for help. He can accept emotional support when it is offered. Typically this support entails his ventilating his frustrations, rather than seeking advice. Consequently, he does not gain different perspectives. Throughout the year he easily falls out of trust with himself and with his employees. With his employees he feels that he must present an image of the omnicompetent, in control, "responsible leader." He cannot seek support from his bosses for fear of losing their approval or esteem.

With his quest for perfection, a leadership role is fraught with additional strain because responsibility means the possibility for blame and blemish. As a leader, he takes responsibility not only for his errors, but also for the errors of his employees. For example, when there is a cash shortage at the store while he is on his vacation, he feels anger, shame, and embarrassment. He said: "I had a real depressed feeling. I thought then that I'd like to just get up and walk out of the whole thing." His reaction is notable because it is his first cash shortage, and it occurred while he was on vacation.

A pattern emerges in his coping and emotion episodes. Almost all have to do with work and they always involve saving face, or preventing errors. His response to errors is also predictable. He

blows off steam, castigates his employees, then feels guilty for having
lost control. Typically he experiences shame and embarrassment
and then depression. He assumes that <u>his</u> loss of control will always
cause his employees to lose control. Every situation is eventually
reduced to a psychological problem or control problem for Mr. Lewis,
where he feels shame over not handling the situation better. Therefore
many of his coping strategies are intrapsychic (see Chart 5.1 for
an example).

His vacations and his home life are viewed as respites and chances
for recovery from the constant stresses at work. They repair his frazzled nerves and allow him to rejoin the fracas. Therefore his leisure
is seldom truly leisure (enjoyment for its own sake; instead his leisure
serves his work). That "many have fallen by the wayside" confirms his
belief that his job is indeed extremely stressful. He believes that his
survival should entitle him to special consideration at home.

On the positive side, he notes that his work has stretched his
decisionmaking abilities. He thinks about stepping down to an instruc-
tor's role before he retires, and upon retirement he dreams of opening
another kind of store. He thinks he will be a much calmer person upon
retirement because he will not have his current level of responsibility.
However, unless his meanings of work change, it is doubtful that he
will have much relief from his fear of making errors.

In summary, he has frequent stress appraisals that are related
to a fear of failure. His strong need to control events at work and his
quest to prove himself prevent him from developing a cushion of
experience, a sense of confidence based upon past successes. The
"effortfulness" of his work is demonstrated in the number of coping
strategies that he marshalls for every stressful episode. (See Chart
5.1 for an example of the number of coping strategies used by Mr.
Lewis.)

" THE EFFICACY OF WORRY IN ACHIEVING GOALS"

Paradigm Case: The Efficacy of Worry in Achieving Goals

Mr. Davis is a 52-year-old, very successful sales representative
for a large company. He has been happily married to his second wife
for 25 years. They have two sons, who no longer live at home.

Mr. Davis is highly work involved. He presents work coping and
emotion episodes in six of the seven coping and emotion interviews. He
mentions work in all of the interviews. Concern for doing well is a
common coping theme in all six of the episodes. Proving himself is

at stake in each episode. In the second interview (first coping interview) he is concerned about doing well on an exam on a particular line of products. He is also frustrated with the assignment because the test is more detailed and difficult than the actual sales situation requires. In the fourth interview he describes anger over an unjust quota. In the fifth interview he describes an episode of irritation in dealing with a difficult customer. In this episode a difficult customer phones his boss and he worries that this call might make it look as if he were not doing his job. In the sixth interview he describes anxiety and concern for doing well with a big sale. Here a large bonus is at stake and Mr. Davis worries about having just the right approach to make a big sale. In the eighth interview Mr. Davis worries over "pulling off a successful" (participant's words) conference. In the ninth interview concern over doing well is once again the issue along with irritation and frustration over a high-pressured sales meeting. Thus, setting high standards and striving hard to achieve them are the predominant meanings of work for Mr. Davis. Consequently the coping and emotion episodes related to work are all tinged with challenge and/or threat. The issue is concern with doing well.

He attributes much of his drive as an attempt to escape the poverty of his childhood and avoid repeating his father's failures. He compares himself to his father in the eleventh interview:

> I lost all respect for my father who was always dreaming about get-rich-quick schemes. He was a dreamer. He always had a scheme for getting rich quick. In 30 years, he was only gainfully employed maybe 12 of those years. So I swore: If anything is going to motivate you to get out of the goddamn ghetto, that was going to do it. Because, you know you can taste what it felt like when your friends came over in their cars and picked you up at the back gate, when you couldn't ask them in because you didn't want them to see where you were living—so that was when I lost all respect for my father.

Work for Mr. Davis is an effortful competitive bid to achieve goals. He draws the analogy of performers and athletes. All meaning is goal oriented. Unlike other participants who see retirement as the reward for years of hard work, Mr. Davis views retirement as death unless he can establish new goals. As he says in the eleventh interview:

> If you just cocoon yourself up, hell, they might as well bury you, because you are dead. You have got to have something interesting. You have got to have a challenge. You have got to have something creative. You have got

to have something where you are meeting a goal. Otherwise, man, pull the blanket over you.

Since Mr. Davis has a goal-oriented structure of meaning, and
thus defines success as becoming, he can never afford to "arrive."
His employer shares his definition and also defines success in terms
of future goals, or this year's quotas rather than last year's. Mr.
Lewis is always meeting a quota and he gets formal written tests on
new material. He can never rest on his past laurels from his perspective, or from his company's.
    He believes that goal achievement requires an "all-out effort."
Therefore he tends to exaggerate the importance of events in order to
ensure his "best" effort. Consequently a sales meeting receives the
same level of attention and anxiety as trying to make his biggest sale
of the year. He spends time psyching himself up, building up all the
reasons that "a lot is resting" on the particular test in question.
For example, in the eighth interview he states: "Well, you always have
a certain amount of apprehension. It's like if you are being invited
to the White House; same idea. Because these are the people that make
or break your future as far as the product is concerned."
    For Mr. Davis, the "White House" experiences are frequent,
and serious. He builds a case for being anxious, is anxious, and then
afterward states that he would not have done anything differently. He
points out that this kind of psyching himself up, getting (in the participant's words) "primed for a performance" is important to his success.
Therefore, he does not even consider being more relaxed. From his
perspective, if he were more relaxed and didn't "psych himself up,"
he would not be as successful. Since he is the most successful salesman, he reasons that his formula for success is accurate. Because he
believes in the efficacy of worry, he heightens the attentiveness and
vigilance normally felt before important events (see Chapter 8, section
entitled "A Physician Who Likes His Work," for comparison). Concern
for doing well is a repeated coping issue throughout the year. In the
ninth interview he talks about the efficacy of worry for doing well at a
sales meeting despite the fact that he has been top salesman for the
past two years:

    [I: Do you feel like you did a good job?] Sure, and maybe
    that is what is necessary—getting all those emotions
    stirred up in order to do a good job. [I: To mobilize
    your . . ?] To psych yourself up. [I: You were quite
    alert, I take it.] You can count on that. [How would
    others feel in the same situation?] I imagine that a good
    many of them felt exactly as I did. I don't know of a single
    person that looks forward in anticipation to a sales

meeting. Because they are downers and that is exactly
contrary to what they are trying to do. They are trying
to psych you up.

In the eleventh interview Mr. Davis points out that he has high
standards for himself both on and off the job. In talking about mowing
and trimming the lawn, he says:

It has got be perfect. I don't know how many times my
mother said to me: "Anything worth doing is worth doing
well." And it stuck! It didn"t matter whether it was in
my professional career or in my singing. I was seldom
happy with a performance because I demanded more
of myself. Same thing is true on the job. You have got
to be number one. There is no other place. . . . [I:
What did the salesman of the year award mean to you
personally, professionally?] Self-satisfaction, ego—that's
about it. It also meant something monetarily. It is the
kind of thing that if you can reach your back, you kind
of pat it and say, "good job." But other than that you don't
make a big deal out of it. Otherwise people think you are
bragging or something. So it is just the kind of standard
that you set for yourself. And if you don't make it,
you are upset.

This excerpt illustrates a goal-oriented structure of meaning.
Setting the standard and reaching for the goal has more meaning than
the actual achieving or arriving at the goal. The actual achieving of
the goal is compared to not making it, which would upset him. Avoiding
failure is as important as being successful. He talks about his
love-hate relationship with the quota: "Anything in sales is always a
challenge because you are always fighting a quota. So every day you
are out in the territory, it is a challenge, because you have to meet
that damn quota."
His reputation with himself and with the company seems to be on
the line all the time. He does not interpret this as a problem. He
interprets this as "the way things are." After all, work is just where
one proves their worth through striving for goals. Mr. Davis lives
out the tenets of the Protestant Work Ethic even during leisure time,
(see Chapter 4). His style does not change on the golf course, as
illustrated in the following interview excerpt:

I had a terrible golf game last Wednesday, but not to the
point of bending clubs around trees and throwing them
into the water. Because when you are a perfectionist you

will not tolerate anything less than perfection. It was
one of those days when it just fell apart completely. The
only thing I didn't do was lose a ball, but I did a lot of
hunting! . . . [I: Picture yourself at that moment. What
went through your mind?] I expressed a very choice
expletive. . . . [I: Do you remember what you were
thinking?] Yeah, it was self-denunciation, because it
is really a game that you are playing against yourself.
You play with others and you are playing against them
too. [I: You are playing against your own record?]
Yes, and you are playing against yourself.

Evaluation, judging, and comparison are repeated themes for
Mr. Davis. He is always "playing against his record," He talks about
performance and makes comparisons whether he is "on duty" or off.
For example, he describes his first marriage, which lasted only four
years, as a source of embarrassment and failure: "Lots of failures
you can hide; the public never knows it. But in those days, in my
family background, divorce was a 'no-no.' So by any criteria, I had
failed, or someone who was better than I which didn't exist, had upped
me. And that is a devastating blow."

It is notable that this divorce is described in terms of a
failure and in terms of losing a competition rather than in terms
descriptive of the relationship. It seems that winning, competing, and
challenge are themes in all spheres of Mr. Davis's life. Mr. Davis
sees himself as a perfectionist, driven for success. Church and religion
support his goal-oriented structure of meaning by providing an ultimate
standard:

It is sort of like having a good rudder on a ship. It gives
stability. It gives you a better sense of values. It gives
you a sense of humility, in that no matter how god dang
good you think you are, there is somebody up there
bigger than you are, and maybe he is directing and maybe
he isn't. . . . If a person can get the same thing through
EST or Buddhism, I say more power to him . . . as long
as they realize that there is something more important
in this world.

The selected emotion episode is typical for Mr. Davis. This
episode reported in the eighth interview is reported as both stressful
and pleasant. The participant had to oversee a meeting in a resort
location. The purpose of the meeting was to report research findings
on a product and thus forecast its future. (See Chart 5.2 for interpretation of the coping episode.)

CHART 5.2

Mr. Davis: Interpretation of Coping Episode

STAKES

    Concern for doing well and making a good impression: "I was concerned with meeting speakers and their wives and presenting a good image of the company and doing the proper things."

APPRAISAL

    Challenge, tinged with threat, but positively toned: "As with most things, you build them up in your mind; you become more anxious before the thing actually transpires, and you find there was really no need for anxiety at all, because everything fits into a nice pattern."

RESOURCES

    Sense of personal efficacy: "I had the innate intelligence to handle it well." Ineffectiveness of social support in the situation: "Well it was something that no one could contribute anything of value . . . it is something that you have to work out in your own mind. . . ."

COPING STRATEGIES

- Direct Action—<u>Careful attention to detail:</u> (He describes a number of details that he watched closely.)
- Information search
- Planning—<u>Advanced planning:</u> He made careful, detailed plans for the meeting.
- Social Support—<u>Use of social skills to give a sense of ease and well-being:</u> "The relaxed atmosphere of camaraderie, cocktails preceding dinner helped me relax."
- Social Influence
- Inhibition of Action
- Cognitive Coping or Palliation—<u>Mentally rehearsed situation:</u> "Mostly posing questions in my mind that I would ask these people regarding our products."
  <u>Psyching self up and reinforcing vigilance by emphasizing the importance of the event:</u> "Well you have a certain amount of apprehension. It's like if you were being invited to the White House; same idea. These are the people that make or break your future as far as the marketing is concerned . . . it means a great deal in your pocket ultimately, too, so there is an

economic factor that you can't overlook. [The economic benefits are indirect and long range, so they will not directly affect Mr. Davis.]

EMOTIONS EXPERIENCED IN EPISODE

Anxiety: He told the interviewer that his anxiety was greatest driving to the conference.

Relaxation, enjoyment: [I: When did your feelings change?] "Five minutes after I met them. . . . It was as though you had invited people into your own home."

Pride, sense of accomplishment: He is pleased with the way the conference but states that he does not dwell on it.

PHYSICAL EXPERIENCE OF EMOTION

Describes having "no emotion" after the conference begins with a social hour. Otherwise, the physical effects of his anxiety before the conference are not described.

EFFECT OF COPING ON EMOTION

Increased anxiety before event; relaxation and smooth preformance during the event. After the conference he does not dwell on the good results.

EFFECT OF COPING ON SITUATION

Performed well in the situation. He said that he would not have done anything differently. The outcomes were good.

Relationship between Work Meanings
and Stress and Coping

It does not occur to the participant to dampen his emotional responses because he believes that butterflies in the stomach are important to a good performance. His coping style and use of emotions are expensive to him physically, but it does not occur to him that a less demanding, less anxious approach could yield equal results. He says that if he were "more blasé" he would not do as well. He does not consider the cost, nor the discomfort; it is simply, from his perspective, the price one pays for success. Unlike the physician in the sample who talks about a lessening of anxiety over time with stressful work episodes (see Chapter 8), this participant does not consider dampening or controlling his anxiety since it is part and parcel of his success, and success is extremely important to him. He does not describe a diminishing level of anxiety over time. When he does not

feel anxious, he prods himself by building a case for how important
the event is; therefore he deliberately extends the number of episodes
where he feels anxious.

In the sample episode, the implications of a goal-oriented
structure of meaning for relaxation is illustrated. The participant
does not discuss his sense of success, nor how well the meeting went.
There is no talk of celebration. Having the meeting over is a signal
to him that he can move on to the next challenge. Arriving, or past
achievement, is not as relevant as a future goal.

"TIME IS MONEY"

A number of participants experienced time pressure as a chronic
source of stress at work. As the next case illustrates, time pressure
is transactional since the source of stress cannot be located totally
outside the person, nor totally within the person. The next participant
is self-employed and could hypothetically restructure his work so that
he did not experience so much time pressure. However, his meaning
of work propels him to work as fast as possible. Time is money for
Mr. Franks and the point of work for Mr. Franks is to make as much
money as possible. He feels that any delay directly affects his earning
power. His work life is lived in quantities. The point is to make as
many calls as possible. Mr. Franks does differentiate about giving
more time to some calls with higher payoff and less time to the smaller
accounts. He treats all calls with equal speed. This creates an anxiety
in him at all times since everywhere he <u>is</u> means that he is losing the
opportunity or possibility of all those places where he is <u>not</u>. Time is
his adversary.

Paradigm Case: Time Is Money

Mr. Franks is a 56-year-old self-employed sales distributor.
He lives in a condominium with his wife and his 88-year-old father-
in-law. He and his wife have been married for 25 years. It is his first
marriage and her second. They have no children. The participant
states that he and his wife are more satisfied with their marriage now.
He says that each has "mellowed." They have "learned to get along
with each other's idiosyncracies." He says he has a short temper and
he sometimes takes things out on his wife when things go badly at work.
His wife also works and he thinks that her job is more stressful than
his. They spend their weekends at a vacation home where they hope to
live when they retire. Mr. Franks's coping and emotion episodes are
related to time delays, and to the father-in-law who was getting more

difficult to live with at the beginning of the year. His father-in-law died toward the end of the interview year.

When concerns come up from other parts of his life, he finds work a welcome relief. It is engaging and challenging. Work is a coping resource. He shows no signs of being alienated from his work. He loves it. "Fighting the clock" creates tension but he is willing to pay the price. For example, when he is hassled in the lawyer's office, he thinks of the "important" work he could be doing if he were not detained in the lawyer's office. He feels hostile and justifies his hostility by estimating his loss of work time. When he is overcome with sadness about a friend's serious illness, he switches to work to get his mind off the sadness.

Mr. Franks is very involved in his work and relates events in other aspects of his life to his work. For example, he procrastinates on doing some paperwork and has to do it on his vacation time. He has car trouble on the way home and worries about all the calls he will have to cancel. He gets a hole-in-one over the weekend and is "more ebullient than usual toward my good customers." He talks about being sad over the serious illness of a close friend. He says: "Your body throws off the sad feelings because you have other things to think about, like my business, Christmas shopping, and all the other rat-race things that go with the holidays." He regrets that he has had little time for recreation until recently when he and his wife started going away for weekends. Nevertheless, taking any extra time off from work distresses him. For example, he gets extremely upset if he has to miss a day of work and finds any delay or interruption distressing.

He does not have difficulty with his work. He knows his merchandise and he has the right contacts. Mr. Franks likes his work and has a great deal of work continuity. His father was a salesman and took him selling with him when he was a boy. His current business is a success. He has been in sales for 30 years. He states that he enjoys meeting people and the challenges of "the selling profession":

> I point out to the customers why they may need the product,
> though with the big stores, they buy according to what
> the computers say and it doesn't make it as interesting
> for me, but it does make it easier. The biggest stress
> about the job is the waiting time. It throws your schedule
> off. But working to sell a big line is a challenge as well
> as a stress, especially in the places where you are all
> crowded in to show. [Here he refers to the competitive
> element of setting up products in a small area to show
> off products.] . . . I enjoy the nice people you meet and
> deal with and the things you learn about merchandising
> and how the stores operate. If you make a good sale it's

a good day all told, especially if you sell a new line. There is no better feeling and satisfaction in life. If you like people it's a good job and a fun job. If not, you'd be miserable. I think that the kind of person you are affects the work. People seem to like me and as a result enjoy dealing with me.

The competitive aspects of sales and racing against time are the challenges that engage Mr. Franks. He uses his "personality" to land sales. Ingratiation is a way of life. In this he is similiar to the other salesman in the study. Both salesmen attempt to influence a police officer when they are stopped for a ticket. They both use their finely tuned interpersonal skills. In the case of the other salesman it works, and he does not get a ticket. But Mr. Franks's ingratiation did not work. His response illustrates an instrumental use of personality; he expects being pleasant to pay off: "I was thinking this one [the police officer] wasn't human. I've found that if you're pleasant it usually pays off. They are pleasant back." [Interviewer notes: It is an interesting commentary about his style, I think. After the interaction with the policeman, he went back to his car and thought about how it hadn't worked out and he felt angry at the cop because he could have been pleasant in return. Thus he felt that he was pleasant for nothing.]

In his first coping episode Mr. Franks describes his chronic stress at work under the heading of "too much to do." He points out that because he is a salesman, he has to schedule as many calls on customers as he can. He recognizes that there is a direct connection between his schedule and his income. Sometimes some clients are late or take longer than anticipated, and Mr. Franks gets frustrated cooling his heels. Inwardly he "fumes." He drives faster and gets home exhausted and frustrated. He feels mentally strained about having to fit everything in. Some clients empathize with him and try to work faster with him. But in any event Mr. Franks says that he has to be nice to all of them because they are his "bread and butter." He always says to himself that he will schedule to allow for delay, but he never does. Sometimes he does lighten his schedule after his wife screams at him about it. Later he resorts back to his old pattern because he feels guilty when he does not push himself as hard as possible. He feels that the solution is to "kill myself to build up the business to be able to hire someone else." He does state that he no longer replaces lost accounts in preparation for retirement. He does not think that he could work differently because "the psychology of a salesman is to make as many calls as you can." [The comment about working as hard as he can to build up the business and then hiring someone else does not seem realistic, since he plans to retire in two years and since he is also "winding" down the business in preparation for retirement.]

The emotion episode selected is typical of the way almost all events are related to Mr. Franks's work. He and his lawyer are meeting with the plaintiff's lawyer over an automobile accident that occurred two years ago. The participant is being sued and is anxious about the meeting. He worries that it might be proven that he was in the wrong and he would have to live with that knowledge the rest of his life. He describes one episode related to his anxiety and one related to his anger at the plaintiff's lawyer:

> I have a lot of respect for the law. [Interviewer's note: but this lawyer was poorly dressed and had a small office. Mr. Franks thought that the matter would take an hour and when the plaintiff's lawyer dragged it out to three hours, Mr. Franks got very angry.] I was short and sarcastic with my answers, and others would have known that I was angry. I'm rarely short with people. I thought about how incompetent the lawyer was. I can excuse anything but dumbness and this was a dummy.

He said that he also thought about the fact that the long procedure was costing him money since it was a busy sales time for him. Mr. Franks indicated that he was mad at the lawyer even before he arrived because the lawyer had, at the last minute, cancelled a previously arranged deposition meeting. This also had wasted a lot of Mr. Franks' time. Thus Mr. Franks was angry before the meeting and his anger escalated during the meeting. (See Chart 5.3 for interpretation of the coping episode.)

Relationship between Work Meanings
and Stress and Coping

Work orders all other events for Mr. Franks. In this episode his sense of time pressure comes to his rescue. He deliberately thinks about how much money he is losing from the delay, and thinks about his work during the meeting. This distracts him from the unpleasant issue at hand. He is able to switch from anxiety to anger, and anger is more comfortable for him than the anxiety. His time pressure serves him in this episode and in others because he uses it to screen out unpleasant aspects of a situation. It also increases his sense of control because the issue is changed from the intolerable problem (for example friend dying, possible outcome of a lawsuit) to the common "liveable" problem of "getting as much done as quickly as possible." This is similar to delaying a difficult task until the last possible moment so that the deadline pressure blocks the anxiety over failing at the task.

Mr. Franks is an extreme example in that his coping strategies are primarily related to working harder and faster. Consequently, his coping becomes a source of stress for him.

CHART 5.3

Mr. Franks: Interpretation of Coping Episode

STAKES
    Being detained under unpleasant circumstances.

APPRAISAL
    Psychological threat.

RESOURCES
    Perceived choices considered inadequate.

COPING STRATEGIES

- Direct Action
- Information Search
- Planning
- Social Support—Followed professional advice: "I had to sit there as long as my attorney wanted me to."
- Social Influence
- Inhibition of Action
- Cognitive Coping or Palliation—Smoked: He stated that he smoked during the meeting.
    Deliberately left the situation: Both he and his lawyer walked out of the meeting.
    Fantasy revenge: "I did consider walking out of the meeting, I did not consider taking a poke at him, something I consider very rarely."
    Use of sarcasm and curt answers to express anger: "I was very short and sarcastic with my answers."
    Distraction: "I thought about what a busy time it was in sales for me, and the fact that this procedure was costing me money. After lunch I got busy and forgot about the meeting."
    Justification of anger: He builds a case for his anger, he thinks about how much the delay is costing him.

EMOTIONS EXPERIENCED IN EPISODE

Anger, frustration, hostility. His derogatory comments about the plaintiff's lawyer seem to be preferable to the anxiety he was feeling over the possible outcomes of the lawsuit.

PHYSICAL EXPERIENCE OF EMOTION

Not described.

EFFECT OF COPING ON EMOTION

His coping increased his anger. He states that he did not want to change his feelings: "I was enjoying being angry, being mad at him."

EFFECT OF COPING ON SITUATION

Mr. Franks's behavior probably made no difference in the situation.

WORK AS LIFE

In the most extreme version of "workaholism" work meanings order all other meanings. In the final paradigm case, work meanings crowd out all other meanings. Work is a substitute for close interpersonal relationships. Except for an ongoing quest to prove himself through work, Mr. Smith embodies many of the meanings of the work discussed thus far. Mr. Smith lives to work rather than working to live

Paradigm Case: Work As Life

Mr. Smith is a 50-year-old self-employed manufacturer. His business is small and, except for one or two employees and the occasional help of his son, he runs the business by himself. He is unhappily married. He and his wife have been married for 22 years (a first marriage for both). They have four children, the youngest is 14 and the oldest is 18. Mr. Smith does not think his relationship with his wife will improve in the future. He states that they drifted further apart when she had major surgery and he was too involved in his work to attend to her needs. Mr. Smith is overweight and keeps extremely busy with his work, his hobbies, and his two civic clubs where he holds responsible, active roles.

Mr. Smith begins the year by stating that he can't stand people "who are on welfare, and who won't go out and work." He notes that he has always had to work and cannot tolerate those who won't. He describes his four teenage children only in terms of their work; he offers very little other personal data about his children. He talks about his work in every interview, and the interviews are conducted mainly at his office. This is notable since the study was not introduced or conducted to be exclusively about work.

Eight of his emotion episodes have to do with work and cluster around being frazzled, overloaded, frustrated, disappointed. Yet he consistently describes his work as important and the one area of his life that is fulfilling. He is good at his work and considers his success worth the hassle. He says he feels best when he is overloaded. He does not think about ways to make his work less demanding. Work is life and he has no competing interests to compel him to work "smarter" instead of harder. It does not occur to him to find ways of delegating more of his work.

Mr. Smith feels competent at his work. In this sense he has "arrived." The challenge for him is putting together the best bid. He figures the possibilities and problems in a situation and manages any anxiety he experiences with the challenge well. He translates any sense of anxiety into a sense of excitement. He talks about his bids much like a team athlete talks about a game. His descriptions are replete with contingencies, chance, skill, and probable outcomes. There is no question that he is able to handle the situation. In the fifth interview he gives the sense of mastery and having arrived when he talks about how he handles his employee:

> If an employee comes up and asks if he can do something
> his way, I say, "Go ahead and do it that way." You don't
> know how it will work out; he might as well do it his way.
> And you have to think of the psychological effect on him
> too. In a sense if he suggests it, he is trying to prove
> himself. I'm not trying to prove anything as much as he
> is. It's better to let him do it his way and get credit for it.

He is one with his work. Work is life. When the interviewer asks him how he is, or how it has been going the past month, he repeatedly gives a brief synopsis of the business, as if that takes care of describing how he is. For example, in interview seven, in response to an opening about how he is, he gives a typical response: "Things have been really hectic this month [Here he goes into details about his contracts]. I can't finish phone calls, or get to the bottom of my desk . . . it makes me frazzled. . . . I even got a little bid in (nearby city). I didn't need it . . . [and more about jobs]."

This kind of synopsis of how the business is going seems to be synonymous with how Mr. Smith is doing. It seems to be a taken-for-granted response when one asks about how he is, that summing up how things are going at work is a reasonable answer.

Another example is sufficient to provide this sense of involvement and identity with work:

> This month has been pretty good . . . being down in Las Vegas two days and then for a weekend, I still haven't caught up . . . and I have to go to town tomorrow to deliver those [goods]. It's cheaper to take them up than to deal with the packing and shipping. [I: What happened to all the bids you had out?] I got contracts on two of them, and am supposed to have two more . . . plus I'm waiting on another rush job . . . if the other two plants come through, I've got my year of work. . . .

Thus Mr. Smith demonstrates and lives out many of the practices of Utilitarianism and the Protestant Work Ethic. He likes being busy, experiences time as an adversary, and thus experiences delays as major coping episodes. He likes the challenge of competing for bids, and he enjoys winning. He does not, however, seem to be trying to prove himself or his capabilities; that seems to have already been settled for Mr. Smith. Since work is his whole life, he does not experience many events related to work as insignificant. His skill and capability do not seem to be issues; he seems clear and settled that he is capable and is no longer testing his capability. He is more preoccupied with winning and demonstrating his skill, exercising it rather than testing it.

However, because work serves as a major coping resource for the less manageable areas of his life, inactivity is a major threat that goes beyond just loss of income. The tension caused by lack of work is extremely difficult for Mr. Smith. He has almost no coping strategies to deal with inactivity. Inactivity signals failure and losing and causes him to lose the major source of his positive emotion. Repeatedly he states that inactivity is far more difficult to cope with than being too busy.

In the twelfth interview the interviewer describes Mr. Smith's ability to cope with being overloaded:

> I arrived at Mr. Smith's factory at a time when his help has usually left and the phone calls have diminished slightly. Today, however, there were three people, rather than the usual one, working in the shop and Jim was in the office going crazy with phone calls. He'd barely start one and another one would come in. He was quoting figures, putting people on hold, and seemed very busy, but on top of it all.

Friends do not play a major role in Mr. Smith's life when compared to his work absorption. Mr. Smith is markedly abstract when he talks about friends. In the tenth interview he said: "Friends are people that you can say what you really mean about the weather, your children, et cetera." He never talks about seeking advice from or giving or receiving help from his friends during the interview year. Friends do not seem to be a source of enjoyment. Instead, his pleasure comes from a successful bid and from his hobbies. As he says in the tenth interview about friends: "If you don't have a [shared] interest, then there is nothing. Like hobbies, it's an interest. One of my bigger interests now is work."

Mr. Smith exhibits less mastery and involvement in other domains of his life. For example, in the second interview, he notes:

> I have a good memory and retention, enough to bring
> thoughts back. I could tell you what happened in a job.
> I could tell you steps but not the prices. I could tell you
> all the materials and needs. It has something to do with
> the subconscious, what you think is important. [When it
> is important] something will register a lot of times.

This statement comes on the heels of describing his inability to remember what he said during an argument with his wife and children, and his inability to remember what he did or said after the argument to make himself feel better. One explanation might be that he just "represses" the arguments at home because they cause him discomfort. But an equally plausible interpretation, and one that the participant offers, is that he is not sufficiently engaged and involved in the arguments at home to remember their details. Throughout the year he seems to have no lingering or intrusive thoughts about the problems at home that cannot be absorbed within a half an hour of applying himself to his work. In comparison to his homelife, work is preeminent and offers an escape from the problems at home.

In the selected coping episode Mr. Smith describes losing a bid. He starts out by describing the context of the event. This episode illustrates many of the typical coping strategies used by Mr. Smith. It also indicates the importance of winning for him:

> There was an indication something was wrong two weeks
> before when the bids were made. It was not that this came
> as a complete surprise. . . . What you were suspecting
> went wrong, did. I had a strong feeling of being upset.
> This month—well the business has not been that good the
> whole past year. It's not a panic situation. We can pull
> in our horns. . . . If I'd gotten all five jobs, that's darn

near, moneywise, half a year's business. I wasn't
surprised. It was disappointing. Here it was January
and I could have half a year's business wrapped up.
. . . [I: How did it feel to you when you got upset?]
Let down, disgusted, and teed-off because I had spent
a good 25 hours in doing it. I'd gotten through enough
barriers. It should have been my job.

(See Chart 5.4 for interpretation of the emotion episode.)

CHART 5.4

Mr. Smith: Interpretation of Emotion Episode

STAKES

Losing a bid in the midst of a good run of success or wins. It is
the context of having "won" a number of bids that makes this loss
particularly disappointing. In his situation, the loss is not because of
the normal legitimate reason for losing a bid, so it is not losing for
the wrong reasons. The issue with putting out the bid is winning.

APPRAISAL

Loss and harm.

RESOURCES

The cushion of experience. An estmate of personal resources,
in which the person feels that experience provides a sense of being
able to handle the current situation. Elsewhere he uses the example
of how he prepares himself, and how he weathers just this kind of
recurring situation. He has lost bids before and he knows how to
handle that.

COPING STRATEGIES

- Direct Action
- Information Search
- Planning
- Social Support

    Presenting a frictionless surface: Again, he calls this not
    burning his bridges behind him, but what he means is that he
    avoids saying anything to antagonize another person. It is not
    clear that his saying anything would, in fact, cause a problem,
    but as a rule he refrains from saying anything in order not to
    rub anyone the wrong way. It is a passive form of ingratiation.

- Social Influence
- Inhibition of Action
- Cognitive Coping or Palliation—Sees personal problem as a part of a larger social problem: "It's the feeling of being stepped on and frustrated by the government. . . . The middle class is getting shafted any way you look at it, etc."
  Positive comparison: [Compares self to others and sees self in a positive light.] He compares himself with the man who lost a multimillion dollar contract because of the environmentalists and with the general contractor who had put in 150 hours to his 25.
  Anticipatory coping, advanced sense of possible disappointment: "I had an inkling that something was wrong, so it was not a cold surprise. I had prepared myself that something was going wrong. It would have been an uplift if I would have gotten it."
  Makes a conscious effort to change mental state: "It's annoying and frustrating, but there is no use in getting upset about it."
  Actively complaining about the unfairness of it all: "I then lose a job and they take 10 percent of my taxes on top of it. I was teed off."
  Accepts situation: "It's useless to rebid. . . . It's final; it's canceled."
  Blames others: "When you have to worry about the owner fouling up, it's annoying."

EMOTIONS EXPERIENCED IN EPISODE
   Disappointment and letdown which turns into anger over the unfairness of the situation.

PHYSICAL EXPERIENCE OF EMOTION
   Not described.

EFFECT OF COPING ON EMOTION
   Changed disappointment and letdown into anger.

EFFECT OF COPING ON SITUATION
   Did not change the situation.

The Relationship between Work Meanings
and Stress and Coping

He presents a "frictionless surface" to those he comes in contact with at work. He says in response to an order not being ready on time:

I was disappointed. [I: But it was unemotional?] I try
not to get upset. I very seldom get really angry and very
seldom with the person I'm angry with. I'd show it
[sometimes], but I would more likely take it out on
someone else.

Presenting a frictionless surface is a rule he follows to avoid
conflict and minimize personal exchanges at work. This coping
strategy might be misinterpreted to be just an inhibition of saying
anything or doing anything to make the situation worse. Yet he never
really assesses whether his saying something will, in fact, make the
situation better or worse. He just follows the rule that he should never
express his anger because it might under some circumstances make
the situation worse.

Interpersonal relationships are difficult for Mr. Smith. He states
in the eleventh interview that his work is his major interest and that it
functions as a substitute for a sex life. He avoids close personal
relationships, and he functions well when he can cut off troublesome
exchanges. For example, he does not work with a company a second
time if he encounters difficulty with a first contract. He states that at
work you can sever and forget about difficult relationships, but you
can't do that at home. He says this explains the advantage of worklife
over homelife.

Work provides a safe arena where interpersonal exchanges are
clear and contractual. Predictability and control are greater than is
possible with friends or family. He keeps interpersonal relationships
as distant and controlled as possible. Thus he has little or no social
support. In fact, social ties are stress provoking for him. He is
subject to work overload as an insurance against inactivity. Like Mr.
Franks, his major coping strategy is to work harder and longer. His
competitive approach to his work adds challenge and excitement but it
also contributes to his work overload since he sometimes wins more
work than he can easily handle.

He describes no positive emotions during the entire year except
for the excitement he felt when his boat capsized on a canoe trip. Thus
he has a narrow range of emotion. He describes frequent episodes of
anger, disappointment, frustration, and no episodes of pleasure, joy,
or pride. Such an emotional profile offers little in the way of recovery
and restoration.

Competition and winning are the most rewarding aspects of work.
They offer him a sense of approval and reward. Winning and work are
so culturally and personally valued that it does not occur to him to
question his passion. His work is his life and it is experienced as a
totally absorbing game. He holds responsible jobs in both of his civic
organizations, and these are experienced much like work.

SUMMARY AND CONCLUSIONS

This chapter has presented four paradigm cases that illustrate the relationship between work meanings and stress and coping episodes. Stress appraisals are determined by the background meanings of work. Dominant meanings of work depicted were work as a way to prove one's worth; a place to strive for goals in order to demonstrate worth; as a place where one works as hard and as fast as possible because time is money; and as a way of life. In each case, these meanings were focal work meanings for the participants and shaped the content of their stressful episodes. The content or stakes involved in a stressful episode determined the coping strategies available for the person.

These paradigm cases were grouped together because they all reflect work meanings that are inherently stressful. For example, the people who are caught in a perennial proving ground can never "relax" in their work. Every new activity is a potential threat because it can signal personal success or failure. Past successes do not count in themselves.

The person who has an extreme version of a goal-oriented structure of meaning is also caught in an endless cycle of setting goals with little facility for enjoying goal achievement. Mr. Davis had an added burden of believing in the efficacy of worry so that he exaggerated his fears in order to ensure the proper level of anxiety for success.

The person who experiences chronic time pressure can never be unhurried with any activity because they feel pressured to accomplish as much as possible in the shortest amount of time. Any task accomplishment is interpreted in light of what they are not accomplishing or could be accomplishing if they could work faster.

Finally, the person who embraces work as life, and who experiences time pressure and a preference for overload as an insurance against inactivity, will do little to make work less demanding. Their emotional life centers around emotions associated with their work. Furthermore the person whose work absorption crowds out love and leisure is cut off from the enrichment and restoration love and leisure can bring. Emotional life shrinks to negative affect (anger, frustration, and so on) or to challenge and excitement, none of which offer much rest.

These cases illustrate the fact that coping is not experienced nor is it available as a list of options or as an antidote to stress. Coping is inextricably bound up with stakes, the meanings inherent in the situation. Therefore, one does not choose coping strategies based upon their merit independent of the meanings and commitments that caused the situation. Because coping is not chosen apart from the understanding and interpretation of the stressful event, coping itself can be stressful. Thus, the person who is caught in a web of hurrying continues to work harder and faster to cope with the time pressure he feels. Also, because coping is bound up with the stakes involved in the situation, the person does not have an unlimited number of choices. Persons do not choose their perceptual lens that determines what is stressful and what is benign nor can they choose coping options independent of their appraisal of the event.

6

WORK MEANINGS IN TRANSITION

Chapter 5 demonstrated that background meanings of work strongly influence what is experienced as stressful, and explained what kinds of coping options are available to the person. However, the meanings themselves can cease to function, and that occurrence is, in itself, another source of stress, because without intact background meanings nothing can be done smoothly. Normally work meanings are invisible to the person. They are the perceptual lens through which the person perceives everything else. A person's background meanings provide the basis for understanding his situation. For example, the meanings "time is money" and "work as life" (see Chapter 5) shaped what work was for the participants and they, in turn, were shaped by those meanings.

When a person's background meanings change, either through personal or cultural change, their expectations and actions no longer proceed routinely. The person whose background meanings no longer support actions or expectations suffers from the inability to choose and act in an uncomplicated, smooth fashion. More and more actions become deliberate choices. The need for too many deliberate choices causes stress and interferes with coping.

When work meanings change, what was once taken for granted now becomes visible. A person's expectations are not met and understanding breaks down. To use the analogy of the perceptual lens, the lens becomes cloudy and therefore becomes noticeable and interferes with, rather than facilitates, perception.

The four paradigm cases in this chapter illustrate a crisis or a transition in the taken-for-granted background meanings of work. These participants talk more self-consciously about their work because their work meanings are changing. While earlier examples illustrated how work meanings can be stressful in themselves, this chapter illustrates that meanings that break down can be even more stressful. For example, Mr. Thomas's circumstances no longer support his expectations for control nor reward him for his diligence. Mr. Collins deliberately seeks to change from a duty to work to a duty to self. Mr. Verdent has had one strong meaning undermined; and Mr. Paul suffers from general meaninglessness in his life.

THE QUEST FOR CONTROL

In a culture that values autonomy and self-control, and where the dream of being the "master of one's own fate" is a common shared meaning, it is not surprising to find distress and disappointment when the limits of control are experienced. The individual is taught to look for the source of responsibility within the self, and that most circumstances can be changed. This ideology works best when circumstances are, in fact, alterable by the individual. With advancing age, increasing career stability, and fewer career options, the sense of controlling one's own destiny is also challenged.

The technological practices of the age also reinforce the value and expectation for control in the form of predictability, precise timing, and coordination. Weber (1958) referred to the "iron cage" of increased rationality, predictability, and control in modern organizational settings. However, the worker may perceive routinization and predictability as a sense of control, so that "control" is felt when the person has a sense of mastery and can predict what will occur. When the work changes, and/or the environment becomes uncertain, the individual may lose a sense of personal control.

As the first paradigm case illustrates, the worker may choose predictability and stability as a means of feeling in control. This feeling might be considered an illusion of control. It is certainly located externally instead of internally, however, and the transactions between the person and the situation are fairly complicated. When the circumstances of the work environment are in great flux, the individual may not perceive any way of controlling events, whereas when things are stable and predictable, personal options for responding and coping can be elaborated as illustrated in the following paradigm case.

"THE LIMITS OF CONTROL"

The first paradigm case illustrates the kind of confusion that occurs when cultural meanings shift and social practices no longer support formerly held meanings. Mr. Thomas clings to a strong duty to work and has a high need for control. His plight illustrates well the stress and coping issues that confront a person during a time of cultural and personal change. Mr. Thomas would like to retreat and live on a mountain. He wants to disengage in the social interactions that cause him confusion and anger.

Paradigm Case: The Limits of Control

Mr. Thomas works for a printing company. He feels stuck in his job after working for the same company for 25 years. He finds it difficult to change jobs because he would lose retirement benefits and because he prefers the known and routine to the novel and risky. He states that he is bored with his job but, despite the boredom, he finds any assignment that is ill-defined or requires discretionary judgment extremely stressful. He has an overriding concern for control and predictability, which causes him to choose assignments that are boring to him.

During the interview year, Mr. Thomas confronts the limits of control. His work and family circumstances no longer match his expectations and meanings. He feels depressed and longs for an earlier time, from 1942 to 1947, when the country was at its zenith and things were clear. He was idealistic then. He states that he has not cast a positive vote for 20 years. He presents a picture of his alienation in the first interview: "Society scares me. I see no discipline, a lack of authority. I was raised to believe in God and to love my country and its leaders. Now nothing is sacred and sometimes I don't know what to tell my kids."

He is bothered by the attitudes of the people he works with who do not seem to care about the quality of the work they turn out. He considers himself an efficient and conscientious worker who takes a great deal of pride in his work. He made a choice not to take a supervisory position because he knows he does not work well with people. He also said that he could never work with the public. He states that he and his wife are not very sociable. His office is crowded and noisy and he wants only the peace and quiet of his home at the end of a day.

His family is important to him. He finds it difficult to relax if all family members are not present and accounted for. His wife works in the home and earns extra money with a home craft. She runs the home and family so well that Mr. Thomas says that he seldom comes home to unsolved problems. He and his wife have been married for 16 years. They have two children, a son, age 11, and a daughter, age 13. His is a traditional marriage. He says: "At work, the final decision must be mine. At home, she is much more involved with the children. She may know things that I don't."

When asked in the third interview about the climate of his home the interviewer expected him to say "happy." Instead he said:

I like to feel that we are a happy family. By and large,
we are content with each other. [He holds up two fingers
in a V.] There is conflict. As a parent, you want your
kids to be independent but when they are, this causes
conflicts. I think we are happy but happiness can be a
delicate balance. You have to work at it. When my
daughter was 11 and she was <u>refusing</u> to admit that she
was wrong about something, I just lost my temper and
I told her that when and if you feel you can't abide our
rules, well, the door swings both ways and it is your
decision. I still feel that way. But those disagreements
are all part of growing up. It's like walking on eggshells.
Sometimes I feel like I am in the circus and I am
walking on a tightrope with a blindfold. I just have to
hope that it will all work out. I know it will get worse
before it gets better, too. [Then with a laugh] I think
we are happy.

The "balance" metaphors are not accidental and recur throughout the year. For example, in the fourth interview he states about
feeling pride, joy, and love:

I had to tell myself to control my exuberance. It's fine
to be happy, but you have to learn to curb it because,
gee whiz, what do you do when you are unhappy. For
every time you climb to the top of the mountain, a
few short steps and you're off the edge and down
into the valley. I like to soften the valleys and the
peaks.

The "balance" metaphors reflect his need for control and his
belief that he must make everything work through his own efforts. He
says repeatedly during times of confusion. "There has to be an answer.
There is always an answer." He is a planner who sees no room for
error or unforeseen possibility in a situation. He says of himself: "I
know that I am the kind of person who has to try out all the options to
try to cover them all and to think how to handle them so that at least
I am mentally prepared. . . . I am not like Scarlett O' Hara, to think
about it tomorrow." Through his advanced planning he hopes to remove
risk, and in predictable circumstances this strategy works well.
However, his current situation is novel and unpredictable, therefore
his advanced planning actually interferes with reading the unexpected
contingencies and possibilities in the situation.
    Outrage, anger, and disgust are frequent emotions for Mr.
Thomas during the year. He has frequent illnesses, colds, flu, and

back problems. He comes home anxious to rest but he is restless on the weekends. In the eighth interview he states: "I am so damn tired, it's just not much fun to live anymore. " The interviewer questions him further:

[I.: What do you mean by things being harder to cope with now? When did it change?] About a year and a half ago, or two years ago. I have noticed a change and my wife has pointed it out, too. I think I'm going through a change of life, very definitely. I have read about that in men around 45-50. [What does it feel like?] It's a combination of things. The first phase I noticed was around work. There has been a recession and so they didn't lay people off, but they didn't replace people when they left. This has been going on for three years and we are overworked and understaffed. One thing else, it is very different with the kids growing up. Our daughter is in her teens and our son will be shortly and there are all the problems with the teenagers and with the church choir. I have noticed my own decreasing lack of interest, not the wife or the kids, just me. [Here he is referring to his disillusionment with the church choir.] It has been going on for a number of years and now with all the unrest at work [that is, the rumor of his company moving]. Perhaps there are physical changes in my body that I am not aware of. But I know it's been very difficult for me the last couple of years, basically psychologically, but now compounded by physical things. I have noticed a growing pessimism within myself.

In the past, his need to control was matched by his ability to control his circumstances until his stable job was threatened; the assignments at work began to change with the decrease in staff; until his children began to be adolescents with opinions and agendas of their own; until the meanings and expectations he participated in were no longer supported in his work group. He feels confused and angry. He states he would like to withdraw and live on top of a mountain with a moat around it. He describes the extent of his despair in the tenth interview:

I sense [the male change of life] in my attitudes and in my general philosophy of life. It's almost like I have a feeling like I am psychologically, emotionally, temper-wise shrinking, pulling in. I have less of a capacity to

handle things. Things that may have bothered me on a
scale of 1-10 around 3 now get to me at 6 or 7. I am
the first to admit that it is out of proportion, but as
yet, I have not been able to get a handle on it. There
has been a slight change in my sleep pattern and I
have always kept up with what is going on in the world
and I don't like what I hear or what I see. I'm getting
older and it has had a disillusioning effect on me.

Mr. Thomas views his world as something that he must create
and control. Because he believes he must make everything happen
himself, he does not rely on others for help. Mr. Thomas has self-
selected a predictable job, and has stayed with it for 25 years. He
has attempted to raise a traditional family but despairs as he contemplates the cultural options open to his daughter that he could not
condone. Thus, his circumstances no longer support his expectations.
Parenting is viewed as extremely effortful, because he believes
that he must "develop" his children just as he must create and control
his world. For example, he talks about the pride he feels at his
daughter's confirmation in terms of an achievement:

I was very proud that she had accepted the challenge of
confirmation, that she did her best and her best is the
best. Moments like this make the hard times worthwhile:
the trying to teach them, to develop them, all to the
point of sheer frustration sometimes.

His need for control precludes faith not only in others but in his
religion as well. He states in the eleventh interview: "My problem is
that I can accept certain concepts up to a point. I cannot accept in
blind faith, it's beyond me, against my basic nature. I don't talk about
it and I don't criticize others for theirs. They have something I don't
and they are infinitely happier for it."
Mr. Thomas's capacity for love and for leisure are severely
disrupted by his effortful attempts to control his world. He feels as if
he must create and shape all events. When he is confronted with the
limits of control (for example, his family out of the house where he
cannot see them, his children becoming teenagers, his job becoming
uncertain), he becomes depressed and his life no longer works well
for him.
Unlike the physician, Dr. Ursell (see Chapter 8), it would not
occur to Mr. Thomas to say: "I try to take things as they come."
Instead he leads an effortful existence trying to cover all the contingencies and "make everything happen himself." This overriding need
for control also makes it difficult for him to deal with novel or unstruc-

tured tasks. He has no cushion of experience (see Chapter 7) working as a resource for him.

His concern for control makes interruptions particularly stressful. He views coworkers and management as potential sources of interruption rather than support. For example, Mr. Thomas was given some new work in which there was a deadline that required him to complete his work in one-fourth the time he usually takes. His first reaction was one of interest and challenge. He welcomed the chance to really get in there and solve a new problem. He told the interviewer:

> What I do is to psychologically prepare myself; to mentally build a wall around myself. I only wish I could physically isolate myself. [Interviewer note: his desk is in a crowded room and he is bothered by the noise and lack of privacy.] I take my breaks at my desk and sometimes eat lunch there too. If I'm working and it's "hot" I just go with it. I get really psyched up. I figure I can mentally relax and goof off when things are slower. I know that I am damn—you'll excuse me—good at it. I take pride in the work I do, and my boss acknowledges this.

In this situation he was frustrated by the delays caused by meetings arranged by management. He also gets upset if the plan he has made for a day's work is thrown off by another request or a coworker's interruption: "One of the bad aspects is how I relate to peers—I don't relate to them."

He is critical of some of his younger coworkers who sit around and talk about their personal lives for 45 minutes in the morning and then complain about being overworked and underpaid. The interviewer asked him how this single-minded purposefulness carries over to his homelife and he told her that it is really hard for him to unwind. Work is only a ten-minute drive and sometimes it takes him another hour to relax. He says that he is tense and edgy and often overreacts to situations at home.

Mr. Thomas likes to work hard. He likes the challenge of the short deadline. It is no sacrifice for him to cut himelf off from his coworkers to focus on work. In fact a legitimate excuse to do so is welcomed. His mobilization may or may not influence the speed at which he does his work, but it does influence his ability to unwind and relax. He finds it difficult to switch from work to leixure. The influence of the Protestant Work Ethic is evident in Mr. Thomas's penchant for working hard. He does his duty diligently and is upset when others around him are less diligent.

Three major emotion episodes related to work have to do with unstructured tasks at work. In the fourth interview he describes how he was asked to draw conclusions in a report he had written. He finds this extremely upsetting and is sure that he cannot draw conclusions that will please his boss. In the eighth and ninth interviews he is very upset over having to clean out files. It is the unstructured nature of the task that bothers him. He finds it extremely threatening to make the decisions about which files to throw away.

The emotion episode about being asked to write a conclusion to a report is representative of three other emotion episodes related to work and is selected as an example. Mr. Thomas completes a lengthy report with many facts and figures and is pleased with his work. However, his boss is not pleased and returns the report to him, explaining that he had asked him to write conclusions to the report. Mr. Thomas responds angrily because he is sure that the boss had not asked for conclusions. Apparently Mr. Thomas usually avoids writing conclusions or making judgments because he is afraid that the boss will disagree with him:

> I am damned if I do and damned if I don't. No matter what
> I come up with, it won't be what he wants. I have worked
> for him nearly 12 years and he is just a so-and-so. He
> was then and he is now. I have been down that road. I
> have been stung enough times to know. That's what got
> me. Anything to do with a conclusion, no matter how
> meticulous, he will find fault with it. Figures are his
> meat and potatoes. I knew it would be an exercise in
> frustration, just mental hell. I have never won it once.
> I thought: "My God, you know you'll do it your way
> anyway. Why the hell get me frustrated when it's your
> ideas that will go to the home office?" No matter what
> you do, it won't be good enough. Plus I just didn't want
> to get back into it. When I am done with a job, mentally,
> I vacuum.

(See Chart 6.1 for interpretation of the emotion episode.)

The Relationship between Work Meanings
and Stress and Coping

Mr. Thomas's work meanings are no longer supported by his work situation. His hard work no longer pays off. Instead he is given assignments he considers difficult because they do not match his preference for predictable, clear tasks that can be controlled. Mr. Thomas's work

CHART 6.1

Mr. Thomas: Interpretation of Emotion Episode

STAKES
Fear of doing an unstructured task incorrectly; fear of having his boss disagree with his conclusions. Distress over having to retrace his steps and therefore waste time. Felt his work was unjustly criticized.

APPRAISAL
Psychological threat.

RESOURCES
Perceived choices considered inadequate.

COPING STRATEGIES

- Direct Action
- Information Search
- Planning
- Social Support
- Social Influence—Argues for his point of view: "I said, 'No, you didn't ask for that.' He said, 'Yes, I did.' I said, 'No, you didn't.'"

  Expressed anger to boss: "I blew my everlovin' cork." Complains about the unfairness and futility of it all: "I felt like he was reprimanding me, and I didn't think he had ever asked for that. I know it would just be an exercise in frustration, just mental hell."
- Inhibition of Action—Delays speaking in order to size up the situation: "I pushed myself back from my desk and didn't say a word. I waited for him to talk."
- Cognitive Coping or Palliation—Defends own competence: "I like to think that I carry out assignments to the best of my ability."

  Blames others: "I have worked for him for nearly 12 years and he is just a so-and-so. He was then and is now. . . . Anything to do with a conclusion, no matter how meticulous, he will find fault with it."

  Absolves self of blame: "If I had known I was supposed to do that, I would have done it when the facts and figures were fresh in my mind."

  Procrastination, passive aggression: "I retreated to an old crutch, 'I'll think about it tomorrow.'

That lets me cool off. . . . You know I still haven't done the damn thing. I took a vacation soon after. And I know from experience that there is no point in rushing, just to have it sit on his desk for weeks."

Follows orders, limits defiance in order to limit conflict: "But I do think that rank has privilege, and I know how far I can go. I'm not going to win, there was no way I wouldn't have to do it. So I shut up."

Try to put it out of his mind: He left his desk. "Leaving my desk represents walking away from the papers, from that assignment. . . . I put another level of bricks on the wall I told you about and the entrance got smaller."

Fantasy revenge: "I felt like poking him one while he was still sitting there talking. . . . Then for about a half an hour, I toyed with the idea of just covering my calculator and going home for the day."

Expresses anger by swearing: "I said out loud, 'You son-of-a-bitch.' I said it loud enough for the individual in front of me to hear it. He couldn't hear me from his office."

Continues with normal routine: [This is coping when effort is required, when it is not automatic to continue with routine.] "Then I went on to another piece of work, some more routine stuff. I didn't have to work that hard, yet I did accomplish something. Routine work is practically soothing."

EMOTIONS EXPERIENCED IN EPISODE

Anger, moral outrage, aggression, frustration, helplessness, hopelessness. The participant was very angry and expressed his anger directly. He felt moral outrage and then felt victimized by the situation. He felt aggressive but had to limit his aggression. He resorted to deliberate delay of the assignment, coming as close to noncompliance as he could. He then felt helpless and hopeless, saying that he was damned if he did and damned if he didn't. Since the issue for him was, in part, doing it correctly and pleasing the boss, he felt that he could not win.

PHYSICAL EXPERIENCE OF EMOTION

"The bottom falls out of my stomach. . . . I got redfaced. I have a tendency to get hot under the collar. I sweat a cold sweat. I did feel slightly physically ill, sort of sick to my stomach when he was first talking to me. It is a feeling that does subside after a while."

EFFECT OF COPING ON EMOTION

His coping altered his emotional state. He went from anger to moral outrage (a sense of unfairness) and then felt aggressive, but when he analyzed the situation and realized that he had to comply, and that it was unlikely that he could please the boss, he felt frustrated, helpless, and hopeless. So his coping enabled him to move from a high-pitched emotional state to a less-intense, acute state, but, nevertheless, an equally negative affect. His coping did not resolve his anger or feeling that he had been treated unfairly.

EFFECTS OF COPING ON SITUATION

His coping got the message across to his boss about how displeased he was. He said, "My boss leaves me alone when he sees that I am upset." His coping did not enable him to learn from the situation. He did not learn how to write the report in a way that would satisfy the boss, and apparently this cycle has been going on for 12 years. The situation was not really improved, and a similar situation will occur again in the future.

---

has become boring and routine but change is difficult for him. He avoids risk and uncertainty. He tries to limit his work to what he knows he can do perfectly.

He feels alienated and isolated because his coworkers do not share his attitudes toward duty. Consequently, he seeks to influence his social network, but he does not seek help or support from them.

His coping strategies are primarily intrapsychic and serve to limit personal change in the situation. He defends his own competence and blames others (see Chart 6.1) so that he does not alter his skill or behavior to cope with the situation. He does not learn from the situation. His coping strategies protect him from the negative impact of the situation but they also prevent him from perceiving options and resources that he does not expect or generate. His strong need for control limits his flexibility.

He has few positive emotions by his own admission and from his reports has little or no "fun." In fact, he deliberately curbs his positive emotions for fear that they will be matched by negative ones. His life is extremely effortful as he seeks to control his life and his family's. With the rumors of his company moving, he says that his work stresses are constant, 35 hours a week. He had confronted the limits of control but does not yet see an alternative other than withdrawal or helplessness and hopelessness.

SEARCHING FOR NEW OPTIONS

While predictability may offer a source of satisfaction for some at the mid-career point, it can be the source of distress for others. But the quest for new horizons is balanced by the need to limit risk and uncertainty, as the next three paradigm cases illustrate. In each case the tension between the stability brought by the adult commitments made thus far are challenged by the desire for new alternatives and a sense of progress in the future. In each of these cases the "progress and promotion" theme discussed in Chapter 5 presents a challenge to the status quo, and the result is troubling for the participants.

"THE SEARCH FOR NEW HORIZONS"

In the second paradigm case the participant, Mr. Collins, struggles with similar cultural changes, but he has a different response. He deliberately tries to change his allegiance from duty to work to a duty to self-fulfillment. However, this shift is still in transition so that his new meanings collide with old meanings. He is unsure what a change toward more self-fulfillment and less preoccupation with work actually entails. He reflects excessively on his behavior. Both Mr. Thomas and Mr. Collins believe that they are in a mid-life crisis.

Paradigm Case: The Search for New Horizons

Mr. Collins is an architect who is relatively satisfied with his profession. However, he feels that he is in a rut and that his life lacks adventure. He regrets that his family keeps him from a more adventurous life, yet he is very committed to them. He is in a transition period and is unsettled about how much time he wants to give to family and how much to work. He seems to be on the outside of his life looking in, trying to decide how to rejoin it. His experiments with his relationships to family and work have produced uneven results. When he tries to give more attention to his 10-, 13-, 14-year-old children, he finds they are unappreciative and do not seem to need it. His attention takes the form of giving them directions or suggesting that they take tennis lessons. But they do not respond the way he expects them to and he feels frustrated.

He wants to be more family-oriented than his father. His father, he states, lived to work, and he wants to be different, but he does not know how. Though he wants to be more family-oriented, he does not want a less traditional role structure in his family. He thinks that it is his "fault that his wife is so caught up in politics and volunteer work."

He says: "If I were into something more dynamic like my own business, she might get more caught up in it, but this 8-to-5 is so undynamic." He says that he tries to be supportive of his wife's activities but finds them annoying. He and his wife have grown apart because of her new activities. They have frequent conflicts that get carried over into the next disagreement.

He reads about mid-life crisis and identifies with what he reads. He has accomplished most of his goals and has no new ones that solicit him. He fondly remembers his twenties and thirties when the world was still out there before him to conquer.

He talks wistfully about more freedom:

> I would like more freedom. I'd like not to be tied down
> to a desk. I envy people who can get a month's vacation
> at a time. Architecture is ongoing service like the
> queen bee, servicing someone all the time. I envy the
> life style of teachers. I find it very hard to get away
> even if I had the dough. I'd like, as time goes by, to
> make a commitment to work only ten months a year.
> That's more desirable to me than extra money. I'd like
> to be able to travel where and when I want. Home is
> like a rubber band. You get so far and then it pulls you
> back. My long-range goal is to travel more.

In the third interview he states:

> My interest in this profession has stabilized. I'll never
> be famous. I don't strive to further myself professionally.
> At this age I'm admitting defeat and I have negative
> feelings about that. My father gave his whole life to
> his profession and did nothing for his family. Well maybe
> he did. The family is still all together. Maybe he wasn't
> so unsuccessful as a parent. But I still see the job and
> being a parent in competition with each other. Ten years
> ago I would have been like a German soldier. I would
> have said work is the most important. Today the home
> means more to me. One thing I saw in my father that
> scared me: He was so resentful of not having been
> recognized as a great man in his profession, he spent
> most of the end of his life making up pipe dreams and
> writing his own obituary. It's awful to think it meant
> that much to him. It's not so important to me, but then
> there is a whole trend worldwide toward shorter work-
> ing hours, et cetera. It is less Germanic than it was.
> Also, I'm somewhat bored with what I'm doing. It's kind

of like cutting weeds. The faster I cut them down the
faster they grow. You never run out of projects. If I
were more professionally oriented I would see It differently. I would say, "Wow, here's an original 'Jones'
design." Now I feel I'm just a piece of a team that I feel
could do well enough without me. What I'm trying to say
is I'm hunting for other values more important than
work and yet can't see where I'm offering so much to the
kids. I talked to my wife about this the other night and
she pointed out that she knew a lot of kids who got even
further without the tennis lessons, et cetera. I have a
guilt complex, but then I have to realize that they are
very involved in their own activities.

Like the majority of other participants, Mr. Collins compares
his worklife with his father's. He longs for a new set of meanings in
his life but they have not yet emerged. He sees the passing of the
old Protestant Work Ethic values, yet he is still caught up in them.
His life was happiest when he had potential ahead and an open horizon;
now that the horizon is closing down and the commitments have worked
themselves out, he is left with little meaning. He is caught in endless
reflection and talks about creating and finding new values. His father
dies during the interview year and this causes more reflection and
contemplation, but initially the importance of his father's death
releases him from reflection and self-consciousness in a way that
enables him to enjoy a party more than is usually possible for him. He
said that his father's death put things in perspective so that he felt
free and could enjoy what he had now.

Mr. Collins has little clarity or settledness, especially in
comparison to Dr. Ursell or Mr. Ingolls (see Chapter 8). He sees
work and home life in competition with one another and is not sure how
much he should give to either. The coping episodes he talks about in
the first interview are typical. He talks about a problem client; hassles
surrounding getting the house ready for company to come; his children
being accused of throwing garbage on a neighbor's driveway; disagreements with his wife on how to discipline the children; worries about
what he didn't do on his vacation. He thinks his vacation should have
been more adventuresome and educational. Even a vacation becomes a
project with criteria for enjoyment much like criteria for performance
at work. That his leisure is so self-conscious and effortful is sympto-
matic of work and play meanings in transition. For example, he
complains that all he does for himself is swim, but can feel guilty for
"wasting his time reading a book."

The coping episode selected concerns an ongoing problem with a
difficult client. His firm serves a client who is very wealthy and
continually orders additions and architectural revisions:

The client is good for the company, work-wise, but that
doesn't make it any less frustrating. The most recent
incident occured this past Friday. The client called and
wanted to change the master bathroom entirely. I had
done all the plans for it. You don't know how much
coordination goes into this kind of work. It's a year's
effort shot to hell. I'd finished with the plans and the
contractors were just about finished with the job and now
we go back to ground zero and start again. I really dread
working with this person. I like to do a job and see it
finished. I like to get someone's approval but with this
client you know as soon as you are done the client will
find new problems and you'll have to do it over 30 or 40
times. This person takes all the fun out of it. I feel kind
of silly bad mouthing because we do get paid for the work.
The client keeps us in business.

(See Chart 6.2 for interpretation of the coping episode.)
He does not mention this as a recurring hassle during the year.
The content of his work does not come up as a stressful episode the
rest of the year. The other work-related episodes are: a misunderstanding with a secretary, which comes up in two different months as
a problem; a problem with a high-pressured salesman.

CHART 6.2

Mr. Collins: Interpretation of Coping Episode

STAKES
Client insists on having her way; it is not the best from the
professional's point of view. Not being able to finish a task.
Have to redo the work.

APPRAISAL
Loss.

RESOURCES
Perceived choices considered as inadequate. He and his company
get paid for the work and they need the business, but working
with her is extremely frustrating and will continue to be so.

COPING STRATEGIES

- Direct Action—<u>Worked longer to get through problem:</u> "Friday I stayed at work overtime to work on the problem because I just couldn't face it on Monday."
- Information Search
- Planning
- Social Support
- Social Influence
- Inhibition of Action
- Cognitive Coping or Palliation—<u>Perspective (see other's point of view, empathy):</u> "I think working on it [the house] keeps her alive. She has no family. She's all alone. Why she's just been left to die. I think she finds it like a breath of life to have young and vital people constantly working for her."

  <u>Acceptance:</u> "Nothing ever gets completed. We just have to accept it. I tried to reason with her in the past but in the long run she gets what she wants— even if I can show her how what she wants isn't the best way of doing something. Now I don't even try to change her mind."

  <u>Recognizes that this will pass:</u> "Things will change. We'll eventually get rid of her, the old bat."

EMOTIONS EXPERIENCED IN EPISODE
<u>Frustration, irritation, hopelessness:</u> "I get frustrated with it. I'm getting tired of it. I just want her to finish and go away."

PHYSICAL EXPERIENCE OF EMOTION
Not described.

EFFECT OF COPING ON EMOTION
Dampened emotional impact.

EFFECT OF COPING ON SITUATION
Enabled him to stick with the task and get what he needed to do done earlier.

Relationship between Work Meanings and
Stress and Coping

Mr. Collins is competent in his work and knows it. For example, in the conflict with the client described above, he does not engage in self-recriminations or self-doubts. He is clear about the issues and this clarity enables him to cope with the frustration. Work runs smoothly and routinely and no other work problems related to the actual content of his work are mentioned during the year. The other work incidents are interpersonal conflicts.

His major work stress is boredom. His work holds little challenge. He imagines what it would feel like if he were more committed to his work or, as he says, "more professional." He no longer gets excited about the projects. They are like "weeds." The more he cuts down, the faster they grow. He contemplates adding interest and the chance for fame to his worklife by going into business for himself, but he lacks the motivation. Because he is searching for "other values more important that work," and has not yet found them, he feels at odds with himself at work and at home, and even at leisure. This search for new values has led to a critical evaluation of his leisure. His self-reflection and deliberate efforts to "enjoy" his vacations more place leisure beyond his reach. His leisure disappears in the face of his critical evaluation of it.

"PROMOTION AS A SIGN OF WORTH"

The third paradigm case illustrates how one strongly held meaning that does not work can diminish social competence and coping effectiveness. Mr. Verdent planned his whole worklife around getting promoted to a particular position. When his former boss retired, and he did not get the promotion, he found the disappointment unbearable. His particular work lost all meaning for him.

Paradigm Case: Promotion As a Sign of Worth

The third paradigm case illustrates how disruptive a lost incentive or meaning can be. Mr. Verdent came to define and understand his success and self-worth in terms of a particular promotion at work.

Mr. Verdent is a 50-year-old man who had worked for a large company for 20 years until the tenth month of the interview year, when he resigned his position of supervisor of a technical division. The entire interview year focuses on an ongoing conflict at work over a woman "less prepared than he" who was promoted instead of him when his supervisor retired. This promotion had occurred one year ago, at the beginning of the interview year. But the conflict was still at a very high level and continued to escalate throughout the year until Mr. Verdent became too distressed to return to work. The year starts out with the participant stating that he is very angry with his "lady boss." At the beginning of the year he is still hopeful of getting a promotion to a different, better position, but this hope wanes by the middle of the year.

He spends a great deal of time on hobbies and with his family. He says: "Now is the time when you ask why you are ridding that bicycle so fast and not getting anywhere. Now you have time to enjoy family and wife." He and his wife have been married for 31 years. It is a first marriage for both. He states that he and his wife have a good relationship. They divide the household tasks, but there is conflict when his wife reminds him to do the dishes. He is a procrastinator, and she, according to his report, is not. He says this will not change; it has been going on for 30 years. He seems to hedge about his relationship to his wife. They have little sexual intimacy. He states that their communication has improved, however, as a result of participation in a marriage enrichment group.

He relies on his wife for advice about work problems throughout the year. Their homelife revolves around their worklife. They talk primarily about their work, he says. Their relationship seems to be satisfactory with effort; but there is little evidence of spontaneity. There is a careful division of labor. Things work, but they do not seem to be a source of great positive emotion during the year.

His wife has an interesting job in which she gets a promotion during the year. They both enjoy the increased freedom involved with her change from working at home to working for pay. He says that he could now quit his job if he wanted and that gives him a new sense of freedom.

Mr. Verdent's understanding of the relative importance of home and family versus work does not match the year's events. He states that family issues and the conflicts with his two daughters are much more important than anything that occurs at work. Yet the problems at work lead to a breakdown and a level of anxiety with which he is unable to cope. He, like others, states that he leaves work at work and separates home and work. But his interviews and the events of the year do not indicate that he is <u>actually</u> able to compartmentalize home- and worklife.

Work is in the forefront of Mr. Verdent's attention and concern throughout the year. He is apparently very good at what he does technically. He gets letters of appreciation and recognition for being able to get things out quickly in his department. His hobby is in the same line as his work and he finds it enjoyable and absorbing.

He seems less skilled at interpersonal relationships at home and at work. He states that he can do without making any new friends, that he has never needed to join social clubs. He has one close male friend who is the only friend he confides in and the only friend he talks about during the year. In the tenth interview he states about his job:

"There is a lot more challenge than frustration in the job when you take away the personalities, but the people make it so negative that you want to leave." So it is not surprising that he was passed over for promotion to a higher level of management. However, he does not perceive himself limited in interpersonal skill. Instead he prides himself on allowing the people in his department room for creativity. He apparently misreads organizational situations, vesting some actions by his superiors with more significance than they deserve, while overlooking the significance of others.

The following excerpt from the second interview provides the background information for coping episodes for the rest of the year. Talking about his position as acting manager he says:

> I made some decisions and I felt good. [I: Had you had previous experience in this position?] The old boss had never had someone take his place. I never approached her directly. I was sneaky. I asked her, "Tell us what will happen when you leave." Both times, on the last day before she left she wrote a memo designating me as her temporary replacement. [I: What happened?] I had different types of decisions. I had to make decisions for the immediate future and for the long term. [I: How did you feel?] I felt elated, solving a problem, assuming a new role. They were decisions I wouldn't have made in my regular position. I had to look at what was good for the whole division in the long run, not just for my particular area. So some of the decisions I made were contrary to my best interests in my regular position. [Interviewer note: He discussed his decisions. Field note: These decisions are not described to protect confidentiality, but they were relatively minor decisions if cost outlay is considered.] I didn't want to be punitive towards people just because I was in this position now. [I: How did you feel when she returned? Did you want to keep the job?] I wouldn't want her job under the current circumstances. [I: Circumstances?] This job could come to me in one of two ways. In seven years she'll have to retire. I'll be 58. I don't feel that it would be more than a slight chance then. Either she retires or is fired as an incompetent. And that doesn't happen around here. You know, it was interesting, when she had me replace her the second time. I look at words. I am very aware of words since I work with forms. She said on the memo that I would be her "acting manager." I liked that. I thought it sounded nice.

This episode is informative for its candor about his power fantasies about being in a formal leadership position. He manages to get himself placed in the position of acting manager, a position that was superfluous in the past. He then expands his sense of the importance of the role by reflecting on the title of "acting manager." This illustrates just how important this particular promotion was to Mr. Verdent. However, it is not the story of one who has a sound grasp on the real power relationships of the organization. He does not view being acting manager as a stepping stone or, even more appropriately, a temporary change of pace. He views it as an entitlement. He relishes the relatively minor decisions that he makes and considers that they convey self-worth and importance.

He predicts that conflicts with his boss will continue and they do. He is gripped by the conflict and by the need to prove his worthiness and his boss's unworthiness. This is illustrated in the fourth interview and monthly thereafter:

> She and I are meeting with the department head on
> Monday for an update. Whenever there are problems,
> she and I talk about the problem and she feels like that
> solves it and then we are back to things as they were.
> But she can't do that; it's like we can't go back to high
> school. Today and yesterday a situation came up. She
> never learns how to deal with a mistake. It's one thing
> to make a mistake, but not the same one over and over.
> I keep telling her to write things in memo form. She
> hadn't and it had caused problems because a clerk was
> doing what she thought the boss wanted. I was talking
> to the clerk, and the boss walked in, said something
> and we went into her office. We discussed it and I said:
> "Listen! Listen!" and I pounded the desk. I told her
> I could tell her anything I want because I am the adver-
> sary and she is the boss.

(See Chart 6.3 for interpretation of the emotion episode.)

The situation at work deteriorated in the fourth month of the interview year. The participant's conflict is polarized and he is locked into proving his boss incompetent and himself worthy of her position. (It is interesting to speculate what might have happened if the position had been given to a man rather than a woman. He might have been able to benefit from comforting phrases commonly used to deal with disappointment. Mr. Verdent might have found a way to legitimize the appointment of a man. He could not even recognize that the new supervisor's position was firm and that his was not.) He expect-ed his position to win out because it was "right." The participant's

CHART 6.3

Mr. Verdent: Interpretation of Emotion Episode

STAKES

Concern over proving immediate boss's inadequacies: "I hoped that they both could see what kinds of problems could be set up [what problems she creates] and what could be solved, areas where she was causing extra work."

Concern over being proven right. Concern over getting a change in the situation: "I wanted the situation changed."

APPRAISAL

Threat.

RESOURCES

Overall balance of power: formal, hierarchical relationships. Being in a one-down or low status position negatively affects access to resources.

COPING STRATEGIES

● Direct Action
● Information Search
● Planning—Advanced planning: "I wrote up a job description, but I couldn't bring myself to hand it to him [the big boss]."
● Social Support—Uses available emotional support: "My feelings got more relaxed before we went out the door because Lee is friendly and says he'll solve it." He talked to his wife for sympathy.
● Social Influence—Argues: "I got argumentative sounding about a point I knew and he knew."
● Inhibition of Action—Inhibits expression of anger: "It is safe to say that I was angry, but I was trying to hide it from the higher ups."

Tries to control physical experience of negative emotion: "The more I tried to control it, the worse it got [shaky knees and dry mouth]."
● Cognitive Coping or Palliation—Imagines hidden power: "I thought I had to be careful not to say anything about my other assignments for him. I'm not feeling puffed up, but I can't mention it because it might be taken the wrong way." [The big boss had given him a minor assignment to do.]

Reads cues in the situation as reassuring: "On the other hand, he took my advice on another situation."

Comforting cognition: Tells himself he is right.

EMOTIONS EXPERIENCED IN EPISODE

Wariness: Participant labels episode as a feeling of wariness, a feeling of having to watch what he says.

Creeping frustration: "It was a very uneasy feeling, not quite like unwariness. You know the facts and you have to deal with them. It's uneasy that you have to wait for a decision. I feel like I'm being dragged along, and I feel like I'll end up with something in the long run—nothing!"

Frustration: "Frustration because you have to use your energy this way [keeping quiet]."

Anger: ". . . bring it out in the open, but I didn't. I controlled my anger."

Hopeless: "It certainly doesn't make you feel hopeful, and I tried to look at the hopeful side and there wasn't any."

PHYSICAL EXPERIENCE OF EMOTION

Nervous, dry mouth, knees shaking. [I: When did your feelings change?] "I got more relaxed just before we went out the door. . . ."

EFFECT OF COPING ON EMOTION

Coping efforts enhance the feeling of wariness. Efforts to control physical experience of emotion increase the physical responses.

EFFECT OF COPING ON SITUATION

The situation, in terms of reconciling or setting things right with the new boss, deteriorates further. But Mr. Verdent's goal is not reconciliation; he wants to prove that the new boss is incompetent. However, Mr. Verdent does not accomplish this goal either. Instead, his own competence comes into question as a result of his coping efforts.

---

efforts to cope with his disappointment and outrage over not getting a promotion that he had counted on getting creates stressful episodes that span a period of almost two years. He is unable to redefine or accept the situation. He stays locked both in the conflict and in his bid to prove himself worthy and his new "lady boss" unworthy. He loses his ability to read the situation correctly. From the fourth interview on, Mr. Verdent continues to have explosive episodes with the boss.

In the eleventh interview the two-year battle is resolved. Mr. Verdent was suffering from acute anxiety and emotional exhaustion. He got up one morning and was unable to go to work because he was shaking uncontrollably. This had happened several times before, but this time it was much worse. His wife asked him what he wanted and he said: "A way out." So she called the office and told them he was too sick to come in. Subsequently, he took a disability leave. He began seeing a psychologist and going to an occupational health clinic. He is now looking for another position within the company. He is willing to take a cut in status and pay but feels depressed because he has no "real" future in the company now. He says that he could have killed himself if it were not for his religious beliefs and the support he receives through a marriage support group.

The Relationship between Work Meanings and Stress and Coping

Worthiness and work are defined for Mr. Verdent by promotion. For two years he was unable to get any distance on the problem and could not recognize it as a situation that he could not change. When he is asked: "What are some of the bad things about being your age?" he responds: "Not being able to accomplish everything you hoped to be able to accomplish. You can't blame it on one person, but at certain times I think I've had too much naive faith in the people above me. I've worked hard because I've enjoyed work and been disappointed when no one noticed." When asked if there was someone who was very important or influential in shaping his life, he responds: "On the bad side, a guy I worked for for 20 years did a bad job on me." He says in the twelfth interview: "One thing I've got to learn is like that alcoholic's prayer—the courage to change the things I can and the patience to bear those I can't and the wisdom to know the difference."

The importance of promotion as a sign of personal worth for Mr. Verdent is similar to the kind of importance that Mr. Roberts experiences related to the process of work (see Chapter 3). Had the meanings of work for Mr. Verdent been the same as those of Mr. Roberts (that is, steady work as an employee), the events of the past two years would not have occurred. Here the issue is confused if the purely cognitive interpretation (usually phrased in terms of "thinking makes it so") is offered. The meaning is a lived one and is not open to reinterpretation or "thinking" until after Mr. Verdent has reached a crisis in his position. Even at the end of the year he is struggling for a reinterpretation of the events of the past two years and states wistfully that he wished he could have recognized this as a battle not to enter. But at the time he could not perceive the events except in terms of losing the promotion. Therefore the stakes of all the coping and emotion episodes at work were to prove his new boss incompetent. When this strategy failed, returning to his old job was untenable. At the end of the year, Mr. Verdent had moved out of his crisis and was seeking to establish a new career. He was trying to reinterpret the events of the past two years. Looking back, it may be difficult for him to understand the strength and meaning of the particular promotion for him, but as long as he was in the situation he was unable to understand his work and his worthiness except in terms of the lost promotion.

The meaning of the events for Mr. Verdent did not permit him to break out of his line of coping (see "Summary and Conclusions" section of Chapter 5). In fact his coping strategies are only understandable in terms of what was at stake for Mr. Verdent. (that is, competing with the new manager instead of adjusting to a disappointment). Mr. Verdent is now trying to discover new meanings of work that allow him to feel committed to his work without the promise of promotions, since it is doubtful that the remainder of his career holds many promotional opportunities. He ends the year in just such a reconstruction process.

This case provides a useful comparison for the next case because one might conclude that holding an untenable meaning is the worst position for coping with stress. However, coping with the stress created by untenable meanings provides more direction and basis for action than a position of meaninglessness or nihilism. The next paradigm case illustrates the chronic stress and diminished coping competence created by nihilism.

"DEMEANING WORK"

The final case illustrates the kind of paralysis that can occur with pervasive meaninglessness. Mr. Paul actively searches for what life means, while nothing in his life seems essential or important to him. He suffers from an advanced stage of nihilism, which interferes with his making a commitment to his current job or finding a new line of work. His work meanings are antithetical to his current work as a bus driver. His work is stressful for him and he constantly searches for a way out. But his search ends in contemplation rather than action, because no alternative stands out as more plausible or more interesting than others.

Paradigm Case: Demeaning Work

Mr. Paul lives in an apartment with his wife and two daughters, ages 10 and 1. He is a bus driver who expected a better career. Prior to driving a bus he was a minister, a teacher, and a real estate salesman. He does not value his work and feels that it is beneath his dignity and ability. He says that his work is "just a job to give me money to support my family. There is nothing creative about it. If I could figure out some way to get out of it I would do that. Work is more frustrating than challenging." He says that the only thing right about the job is the pay. He stuck with teaching for a year but it made him so tense that he had physical symptoms. None of the jobs he has tried has worked out for him. He thinks of going back to school to be a lawyer or an accountant. He says that his self-image is not as high as it was. He states: "I am not using the talents I have." His job does not match his expectations. He has never thought of himself as a bus driver and cannot think of being a bus driver the rest of his life. He does not communicate or associate with other bus drivers, and does not want to identify with them because "they are not the type of people I would ask to come home to share a meal."

He says that he feels trapped on the bus with the frequent conflicts that occur there. He also feels trapped in their small apartment where conflicts can escalate over any number of routine daily activities.

He feels that his work is meaningless except as a way of providing for his family. But his sense of meaninglessness does not stop with his job. Mr. Paul's life is collapsing inward. He is lost in endless self-analysis, none of which helps him to love or be loved, or make any commitments whatsoever. He is the only participant to state that the best time in his life was grammar school and high school—the time in his life prior to any adult commitments. When he was asked whether he would choose to have children if he could start all over, he said:

> That's a real hard one. You can't really see the loveliness of the children. You can't really separate it away from the energy and effort consumed in raising the children. I would do it again if I could have my same two children because they are beautiful children. Once again, you get into the question what does it all mean? Is having leisure time what living here on this earth is all about? Or is it for moral growth and humanizing yourself to the greatest extent? Then it would be more important to have the children. This is what I haven't solved . . . being human is why we are here, the children are important.

Even though he loves his children, he can still wonder whether he made the "right" choice. "What does having childen mean?" he asks himself as a part of his endless reflection. In any particular situation he wonders if he would be happier and feel more worthwhile if he were doing something else.

He is not solicited by any important tasks and cannot seem to commit himself fully to any endeavor in the present. In the Life Cycle and Aging Interview (tenth interview) he wonders if he should have given himself to a larger community instead of a family. This is said in the context of a chaotic and unhappy family situation. His wife was severely depressed and suicidal for three years. While she is functioning better now, running a household is still difficult for her. He is caught in endless reflection and analysis about the other possibilities he might have chosen. "Caring" and giving in the abstract, or more impersonally in a larger community seems more feasible. Close relationships and intimacy seem fraught with tension and seem to be beyond Mr. Paul's reach. He is not available in the concrete situation to participate in the give and take of close relationships. The commitments he has taken up are not very meaningful to him and he wonders what it would be like if he had taken a different path. He would like to have extramarital affairs but says he could not handle the guilt psychologically. Everything seems possible to reflect upon and contemplate, but almost nothing seems possible to do. Abstractions and intellectualization are prevalent in all his interviews. For example, in the eleventh interview when he was asked what he thinks about the time of _his_ life, he answered about time in general:

> The future is hope, nothing else . . . maybe something will happen [Interviewer note: He interpreted this question to apply to time in general, rather than _his_ time.] The past . . . had a larger human quality to it because it was closer. Maybe this is fantasy. Maybe being close to a land-type economy, even if there was oppression there, there was a chance for humanism. Now everything is collapsing inward. As for the future? The hope says this will break apart, open up, have a future ever expanding of which humanism is a part. I don't expect this to happen before I die.

This answer contrasts starkly with other participants' answers, which usually concerned their own life experience. His answer reflects the way Mr. Paul lives and understands his life. As he says in the tenth interview: "I'm stuck where I am. It's the same thing over and over. Is it possible to change 47 years of patterns?"

Most of his emotion and coping episodes concern conflicts at home and his dissatisfaction with his marriage. His coping and emotion episodes are negative except for one joyful episode with his daughter, during a soccer game. He was able to forget himself and enjoy the moment. After the game he concludes that he had enjoyed the game because he had received so much approval from the parents and that he needs adult reward. His interpretation seems at odds with his description of exhilaration during the game and his description of losing himself in the moment.

The emotion episodes he described with the family were anger, resentment, frustration, depression, hurt, and anxiety. Episodes related to work had to do with frustration and fear with a busload of unruly kids; frustration, anger, and depression over the union contract settlement after a long strike; and finally anxiety in general related to his bus driving and to his selling real estate. Actually, he has frequent difficult episodes at work with unruly riders, smokers, tight schedules, but he mentions these only in passing, saying that he is learning to handle them better. The real issues are at home, and work pales compared to the difficulty he experiences at home. When the interviewer commented that most of his episodes were focused on the home he said: "Perhaps it is the type of job I have. I'm by myself. I'm just out there driving my bus with these people I'm driving around. It's kind of independent. All my hassles come at home."

The interviewer cannot get a "story" with chronology and real events from Mr. Paul, because his description of events contains so much self-doubt and analysis that most of the dialogue and turmoil are internal. For example, one episode he described relating to his job selling real estate is very convoluted because he is confused about the ethics of selling. He worries that his lack of knowledge prevented a loan from going through at the bank. When he heard that the loan had been refused, he looked at the floor in embarrassment. He told the interviewer that he was able to reestablish eye contact—that he is good at this. He said: "I felt that I could at least look at them." The rest of the episode is a complicated story about wanting to make up the money the couple lost, getting into an argument with his wife over this, and discussion about guilt and embarrassment. The clients were not angry with him and the interviewer notes: "This episode, as others in his life, went on within him."

He imagines that he is most adept in situations dealing with human beings, but the example of self-conscious attempts at maintaining eye contact would indicate that interacting and communicating with people do not come easily for him. If he were more facile, he would probably not have to consciously try to maintain eye contact. In fact, his extreme self-consciousness and excessive reflection probably prevent him from having spontaneous fluid interactions with others. This is probably why the times at the soccer games where he is able to lose himself in the moment stand out as high points for him. When the bus driving goes well, it provides him with something to do that does not require a lot of interpersonal interaction and thus offers him an asylum from self-conscious concern for doing well and from difficult troubled interactions with others.

Mr. Paul still dreams of finding a more pleasant, satisfying line of work; but considering other jobs leaves him confused because he does not know what he would like. Dreaming about other possibilities offers him comfort and escape amidst the difficulties of driving the bus. He fears that he will not trade his job for one more commensurate with his education and status expectations because he is caught by the retirement and pension plan.

He is also caught by his inner turmoil so that a relatively structured job with minimal interpersonal demands is all that he can handle given his level of confusion. Bus driving, while not up to his education and aspirations, does allow him to function as a provider for his family.

Bus driving is extremely taxing for him physically and emotionally. He gets very angry with loud passengers, passengers who smoke on the bus, and he is terrified by unruly adolescents. He worries that he is developing racial prejudice, as he comes to hate the blacks who ride his bus and cause disruptions.

His one description of terror and frustration on the bus illustrates the level of chaos and fear to which a bus driver is subject and illustrates this participant's response to these most extreme work stressors. In this episode the participant was driving an unusual route. The bus was crowded and many of the kids had to stand. The problem started immediately, with kids shooting firecrackers, screaming, and running around the bus. He walked back and told the kids that he would wait until they stopped since he was paid whether or not the bus was moving. The bus had no radio so he could not phone in for help or phone for the police. This made him furious:

> The whole time I talked to them, the girls were shrieking and yelling. I went back to drive and they started all over again. I became determined to get them where they were going and get it over with. The noise got worse, and I dealt with it less. My knees got shaky, and I worried about being able to control the bus. I also worried about the safety of the small children. By the time the kids got off, they had kicked out four windows, and pushed one totally out into the street. I wanted to slam on the brakes and throw them [the kids] up against the window, but I didn't. . . . Incidents like this churn up antiblack prejudice since most of the kids were black.

His conscience bothers him for hating the kids and for seeing them as animals. He says that he is used to blocking out the blaring music but can't stand the "animal" behavior. He used to get into a rage over the music but psyched himself out because he feels totally impotent when he is in a rage.

(See Chart 6.4 for interpretation of the coping episode.)

CHART 6.4

Mr. Paul: Interpretation of Coping Episode

STAKES
> Fear of physical harm to himself and to his passengers.
> Fear of his own loss of control. Anxiety over helplessness in
> the situation.

APPRAISAL
> Physical threat; psychological threat.

RESOURCES
> Perceived choices considered inadequate.

COPING STRATEGIES

- Direct Action—He stopped the bus during the worst of the
  behavior.
- Information Search
- Planning—Makes a plan to deal with a similar situation in the future:
  "I told the assistant superintendent not to send that bus out
  without a radio again." In the future he would insist on a radio.
- Social Support—Seeks active assistance: He talked with the
  superintendent.
- Social Influence
- Inhibition of Action
- Cognitive Coping or Palliation—Makes a conscious effort to change
  his mental state: "I used to get into a rage over the music."
  But he now "psychs" himself out.
  Concentrated on getting through the
  event: "I became determined to get where we were going and
  get it over with."
  Fantasy Revenge: "I wanted to slam
  on the brakes and throw them [the kids on the bus] out the
  window."

EMOTIONS EXPERIENCED IN EPISODE
> Anger, concern, fear, frustration, helplessness, guilt. He felt
> angry and frightened over the kids' behavior. He was worried
> about the little children on the bus. He felt frustrated that he
> could not control the kids' behavior. He felt helpless, and just
> tried to get through the situation. Finally, he felt guilty for per-
> ceiving the kids as animals, since he was afraid that these feel-
> ings demonstrated prejudice on his part because the kids were black.

PHYSICAL EXPERIENCE OF EMOTION
His knees were shaky and he felt tense.

EFFECT OF COPING ON EMOTION
He controlled his rage but did not change his anger or frustration, helplessness or guilt.

EFFECT OF COPING ON SITUATION
He was ineffective in the situation in terms of changing the behavior of the children; however, he did arrange it so that this would not happen again. His self-blame and self-recriminations added to his sense of guilt and helplessness.

The Relationship between Work Meanings
and Stress and Coping

Mr. Paul's work meanings are antithetical to his job. The work meanings he has are divorced from his capabilities and his situation. He has remnants of his ministerial self-definition, which make his responses as a bus driver or a real estate salesman confusing and even more stressful. Therefore, he does not talk about skills or "tricks of the trade." He does not trade talk or gather survival tips from other bus drivers. He is not sufficiently engaged in being a bus driver to improve his coping skills on the bus. His coping strategy for dealing with blaring radios and unruly passengers is to ignore them. When that strategy fails to insulate him, he feels guilty over his anger and hostility.

Because of the pervasive meaninglessness in his life, he has lost his clarity and therefore few of his coping strategies are automatic. He can contemplate almost any career option (for example, hanging wallpaper, being a travel agent, working for another department in public transportation, and others). However, he has no basis for sorting out which might be well suited to him.

No one set of meanings can prevent stress or provide optimal coping strategies for every circumstance. However, meaninglessness is the most stressful position. The person without meanings has no basis for guiding choices and no incentive for developing coping strategies. Since the person has no clarity about his goals, he can contemplate many choices without having any stand out as more or less important. It can seem as if he has an infinite number of choices and this proliferation of choices paralyzes his ability to act. Mr. Paul engages in excessive reflection, which prevents him from making any particular commitments. A certain level of commitment is required for situational adjustment (Becker, 1964, see discussion on situational adjustment, pp. 35-36). Mr. Paul is not engaged in work as a bus driver, and therefore most of his coping strategies are intrapsychic measures to distance himself further from the situation.

SUMMARY AND CONCLUSIONS

These four participants have disrupted work meanings that affect their stress appraisals and coping options. The first participant clings to his meanings of work as duty. He believes in being diligent and doing a job well regardless of his interests and talents. For Mr. Thomas, doing a job well requires that he be able to predict the outcome and make no mistakes. In the past his work was more predictable and matched his preference for clarity and control. Also, his coworkers shared his beliefs and expectations about duty. However, his company is changing. Now he gets novel assignments. His uncertainty at work is compounded by new uncertainties at home as his children become adolescents. His response to these changes has been to increase his efforts to control and balance his life. He avoids excitement or positive emotions because he fears he will feel depressed afterward. Consequently he has few positive emotions. He carefully tries to balance and control his emotional life, his work life, and his family life. As balance and control become more tenuous, his life becomes more and more effortful, and he responds by limiting his endeavors. His mental image of the ideal setting is a house on top of a mountain with no access.

The second participant is much less distressed than Mr. Thomas. However, Mr. Collins is struggling with similar personal and cultural changes. He is deliberately trying to change his work meanings. He wants to be less work involved and to seek his fulfillment outside his work. His main source of distress stems from the confusion that this change creates and the depression that his loss of work interest causes. His coping strategies often do not match his new desires and interests because they are remnants of his old work meanings.

The third participant ends the year in a reconstruction stage. For two years Mr. Verdent's work meanings were reduced to winning one promotion. He could not accept the loss and after two years of frequent stressful episodes he left his job in a state of exhaustion. Mr. Verdent's coping strategies were defined by the stakes, the meaning of the event for himself. Since his goal of unseating the new manager was unrealistic, his coping efforts were also unrealistic.

The final case illustrates that the position of nihilism is the most bereft of coping options for several reasons. First, Mr. Paul lacks the commitment to any particular situation to either change himself or the situation. A certain level of commitment is required for situational adjustment. Second, the person's ability to act is paralyzed because he perceives that he has unlimited choices and all those choices seem equally plausible. Since meaninglessness disrupts coping, it is potentially the most stressful position. No position is immune from stress; however, it would be naive to conclude that one would be better off to participate in no meanings. Meanings and involvement give rise to stressful appraisals but they also provide the basis for coping with the situation.

7

THE CUSHION OF EXPERIENCE AS
A COPING RESOURCE

In contrast to the eight cases presented in Chapters 5 and 6, work has become less stressful for seven participants. Their work meanings are integrated with their work practices and experience so that what was once stressful is no longer. These participants have a backlog of similar situations that they rely on in a way that prevents stressful appraisals. This study calls this "preappraisal resource" the cushion of experience, which will be contrasted to comforting cognitions (see Mechanic, 1962) that are used after a stress appraisal, and with the illusion of control that, like a cushion of experience, can also serve as a coping resource.

This chapter presents a thematic analysis and description of the cushion of experience. When a person's prior experience makes events that were once perceived as threatening into nonthreatening events, then the person is drawing on a cushion of experience as a coping resource. This is termed a cushion of experience because the person is not drawing on a particular talent or competency that can be isolated. Instead they are relying on a global perception, the confidence acquired in reading whole situations. They are relying on their ability to recognize whole situations as similar and dissimilar to past situations. They are not relynig on precise procedures or rules for handling the situation, nor do they necessarily believe that they can control the outcomes. They do believe that their efforts can make a difference, and if not, they believe they can handle the outcomes.

THE PERCEIVED RESOURCE OF EXPERIENCE

Seven participants claimed that the perspective of experience limits their emotional distress in complex, ambiguous circumstances

(Mr. Collins, Mr. Gough, Mr. Ingolls, Mr. Kemp, Mr. Morris, Mr. Smith, and Dr. Ursell). Three interview excerpts illustrate the perceived resource of experience that prevents a stressful appraisal. A successful business executive talks about the pros and cons of going into business for himself:

> [I: Hypothetically, what would happen if the business did fail? Note: Here the participant offered three concrete options if the business failed. Then the interviewer asks: "What would it mean to you personally if the business failed?"] I think that there would be a lot of bad feelings to the point of tears. I'm sure there would be a lot of that. There would be a lot of talking in the family as to what the next step would be. I'd feel bad a reasonably short time unless I couldn't correct the situation in any way. [I: And then?] I don't worry about things like that. I've had lots of disappointments in 51 years and I can't remember any of them lasting longer than three weeks.

This participant does not know <u>how</u> things will work out, but he is confident that they will, and that life will still be livable. He knows that he can recover, because disappointments do not last forever. He has a number of reliable external and internal resources.

Another participant, a physician, talks about a complicated situation where disciplinary action against a colleague was required. The interviewer asks about how he could remain so calm; the participant credits past experience: "It used to be a major event when things like that happened. It's a step-by-step process where you get used to handling situations. It's like a comment I heard at a lecture yesterday: 'Good judgment comes from experience and experience comes from bad judgment.'"

Both of these participants endorse what they have learned from failures as well as from successes. Implicit in their definition of experience is the surprise, disappointment, or bad judgment that taught them something useful. Thus, people who possess a cushion of experience expect not only to survive but also to learn from <u>any</u> experience. This expectation is illustrated in the next interview excerpt. The participant, a safety engineer, stated after describing some difficulty he had in correcting a safety hazard: "I can adapt to any situation. You don't spend 15 years in the Navy without learning how." [I: Could you clarify that for me?] "I make friends and take things as they come."

These three examples of a cushion of experience support the following definition: <u>A cushion of experience as a coping resource is</u>

a perceptual stance that prevents a stressful appraisal in uncertain situations where a person's prediction and control may be limited. This is a preappraisal expectancy that reassures people that despite uncertainties and change they will be able to alter their response. It is based on an understanding that good outcomes can be achieved in a number of ways. People with a cushion of experience as a coping resource trust that their past concrete experiences in similar situations will guide their decisions and actions. Thus, a cushion of experience, when it is available as a coping resource, prevents a stressful appraisal.

The stress-prevention function of the cushion of experience becomes clearer when one examines cases where it is absent. Decreased stress, or stress prevention due to prior experience, is the expected norm. One expects a person to gain a sense of assurance, if not wisdom, from experience. Since study participants had at least 20 years of work experience, it was expected that most would have a cushion of experience as a coping resource. However, ten participants lacked this coping resource. Six participants lacked a cushion of experience primarily because of beliefs about the self, and four lacked it primarily because of situational characteristics. Each is discussed in the next sections.

BELIEFS ABOUT THE SELF THAT LIMIT A CUSHION OF EXPERIENCE

Seven participants have beliefs about the self that limit their cushion of experience (Mr. Adams, Mr. Davis, Mr. Franks, Mr. Lewis, Mr. Narring, Mr. Verdent, and Mr. West). This section examines why these beliefs prevent the development of a cushion of experience. Each of these participants chose to talk about work frequently. Prior successes did not reassure them. For three of these participants, a fear of failure and a belief in the efficacy of worry prevent the development of a cushion of experience. Like most people, they fear making an error, but they carry this fear to the extreme of believing that making an error cancels out past successes. Past success does not offer any assurance of future success. These participants also believe that worry is, in itself, an effective strategy. This belief is best illustrated by interview excerpts. For example, Mr. Davis, a successful salesman, talks about the value of psyching himself up:

> Well you have a certain amount of apprehension. It's
> as if you were being invited to the White House; same
> idea. Because these are the people that make or

> break you. . . . [On another occasion he states in
> response to the interviewer's question: "Do you feel like
> you did a good job?"] Sure, and maybe that is what is
> necessary—getting all those emotions stirred up in order
> to do a good job. [I: To mobilize your . . ?] To psych
> yourself up. [I: You were quite alert, I take it.] You
> can count on that.

In retrospect he can acknowledge that things do usually fit into a
nice pattern and that he is usually successful, but he avoids drawing
on reasurring thoughts in advance because he is afraid that he will
not have "enough" anxiety to give a good performance. He draws on the
analogy of stage performers who perform best with butterflies in their
stomach. Thus, past experience does not prevent stress appraisals
because he operates from the personal paradigm that anxiety breeds
success, and success is totally up to the individual. He believes that
his performance will fall apart if he is calmer. Anxiety has a magical
quality that goes beyond the attentiveness called for by the task. He
accentuates his anxious feelings to ensure his success.

Two other participants, a carpenter and a store manager, have a
fear of failure that prevents them from experiencing a cushion of
experience. Both find it noticeably difficult to talk about coping
with errors; they actually seem to lack the language necessary for such
a discussion. This is depicted in the carpenter's description of a
bad day:

> Today when I was measuring elevations, there was no one
> to say it was all right, and it bothered me. . . . Other
> than measuring, all I have to do now on this project is to
> sit there and watch a guy excavate. I was watching him
> get a half a load at a time and I thought he should get
> more. That's how I was today, worrying about little things
> that aren't my job. [I: How did you feel when you were
> measuring the elevations?] My stomach was in knots. It
> really grabbed me fast like an accident . . . I thought,
> "If something really happened, what would I feel if I really
> blow it someday?" I was thinking of the other house and
> the angle we had wrong, but that we had caught in time.
> [That he caught the error in time before does not reassure
> him. It only prods him to recheck his measurements.]

Normally, one would expect that a carpenter, with as much
experience as Mr. West, has to have a language to talk about errors.
For example, one expects phrases such as "Errors are usually caught"
or "Errors are seldom made if measurements are checked twice";

or statements of acceptance of errors such as "Things can go wrong and sometimes you just have to redo your work." But Mr. West has no such ways to talk about errors. Instead he mentally rehearses the consequences of making an error as if to increase his vigilance. He has little acceptance of the limits of control and perfectionism.

The store manager (Mr. Lewis, see Chapter 5 for paradigm case) has a similar fear of making errors. He states that he usually has an "on-guard" feeling when he is at work. During the interview year he has his first notable cash shortage in 22 years. He is extremely threatened and falls out of trust with himself and his employees. He states:

> I had a real depressed feeling. I thought I'd just like
> to get up and walk out of the whole thing. I've always been
> very intense and precise with the procedures with the
> money and I feel depressed about it. It may be a
> reflection on my always having maintained a good record
> for cash control.

Actually, the cash shortage was relatively minor and he was told by his boss not to worry about it. Like the other six participants who lack a cushion of experience, his coping and emotion episodes focus primarily on work. Coping episodes at work usually relate to saving face or preventing errors. Mr. Lewis reduces most situations to a psychological problem or an internal control problem where he feels shame over not handling the situation better. He tends to overestimate personal responsibility and underestimate external resources and constraints. Past success records do not reassure him. They only make him feel that he must try harder to avoid failure and that his success is dependent primarily on his own efforts.

These three participants do not have a cushion of experience because they fear failure, and because they believe that their performance is best when they have exerted extreme effort. They believe in the value of hard work, and their particular notion of working hard includes feeling tense, worrying about failing, and being vigilant.

Mr. Narring shares these three participants' need for control, but he further limits his cushion of experience because he deliberately shuts out the immediate and distant past. Mr. Narring is a purchasing agent for a large company. He also worries about what his superiors are thinking of his work. He finds relief from his worry when he is busy at work. He states that he spends much of his time daydreaming about the future and shutting out his past. He fears that he might be doing this excessively because occasionally he feels remote and lonely. He takes great pride in his work, but he worries that others will bypass his department, do their own purchasing, and thus threaten his job.

He, like the three participants just described, also has a strong need to feel that he is in control of events. When things go wrong at home or work, he looks for the source of the problem within, and then feels better because he can "do something about the problem if the source of the problem is within." He attributes his habit of shutting out past events to having learned as a child to shut out immediate past events in order to overcome a reading disability. The combination of his shutting out the immediate past and his need for control interferes with his development of a cushion of experience. He has little sense that things will work out. His description of coping and emotion episodes at work sound more like those of a beginning worker than someone who has held the same job for 17 years. In one example he takes a stand against his boss and worries all weekend that he will lose his job. This worry seems excessive considering his number of years with the company, and considering the fact that he performs well in his job. Nothing came of the disagreement and his job, in fact, was not threatened.

Unlike the participants above, Mr. Franks (see Chapter 5 for paradigm case) does not worry about failure, but, like the others, his job has not become easier with years of experience. Mr. Franks, a salesman, lacks a cushion of experience because he approaches his work in terms of how many contacts he can make in the shortest time. He has a persistent sense of time urgency related to work. He does not talk about qualitative strategies for dealing differently with his work. Instead he just works faster and harder. His sense of time urgency is so extreme that he finds it difficult to focus on any particular task at hand without feeling tense about what he is not doing. For him, time is money, and he does not seek to work with greater ease but with greater speed. He does not talk about qualitative differences in sales situations, or in his work days.

In each case, these participants are prevented from taking in evidence from the situation that can disconfirm their expectations or preconceptions because they have beliefs about the self that interfere with this process. The belief in the efficacy of worry, the fear of making an error, the deliberate shutting out of immediate past events, and chronic hurry prevent these participants from attending to the situation sufficiently to reconsider and refine their preconceptions.

Finally, Mr. Adams, a carpenter, does not have a cushion of experience because he is so alienated from his work. He hates his work and is not sufficiently engaged in it to learn from specific work incidents. A certain level of commitment to the tasks of one's work is required to attend to them sufficiently to develop an advanced level of skill (see Dreyfus and Dreyfus, 1980, for a discussion of skill acquisition.) A certain level of engagement is required in order to develop the cue sensitivity to recognize and remember salient aspects of situations (see Wrubel, Benner, and Lazarus, 1981). Mr. Adams lacks this level of engagement. He prefers his work to require as little attention and responsibility as possible. For example, when he discovers an error, he is angry that his superior did not discover it first. He does not expect to discover problems. He states that he does not know from one hour to the next what will happen at work. He has lost at least 15 jobs (these losses were unrelated to the seasonal nature of the work). He says: "But construction is that way. If they don't like the way you part your hair they give you your walking papers." His years of experience have not made him feel more secure on his jobs nor has he increased his sense of mastery with time. Thus, he does not talk about things getting easier (see Chapter 3 for case study).

In summary, these seven participants stand out because, despite their relatively stable jobs and their levels of experience, they all lack a cushion of experience. Several beliefs about the self were identified as probable barriers to a cushion of experience: a fear of failure coupled with perfectionism, a high need for control, blocking out the immediate past, time urgency, and a lack of commitment to work. This section has examined why these beliefs prevent the development of a cushion of experience. The next section examines situational characteristics that limit a cushion of experience.

SITUATIONAL CHARACTERISTICS THAT LIMIT A CUSHION OF EXPERIENCE

Four participants (Mr. Evans, Mr. Paul, Mr. Roberts, and Mr. Thomas) lack a sense of confidence based on prior experience probably because their circumstances were novel and hence extremely uncertain. The cushion of experience is a transactional variable, not a talent or trait that can prepare the individual for any circumstance. For there to be a cushion of experience, the current situation must be comparable at least on a global level with past situations.

Some situations are so disparate that prior experience is irrelevant. For example Mr. Roberts (Chapter 3 for paradigm case), a 49-year-old heavy equipment operator, was unemployed for much of the past two years. He finally went into business for himself as a heavy equipment operator toward the end of the interview year. He did not have prior experience in running a business, nor had he ever been out of work for such a long period of time. His prior experience could not insulate him from such persistent uncertainty. Furthermore, he preferred a stable, routine job and did not like the risks of being in business for himself. His new circumstance was foreign to him, thus his prior experience was irrelevant.

Two participants lacked a cushion of experience because they had held a series of unrelated jobs. The first, a photographer (Mr. Evans), had an extremely discontinuous work history and was also out of work for most of the year. He had no assurance from his past work history that things would work out. The skills from one job contributed little to the next. His last job was his first and only satisfying job. He made no statements that indicated he had a cushion of experience. Mr. Paul, a bus driver (see paradigm case in Chapter 6), also lacked a sense of continuity in his work history. His past experience as a minister and as a teacher did not contribute to his current work as a bus driver. He was distressed about being a bus driver and wanted to find a better job. He lacked sufficient commitment and time on his current job to have gained a cushion of experience. He saw little connection between his past and his future.

Finally, Mr. Thomas (see paradigm case in Chapter 6) had little benefit from his past 25 years with his company because his company was reorganizing and cutting back. The future was extremely uncertain. So even though Mr. Thomas had worked for his company for 25 years, his work was changing and he now faced an uncertain future. The problem was exacerbated for Mr. Thomas because he preferred routine, certainty, and personal control in his work. If a work assignment required discretionary judgment, he found it distressing. He was sure that his judgment would not be acceptable. While Mr. Thomas's insecurity about using his own judgment was increased by the current uncertainty in the company, he had always experienced anxiety over drawing his own conclusions. He stated that he had felt distressed over writing reports for his current boss for the past 12 years.

Tasks that can be performed according to precise specifications do not require the global recognitional skills that are required for discretionary judgment. Therefore they do not rely on prior experience for task performance. Instead they require precise adherence to the specifications for the task. Thus, Mr. Thomas's work did not require the development of a cushion of experience in order to perform most of his tasks. When tasks that required discretionary judgment came up he was apparently able to avoid them until the company began changing. Consequently he had not developed a cushion of experience.

In summary, unlike the other participants, ten participants did not describe or demonstrate that complex, uncertain situations at work were becoming easier for them. They did not demonstrate that they had a cushion of experience that prevented stressful appraisals.

Five participants are excluded from this discussion (Mr. Baker, Mr. Harris, Mr. Jarvis, Mr. Overton, and Mr. Quest) because it could not be determined from their interviews whether they had a cushion of experience. These participants did not report work-related coping or emotion episodes as frequently as those cited above who did not have a cushion of experience. It could be that a cushion of experience was operating to prevent stressful episodes at work, but these participants did not offer statements indicating whether or not their work had become easier over the years, so they were excluded from this analysis.

This discussion of the role of experience as a coping resource is completed by comparing it with the use of experience as a coping strategy and by comparing it with the concept of personal control.

COMFORTING COGNITIONS: THE USE OF
EXPERIENCE AS A COPING STRATEGY

When a cushion of experience does not work to prevent a stressful appraisal, the person may purposefully recall past examples where difficult or threatening circumstances have worked out well. This use of prior experience to provide comforting cognitions is a coping strategy instead of a coping resource and has been described by Mechanic (1962). The person diminishes his threat by deliberately remembering past difficult situations and remembering that he came through it. The use of prior experience as a coping strategy does not prevent stressful appraisals, nor does it indicate that the person's work is getting less stressful.

This distinction between the use of prior experience as a coping resource and as a coping strategy is best illustrated by an example. The store manager, Mr. Lewis, calls on his past experience in order to reestablish trust in himself and in his coworkers after he had discovered slight changes in the money-handling procedures. In his anger he had felt that he was the only reliable person in his store. "He had to do all the work himself." As a means of counteracting this perceptual distortion, he then talked to himself sternly. He tells himself that things always work out. He says: "How asinine. Why let this bother you?"

A combination of this comforting cognition that things have worked out in the past, his activity, and the passage of time allowed him to calm down and reestablish contact with his employees. Thus, his past experience works for him as a coping strategy, but it does not work as a personal paradigm or perceptual lens to prevent stressful appraisals.

DISTINCTIONS BETWEEN THE CUSHION OF
EXPERIENCE AND LOCUS OF CONTROL

A cushion of experience as a coping resource should be confused with neither the concept of "internal and external locus of control" (Rotter, 1975) nor the concept of "illusion of control" (Langer, 1975; Lefcourt, 1973). A person is said to have an internal locus of control when he perceives that the outcome of an event is contingent upon his own actions. In contrast, the person has an external locus of control when he perceives that the outcomes of a situation are not entirely contingent upon his own actions. When a person views a situation as being under the control of a powerful "other" or as the result of chance or luck, he is said to have an external locus of control for that situation. He is said to have an illusion of control when he misreads chance situations as situations amenable to his control.

People who have an overriding need for control may limit the development of a cushion of experience. An excessive need for control may cause the person to have a means-ends displacement so that they do not recognize a good outcome that does not come from their effort or that does not follow their plan.

People who have a cushion of experience do not necessarily have an illusion of control, nor do they necessarily perceive the situation as one where the outcome is dependent entirely upon their own actions. Despite this, they do not perceive the event as entirely outside of their influence either. A sense of control implies that the person will be able to influence events in a predictable direction, whereas with the cushion of experience, the person relies on both internal and external resources. He has a sense of possibility in the midst of limited control. This sense of possibility stems from one's past memories of surviving similar difficult circumstances. Thus, a cushion of experience is not limited to one's estimated ability to control external circumstances. But a cushion of experience can prevent stressful appraisals in uncertain circumstances where the person can call on their ability to relate their past experience to similar and dissimilar uncertain situations.

THE IMPLICATIONS OF A CUSHION OF EXPERIENCE FOR STRESS MANAGEMENT

In complex social situations typical of worklife, seven participants accounted for decreased stress over time as a result of the confidence they gained from their prior experience. These participants did not rely solely on a sense of control. Those who have a cushion of experience as a coping resource have learned from their experience. They are confident of their ability to find possibility in the midst of unstructured circumstances.

The question of what facilitates learning from experience so that threat is diminished over time warrants further study. However, it may be easier to find out what inhibits a cushion of experience than to discover what contributes to it. For example, those participants who had an excessive need for control, who were perfectionistic, who were not committed to their work, or who found themselves in extremely discontinuous experiences did not have a cushion of experience. Yet a person could be free of these personal beliefs and situation characteristics and still not have a cushion of experience.

The cushion of experience is based on the ability of highly skilled decisionmakers to read whole situations and to interpet events in rapidly changing circumstance without resorting to rules or formulas (see Dreyfus and Dreyfus, 1980; Benner, 1982). These people do not rely solely on internal resources nor do they locate <u>all</u> the responsibility for outcomes internally. They believe that they can influence situations, and their ability to read whole situations enables them to recognize solutions and alternatives that they neither expect nor generate.

The cushion of experience and its absence in experienced employees offer a rich avenue in the study of work-stress prevention. To date, much attention has been given to the value of an internal locus of control for social competence (see Wrubel, Benner, and Lazarus, 1981) and for stress management. An ability to develop a cushion of experience and circumstances that permit a cushion of experience are probably more important to stress prevention in complex social situations than are either an internal locus of control or an illusion of control. This can be illustrated with parenting. Parents of a second child seldom experience the same level of anxiety and uncertainty with the birth of the second child as with the first. However, few parents would attribute this increased sense of ease with the second child to an increased "internal locus of control."

Having children typically confronts parents with the limits of control. Yet experience provides assurance in the face of limited control and uncertainty. The ability to gain a cushion of experience, or the lack of this ability, is probably much more important to stress prevention and stress management in complex social situations than the more researched question about the relative merits of internal and external loci of control. The cushion of experience is a transactional variable (see Chapter 2 for a discussion of transactional variables). Thus it is not a trait that can be studied out of the context of a person's particular history and situation. Both person and situation characteristics can promote or prevent a cushion of experience. Thus, this concept will need to be studied by methods that capture the transactional nature of a cushion of experience.

This chapter has presented the cushion of experience as a personal meaning derived from experience that <u>prevents</u> stressful appraisals in complex work situations. In Chapter 8, paradigm cases where the meanings of work prevent recurrent stress appraisals and facilitate coping with work stress are presented. The participants in each of these paradigm cases have a cushion of experience.

8

MEANINGFUL WORK

No one set of meanings can prevent all work stress or guarantee effective coping in stressful situations. However, participation in meaningful work does influence what is experienced as stressful. Because a meaningful relationship to work is transactional and context-dependent it can be recognized only by studying examples in their context. Decontextualized characteristics and traits alone cannot capture this relationship. The four cases in this chapter present examples of meaningful engagement in work. These four participants all embrace the meanings of work handed down in Utilitarianism and the Protestant Work Ethic; however, they do not have the same means-ends displacement evident in the cases presented in Chapter 5. Instead the goals and tasks of the work itself solicit them. Different aspects of their work stand out as more or less important because they are able to draw on past experience in a meaningful way. Such a meaningful relationship to work cannot be termed "intrinsic" meaning because the meaning does not reside only in the work itself but also in the particular way the person is engaged in his work.

A transactional perspective that acknowledges that the person both changes and is changed by the situation is required because just such a dynamic relationship is requisite for learning from experience, as defined by Heidegger (1962). Under Heidegger's notion of experience, experience turns around preconceptions, or disconfirms expectations (see also Gadamer, 1975; Macomber, 1967). Therefore, the person must be engaged in their work so that they test and refine their preconceptions and expectations repeatedly in concrete situations. Some meanings, such as "time as an adversary" or the fear of failure in the proving ground stance, block out some meanings in the situation so that the person's meanings actively prevent his perceiving aspects of the situation. When personal meanings block out relevant evidence in the situation, the person does not learn from experience.

Aside from innate ability, a certain level of commitment to one's work is required in order to acquire skill. If the person is not engaged in his work, he is not likely to be motivated to do all the things necessary to master his work (for example, practice, seek advice, and so on). Also he will not have sufficient cue sensitivity to attend to and thus recognize with experience important aspects of the situation. Dreyfus and Dreyfus (1980; S. E. Dreyfus, 1982) determined that the perceptual ability to recognize relative aspects of situations without deliberate analysis requires a "sense of salience" that can come only with experience. A sense of salience is required for a competent level of performance. Salience is absent for the beginner, or one with little skill (see case study on Mr. Adams, Chapter 3). Thus, salience requires both commitment and experience (see Polanyi, 1958; Wrubel, Benner, and Lazarus, 1981; Benner and Wrubel, 1982). Meaningful engagement in work provides an experience-based perceptual lens that determines both primary appraisals (that is, what is perceived as stressful) and coping options or notions about what to do in a situation (secondary appraisals). People who hold meanings that prevent them from refining their preconceptions do not gain a cushion of experience so that their work becomes less stressful over time. This was evident in Chapter 5, where the store manager's background meanings of proving his worth prevented him from appropriating past experience. It was evident in Chapter 7, where participants described decreased stress with experience. The individual does not choose or determine what will be stressful; that is a given in their perceptual lens. Neither does the individual choose coping strategies in isolation from the primary appraisal. The question foreshadows its solution.

People who lack these obstructive meanings can gain a cushion of experience if their current work can be understood in terms of past concrete work experiences. Furthermore, some people's meanings not only don't block but seem to enhance the stress-reducing effects of experience. The four participants in this chapter serve as exemplars of such a meaningful relation to work. Each case illustrates how work that is meaningful in itself limits stressful appraisals and increases fiexibility in coping with stressful events. These participants do not suffer from a means-ends displacement from the work itself. Though they are deeply involved in their work, they are not compulsive workers. Work does not entirely consume their interests and energy.

These participants share the following unifying characteristics: they each have a cushion of experience so that past experience works as a coping resource. All four cite the present as the best time in their life. They do not interpret the present merely in terms of future rewards. Their stressful episodes at work are varied and get resolved. In other words, a stressful episode does not linger on and come up again as an issue at another time. These participants do not present work stress and coping episodes on a monthly basis to the interviewer. When they do present stressful work episodes, they are not always presented as the most important issue in the person's life.

Personal meanings such as a high need for proving themselves does not prevent them from reading the situation accurately, nor from gaining a new perspective when the problem or situation does not change with their coping efforts. Coping typically serves to change distressing emotions into less distressing ones (see Charts 8.1-8.4) and, typically, coping either improves the situation or at least doesn't make the situation worse. The coping strategies and resources used seem to allow the participant to learn from experience and be flexible in stressful situations at work. In each case, work does not crowd out other life concerns. The participant is able to enjoy leisure, love, family, and friendships as well as work.

These unifying characteristics cannot alone define the conditions necessary for a meaningful relationship to work. A person would not necessarily achieve a meaningful relationship to their work by pursuing these characteristics as aims. A meaningful engagement in work cannot be taught by precept since it is the way one takes up his work that makes it meaningful. Should the social context change for any of these participants, the meaningfulness of their work could also change for better or for worse.

Meaning, by its very nature, is vulnerable to change. Meaning is not a talent or trait that lies within the individual, nor is it a characteristic of the situation that can be isolated and defined. Meaningful work serves the person well in terms of stress and coping because work meanings and work practices are integrated. Therefore, the above summary description can only present the similarities and differences that make these four cases stand out.

These participants manage their work with less distress than they did earlier in their careers. This is what one would expect, but it differs from those participants who experience their work as a perennial proving ground where the stress experienced at work has not lessened over the years (see Chapter 5).

PARADIGM CASE: A PHYSICIAN WHO LIKES HIS WORK

Dr. Ursell is a happily married physician and father of three children. His father and grandfather were physicians, and he wanted to be the kind of physician that they were, except that he wanted to give more time to his children. He and his wife have experienced a romantic renewal in their marriage since the children have left home. They both come from stable families and have established a stable family. Life has become better for Dr. Ursell over the years. There are now more peaks than valleys, he says, and events that were peaks ten years ago are now the valleys. He likes his work and thrives on it. He gets satisfaction from his patients and from his peers, and he says he has learned a lot about the human condition by being a physician.

His life is not free of conflict. He states in the third interview that work takes up so much of his time that it often conflicts with other things. He accepts the busyness and tries to arrange as much time for leisure and family as possible. For example, he managed to work with his sons in the Boy Scouts. He states that work is the main course in his life, family is the dessert, and friends are the "hors d'oeuvres." He uses detachment and humor as coping strategies and states that he is not so ego-involved in his performance or how things turn out. A good day is "when he successfully meets the challenges," and a bad day is "when the outcomes of the challenges are unsuccessful, or still precarious or when I push papers all day long."

In addition to his busy medical practice, he is involved in hospital administrative committees. He apparently is asked to chair committees and is sought out to handle controversial situations.

He views stress as change and thinks that one cannot really reduce stress. His emphasis is on coping. He thinks that ego strength is the key and that it comes early in life. That is why he has chosen to work with the Boy Scouts. When asked about his religious beliefs, he states that he believes in "doing" here on earth. His active life supports that statement. He is pleased with his work and with his life. That he is frequently overloaded is his biggest work stress except for occasional political hassles with his committee work at the hospital. When asked if his job is more challenging or more frustrating he states, "I have tended to look at every new situation as a challenge. I have kind of evolved that philosophy, I guess. I don't get frustrated nearly as often as I did. I have a tendency to become less ego-involved in my frustration. Life is a lot more fun that way."

With work overload, his one main strategy is working harder. He states that his work "has not become onerous yet," and acknowledges that the practice of medicine tends to become onerous. He is solicited and challenged by his work. His overall life satisfaction seems high. He is committed and involved in the content of his work. He says about the advantages and drawbacks to his work:

> I'm able to do a lot of things I like to do and I'm able to
> decide what I do to a large extent. I have lots of choice.
> I like that. To be able to take off of work; to decide how
> I am going to work or play. I think I am very fortunate

that I am able to do that. [I: What are the drawbacks?]
I don't think about that very much.

His statement about his freedom to control his schedule is
contradicted by the <u>actual</u> demands of his work as he describes them
month by month. He is frequently overscheduled. His schedule was
changed by the vacation plans of other physicians at least twice, and
he describes missed dinners and days that begin at 6:00 A.M. and end
at 10:00 P.M. Even so, he does have one afternoon off during the week
and he goes skiing when he has a weekend off.

In reading the month-by-month episodes, one is struck by the
mix of episodes described from home and work and volunteer activities. Each month there is a mix of positive and negative emotions and
a variety in the content of the stressful episodes. In each case he does
not try to avoid the particular problem and it is resolved so that it
does not come up again. Dr. Ursell has a compelling interest in his
work that brings him satisfaction. He also has other compelling
commitments that take him away from the demands of his work.

An episode of work overload is selected as representative of his
stress and coping at work. (See Chart 8.1 for interpretation of the
coping episode.)

The Relationship between Work Meanings
and Stress and Coping

The selected coping episode illustrates the variety of coping
strategies used by Dr. Ursell. It also illustrates a cushion of
experience. He accepts the work overload as temporarily necessary
and does not increase it by his own coping style. He is not alienated
from his work, and therefore he is solicited by the demands in a way
that calls forth his best effort. In the midst of his heaviest period of
workload he becomes intrigued by an unusual case that challenges him.
While he fantasizes and mentally rehearses his upcoming recreation,
much like a reward, he does not talk about wanting to escape permanently. He does not feel overwhelmed by the demands and is
confident that he can manage. He makes a positive comparison of the
present with past overload during his internship. Dr. Ursell's response
can be compared to that of Mr. Lewis (see Chapter 5) who does not
have a cushion of experience, and to Mr. Smith (see Chapter 5) and
Mr. Gough (see later in this Chapter) whose coping styles increase
their work overload.

He describes one other unusually busy day during the course of
the year. The other topics of his coping and emotion episodes were
nonrecurring events that related to his family, recreation, and work.

CHART 8.1

Dr. Ursell: Interpretation of Coping Episode

STAKES
> Managing an increased workload in a schedule that is already
> full. Concern over getting work done.

APPRAISAL
> Challenge.

RESOURCES
> Cushion of experience: a sense from past experience with similar
> situations that things will work out O.K. Finds reward and
> interest in the nature of the work: "And just when you are knee
> deep in crisis, some fascinating medical situation will come up
> and you want to spend your time gnawing over that."

COPING STRATEGIES

- Direct Action—<u>Works harder and longer:</u> He misses lunch, starts
   work earlier, and works later.
   <u>Cuts corners to save time and work:</u> "I carry things
   that can't be postponed. . . . I would try to get a feel for the
   situation on the phone and if they had to be seen, I would see
   them. I might make rounds at six o'clock before patients have
   had time to organize their complaints."
- Information Search
- Planning
- Social Support
- Social Influence
- Inhibition of Action
- Cognitive Coping or Palliation—<u>Perspective:</u> "Things go in fits and
   starts. There is a slack time now." This has the quality of
   "this too will pass, it will not last forever."
   <u>Positive assessment of performance;</u>
   <u>seeks an indicator that he's making it:</u> "And I don't think that
   I was ever more than one hour behind at the office. I was two
   behind at Hospital X the other day when the bus stride ended.
   <u>Mentally rehearses upcoming recre-</u>
   <u>ation:</u> "I keep thinking how nice the snow would be over the
   weekend, and how nice it would be to get away from the phone
   and where it is quiet."

<u>Reaffirms commitment to situation:</u>
"Really, what can you do? You can't tell people to go away
and be sick some other time."

<u>Rest; sleep:</u> "I try to get a good
night's sleep the night before."

EMOTIONS EXPERIENCED IN EPISODE

Irritation, fascination, challenge. He is challenged by balancing
all the demands. This comes through in the discourse. He seems
to relish the strategies he uses, and he describes with some
excitement the multiple demands. He notes that he gets irritable
with his office staff. And in the midst of the busyness, he becomes fascinated with an interesting case.

PHYSICAL EXPERIENCE OF EMOTION

Edgy and short-tempered; fatigued, sleepy. He falls asleep
during a meeting.

EFFECT OF COPING ON SITUATION

Coping leaves him open to fascination and interest in the midst
of demands; since he is not alienated from the situation, he
accepts and affirms the busyness as necessary and worthwhile.
His working harder increases his sense of mastery and challenge.

They included positive as well as negative emotions. His array of
coping and strong emotion episodes presents the picture of a person
who is involved and committed in a number of different arenas. He
does not find his work onerous or overwhelming. He sees the challenge
in it. The risks and responsibilities call forth herculean effort at
times. Trying harder is a part of his Work Ethic meanings. However,
his efforts do not seem to be greater than the situation requires. For
example, he attempts to limit his "ego-involvement," which seems to
mean that he does not get caught up in proving himself. As a result of
his experience, he can afford to take risks. He manages his fear of
mistakes with statements such as: "You know what they say . . . good
judgment comes from experience and experience comes from bad
judgment." He repeats this phrase during the year. He sees the
present as the best time of his life and says: "I like to live in the
present, that's where the action is."

He actively seeks advice and support during stormy and complicated political situations. For example, he talked about his concern
over an administrative task with his colleagues at the hospital, with
other staff, and with his wife. He says: "I let steam off that way and I

kind of figure that what can be done mostly is done or will be. So I am just going to wait and see." Apparently he is astute in reading political situations in the hospital and knows how to use informal channels. Thus he clearly does not overestimate his personal control in complex social interactions and deliberately tests his interpretations and assumptions.

This case study permits a distinction between the dynamics of control and commitment in relation to stress and coping. He is committed to his work without having an overriding concern for control. Commitment allows him to be engaged in the situation in a transactional way. It allows his expectations and preconceptions to be tested by the situation. He actively seeks opinions and evidence that will confirm or disconfirm his position. In contrast, a person with an overriding concern for control chooses the position that gives the greatest sense of control and tends to overestimate his impact on a situation and thus tends to overlook solutions that he does not anticipate. People with an overriding concern for control are susceptible to feelings of helplessness and hopelessness when they confront the limits of control because they believe control is the only alternative and that they should be able to control their circumstances. Dr. Ursell is able to assess his impact on a situation accurately and draw on both internal and external resources.

In sum, Dr. Ursell is very committed to his work, but he is also very committed to his wife and family. He manages to both love and work. He is at home in the situations in which he finds himself, is pleased with what he is able to accomplish, and can live with what he cannot accomplish. He has a great deal of clarity about his life and is not confused or too conflicted over competing interests.

PARADIGM CASE: A CREATIVE ADVERTISING EXECUTIVE

Mr. Ingolls is a 50-year-old advertising executive for a large corporation. He has been married for 28 years. He has three sons, two in college and one in high school. He seems happily married. His wife works in the home and does volunteer work. He talks over work problems with her frequently. He changed jobs within the same company early in the interview year. At the time of the change, he contemplated going into business for himself but decided against it because he did not want to lose his benefits with the company. Even though the transfer was fraught with uncertainty, he says: "I tried to adopt a pretty positive attitude about the whole thing in the way I dealt with the people around me. I tried to be outgoing and enthusiastic. For example, I said: 'It's great to be back.' . . . It was just a matter of accepting it in an adult manner."

This illustrates that he can read situations and can get enough distance on his own feelings to behave in an interpretable and positive manner. He is clear about his work prioritees and preferences. When he first heard of the job change at work he was very unhappy. He said his wife's counseling helped him look ahead past the problem into the future and this reassured him. At the end of the year he stated that his job change turned out well for him.

He is very involved in his work and has frequent work coping and emotion episodes, but work does not crowd out other interests as it does for Mr. Smith (see Chapter 5). However, like Mr. Smith, the major stakes involved in his work coping and emotion episodes relate to winning his point. Unlike Mr. Smith, however, Mr. Ingolls can sustain his relationships in the face of disagreements, whereas Mr. Smith relies on presenting a frictionless surface or breaking off relations where disagreements arise. Unlike Mr. Smith, friends enrich and support Mr. Ingolls:

> Friends are very important, sharing fun times; sharing emotional ups and downs. Doing things together, being able to rely on one another. Having someone to share family-oriented times. So friends have become like family to us. As our children have grown older, we've become closer.

He enjoys his work. He says he can express his creativity at work even though he cannot always sell his ideas there. If money were no object he would resign, do something more creative, and work at his own pace. He describes work as a way to maintain a way of life and hopefully to improve his own and his family's position in life. His challenge comes from selling his ideas. He becomes distressed when he cannot sell an idea that he is convinced is correct. Work overload is not a problem for him.

Mr. Ingolls views this as the best time in his life:

> Right now is the best time. It's my ability to learn and to express myself. They are at their greatest now, and I treasure my observations. The disadvantages are that professionally I am not as competitive for job opportunities as I once was. And I suspect that management has you labeled as you attain a certain age, they look at you as being there a certain time rather than as having something to contribute.

He does expect advancement before retirement and the above statement does not indicate that he has ceased making contributions;

it is an observation of the way aging is viewed in most companies.
Good days at work are those days when his plans are adopted or
implemented, and on bad days his plans are rejected despite a great
deal of personal effort. He is satisfied with his life and with his
work. He states:

> [I: Does your job match your expectations?] Yes, it
> allows me to express my thoughts in writing and in
> graphic displays, but not totally because of an inability
> to do everything I think should be done because of the
> politics. . . . The major rewards and satisfactions
> have been the acceptance of things and ideas I've
> generated and brought into commercials and the monetary
> rewards. [I: What will be easy for you to give up?]
> Getting up and commuting 20 miles each way. [I: What
> will be hard for you to give up?] The close relationships
> with the people and the enjoyment of what I do.

His job improved markedly over the year. He states with some
tongue-in-cheek humor that he went from a dissatisfying job to an
"almost satisfying one." His year is an eventful one. In addition to
his job change, his in-laws were ill and lived with the participant's
family for a period of time. One of his sons was injured, and his wife
had surgery. But he notes: "On the positive side, my son graduated
from college." At the end of the year he reflects back on the events
of the past 12 months and states: "I am not lacking in [stressful]
emotion, but I react in a controlled way, and in short order return to
a pre-stress state of mind."

Three work coping and emotion episodes concern winning his
point of view with his boss. The one selected is similar to the other
two other episodes. He talks about his anticipation of the event:

> In situations like this, in which I know I'll be challenged
> and on display, I get "up" [mobilized]. My pulse goes
> up and I am eager to talk to them. I get excited, and the
> adrenalin really gets pumping. . . . It seemed like an
> eternity before the afternoon meeting. I felt quite "revved
> up" and confident. I knew what I had to say made a lot
> of sense. . . . [When he went to see the boss, the boss
> commented almost immediately after he had sat down in
> his office that he had read the report and that he couldn't
> buy it.] I thought the statement bordered on stupidity,
> but maintained a nonaccusatory rational and quiet
> businesslike tone.

(See Chart 8.2 for interpretation of the coping episode.)

While winning is very much the point with Mr. Ingolls, the winning is not related to proving himself. For example, in the eighth interview, when his boss turns down another one of his proposals, the participant backs off and thinks about a new line of action. He does not interpret the refusal as a reflection on his ability or worth:

> What can I say to convince him that he's wrong
> without jeopardizing myself? [I: How long did this
> feeling of extreme frustration last?] I'd say maybe
> five minutes and we just began talking it out and it
> became obvious that he wasn't going to change his mind,
> and I just sort of came down to an acceptable, manageable
> level of frustration due to the talking. I'm mature
> enough [laughs] to realize that you can't beat a dead
> horse. I had tried several tacks in that five minutes.

He says of his frustration with this event: "If anything it has made us more determined to make it go [laughs]." He does not engage in self-recrimination over losing.

CHART 8.2

Mr. Ingolls: Interpretation of Coping Episode

STAKES
   Winning his point, selling his recommendations to the boss.

APPRAISAL
   Challenge.

RESOURCES
   Sense of efficacy, a general sense that "I can do that. I felt quite confident and 'revved up' about it."

COPING STRATEGIES

- Direct Action
- Information Search
- Planning
- Social Support
- Influence Attempt—Retaliation: He discusses his boss's flip-flop in his decision; this seemed to be an effort to undermine his boss and to save his own face with his coworkers.

Makes a direct effort to change another's mind by marshalling support for his position: "I explained that their company had only five persons to work on this project, while the other agency had far greater resources. I gave other examples of what this agency had already done before."

Manages expression of emotion in order to be effective in the situation: "I maintained a nonaccusatory, rational, and quiet business-like tone as he made the statement."

- Social Influence
- Inhibition of Action—"Then I shut up because there comes a time and a point where he's the boss and your're not, so you shut up."
- Cognitive Coping or Palliation—Psyching self up: "When I know that I am going to be on display, I get up."

EMOTIONS EXPERIENCED IN EPISODE

Excited, eager, frustrated, helpless, confused (scared), irritated. Before the event he felt up, excited, and confident of his case. When the boss was persistent in his refusal, he felt frustrated, and then helpless because the boss is boss. He felt confused when the boss did a flip-flop on his decision. He said he thought that was scary because he did not feel that the boss should vacillate in his decisions. Then he felt irritated when he concluded that the boss was only trying to placate him by appearing to listen to him and take his advice seriously by setting up a meeting with the other agency that he had recommende This he found irritating because it was only delaying the inevitable negative action. He knew he had not won a victory.

PHYSICAL EXPERIENCE OF EMOTION

EFFECT OF COPING ON EMOTION

His coping increased his feeling of challenge and limited his sense of threat. It probably increased his frustration when his program was blocked.

EFFECT OF COPING ON SITUATION

He handled the situation well. He did not alienate his boss, even though he was very upset with him. He presented a well-thought out case.

Relationship between Work Meanings
and Stress and Coping

Mr. Ingolls lives and participates in a network of meaningful
relationships. His attitudes and statements about himself resemble
Kobasa's (1980, p. 14) description of the hardy personality (that is,
intact work ethic meanings). He can accommodate change in his life.
For example, he can imagine setbacks, but he says he cannot
imagine failing. If he failed in business, he knows that his family
would still be "successful." His wife would get a job; his sons
would work and pitch in and help; and he would get another job. He is
a self-confident risk taker who believes that he can influence his
circumstances even if they change. Winning is important to him
personally, and it is a frequent stake in his coping and emotion episodes.

Mr. Ingolls's work structure and practices are integrated with
his work meanings so that his past experience guides his actions in a
meaningful way. He moved to a position that was more challenging and
rewarding for him during the course of the year. This transition
attests to his coping skill because he did not expect the new position
to be better. He did not choose it, it was a transfer. At first he
thought of resigning and going into business for himself; but as he
said, he adopted a positive attitude and made new ties for himself in
the new office. At the end of the year he compares his "old" job less
favorably than his current one.

Though winning and success are important to Mr. Ingolls, he has
domains in his life where winning and control are not the point.
Friends, family, and leisure activities are frequent sources of
positive emotion throughout the year. It would seem that though Mr.
Ingolls's high standard of living places demands on him, these are
demands he has been able to meet and still have interest nad energy
for love and leisure. The possible eventuality that he fears the most
is incapacity, or prolonged ill health. Given his self-definition as
a provider, and as an active, successful worker, it is understandable
that physical disability is an unthinkable eventuality.

The next paradigm case is similar in that the participant's work
life improves over the year. His work is recognized and he moves
from feeling frustrated at work to feeling entitled.

PARADIGM CASE: AN ELECTRICIAN WHOSE GOOD
WORK IS REWARDED

Mr. Gough is a 54-year-old maintenance electrician. He lives
with his wife and is satisfied with his marriage. He supports his adult
son who has been the source of frequent problems related to drinking
and temper tantrums. In the twelfth interview he states that his opinion

about his son has changed over the year from being pessimistic to being hopeful, because his son is going to school and applying himsel

Mr. Gough has had one major illness and now a main concern i staying healthy. He cites his illness as a turning point in his life:

> I almost damn near died when I was 44 from an operation for a ruptured appendix, or colon. They told my wife that I had eight hours to live. . . . It's hard to say how I changed. I had been a cheerful happy-go-lucky guy. Nothing could faze me. After the near death I worried about everything, little things like my wife being two minutes late in getting home. To a degree that seriousness and fretfulness has stayed with me to this day.

He says his health problems developed as a result of the difficulty he had adjusting to his new job ten years ago:

> I didn't know what I was doing. I was 44. There was too much to learn. I expected to carry my weight and I found out it was harder than I thought. . . . I realized nobody but nobody could learn it all in a year but I still struggled to learn as much as I could. All of a sudden I inherited the whole place due to the illness of the other guy. But as a result it made me a better person. I learned thoroughly and completely. After you have been there five years everything falls together.

Mr. Gough is very good in his work. He repairs equipment that others cannot repair and he makes suggestions for improving work. H starts the year off by describing two work incidents where he wants a change made for improved safety. In both cases he runs into problem; with management. He states that his new boss is one of those "hotsho with a degree who has had little practical experience and knows little. "He expects me to carry him, yet at the same time he is removing privileges." Mr. Gough is quite frustrated with both incider and talks to his wife who restores his sense of confidence. He manage his frustration at work and refrains from vindictive behavior such as not doing his job or taking the problem to the national union.

Work is central to him, and he values doing a good job. He is rewarded for his effort and expertise in the eighth month of the interview year by a promotion, which changes his general outlook on life. The nature of his work hassles changes. He now has problem; with fellow employees who used to be friends. But he states that he feels better about himself:

Work for me is an opportunity to create and to improve
things. I can do many things to earn a living but now
I can improve the conditions and production of the
workers. . . . Something recently changed with my new
job—the situation has changed. My attitude and outlook are
optimistic and pleasant and generous, the better things
of a character. My attitude toward everything, people
and work. [I: What sort of things have changed most?]
My job has changed from my being a union man to manager,
a supervisory foreman.

Before his promotion, his level of involvement and concern with
larger safety issues created problems for him because he did not have
enough authority to support his concern and involvement. This is
illustrated in his first two work coping and emotion episodes. After
his promotion his general sense of well-being and satisfaction improves.
His new job requires new skills and makes new demands that he finds
challenging.

Mr. Gough prides himself in modulating the highs and lows in his
life, trying to keep things in balance. Nevertheless he seems to experience the threats and fears of his life deeply, and he describes feelings
of elation and despair during the year. He believes that there is an
answer to everything and worries a problem through until he has sorted
out all the possible ramifications and options available to him. As
the interviewer describes him: "He is an introspective man, always
questioning, sifting, sorting, analyzing, dissecting, and seeking out
every angle and detail meticulously."

His style makes it difficult for him to sleep at times as he sorts
through a problem. Mastery is important to him and he is highly
invested in the situations he describes. The quality of his reflection
however is different from Mr. Thomas and Mr. Paul who reflect on
why or whether they should experience what they are experiencing. Mr.
Gough's beginning point seems to be an acceptance of his situation. He
actively tries to "learn from the situation" (his words) and looks for
solutions from within and without. He is able to receive solace and
support from others and remains actively engaged in highly charged
events until they are resolved.

A sample episode was selected after his promotion to illustrate
the stress and coping linked with his new position. After he was promoted to foreman, his coworkers tested him by playing cards on duty.

[I: What went through your mind when you felt the
most frustration and anger?] About how far the
confrontation would go. Would they [the workers] start
swinging at me? [I: What did you feel frustrated with?] I

had to treat them all the same in the group even though
some were friends. The thought went through my mind
was that "you've got a job to do, don't back down on it.
Do it." [Raps his finger on the table in cadence with his
words for emphasis] [I: What were you angry at?] At first
the fact that they betrayed me in a sense. They were
treating me badly, testing me, and I thought that
they were on my side and then the attitude that
they should be allowed to play cards, and then the fact
that they used all kinds of weak excuses for playing.
[I: How long did you feel anger?] Five minutes.
[I: What did the feeling change to?] When rehashing what
happened in my mind, then it changed to disappointment
that they tried to embarrass me and jeopardize my position
after working for me for eleven years, then they
decided to test me, the whole crew.

(See Chart 8.3 for interpretation of the emotion episode.)

CHART 8.3

Mr. Gough: Interpretation of Coping Episode

STAKES
   Maintaining his authority and friendship with his coworkers;
   passing the "test" of his new position. Concern for doing well
   and maintaining his integrity.

APPRAISAL
   Psycholohical and physical threat.

RESOURCES
   Sense of purpose and sense of importance of "doing what was
   right" in the situation. "You've got a job to do, don't back down
   on it."

COPING STRATEGIES

● Direct Action—Acts directly at the time of the episode by saying
      something to deal with the problem: "They knew I meant what
      I said because they threw the cards away. My voice was stern
            Normalizes situation to deescalate the conflict:
      "They'd speak to me and things got back to normal. I went

along as if nothing had happened and I couldn't do in any other way."
- Information Search
- Planning
- Social Support—Seeks active assistance-support: "I told her [his wife] how I felt, and she said I was right in handling it and how I handled it and she confirmed what I thought. . . . She restored my confidence. . . . She is the type who'll tell me if she thinks I'm wrong."
      Controlled expression of emotion to be effective in the situation: "I don't think that they could tell that I was angry."
- Social Influence
- Inhibition of Action
- Cognitive Coping or Palliation—Prayer: "I asked God's forgiveness if I was wrong and questioned how to handle it. I realized it was O.K. and developed confidence so that I could relax."
      Relies on a principle (in this case a principle of fairness and even-handedness) to handle the conflict: "I had to treat them all the same in the group even though some were friends."
      Goes over problem in mind: "You rehash the situation all over again."

EMOTIONS EXPERIENCED IN EPISODE
Anger, disappointment, sadness, apprehension, tension, relaxation. The testing made him angry initially, then he felt betrayed by his friends and, therefore, disappointed and sad. He felt apprehensive and tense until the conflict was resolved and normal relations were reestablished. There were no lingering hard feelings after the situation improved.

PHYSICAL EXPERIENCE OF EMOTION
"The blood pressure goes up. My face feels flush. My pulse races, and I'm telling myself to stay cool." He was wakeful: "It took an hour to get to sleep." He had recurring intrusive thoughts and tension, "It stayed with me for three or four days with a recurrence of anger when I thought about it during those days."

EFFECT OF COPING ON EMOTION
Coping enabled him to experience feelings while controlling the expression of emotion in the actual situation in order to be effective. His coping allowed him to work through his feelings so that there were no apparent residual feelings after the conflict was resolved (after about one week).

EFFECT OF COPING ON SITUATION

> Managed the situation well. He maintained his authority and did not break off communication with his friends. He apparently "passed the test."

Relationship Between Work Meanings
and Stress and Coping

Mr. Gough is very committed to his work, and when problems arise he stays engaged and actively seeks solutions, while he makes the most of the situation. He does not use much distancing or avoidance. His work is meaningful to him. He is a worrier, but his worry is focused on the problem at hand. His stressful episodes at work concerned major safety issues before his promotion and management issues after his promotion. He is a safety engineer and describes both positive and stressful episodes. He learns from his experience. He does not get caught in self-doubt and confusion. He uses prayer to keep himself open to change in the situation and himself (see Coping Strategies, Chart 8.3).

Mr. Gough has a cushion of experience. He has a lot of continuity in his work, so that his past experience can guide his current decisions. He has confidence that he can weather situations. He learned that from his 15 years in the Navy. He uses his feelings to mobilize himself to search for solutions and to deal with the problem. He seems to go for solutions to the problem that will hold up over time. For example, he wants a total solution with the work situations so that they do not recur, and he wants the problems with his son dealt with so that they do not recur. At the end of the year, the problem that he has confronted during the year seem to be resolved. Thus his style works for him. He does not become entangled in repeated situations that are made more difficult by unresolved problems or feelings from prior situations.

Mr. Gough's reflection is focused on the problem itself rather than whether or not he should be experiencing the problem. His reflection does not cause him to withdraw, instead it offers him new options for dealing with the problem at hand. He is good at his work and his reflection helps him come up with solutions to the problems he encounters.

He is able to use the social support that is offered him, but he also seeks out support. For example, he went to a former coworker/friend to talk over the promotion. His friend's perspective and advice helped him confirm his decision to accept the promotion. He is careful to maintain his relationship with his coworkers and enjoys the sense of trust he has built up. When his former coworkers tested him he was able to maintain his integrity as a manager and still keep his relationship with the workers.

His promotion supports his concerns and involvement, so that he is more satisfied with his work at the end of the year than he was at the beginning of the year. This too attests to his coping skills.

PARADIGM CASE: A TRUCKER WHO ENJOYS A SMOOTH RUN

Mr. Morris is a 50-year-old truck driver who drives a 20-foot truck. He has worked for the same company for the past 18 years, and has had the same boss for the past five years. He lives with his wife and daughter. Two adult sons live in the area. Mr. Morris is satisfied with his marriage and is surprised that it has lasted so long. He feels disappointed that he cannot afford to get a better house in a better neighborhood. The interviewer asks him whether he thinks that it is a reflection on him that they cannot buy a more expensive house and he responds that maybe that is the way both he and his wife feel. He says: "Maybe if I'd been a lawyer or a doctor . . . [drifts off]." His wife is a librarian who works part time. Sometimes the participant does not live up to his wife's expectations socially. This is the issue involved in one of his coping episodes.

He says that he gets angry every day in the traffic and swears or says things that he wouldn't ordinarily say. Every day he "boils a little," but at the end of the day he feels great after he "shoots the breeze with his friends, unwinds, and drinks 2-3 beers."

His stressful episodes at work involve too little to do, waiting to unload freight, and traffic incidents that upset him. All are persistent sources of stress that are repeated throughout the year. The episodes related to traffic and delay in unloading freight seem more transitory and self-contained, whereas the lack of work also affects his mood off work.

He also has good days at work. For example, in the seventh interview he describes a good day: "Yesterday was unusually happy at work. Four of us were telling stories about people we've known. We had a lot of laughs. It was at a coffee shop at the end of the day." He likes his boss, he says, because "he compliments people and is easy to work for." Mr. Morris states that his boss is "the same as he would like to be. I can do more for him than for other people."

A smooth day is when his route is clear, and there are specific procedures for unloading the freight. He likes for the day to go smoothly, with no delays and enough work to keep him busy.

He reads inspirational books about making money and says: "Maybe someday I'll fulfill some of the things I've dreamed about.

[I: How?] Having some property, being a man of means, being able to go out of here in dignity. That would be a major thing for me to accom plish." He dreams of building homes when he retires.

In the eleventh interview he states that most of the time he enjoys his work:

> I like what I'm doing. For a working guy, I make a pretty
> good living. It is a means to an end, something I enjoy
> and a way to earn a living. There are frustrating days,
> but it is more challenging than frustrating. [I: What is
> challenging?] Getting materials to the companies on
> time, and returning them on time; knowing how long it
> takes me to do certain things.

Mr. Morris reports frequent positive emotions at home and at work. For example, in the fourth interview he talks about a feeling of pride that he had from helping a nephew build a planter box. In the fifth interview he talks about the joy in attending a friend's wedding. He exchanged loving greetings and that made him feel good. He describes good feelings about a day that went smoothly at work, and an unusually happy day at work with his friends at a coffee shop at the end of a day. He seems to be able to both work and enjoy leisure. At the end of the year his major concerns were still about finding a new place to live and over not having enough to do three or four times a month.

An episode described in the sixth interview is typical of his frequent episodes of anger with other drivers. He was in his car on his way to the coffee shop to have his morning get-together with his friends. He describes the incident:

> A guy pulled out from a stop sign, as I was coming down
> the street. I felt like I should hit him. I came as close
> as I could; I wanted to hit him. I swore, something like
> you dirty so and so and then dropped it. . . . [I: What
> were you thinking about?] That that guy's not going to
> stop and I'm almost on top of him. He didn't even know
> I was coming. . . . [I: What made you really mad?] The
> fact that that guy wasn't aware and he didn't stop for a
> stop sign. Complete oblivion. . . . Someday I'd like to
> hit the car just for the sheer joy of . . . [I: joy of what?]
> just hitting the car, because people do not care
> sometimes. . . I thought if I hit the guy that would have
> taught him a lesson. I wanted him to be aware that I was
> there, and he wasn't even aware.

The violation of road courtesy and safety rules amounts to an assault on Mr. Morris. He reacts personally with drivers. He personalizes them, trying to teach them lessons even though he will never see them again, or get the benefit of the improved driving. He describes the event as if it were clear and well punctuated: "Instead of stopping, this guy just drove across the street." When the interviewer asked what kind of guy the driver was, the question seemed reasonable to Mr. Morris. He responded. "He was an older guy, about 50, about my age, the dumb jerk." He states: "If someone had been with me, I would not have done this [swearing, coming as close to the driver as possible] because it would be showing my ignorance." His reactions come from his involvement with what he is doing, so he might not benefit distancing himself from the meanings that generate these reactions. It might be more difficult for him to handle full-time driving if he considered driving completely routine, impersonal, and he was indifferent to the driving habits of others. That driving matters to him, and that other drivers matter to him, may be more important to his coping with daily work than the episodes of brief anger and feelings of aggression. He says that he felt great just after this incident and enjoyed shooting the breeze with his friends.

The other recurring work stress for Mr. Morris is not having enough work to do. It occurs three or four times a month. The following episode is representative:

> Today was one of the bad days and I know it. [I: Why?]
> Not enough work for me to do. It happens three or four
> times a month. Not enough to keep me going. [I: What
> do you do?] Nothing. That bothers me. I get lazy. Today
> I knew that I had just so much to do and that I would run
> out. I called when I was done. [I: When was that?]
> 1:15 P.M.

He goes on to describe the aggravating, frustrating afternoon that troubled him. He cannot drum up the business, but it makes him feel guilty that he is not working. He says it makes him feel like he is cheating the company. He describes his feelings:

> [I: Did anyone know how you were feeling?] Yes,
> the dispatcher. I ask him how he can justify the mileage.
> [How does he?] I don't know. He always says, "Don't
> worry about it." He's not concerned. Just as long
> as he knows where I'm at. [I: Do you mean at the
> coffee shop?] Yes. [I: Is it the feeling of not being
> productive that is the main factor?] I am not sure.
> [I: Or is the main factor that they might not need you?]
> The main factor is not being productive for the day.
> Or the fact that they'll wake up and say one day that

they don't need me. But they have been leasing trucks for
24 years and it has been the same way always. . . . At
the end of the day I figure I've been there eight or nine
hours and that I've done something, just going there. In
other words, I've given them the hours. I've put in a day's
eight hours, not done a day's work. I look forward to the
next day. I hope that there will be something to do
tomorrow. It could happen two days in a row. Tomorrow
could send me to—, or any place. That's an all-day job
with a lot of driving. [I: You would rather do that?]
Oh yeah.

(See Chart 8.4 for interpretation of the coping episode.)

Relationship Between Work Meanings
and Stress and Coping

Mr. Morris gets frustrated with the coping questionnaire because it doesn't work for him. He says: "It's hard trying to find things
that bother me. Not too many things bother me. I just have petty little
things that bother me. My petty things are people on the road. I've
learned to deal with it by swearing." He is not very reflective. His
biggest worries are not having enough to do or getting delayed in his
deliveries so that he doesn't have a smooth efficient day. He describes
good days at work. He seems to enjoy the process of work, and having
things come off smoothly:

Today was a typical good day. It is an example of working
and enjoying it. I'm in the truck, and went to work, waited
around while it was loaded, and then took a nice long ride.
It made my day good. It was a nice and easy day. I was
doing something. [I: What was nice about it?] I felt like
I had a real good pay load. [I: What do you mean by that?]
I was full to capacity, and had two deliveries. . . . Everything went off beautifully, it was a good day. They were
almost waiting for me to unload and get me going again.

The description of a good day rounds out the picture of the
frustration and damage he feels when he is not busy. He is ashamed of
not being busy and does not tell his wife because he wants her to think
that he is working when he goes to work.

He is not very reflective about his work. He is committed to it.
This is evident in his descriptions of good days. It was also evident
when he brought his large truck home to show it to the interviewer. He
enjoys his work, when he has enough to do, and when he is not delayed

CHART 8.4

Mr. Morris: Interpretation of Coping Episode

STAKES

Feels guilty over not working. Fears that inactivity means that his job is threatened. Disappointed that the day does not go as planned: "I haven't accomplished the task. God, to do a day's work is what's in my mind, to be productive."

APPRAISAL

Psychological and material threat.

RESOURCES

Perceived choices considered as inadequate.

COPING STRATEGIES

- Direct Action
- Information Search
- Planning
- Social Support—Uses available emotional support: "[I: Did anyone know how you were feeling?] Yes, the dispatcher, I asked him how he can justify the mileage. He always says, 'Don't worry about it.'"
- Social Influence
- Inhibition of Action
- Cognitive Coping or Palliation—Justification: "I've put in a day's eight hours."

  Eating and drinking coffee: He drinks about 30 cups of coffee during this day while waiting at the coffee shop. He goes and has a couple of beers with a friend after work, but he says that he ordinarily does this regardless of the kind of day.

  Mobilizes hope: "I look forward to the next day. Tomorrow they could send me to———, or any place.

  Diminishes severity of threat: "But they have been leasing trucks for 24 years and it has been the same way always."

  Defends own competence: "I try to get the materials to a specified place at a specified time."

EMOTIONS EXPERIENCED IN EPISODE

Guilt, frustration, boredom, worry: He feels guilty for being nonproductive even though he does not produce the work. He feels frustrated and worried when the dispatcher cannot find work for him. He also feels restless boredom and looks forward to a busy day, perhaps tomorrow.

PHYSICAL EXPERIENCE OF EMOTION

Not described.

EFFECT OF COPING ON EMOTION

His coping keeps him in the situation and helps him tolerate it. It keeps his emotions in check. He defends and rationalizes, seeks support, and feels better for it. However, the feelings are not resolved and do not go away. They come the next time he does not have enough to do.

EFFECT OF COPING ON SITUATION

Manages situation as well as it can be managed. He is actually powerless to do anything about the situation. He stays available and stays responsible to the dispatcher, continues to check in and let him know where he is.

---

unnecessarily. He has a network of friends who are also truckers. He talks about meeting with his trucker friends at a coffee shop and exchanging stories and laughing with them. He has a range of positive as well as negative emotions both on and off work.

During the year he has a variety of work and nonwork coping and emotion episodes. His life has its struggles, but he is happy with it. He does not drink as much as he did in the past. He has learned to stop at three drinks. Participating in the study made him realize that he is happy most of the time. Meaningful work does not prevent stressful episodes, it allows them to show up. Being engaged in work so that some things stand out as more or less important facilitates coping (see "Summary and Conclusions" Section of Chapter 6). Also a certain level of commitment motivates the person to develop coping skills. Mr. Morris provides a contrast to the bus driver, Mr. Paul, (see Chapter 6) who was not sufficiently committed to his work to learn the tricks of the trade to make his work easier.

SUMMARY AND CONCLUSIONS

These paradigm cases were selected because they portray the stress and coping benefits of meaningful work. They so not portray "stress-free" work, but rather work that is satisfying because of the way these participants are engaged in their work and the social participation they experience in their work. Their work meanings and practices are integrated. In each case, the worker is neither consumed by his work nor is he alienated from it. These participants do not stand out because they "believe" different things about work. If they were asked what they believe about work, they might sound similar to the participants in Chapter 5. For example, they might say that they believe in doing their duty, but their work is more than a duty. They stand out because of their particular involvement and relationship to work that is evident as they describe their coping and emotion episodes related to work across the year. This particular relationship to work is transactional and cannot be explained by decontextualized personality or situational variables.

They share the meanings of work handed down in the Protestant Work Ethic and they believe many of the same things about their work that the participants in Chapter 5 believe. These participants are not primarily engaged in meanings peripheral to the work itself. For example, they are not trying to prove themselves. They are not overcome with a sense of time pressure. They all share a commitment to the present and to the future but they do not understand their present activities merely in terms of future goals and rewards. They look neither to the past nor the future as the best times in their lives. Work Ethic meanings serve work goals and tasks instead of becoming ends in themselves, as was the case in Chapter 5.

Commitment to work can produce stress when one's commitments are not supported by the structure of one's work, the work group, and significant others. These four participants can be considered "fortunate" in that their commitments are supported by their work situations. The stressful consequences of a mismatched level of commitment was illustrated in Mr. Gough's frustration and moral outrage when he was powerless to influence his work situation, and when it was evident that promotion came to those less knowledgeable than he. After his promotion, however, his work satisfaction returned because once again the work environment supported and sanctioned his level of interest and commitment. He traded the stress of moral outrage and helplessness for a sense of entitlement and a new set of stressful transactions created by his role transition and lack of management skills. He moved from distressing emotions to a sense of challenge and entitlement. As he noted, he "felt better about himself and about the world" after his promotion.

Mr. Ingolls also moved from a dissatisfying work situation to a satisfying one. His current work is not without stress, but the stress is manageable from the participant's perspective. His work has become easier and less stressful over time. He is not tyrannized by the fear of failure in the midst of his success.

The physician, Dr. Ursell, experiences work overload, but he does not add to his overload by deliberately filling his off-duty hours with work activity, and he has developed a number of strategies for smoothing his workload. An interesting case can show up in the midst of the busy schedule and engage him, so that he does not experience his work as drudgery. Work has become less stressful for him over the years, too. Meaningful work causes some events to show up as stressful and pleasurable. For example, the truck driver's engagement with his work causes him to get angry daily at poor drivers; however, it also allows him to get pleasure from a day that goes smoothly. He is threatened by inactivity both because it is a threat to his job security and because it prevents him from feeling that he is earning his pay. He is rewarded by a network of fellow truck drivers who meet and joke and shoot the breeze while they wait for their dispatcher to call. He reads books on making money and dreams of finding the right angle to strike it rich and go out with some dignity. But he is happy with his life now.

Work that is meaningful to the person is not necessarily the most self-actualizing, psychologically rewarding, or expressive work. People can value the work they do without having found their most fulfilling work. For example, the truck driver still dreams of making a lot of money so that he "can go out with some dignity." He also states that he and his wife would be prouder of his station in life if he were a doctor or a lawyer. Nevertheless, driving a truck is meaningful to him. He feels that his work is worthwhile. He takes pride in a day that runs smoothly and according to schedule. He describes fun and companionship with his fellow truck drivers whom he has been meeting in coffee shops for 14 years. He experiences his work as social participation. Thus, meaningfulness allows participation and engagement in what may or may not be considered the most self-actualizing line of work for him. The meaningfulness of the work allows events to show up as stressful (for example, the anger the truck-driver experiences over poor drivers) and it provides a sense of options or possibilities in the situation. Meaningfulness enables the person to take action in a situation because some action stands out as relevant (that is, more or less important or salient to the problem at hand).

When stressful events arise, these participants are not distracted by side issues. Their commitment to their work and their expertise give them a sense of salience (see Dreyfus, 1982; Benner, 1984;

Dreyfus and Dreyfus, in press). That is, some things stand out as inportant relative to other things as they go about their work. A sense of salience mades one's work easier because it allows the person to attend to the most relevant issues in a situation without a lot of wasteful consideration of irrelevant facts. A sense of salience prevents unnecessary stress appraisals or at least limits false alarms. A sense of salience helps a person grasp what coping options are available in the situation. They are not limited to the solutions they anticipate but can recognize solutions that present themselves in the situation. Because the person is engaged in his work in a particular way, he accumulates coping skills from prior experience.

These participants do not get sidetracked as easily into proving themselves or controlling events. The task itself has meaning for them so they can respond directly to the demands, resources, and constraints in the task itself, For example, Mr. Ingolls does not get distracted by the side issue of "pleasing his boss" or "proving his boss is less capable or worthy than himself." Instead, in one situation he backs off when he sees that he cannot alter the situation. In another situation he backs off to regroup and try another approach. In both instances he is convinced of the merits of his ideas and does not engage in retaliation or self-recrimination.

Work satisfaction is of course more than the absence of stress. It seems to help the individual tolerate and minimize stress. Mr. Ingolls becomes alert and mobilized prior to presenting an important case to his boss, but he does not try to potentiate that anxiety by psyching himself up and he, unlike one salesman in the sample, does not respond to his golf game with the same level of intensity as he does to major presentations. Each of these participants draws satisfaction from doing his work. The physician gets intrigued by an interesting case during a busy time. The maintenance electrician derives great pride and satisfaction from making a machine work better. The advertising executive enjoys seeing his ideas worked out. The truck driver enjoys a good day's run where everything goes smoothly. All of these satisfactions are repetitive and do not exact high personal costs. They also indicate a level of involvement with the work itself that allows them to develop a cushion of experience as a coping resource.

When work is meaningful in itself to the person and when the person does not have other overriding personal and cultural meanings that interfere with performance, the person is free to attend fully to the work at hand. They are also free to develop a sense of salience. They experience fewer stressful episodes at work over time even though they may be very involved in their work.

9

SUMMARY AND CONCLUSIONS: IMPLICATIONS FOR STRESS MANAGEMENT

The coping and emotion episodes of these 23 participants illustrate that background meanings influence what is experienced as stressful and what coping options are available to the person. Background meanings function as a perceptual lens and thus are invisible to the person. These meanings show up in daily activities and choices and in what is experienced as stressful.

Meaningfulness is transactional. It neither stands in the culture alone nor is it located only within the individual. It is neither a talent nor a trait nor is it a characteristic of a social system that can be adequately described out of context. For example, it was posited that should the social context change for any of the participants, the meaningfulness of their work could also change for better or for worse

It is easier to describe the impact of powerfully held background personal meanings on stress and coping when the meanings are changing, because when meanings are working best they are invisible. They are taken for granted, just as the researcher takes his paradigm for granted (see Kuhn, 1970). Therefore it is difficult to describe the positive impact of intact meanings and their impact on stress and coping. Kobasa (1979) demonstrated in an empirical study that participants who demonstrated "hardiness" suffered less illness during a period of high stress than those who did not demonstrate hardiness. She defined hardiness as a strong commitment to self, an attitude of vigorousness toward the environment, and a sense of meaningfulness and internal locus of control. Her description probably captures intact Utilitarian and Work Ethic meanings. Regardless of their label, she observed differences between those who have a sense of meaningfulness and those who do not.

STRESS AND COPING: A LINKED
INTERPRETATIVE PROCESS

The stimulus-response paradigm of behavior is all but abandoned, yet the hidden assumptions of that paradigm still hold powerful sway in the methodological strategies used in studying stress and coping. Most studies formulate causes, antecedents, mediators, and outcomes of stress and coping. Despite attempts to break beyond these methodological strategies, because they miss the complexity and transactional nature of stress and coping (Lazarus, 1981), stress and coping are still studied as if they were not linked. Thus, coping gets defined as that which mediates, ameliorates, and alters stress without considering the relationship between the stressful transaction and the coping response. Consequently coping can be misconstrued to be a general antidote to stress. In actuality, coping always relates to the issue at stake for the person in a particular situation.

Stress management programs reflect this confusion by teaching general coping strategies. They offer a variety of stress-reduction techniques with little or no diagnostic assessment of the nature of the individual's recurring stressful episodes.

Because the background meanings of work determine stress appraisals, stress and coping are linked interpretive processes, and they both must be studied in a way that maintains the meaning of an event for the person. Coping stems from a secondary appraisal, or an assessment of how to respond to the stressful situation. Therefore coping strategies are tied to the stress-laden interpretation of an event and can be understood only in relation to the meanings of the event for the person. Coping may ameliorate or exacerbate the stressful transaction. This dooms all context-free prescriptions or recipes for how to cope with stress. For example, recommendations that one use direct action or avoid wishful thinking simply do not hold up because in some situations wishful thinking is more useful than direct action.

More to the point, wishful thinking may be the only coping option available, from the perspective of the person in the situation (that is, from a particular understanding of the situation). This perception is illustrated in the analyses of the coping and emotion episodes (see Chapters 5, 6, and 8). Mr. Davis's coping strategy of psyching himself up in order to produce a successful performance is based upon the lived interpretation that work is a competitive bid, which requires total concentration, marshaling of resources, and use of self. Work is a challenge laced with threat, therefore one copes by marshaling all resources as if work were a battle. These coping strategies combat the stress of the challenging, threatening event. But the coping strategies create damage and stress in themselves. They become stress to be coped with.

Mr. Verdent's case study also illustrates the interrelationship between meanings and stress and coping. Mr. Verdent's self-definition was tied to a particular promotion. The meaning of promotion was a lived one and not open to reinterpretation or "thinking" until after he had reached a crisis in his position. Even at the end of the year, he was struggling for a reinterpretation of the events of the past two years and stated that he wished he could have recognized this as a battle not to enter. At the time, however, because his sense of worthiness and his self-definition were tied to promotion, he could not perceive the events except in terms of winning or losing the promotion. Being promoted was just what it meant to be a worthy person.

This meaning functioned much like the researcher's paradigm described by Kuhn (1970). Counseling, to be effective, would have to clarify the options available in his current paradigm and offer the participant the option of changing his paradigm, or embarking on a personal "conceptual" (that is, perceptual) revolution. It is doubtful that any advice that did not assist the participant in a paradigm switch could have interrupted Mr. Verdent's stressful cycle.

However, one cannot be educated into a perceptual revolution. A person has to be in a situation ripe for discovery. Information alone is usually not helpful. A person caught in this sort of stressful cycle could only benefit from experiential learning, much like cross-cultural training programs that have been used to promote an encounter with alternative cultural meanings (see Oberg, 1960; Kramer, 1974).

Without a paradigm switch, the participant is limited to coping options that comfort and allow escape or tolerance of disappoinment. Transformation or change that promotes a restored sense of well-being are not possible without success within his old paradigm, or a new paradigm.

Stress management cannot help in these two examples if it ignores the background meanings that are causing the stress and dictating the coping responses. An assessment of stressful episodes is needed in order to design experiential learning that makes current work meanings visible and offers new alternatives. Thus the view of stress and coping as a linked interpretive process not only has implications for the way stress and coping are studied, it also has implications for theories and programs of stress management. Stress intervention programs aimed at enhancing the individual's coping strategies typically comprise relaxation techniques, biofeedback, psychodynamic therapies, behavior therapies, and planning. Except for psychodynamic therapy, each of these strategies is based upon the premise that the person is committed to his work and is motivated to find ways to cope with the stress that they experience because of the demands of their commitment.

Thus, current stress management programs are unidimensional. They simply seek to give the person greater distance and less engagement in the stressful situation. They work well for overextended workers who need to gain distance from their work in order to revise their approach to work. They also help the temporarily beuned-out workers, who need to gain distance from their work in order to recover energy and interest. However, recovery from burnout is signaled only by reengagement and involvement. If burned-out workers come to believe that they must avoid involvement and commitment in order to prevent burnout, then their coping strategies will perpetuate their loss of caring, their loss of meaningfulness.

Thus, distancing and control strategies have little to offer to workers whose work is meaningless. Nor can they help workers who suffer from pervasive meaninglessness. They offer little to the workers who are bored with their work. Nor can they help workers whose overriding concern for control has reduced their ability to cope with novel, ambiguous tasks.

For example, work has lost its edge and interest for the architect, Mr. Collins, and further distance is not going to renew his zest for work. Work has become boring for Mr. Thomas, the technical writer, but his need for control and predictability prevent him from seeking new assignments. Traditional insight therapy alone will not suffice because it is predicated on freeing and disentangling the person from untenable commitments rather than enabling the person to find new commitments. Letting go of restrictive meanings around the need for control does not guarantee increased work satisfaction.

Often work structures and meanings associated with work cut the person off from the meanings embedded in the work itself. These meanings can be recovered by focusing specifically on work situations that are particularly satisfying. Attention to skills developed, but which may go unnoticed and uncharted by the person, can restore interest in the mastery associated with work. It is not always possible for the person to change jobs or learn new skills to restore interest, in which case attending and enhancing existing skills can be a source of renewal.

Mr. Collins has begun a shift in his work emphasis that may open new interests and begin a new relationship with his work. Such a pattern was described by Bray, Campbell, and Grant (1974) in mid-career managers. Further ethnographic studies would be helpful to understand how work can shift to the background without becoming meaningless. A gap exists between the interpretations based on early childhood experiences offered by traditional insight therapy and the work meanings taken on by the adult worker. An insight approach based on an assessment of recurring stressful episodes is needed so that stress management programs can also be based upon individual stress patterns acquired in adulthood.

WORK AS A COPING RESOURCE

It is a common understanding that work can be soothing or distracting during difficult times. However, researchers frequently study work stress in a way that makes them overlook work as a coping resource. In addition to the obvious function of providing a financial means of living, work was a vital coping resource for all of the participants in this study. Work in this culture is self-definitional and linked to self-esteem. Therefore even stressful work is less stressful for the individual than unemployment.

Work can provide a stable background and sense of mastery that provides reassurance for more difficult life domains that are less subject to skill and control. After all, work is the area of life that is most amenable to mastery. Work tasks respond to skill acquisition. Work expectations and contracts are also clearer than most other social situations. Work expectations and performance criteria, while never completely explicit, are much clearer that they can be in family and other interpersonal domains. Thus work can become easier over time (see Chapters 7 and 8).

Mr. Kemp stood out because he had no coping episodes at work for the entire year. Work provided a stable background and sense of mastery that constantly reassured him during the difficulties and distress he experienced in his personal relationships (see Chapter 3 for sample case study).

Work also provides a sense of boundaries and structure for most people in this culture. However, this function of work is so basic that it is less apparent than the other meanings of work. This was most dramatically illustrated by Mr. West who had few meanings relating to his work other than the sense of authority and boundaries his work created for him (see Chapter 3 for case study). Mr. West, a carpenter hated his work. However, when he was temporarily unemployed, he became irritable and spent his time drinking and napping. He knew that his employment was temporary and that he was only trying to get enough hours in for retirement. Yet being off work and home alone was extremely distressing in a way that he could not understand. His daily patterns and stress and coping episodes charted over the study year support the conclusion that he had lost his sense of structure that his workday provided for him and he had none to substitute.

Work was not a major source of stress for eight of the participants of this study. For them, work served as a source of self-esteem provided distraction, structured time, and provided boundaries and authority. Work has multiple functions and meanings in our culture, many of which the worker is unaware. That is why unemployment and retirement can be so disruptive. Their impact is not limited to the obvious difficulties associated with earning a living, but also affects self-definition and coping itself.

It is an untested assumption that retiring or changing jobs after a heart attack or other stress-impacted illnesses will yield the desired goal of stress reduction. Work is not only a demand, it is also a coping resource. Giving up one's job may lead to a cycle of self-defeat and depression that is more difficult to cope with than the excessive mobilization involved in the work situation. Changing jobs may lead to even more stress if the person transfers inherently stressful work practices, expectations, and meanings. Work is a culture and the person takes up practices, expectations, and meanings tacitly. They then transfer their acquired culture of work to new work settings. Changing jobs may only obscure the need for change at a personal level because, initially, the new job may seem easier and the person may feel less encumbered by past demands. However, in time, the same work practices and meanings from prior work experience tend to be reinstated in the new setting.

Even though the need for a high-level mobilization may <u>not</u> exist in the "new" job, the person may understand their work demands in terms of their past experience. I am reminded of a friend who visited just after retirement. She had retired early due to a heart condition and had every intention of taking it easy. However, her past high-pressured job and work meanings spilled over into her leisure. She was trying to visit <u>all</u> the national parks and had a series of mementos she wanted to collect from each each park. Each tour was spent with great concentration, haste, and attention on the getting to the next park. It is not that easy to shed past work meanings, even when the circumstances are different.

If the work situation itself is not excessively demanding, the person may experience fewer demands and a greater sense of well-being by remaining in his or her current work setting and embarking upon a program to alter work attitudes and approaches. By keeping the work setting constant, the person can better judge the impact of his or her own personal change. In other words, the person will know what to attribute to changes in the situation and what to attribute to personal change. Also, it is easier to focus on personal change if the individual already has mastered the skills inherent on the job and already knows coworkers and how the system works. If a person is working in a highly demanding work situation, such as a large brokerage firm or a large, busy emergency room, he or she may need to find a smaller, slower office or a different health-care setting. The person cannot afford to overlook the demands of the situation itself, nor can he or she assume that changing the situation will necessarily ensure personal change and stress reduction. Old work practices and meanings are frequently transferred unwittingly.

Futher research is needed to determine the relative merits of early retirement, job change, or a program of personal and situational change in the old work setting for the purpose of stress reduction for health. However, this research question will need to consider the possibility that work serves as a coping resource as well as a coping demand. Too often research in this field has begun with the premise that work is primarily stressful. The researcher will need to evaluate the extent to which work meanings are a positive coping resource and are inherently stressful. In the end, the individual will have to weigh the personal costs of altering his or her approach to work, changing jobs, or giving work up altogether. Such a complex decision is probably best made in stages so that the person can alter their decision should they find that their choice has unexpected negative ramifications. The person who trades excessive mobilization for a cycle of defeat and sense of helplessness merely trades one set of stressful emotions for another.

STRESS AT WORK IS EASED BY MEANINGFUL WORK

Four case studies in this study illustrated the positive effect of meaningfulness on stress and coping related to work (see Chapter 8). The participants were selected because their work meanings did not create frequent stressful episodes and because they were able to work, love, and have leisure. They are satisfied with their work, and typically their coping efforts both improved the situation and made them feel less distressed or less mobilized (See Charts 8.1-8.4).

The physician finds satisfaction and interest in his work. In the midst of work overload he gets intrigued with an interesting case and explains that this renewed interest helps him cope with the overload. As he says, his work has not become onerous. He does not suffer from chronic time pressure. He has developed a number of skills and strategies for smoothing his workload. He has a strong sense of priorities and does not compulsively try to do everything.

The advertising excutive, Mr. Ingolls, simply states that he does not experience work overload. Probably the structure of his work permits a smoothing of workload, but his own work habits do not create unnecessary overload. His work stresses stem from trying to sell his ideas. However, when he fails to sell his ideas, he does not engage in self-doubt as did the participants caught in a perennial proving ground. He does not link winning to proving his worth.

Mr. Ingolls is mobilized so that he is attentive prior to presenting his ideas, but his level of mobilization seems appropriate to the event. This contrasts with other participants who "psyched themselves up" for any number of work situations and for leisure activities. For example, Mr. Davis exaggerated the importance of some work situations so that he would have "butterflies in his stomach" to ensure a good performance. The store manager worried about counting a relatively small amount of cash for a pancake breakfast despite the fact that he has handled large sums of money for over 20 years.

Work has become easier over time for all four participants with meaningful work. Their work meanings are integrated with their work practices. All have a cushion of experience. They each have enough continuity in their work so that their past experience affects their current work practices. And they do not have other work meanings such as "time as an adversary" or work as a perennial proving ground that interferes with appropriating their past experience for their current situation.

All four participants are committed to their work; but their engagement with their work is not limited to a sense of personal control. Because they do not have an overriding concern for control, they can be open to alternatives that they do not generate themselves. They successfully influence their work situations, but they also expect to be influenced by the situation. They not only seek to influence their coworkers and friends, they also seek and receive advice and emotional support from them. They provide a contrast between work involvement based on commitment and work involvement based on control. Their commitment provides a type of involvement that enables them to be both flexible and effective in their work.

All four cite the present as the best time in their lives. They are rewarded by their work now and do not experience their work as drudgery to be endured until retirement. They plan for the future but they do not look to the future to make up for current deficits.

The meaningfulness of work allows events to show up as stressful (for example, the truck driver's anger over poor driving), and it provides a sense of options or possibilities in the situation. Meaningfulness enables the person to take action in the situation because some action stands out as being relevant to the problem at hand. Also a certain level of commitment (that is, personal meaning) is required to motivate the person to develop coping skills and strategies (see also Becker, 1964). In the long term, involvement facilitates the development of a cushion of experience as a coping resource and the development of coping skills. Detachment may reduce stress in the short term but may actually hinder stress management because detachment hinders the development of coping skills and resources.

WORK MEANINGS PRONE TO STRESSFUL TRANSACTIONS

Some meanings of work are inherently stressful regardless of the particular nature of the work. Though the person can find lesser or greater "person-situation fit," the way they understand work and their personal meanings in relationship to work may either cause repeated stressful transactions or render some work demands nonstressful. For example, the person caught up in a perennial proving ground can never "relax" in his work. Every task or activity can threaten to lower self-esteem, through either making an error or not achieving a particular goal. The person with a particularly singular commitment to promotion is vulnerable to crisis when expected promotions are not forthcoming.

The person who requires the process or activity of work as a source of self-esteem is extremely vulnerable to stress from underload or unemployment. Inactivity will be a repeated stress if he is in circumstances where he does not control the amount or pacing of work. If he does control his work pace, he may choose overwork to avoid inactivity. The person who experiences time as an adversary and equates time with money, and who is committed to earn as much money as possible, will find any delay stressful. The person who carries this position to the extreme cannot value any activity for itself. Even task related to earning can be a source of irritation because the person races ahead to think of all that he is not accomplishing.

The person who has an overriding concern for control is subject to stress when he finds himself in situations beyond his control. When the situation does not permit control, the person may inappropriately resort to strategies that promote an increased sense of personal control, or an illusion of control so that any threatening situation can become defined as an internal or psychological problem (see case study on Mr. Lewis, Chapter 5). Thus the person locates the source of the problem within himself so that he can gain a sense of control. He "controls" the meaning of the situation for himself. But locating the problem within and altering its meaning to increase a sense of personal control prevents the person from attending to the meanings inherent in the situation. It prevents him from having his notions of the situation turned around so that he learns from the situation.

Perfect control puts one beyond learning from experience. Experience is gained only when preconceptions are turned around (see Heidegger, 1962). In order to learn from experience the person must be able to have his preconceptions challenged and still be able to see alternatives that present themselves in the situation. An extreme concern for control precludes this kind of flexibility. It also precludes recognizing the unexpected possibilities and constraints in the situation. People who have a strong need for control are prone to feelings of helplessness and hopelessness, because they believe that they should be able to control situations (See Glass, 1977). When they cannot control events and when they are unable to create an illusion of control for themselves, they feel helpless because they do not expect or believe that a solution outside themselves exists.

Of course, to say that one cannot <u>control</u> a situation does not mean that one is absolutely passive, with no alternatives, it just means that all the alternatives and possibilities are not self-generated. But poeple who believe that they must completely control their options will not expect to find alternatives that they do not generate. They will not see possibility in the unplanned or the risky; instead, they will perceive threat. Thus their very need for control may render them incapable of perceiving the options and opportunities that just present themselves in the situation. They will be less prone to work stress than other people when they can select situations that are within their control but when they confront the limits of control they will be extremely stressed.

The participant for whom work is life (see Chapter 5, Mr. Smith's case) to overwork, and the range of his emotional life is limited to what his worklife offers. For example, Mr. Smith's worklife replaces love and friendships. Mr. Smith described no positive emotions outside of his work except for "excitement" during one weekend outing. His hobby is acquiring several collections that require the same kind of bargaining and searching skills that he enjoys in his work. He also participates in civic clubs where he has active responsible roles. By his report, he has no close friendships or intimate relationships. His work stress stems from overwork, but he keeps his workload as heavy as possible to protect himself from inactivity. Even so, Mr. Smith does not feel distressed about his life. He states that his work has replaced interest in and need for sex. The "work as life" attitude is stressful because the positive emotions found in love and leisure are crowded out and because the person is chronically pressured because he overschedules his time. His excitement and enjoyment of work come from winning contracts rather than from the process of doing the work associated with the contracts. Therefore, much of his actual work is experienced as drudgery rather than as a satisfying way to spend his time. Thus, his work is burdensome much of the time, and he has few positive emotions that give him respite from his work absorption.

The person who believes in the efficacy of worry will exaggerate the importance of some events in order to generate anxious feelings to ensure success. These anxious feelings are in themselves stressful. This was contrasted earlier to the person who found himself anxious before an important meeting, but who did not try to increase that anxiety nor to emphasize deliberately the event's importance in order to increase his vigilance.

To summarize, some work meanings lead to stressful appraisals. The person who requires activity for a sense of well-being but who does not control the pacing of his work will be distressed with enforced inactivity or unemployment. The person who does control his workload will choose overload to insure against inactivity. People who have an overriding concern for control will be extremly stressed in novel and risky situations. They will fail to gain a cushion of experience that would decrease their work stress over time. People who experience work as life will have few positive emotions and support systems outside of their work. The person who believes in the efficacy of anxiety will be more vigilant than necessary in many situations. The person who experiences time as an adversary will experience chronic time pressure, and his coping strategies of working harder and longer will be stressful in themselves. In each case, if these meanings are ascendant, a means-ends displacement occurs that prevents the person from finding meaning in the work itself. These meanings all lead to frequent stress appraisals and to coping strategies that may be stressful in themselves.

This finding that certain work meanings are inherently stressful has implications for stress management programs. Currently most of these programs teach participants distancing and distraction techniques, exercise and meditation. Frequently they focus on increasing the person's sense of control in their work situation. But the person who already has an overriding concern for personal control might be better helped by participating in training courses where they could experientially learn the limits to control and by practicing ways of listening and perceiving alternatives that present themselves in the situation. This kind of consciousness raising has been successfully used in cross-cultural training programs (Oberg, 1960; Kramer, 1974). Similar strategies of consciousness raising and experiential learning would be useful for the time-urgent person. In fact, just practicing meditation may restructure one's relationship to time and time use (Roskies, 1983).

The person who chooses work as life may not choose to participate in a stress management program. Should Mr. Smith find himself in a stress management program, it is unclear what he would want out of it. Short of insight therapy, his stress management would need to be geared to relaxation, diversion, and restructuring his work so that it would be less chronically demanding. We do not know how prevalent the kind of work addiction embraced by Mr. Smith is, nor what the health consequences of such an addiction are.

However, stress management programs should not blindly prescribe the shedding of stressful work meanings without assessing how these meanings function in actual stressful episodes. As illustrated in the next section, unless the person is able to replace his current paradigm with a new one, he may be left with fewer coping options because he will not have a functioning understanding of his work. Also, since meanings do not reside only within the person but also within his work situation, in some cases the structure and practices of work will have to be changed before the meanings of work are changed. For example, the company for which Mr. Davis works would probably have to change its testing and evaluation procedures that indicate that a successful sales record does not suffice, and that the company, even after 20 years, does not view the salesman as a colleague with internal motivation. One could imagine the restructuring of sales meetings where sales persons gave their recommendations and accumulated wisdom to management instead of always having the "training" flow from the top down.

MEANINGS IN TRANSITION AND MEANINGLESSNESS

When a person does not have a rich background of meaning to support his or her actions, he or she suffers from the inability to choose and act in an uncomplicated, smooth fashion. Actions that were once automatic become issues for thought and deliberation. What was once easy now becomes effortful. The problem of a lack of smoothly functioning background meanings is similar to the difficulty encountered when conducting business in a foreign culture. This disorientation created by a radical disruption in background meanings has been described as "culture shock" by Oberg (1960). The person experiences anger and surprise when things do not go according to his or her assumptions about what is appropriate, decent, courteous, and so on. On a long-term basis, the person in a foreign culture experiences culture fatigue, which comes from having daily to make decisions about how to act or respond in situations that are ordinarily taken for granted or automatic.

The meanings of work were in crisis for four of the participants in the sample. The meanings of work were in crisis for one participant because he did not get a long-awaited promotion. For years he performed his job in light of moving into his supervisor's position when the supervisor retired. His efforts were all linked to that goal. When that goal became untenable because someone else was appointed to the position, he was angry and disappointed, and his work was no longer meaningful to him.

Two of the four participants talked about being in a mid-life crisis. The meanings of work by which they had lived had gone flat on them. Mr. Collins, the participant whose meanings of work had shifted from that of the duty ethic to a duty to self, found it difficult to engage fully in work or leisure because work had become routine and boring and his vacations did not live up to his expectations of adventure and challenge. He had not yet found new meanings and commitments to replace the old. Mr. Thomas still clung to his duty ethic, but he felt alienated from his coworkers because they did not share his expectations and practices at work. He felt himself shrinking inwardly and wanting to retreat from a society that no longer shared his concerns and practices.

Work meanings were limited for the fourth participant (Mr. Paul), because his life had a general condition of meaninglessness. Mr. Paul had lost his ability to make concrete, specific commitments. Commitment is required in order to have personal meanings that operate as a paradigm or perceptual lens. Without commitment (personal meaning), the person must resort excessively to deliberate analysis and calculation of values and preferences so that smooth functioning breaks down.

The shift in meanings in each case leaves confusion in its wake, and this confusion shows up in the emotion and coping episodes of the participants. All four of these participants end up with excessive reflectiveness that does not lead to resolution or action. They talk self-consciously about their work meanings because their meanings are no longer working well and therefore the participants are examining them. They have lost their clarity about daily choices and about their lives in general. Old work meanings clash with their new work circumstances. Consequently many of their coping and emotion episodes end without being resolved, and they contribute to future stress and coping episodes. They all have frequent episodes of frustration, anger, impatience, and irritation. Except for Mr. Collins, whose main difficulty is boredom, all have a sense of hopelessness. In other words, three of these participants do not expect things to get better.

When meaning breaks down, coping can no longer be anchored in compelling preferences; therefore, people are confused and in conflict about what they want in any given situation. Problem solving no longer makes sense because they are not sure what the problem is, nor what constitutes an adequate solution.

When people experience pervasive meaninglessness in their lives, stress is also pervasive. Furthermore, coping options are not readily apparent because all options seem equally plausible. When one's primary appraisal does not come from personal commitments—for example, to be a good bus driver, or to do one's duty—then it is difficult for the person to mobilize his efforts to cope with the situation. Pervasive meaninglessness leads to the alienated positions of "not me," "not here," "not now," and this alienated stance offers no direction or even motivation to come to terms with the situation.

The person who suffers from meaninglessness temporarily is said to be "burned out." Meanings have gone flat so that the commitments that once facilitated caring are no longer available. Nothing stands out as important or seems worth doing. The person who has lost deeply held personal commitments (that is, personal meanings)

feels depressed (Klinger, 1975; Wrubel, Benner, and Lazarus, 1981).
The person who suffers from a pervasive sense of meaninglessness is
said to be suffering from nihilism and anomie. Most stress management
programs are predicated on the assumption that coping makes sense
to the person and is recognizable whether it is in the form of making
themselves feel better or of doing something about the situation. These
programs have little to offer a person beset by meaninglessness,
because before people can choose their actions, they must be situated
in a network of meaning. While no one is ever totally bereft of meaning,
one's sense of meaning can be so disrupted that stress is pervasive,
and the ability to act in any deliberative way is blocked (see Benner,
Roskies, and Lazarus, 1980).

STRESS AND COPING AND STRESS MANAGEMENT:
SUMMARY AND CONCLUSIONS

The empirical studies linking various sources of work stress to
health have been yielding positive results faster than the theoretical
notions of stress can accommodate. Increasingly stress is understood
as a complicated and broad process (Lazarus, 1981; Pearlin et al.,
1981). Stress research illustrates the human science predicament
that Heidegger (1962) points out: There is no privileged position from
which to study self-interpreting human beings. There are no deep or
hidden rules, needs, drives, or traits that are interpretation-free. If
there were needs or traits that were basic (that is, interpretation-free),
then it would be plausible to design environments from the ground up
that would accommodate these needs with the least amount of frustration
and tension. This would be the world of total control and meaning
would cease to be important. Such a totalitarian stance is steadfastly
rejected even by social planners and for good reasons (see H. L.
Dreyfus, 1980, 1981). The problem is not circumvented by studying
beliefs or values because these cannot be studied from an objective or
value-free stance. The stress researcher cannot stand outside the
human condition and look in and discover that there is a perfect personality or perfect environment for perfect health, or even for homeo-
stasis (see Benner, Roskies, and Lazarus, 1980).
Stress research also illustrates the limits of formalism in studying everyday human practices, because these practices are nonobjec-
tifiable. This problem is not limited to the impossibility of listing
context-free variables; the limits of formalism are also encountered
when the researcher attempts to establish all the possible causal links,
interactions, additive impacts, buffers, and other mediaters between
the individual and the situation.
Work meanings and involvement are two transactional variables
that permit the study of the person in the situation. Synthetic interpre-

tive strategies allow the researcher to maintain the context of events so that transactional variables such as commitment and involvement can be considered. Such interpretive research is needed to augment quantitative and empirical research so that the interrelationship between meanings and stress and coping can be better understood. If quantitative and empirical research are not augmented by interpretive strategies, stress and coping researchers run the risk of further contributing to the stress endemic in the modern utilitarian who seeks to control his existence out of fear and loss of faith in the human condition. The final lament may well be that the impetus or zeitgeist behind the study of stress and coping may be causing the problem, and the intensive study of stress and coping may itself be a symptom of our modern dilemma. As Lewis Thomas (1975, pp. 1245-46) notes:

> Tennis has become more than the national sport; it is a rigorous discipline, a form of collective physiotherapy. Jogging is done by swarms of people, out onto the streets each day in underpants, moving in a stolid sort of rapid trudge, hoping by all these means to stay alive. Bicycles are cures. Meditation may be good for the soul, but it is even better for blood pressure. As a people, we have become obsessed with health. There is something fundamentally, radically unhealthy about all this. We do not seem to be seeking more exuberance in living as staving off failure, putting off dying. We are losing confidence in the human form. The new consensus is that we are badly designed, intrinsically fallible, vulnerable to a host of hostile influences inside and around us, and only precariously alive. We live in danger of falling apart at any moment, and are therefore always in need of surveillance and propping up.

Stress management programs based on correlational research can generate formulas for coping with work stress that are unrelated to the individual's work meanings. They may unwittingly foster the perceptual lens or personal paradigm that the individual must base their lifestyle on scientifically calculated attributes that promote health. The individual in this view is a collection of needs, desires, and potentials that must each be met individually and rationally. Such a position actively removes the person from integrative meanings. To embrace such a personal paradigm would be to abandon the cultural and personal meanings that allow understanding and smooth functioning without rational calculation. The calculating individual is also cut off from meaningful social ties. The attributes and characteristics that can be detected in epidemiological research are not the whole story.

They point to cultural meanings, and meanings work as a network of practices, expectations, beliefs, and commitments. If persons designing stress management programs mistakenly recommend the adoption of general, personal, and situational characteristics correlated with less stress, they may unwittingly foster a more stressful, calculating relationship as a result. Superimposing isolated characteristics on one's life is not the same as partaking in these meanings. A totally calculative position would place the individual outside of culture and meaningfulness.

Stress management programs can avoid prescribing context-free coping strategies by assessing individual coping episodes as was done in this study and designing stress management programs based upon the person's work meanings. This approach will require more interpretive studies of the interrelationship between stress and coping of people in real work settings. It will also require a nonpathological model of work stress so that work as a coping resource and the positive functions of work meanings are not overlooked due to the assumption that all workers are alienated or that work is inherently stressful. Also more study is needed to understand what facilitates and what hinders the acquisition of a cushion of experience. We have much to learn from those whose work has become less stressful over time in addition to those who have become more stressed.

Despite an increased academic understanding of the relationship between stress and coping, stress management programs remain limited and are valuable only for certain kinds of stress-related problems. Other stress and coping problems, although understood theoretically, aren't attended to practically. Furthermore, stress management interventions that fail to treat stress and coping as linked interpretive processes and that recommend coping strategies as an antidote to stress regardless of the person's background meanings and context will have minimal impact at best. At worst, they will actually add to the person's stress. This research has presented strategies for broadening the perspective of research on work stress and coping and has pointed to new approaches to the design of stress management programs.

APPENDIX: INTERVIEW SCHEDULE

Interview	Tasks for the Interview	Materials To Be Left with Participants

First	Explain study
	Recent Life Events Question update
	Fill out Calendar of Anticipated
	  Events*
	Give Cantril Current Concerns
	Obtain consent
	Answer questions about mailed
	  materials
	Explain and/or demonstrate:
	  Hassles*
	  Uplifts*
	  Daily Log*
	Bradburn-Beck Scales
		Hassles Scale*
		Uplifts Scale*
		
		Bradburn-Beck Scales
		Daily Log* (4 copies)

Second	Review and answer questions about
	  materials left with participant
	  previous month
	Conduct Coping Interview*
	Explain and/or demonstrate:
	  Coping Questionnaire*
	  Heimler Scale of Social
	    Functioning
	Symptom checklist
		Hassle Scale*
		Uplifts Scale*
		Daily Log (4)*
		Bradburn-Beck Scales
		Coping Questionnaire*
		Heimler Scale of Social
		  Functioning
		Symptom checklist

Third	Review and answer questions about
	  materials left with participant
	  the previous month
	Administer Social Support Question*
	Conduct Family Relations Interview*
	Explain:
	  Jenkins Activity Survey
		Hassles Scale*
		Uplifts Scale*
		Daily Log (4)*
		Bradburn-Beck Scales
		Coping Questionnaire*
		Jenkins Activity Survey

Fourth	Review and answer questions about
	  materials left with participant
	  previous month
	Conduct first Emotion Interview*
	Administer Ways of Coping*
		Hassles Scale*
		Uplifts Scale*
		Daily Log (4)*
		Bradburn-Beck Scales

Fifth	Review and answer questions about
	  materials left with participant
	  previous month
	Conduct second Emotion Interview*
	Administer Ways of Coping*
		Hassles Scale*
		Uplifts Scale*
		Daily Log (4)*
		Bradburn-Beck Scales
		Fe scale from California
		  Psychological Inventory
		Personal Attributes Scale
		Coping Questionnaire*

*Developed By Stress and Coping Project.

Interview	Tasks for the Interview	Materials To Be Left with Participants
Sixth	Review and answer questions about materials left wirh participant previous month Conduct third Emotion Interview* Administer Ways of Coping*	Hassles Scale* Uplifts Scale* Daily log (4)* Bradburn-Beck Scales Coping Questionnaire*
Seventh	Review and answer questions about material left with participant previous month Conduct fourth Emotion Interview* Adninister Ways of Coping*	Hassles Scale* Uplifts Scale* Daily Log (4)* Bradburn-Beck Scales Coping Questionnaire*
Eighth	Review and answer questions about materials left with participant previous month Conduct fifth Emotion Interview* Administer Ways of Coping*	Hassles Scale* Uplifts Scale* Daily Log (4)* Bradburn-Beck Scales Coping Questionnaire*
Ninth	Review and answer questiona about materials left with participant previous month Conduct Sixth Emotion Interview* Administer Ways of Coping*	Hassles Scale* Uplifts Scale* Daily Log (4)* Bradburn-Beck Scales Coping Questionnaire*
Tenth	Review and answer questions about materials left with participant previous month Administer Buhler Life Goals Inventory Conduct Aging and Life Review Interview*	Social Environment Questionnaire* Symptom checklist Health Status Questionnaire Recent Life Events Question Heimler Scale of Social Functioning
Eleventh	Review and answer questions about materials left with participant the previous month Conduct Developmental Interview* Administer Intelligence Scale (Ammons and Ammons) Adjective Checklist	Hassles Scales* Uplifts Scale* Bradburn-Beck Scales Daily Log (4)* Coping Questionnaire*
Twelfth	Administer Social Supports Question* Year-in-review: Pick up loose ends, review earlier themes, persistent failures and major successes, emotions not apparently experienced. Prepare for participant follow-ups	

REFERENCES

Antonovsky, A. Health, stress, and coping. San Francisco: Jossey-Bass, 1980.

Ashford, N. A. Crisis in the workplace: Occupational disease and injury. A Report to the Ford Foundation. Cambridge, Mass.: MIT Press, 1976.

Becker, H. S. Personal change in adult life. Sociometry, 1964, 27, 40-53.

Beehr, T. A., Walsh, J. T., and Taber, T. D. Relationship of stress to individually and organizationally valued states: Higher order needs as a moderator. Journal of Applied Psychology, 1976, 61, 41-47.

Benner, P. From novice to expert: Excellence and power in clinical nursing practice. Menlo Park, Calif.: Addison-Wesley, 1984.

____. Reality testing a reality shock program. In M. Kramer, Reality shock: Why nurses leave nursing. St. Louis: C. V. Mosby, 1974.

____. From novice to expert. American Journal of Nursing, 1982, 82, 402-407.

Benner, P. and Benner, R. V. The new nurse's work entry: A troubled sponsorship. New York: Tiresias Press, 1979.

Benner, P., Roskies, E., and Lazarus, R. S. Stress and coping under extreme conditions. In J. E. Dimsdale, ed., Survivors, victims, perpetrators: Essays on the Nazi holocaust. Washington, D.C.: Hemisphere, 1980.

Benner, P. and Wrubel, J. Skilled clinical knowledge: The value of perceptual awareness. Nurse Educator, 1982, 7, 11-17.

Berger, P., Berger, B., and Kellner, H. The homeless mind. New York: Vintage Books, 1974.

Blau, P. M. and Duncan, O. D. The American occupational structure. New York: John Wiley, 1967.

Borland, D. C. Research on middle age: an assessment. The Gerontologist, 1978, 18, 379-86.

Bray, D. W., Campbell, R. J., and Grant, D. L. Formative years
in business: A long-term A. T. & T. study of managerial lives.
New York: John Wiley, 1974.

Brennan, A. J. J. Health promotion in business: Caveats for success.
Journal of Occupational Medicine, 1981, 23, 639-42.

Brief, A. P., Shuler, R. S., and Van Sell, M. Managing job stress.
Boston: Little, Brown, 1981.

Brim, O. G. & Wheeler, S. Socialization after childhood. New York:
John Wiley, 1966.

Burke, R. J. and Belcourt, M. Managerial role stress and coping
response. Journal of Business Administration, 1974, 5, 55-68.

Burke, R. J. and Weir, T. Coping with the stress of managerial
occupations. In C. L. Cooper and R. Payne, eds., Current concerns in occupational stress. New York: John Wiley, 1980,
pp. 299-335.

Campbell, D. B. A program to reduce coronary heart disease risk
by altering job stresses. Doctoral dissertation, The University
of Michigan, 1973.

Cantril, A. H. and Roll, C. W. Hopes and fears of the American
people. New York: Universe Books, 1971.

Caplan, R. D. Organizational stress and individual strain: A social-
psychological study of risk factors in coronary heart disease
among administrators, engineers, and scientists. Doctoral
dissertation, The University of Michigan, 1971.

Cassel J. The contribution of the social environment to host resistance.
American Journal of Epidemiology, 1976, 104, 1458-63.

Cherniss, C. Professional burnout in human service organizations.
New York: Praeger, 1980.

Chesney, M. A. and Rosenman, R. H. Type A behavior in the work
setting. In C. L. Cooper and R. Payne, eds., Current Concerns
in Occupational Stress. New York: John Wiley, 1980, pp. 187-212.

Chesney, M. A., Sevelius, G., Black, G. W., Ward, M. M., Swan, G. E., and Rosenman, R. H. Work environment, Type A behavior, and coronary heart disease risk factors. Journal of Occupational Medicine, 1981, 23, 551-55.

Cobb, S. Social support as a moderator of life stress. Psychosomatic Medicine, 1976, 38, 300-14.

Cohen, J. B. The influence of culture on coronary-prone behavior. In T. M. Dembroski, S. M. Weiss, J. L. Shields, eds., Coronary-prone behavior. New York: Springer-Verlag, 1978, pp. 243-52.

Cooper C. L. and Marshall, J. Occupational sources of stress. A review of the literature relating to coronary heart disease and mental ill health. Journal of Occupational Medicine, 1976, 49, 11-28.

Cooper, C. L. and Payne, R. Stress at work. New York: John Wiley, 1978.

Davidson, M. J. and Cooper, C. L. A model of occupational stress. Journal of Occupational Medicine, 1981, 23, 564-74.

Dewe, P., Guest, D., and Williams, R. Methods of coping with work-related stress. Unpublished paper presented at a conference of The Ergonomics Society on "Psychophysiological Response to Occupational Stress," held at The University of Nottingham, September 20-21, 1978. Work Research Unit, Department of Employment, London, England.

Dewey, J. and Bentley, A. F. Knowing and the known. Boston: Beacon, 1949.

Dilthey, W. Selected writings, ed. H. P. Rickman. Cambridge: Cambridge University Press, 1976.

Dreyfus, H. L. Knowledge and human values: A genealogy of nihilism. Teacher's College Record, 1981, 82, 508-20.

_____. Holism and hermeneutics. Review of Metaphysics. 1980, 34, 3-23.

_____. What computers can't do, 2d ed. New York: Harper & Row, 1979.

____. Lecture notes: Heidegger's existential phenomenology. University of California, Berkeley, 1977.

Dreyfus, H. L. and Dreyfus, S. E. Putting computers in their place: The primacy of intuition in education and management. New York: Morrow Books, in press.

Dreyfus, S. E. Formal models vs. human situational understanding: Inherent limitations on the modeling of business expertise. Office: Technology and People, 1982, 1, 133-55.

Dreyfus, S. E. and Dreyfus, H. L. A five-stage model of the mental activities involved in directed skill acquisition. Unpublished report supported by the Air Force Office of Scientific Research (AFSC), USAF, under Grant AFOSR-78-3594 with the University of California, Berkeley, February, 1980.

Elder, G. H., Jr. Children of the great depression. Chicago: University of Chicago Press, 1974.

Erikson, E. M. Childhood and society, 2d ed., New York: Norton & Simon, 1963.

Feather, N. T. Values in education and society. New York: The Free Press, 1975.

Festinger, L. A. A theory of social comparison processes, Human Relations, 1954, 7, 117-40.

Folkman, S. Analysis of coping in an adequately functioning 45-to-64 year-old population. Doctoral dissertation, University of California, Berkeley, 1979.

Folkman, S. and Lazarus, R. S. An analysis of coping in a middle-aged community sample. Journal of Health and Social Behavior, 1980, 21, 219-39.

Folkman, S., Schaefer, C., and Lazarus, R. S. Cognitive processes as mediators of stress and coping. In V. Hamilton & D. M. Warburton, eds., Human stress and cognition: An information-processing approach. London: John Wiley, 1979.

French, J. R. P. and Caplan, R. D. Organizational stress and individual strain, In A. J. Marrow, ed., The failure of sucess. New York: AMACOM, 1972.

French, J. R. P. and Kahn, R. L. A programmatic approach to studying the industrial environment and mental health. Journal of Social Issues, 1972, 18, 1-47.

French, J. R. P., Rodgers, W., and Cobb, S. Adjustment as person-environment fit. In J. G. Coelho, D. A. Hamburg, and J. E. Adams, eds., Coping and adaptation. New York: Basic Books, 1974.

Friedman E. A. and Havighurst, R. J. The meaning of work and retirement. Chicago: University of Chicago Press, 1954.

Friedman, M. and Rosenman, R. H. Type A behavior and your heart. New York: Knopf, 1974.

Fromm, E. Escape from freedom. New York: Farrar & Rinehart, 1941.

Gadamer, H. Truth and method. New York: Seabury Press, 1975.

Glass, D. C. Behavior patterns, stress and coronary disease. Hillsdale, N.J.: Lawrence Erlbaum, 1977.

Glock, C. Y. and R. N. Bellah, eds. The new religious consciousness. Berkeley: University of California Press, 1976.

Gouldner, A. The coming crisis of western sociology. New York: Avon Books, 1971.

Greenwood, J. W. Exploring executive stress: A general systems approach. Ph.D. dissertation, Pace University, 1977.

Guralnick, L. Mortality by occupation and cause of death (No. 3), Mortality by industry and cause of death (No. 4), Mortality by occupational level and cause of death (No. 5), Among men 20 to 64 years of age, U. S. 1950. USDHEW PHS. Vital Statistics-Special Reports, Vol. 53, 1963. (As cited by S. L. Kasl, Epidemiological contributions to the study of work stress. In C. L. Cooper and R. Payne, eds., Stress at work. New York: John Wiley, 1978.

Hall, D. T. Careers in organizations. Pacific Palisades: Calif., Goodyear, 1976.

Harrison, R. V. Person-environment fit and job stress. In C. L. Cooper and R. Payne, eds., Stress at work. New York: John Wiley, 1978.

———. Job demands and worker health: Person-environment misfit. Doctoral dissertation, The University of Michigan, 1976.

Heidegger, M. Being and time. Trans. J. Macquarrie and E. Robinson. New York: Harper & Row, 1962.

Hochstim, J. R. Health and ways of living. In I. J. Kessler and M. L. Levin, eds., The community as an epidemiological laboratory. Baltimore: Johns Hopkins University Press, 1970, pp. 149-76.

Holland, J. L. Making vocational choices: A theory of careers. Englewood Cliffs, N. J.: Prentice-Hall, 1973.

Holmes, T. H. and Rahe, R. H. The social readjustment rating scale. Journal of Psychosomatic Research, 1967, 11, 213-18.

House, J. S. The relationship of intrinsic and extrinsic work motivations to occupational stress and coronary heart disease risk. Doctoral dissertation, The University of Michigan, 1972.

House J. S. and Jackman, M. F. Occupationsl stress and health. In P. Ahmed and G. Coehlo, eds., Toward a new definition of health: Psychosocial dimensions. New York: Plenum, 1981.

Jenkins, C. D. Recent evidence supporting psychological and social risk factors for coronary disease, Part 2. The New England Journal of Medicine. 1976, 294, 987-94, 1033-38.

Kahn, R. L., Wolfe, D. M., Quinn, R. F., Snoek, J. D., and Rosenthal, R. A. Organizational stress: Studies in role conflict and ambiguity. New York: John Wiley, 1964.

Kanner, A. Specificity in the impact of daily hassles and uplifts: An analysis of gender, employment status, and Type A behavior. Doctoral dissertation. University of California, Berkeley, 1981.

Kasl, S. L. Epidemiological Contributions to the study of work stress. In C. L. Cooper and R. Payne, eds., Stress at work. New York: John Wiley, 1978, pp. 3-48.

Kerr, W. The decline of pleasure. New York: Simon and Schuster, 1962.

Klinger, E. Consequences of commitment to and disengagement from incentives. Psychological Review, 1975, 82, 1-25.

Kobasa, S. Stressful life events, personality, and health: An inquiry into hardiness. Journal of Personality and Social Psychology, 1979, 37, 1-11.

Kobasa, S., Maddi, S. R., and Courington, S. Personality and constitution as mediators in the stress-illness relationship. Journal of Health and Social Behavior, 1981, 22, 368-378.

Kohn, M. L. Class and conformity. Homewood, Ill.: Dorsey, 1969.

Kohn, M. L. and Schooler, C. The reciprocal effects of the substantive complexity of work and intellectual flexibility: A longitudinal assessment. American Journal of Sociology, 1978, 84, 24-52.

Kramer, M. Reality shock. St. Louis: Mosby, 1974.

Kroll, A. M., Drinklage, L. B., Lee, J., Morley, E. D., and Wilson, E. H. Career development: Growth and crisis. New York: John Wiley, 1970.

Kuhn, T. The structure of scientific revolutions, 2d ed. Chicago: University of Chicago Press, 1970.

Langer, E. J. The illusion of control. Journal of Personality and Social Psychology, 1975, 32, 311-28.

Lasch, C. The culture of narcissism. New York: W. W. Norton, 1978.

Lazarus, R. S. The stress and coping paradigm. In C. Eisdorfer, D. Cohen, A. Kleinman, and P. Maxim, eds., Conceptual models for psychopathology. New York: Spectrum, 1981, pp. 173-209.

_____., Unpublished general plan for research analysis. University of California, Berkeley, July, 1978, p. 1.

_____. Psychological stress and the coping process. New York: McGraw-Hill, 1966.

Lazarus, R. S. and Cohen, J. B. Theory and method in the study of stress and coping. Paper presented at the 5th World Health Organization Conference on Society, Stress and Disease: Aging and Old Age. Stockholm, June 14-19, 1976.

Lazarus, R. S. and Launier, R. Stress-related transactions between person and environment. In L. Pervin and M. Lewis, eds., Perspectives in interactional psychology. New York: Plenum, 1978, pp. 287-327.

Lazarus, R. S. and McCleary, R. A. Autonomic discrimination without awareness: A study of subsception. Psychological Review, 1951, 58, 113-22.

Lefcourt, H. M. The functions of illusions of control and freedom. American Psychologist, 1973, 28, 417-25.

Levinson, D. J. Seasons of a man's life. New York: Knopf, 1978.

Levinson, D. J., Darrow, J. C., Klein, E., Levinson, M., and Mc Kee, B. The psychological development of men in early adulthood and the mid-life transition. In D. F. Hicks, A. Thomas, and M. Roff, eds., Life history research in psychopathology, Vol. 3. Minneapolis: University of Minnesota Press, 1974.

Lewin, K. Behavior and development as a function of the total situation. In L. Carmichael, ed., Manual of child psychology. New York: John Wiley, 1976.

_____. Field theory in social science. New York: Harper & Row, 1951.

Lin, N., Ensel, W. M., Simeone, R. S., and Kuo, W. Social support, stressful life events, and illness: A model and an empirical test. Journal of Health and Social Behavior, 1979, 20, 108-19.

Love, K. G. and Beehr, T. A. Social stressors on the job: Recommendations for a broadened perspective. Group and Organizational Studies, 6, 1981, 190-200.

Macomber, W. B. The anatomy of disillusion, Martin Heidegger's notion of truth. Evanston, Ill.: Northwestern University Press, 1967.

Marmot M. G. and Syme, S. L. Acculturation and coronary heart disease in Japanese Americans. American Journal of Epidemiology, 1976, 104, 225-47.

Mechanic, D. Students under stress. New York: The Free Press, 1962.

Merton, R. K. Social theory and social structure. New York: The Free Press, 1968, pp. 203-07.

Myers, J. K., Lindenthal, J. J., and Pepper, M. P. Life events, social integration, and psychiatric symptomatology. Journal of Health and Social Behavior, 1975, 16, 421-427.

Myers J. K., Lindenthal, J. J., Pepper, M. P., and Ostrander, D. R. Life events and mental status: A longitudinal study. Journal of Health and Social Behavior, 1972, 13, 398-406.

Murray, H. A. Explorations in personality. New York: Oxford University Press, 1938.

Nuckolls, K. B., Cassel, J., and Kaplan, B. H. Psychosocial assets, life crisis and the prognosis of pregnancy. American Journal of Epidemiology, 1972, 95, 431-41.

Oberg, K. Cultural shock: Adjustment to new cultural environments. Practical Anthropology, 1960, 4, 177-82.

Palmore, E. B. Physical, mental and social factors in predicting longevity. Gerontologist, 1969, 9, Part I, 103-08.

Pearlin, L. I., Lieberman, M. A., Menaghan, E.G., and Mullan, J. T. The stress process. Journal of Health and Social Behavior, 1981, 22, 337-56.

Pearlin, L. and Schooler, C. The structure of coping. Journal of Health and Social Behavior. 1978, 19, 2-21.

____. Overview of the internal-external issue. In L. A. Pervin & M. Lewis, eds., Perspectives in interactional psychology. New York: Plenum, 1978.

Pinneau, S. R., Jr. Effects of social support on psychological and physiological strains. Doctoral dissertation, The University of Michigan, 1975.

Polanyi, M. Personal knowledge. London: Routledge and Kegan Paul, 1958.

Reich, C. The greening of America. New York: Random House, 1970.

Rohrlich, J. B. Love and work: The crucial balance. New York: Summit Books, 1980.

Roskies, E. Stress management for Type A individuals. In Meichen-baum, D. and Jaremko, M. E., eds., Stress reduction and prevention. New York: Plenum, 1983, pp. 261-88.

Roskies, E. and Lazarus, R. S. Coping theory and the teaching of coping skills. In P. Davidson and S. Davidson, eds., Behavioral medicine: Changing health life styles. New York: Brunner/Mazel, 1980, pp. 38-69.

Rotter, J. B. Sone problems and misconceptions related to the construct of internal versus external control of reinforcement. Journal of Consulting and Clinical Psychology, 1975, 43, 56-67.

Sarason, S. B. Work, aging and social change: Professionals and the one-life, one-career imperative. New York: The Free Press, 1977.

Schachter, S. The psychology of affiliation. Stanford, Calif.: Stanford University Press, 1959.

Schaefer, C., Coyne, J., and Lazarus, R. S. The health-related functions of social support. Journal of Behavioral Medicine, 1982, 4, 381-406.

Schein, E. H. How to break in the college graduate. Harvard Business Review, 1964, 42, 68-76.

Sheehy, G. Passages: Predictable crises of adult life. New York: Bantam Books, 1976.

Shils, E. Tradition. Chicago: University of Chicago Press. 1981.

Super, D. E. The psychology of careers. New York: Harper & Row, 1957.

Super, D. E. and Bohn, M. J., Occupational psychology. Belmont, Calif.: Wadsworth, 1970.

Task Force Report. Work in America. Report of a Special Task Force to the Secretary of Health, Education and Welfare, Cambridge, Mass.: The MIT Press, 1973.

Tausky, C. and Piedmont, E. B. The meaning of work and unemployment: Implications for mental health, International Journal of Social Psychiatry, 1967-68, 14, pp. 44-49.

Taylor, C. Interpretation and the sciences of man. The Review of Metaphysics, 1971, 25, 3-34, 45-51.

Thomas, L. Notes of a biology watcher, New England Journal of Medicine, 1975, 293, 1245-46.

Tipton, S. M. Getting saved from the sixties. Berkeley: University of California Press, 1982.

Williams, A. W., Ware, J. E., and Donald, C. A. A model of mental health, general life events, and social supports applicable to populations, Journal of Health and Social Behavior, 1981, 22, 324-36.

Weber, M. The Protestant ethic and the spirit of capitalism. New York: Charles Scribner's Sons, 1958.

Wrubel, J., Benner, P., and Lazarus, R. S. Social competence from the perspective of stress and coping. In J. Wine & M. Smye, eds., Social competence. New York: Guilford, 1981, pp. 61-99.

Yankelovich, D. The work ethic is underemployed. Psychology Today, 1982, 16:5, 5-6.

____. New rules in American life: Searching for self-fulfillment in a world turned upside down. New York: Random House, 1981.

Yates, J. E. Managing stress. New York: AMACOM, 1979.

INDEX

ABOUT THE AUTHOR

PATRICIA BENNER is an Associate Professor at the University of California School of Nursing, San Francisco. This work was developed as a part of a larger study on stress and coping directed by Richard S. Lazarus, Professor, Department of Psychology, University of California, Berkeley.

Dr. Benner has published in the fields of stress and coping, occupational socialization, and skill acquisition. She holds a B.A. from Pasadena College, an M.S. from the University of California, San Francisco School of Nursing, and a Ph.D. from the University of California, Berkeley.

A PREFACE TO MORALS

BY

WALTER LIPPMANN

A PREFACE TO POLITICS
DRIFT AND MASTERY
THE STAKES OF DIPLOMACY
LIBERTY AND THE NEWS
PUBLIC OPINION
THE PHANTOM PUBLIC
MEN OF DESTINY
AMERICAN INQUISITORS

WALTER LIPPMANN

A
PREFACE
TO
MORALS

THE MACMILLAN COMPANY
NEW YORK   MCMXXXI

Printed in the United States of America by
THE STRATFORD PRESS, INC., NEW YORK

CONTENTS

PART I

THE DISSOLUTION OF THE ANCESTRAL ORDER

[v]

CONTENTS

CONTENTS

PART III

THE GENIUS OF MODERNITY

CONTENTS

PART I

THE DISSOLUTION OF THE ANCESTRAL ORDER

"Whirl is King, having driven out Zeus."

ARISTOPHANES.

A PREFACE TO MORALS

CHAPTER I

THE PROBLEM OF UNBELIEF

1. *Whirl is King*

AMONG those who no longer believe in the religion of their fathers, some are proudly defiant, and many are indifferent. But there are also a few, perhaps an increasing number, who feel that there is a vacancy in their lives. This inquiry deals with their problem. It is not intended to disturb the serenity of those who are unshaken in the faith they hold, and it is not concerned with those who are still exhilarated by their escape from some stale orthodoxy. It is concerned with those who are perplexed by the consequences of their own irreligion. It deals with the problem of unbelief, not as believers are accustomed to deal with it, in the spirit of men confidently calling the lost sheep back into the fold, but as unbelievers themselves must, I think, face the problem if they face it candidly and without presumption.

When such men put their feelings into words they are likely to say that, having lost their faith, they have lost the certainty that their lives are significant, and that it matters what they do with their lives. If they deal with young people they are likely to say that they know of no compelling reason which certifies the moral code they adhere to, and that, therefore, their own preferences, when tested by the ruthless curiosity of their children, seem to have no sure foundation of any kind. They are likely to point to the world about them, and to ask whether the modern man possesses any criterion by which he can measure the value of his own desires, whether there is any standard he really believes in which permits him to put a term upon that pursuit of money, of power, and of excitement which has created so much of the turmoil and the squalor and the explosiveness of modern civilization.

These are, perhaps, merely the rationalizations of the modern man's discontent. At the heart of it there are likely to be moments of blank misgiving in which he finds that the civilization of which he is a part leaves a dusty taste in his mouth. He may be very busy with many things, but he discovers one day that he is no longer sure they are worth doing. He has been much preoccupied; but he is no longer sure he knows why. He has become involved in an elaborate routine of pleasures; and they do not seem to amuse him very much. He finds it hard to believe that doing any one thing is better than doing any other thing, or, in fact, that it is better than doing nothing at all. It occurs to him that it is a great deal of trouble to live, and that even in the best of lives the thrills are few and far between. He begins more or less consciously to seek satisfactions, because he is no longer satisfied, and all the while he realizes that the pursuit of happiness was always a most unhappy quest. In the later stages of his woe he not only loses his appetite, but becomes excessively miserable trying to recover it. And then, surveying the flux of events and the giddiness of his own soul, he comes to feel that Aristophanes must have been thinking of him when he declared that "Whirl is King, having driven out Zeus."

2. *False Prophecies*

The modern age has been rich both in prophecies that men would at last inherit the kingdoms of this world, and in complaints at the kind of world they inherited. Thus Petrarch, who was an early victim of modernity, came to feel that he would "have preferred to be born in any other period" than his own; he tells us that he sought an escape by imagining that he lived in some other age. The Nineteenth Century, which begat us, was forever blowing the trumpets of freedom and providing asylums in which its most sensitive children could take refuge. Wordsworth fled from mankind to rejoice in nature. Chateaubriand fled from man to rejoice in savages. Byron fled to an imaginary Greece, and William Morris to the Middle Ages. A few tried an imaginary India. A few an equally imaginary China. Many fled to Bohemia, to Utopia, to the Golden West, and to the Latin Quarter, and some, like James Thomson, to hell where they were

> gratified to gain
> That positive eternity of pain
> Instead of this insufferable inane.

They had all been disappointed by the failure of a great prophecy. The theme of this prophecy had been that man is a beautiful soul who in the course of history had somehow become enslaved by

> Scepters, tiaras, swords, and chains, and tomes
> Of reasoned wrong, glozed on by ignorance,

and they believed with Shelley that when "the loathsome mask has fallen," man, exempt from awe, worship, degree, the king over himself, would then be "free from guilt or pain." This was the orthodox liberalism to which men turned when they had lost the religion of their fathers. But the promises of liberalism have not been fulfilled. We are living in the midst of that vast dissolution of ancient habits which the emancipators believed would restore our birthright of happiness. We know now that they did not see very clearly beyond the evils against which they were rebelling. It is evident to us that their prophecies were pleasant fantasies which concealed the greater difficulties that confront men, when having won the freedom to do what they wish—that wish, as Byron said:

> which ages have not yet subdued
> In man—to have no master save his mood,

they are full of contrary moods and do not know what they wish to do. We have come to see that Huxley was right when he said that "a man's worst difficulties begin when he is able to do as he likes."

The evidences of these greater difficulties lie all about us: in the brave and brilliant atheists who have defied the Methodist God, and have become very nervous; in the women who have emancipated themselves from the tyranny of fathers, husbands, and homes, and with the intermittent but expensive help of a psychoanalyst, are now enduring liberty as interior decorators; in the young men and women who are world-weary at twenty-two; in the multitudes who drug themselves with pleasure; in the crowds enfranchised by the blood of heroes who cannot be persuaded to take an interest in their destiny; in the millions, at last free to think without fear of priest or policeman, who have made the moving pictures and the popular newspapers what they are.

These are the prisoners who have been released. They ought to be very happy. They ought to be serene and composed. They are free to make their own lives. There are no conventions, no tabus, no gods, priests, princes, fathers, or revelations which they must accept. Yet the result is not so good as they thought it would be. The prison door is wide open. They stagger out into trackless space under a blinding sun. They find it nerve-racking. "My sensibility," said Flaubert, "is sharper than a razor's edge; the creaking of a door, the face of a bourgeois, an absurd statement set my heart to throbbing and completely upset me." They must find their own courage for battle and their own consolation in defeat. They complain, like Renan after he had broken with the Church, that the enchanted circle which embraced the whole of life is broken, and that they are left with a feeling of emptiness "like that which follows an attack of fever or an unhappy love affair." Where is my *home?* cried Nietzsche: "For it do I ask and seek, and have sought, but have not found it. O eternal everywhere, O eternal nowhere, O eternal in vain."

To more placid temperaments the pangs of freedom are no doubt less acute. It is possible for multitudes in time of peace and security to exist agreeably—somewhat incoherently, perhaps, but without convulsions—to dream a little and not unpleasantly, to have only now and then a nightmare, and only occasionally a rude awakening. It is possible to drift along not too discontentedly, somewhat nervously, somewhat anxiously, somewhat confusedly, hoping for the best, and believing in nothing very much. It is possible to be a passable citizen. But it is not possible to be wholly at peace. For serenity of soul requires some better organization of life than a man can attain by pursuing his casual ambitions, satisfying his hungers, and for the rest accepting destiny as an idiot's tale in which one dumb sensation succeeds another to no known end. And it is not possible for him to be wholly alive. For that depends upon his sense of being completely engaged with the world, with all his passions and all the faculties in rich harmonies with one other, and in deep rhythm with the nature of things.

These are the gifts of a vital religion which can bring the whole of a man into adjustment with the whole of his relevant experience. Our forefathers had such a religion. They quarreled a good deal about the details, but they had no doubt that there was an order in the universe which justified their lives because they were a part of it. The acids of modernity have dissolved that order for many of us, and there are some in consequence who think that the needs which religion fulfilled have also been dissolved. But however self-sufficient the eugenic and perfectly educated man of the distant future may be, our present experience is that the needs remain. In failing to meet them, it is plain that we have succeeded only in substituting trivial illusions for majestic faiths. For while the modern emancipated man may wonder how any one ever believed that in this universe of stars and atoms and multitudinous life, there is a drama in progress of which the principal event was enacted in Palestine nineteen hundred years ago, it is not really a stranger fable than many which he so readily accepts. He does not believe the words of the Gospel but he believes the best-advertised notion. The older fable may be incredible to-day, but when it was credible it bound together the whole of experience upon a stately and dignified theme. The modern man has ceased to believe in it but he has not ceased to be credulous, and the need to believe haunts him. It is no wonder that his impulse is to turn back from his freedom, and to find some one who says he knows the truth and can tell him what to do, to find the shrine of some new god, of any cult however newfangled, where he can kneel and be comforted, put on manacles to keep his hands from trembling, ensconce himself in some citadel where it is safe and warm.

For the modern man who has ceased to believe, without ceasing to be credulous, hangs, as it were, between heaven and earth, and is at rest nowhere. There is no theory of the meaning and value of events which he is compelled to accept, but he is none the less compelled to accept the events. There is no moral authority to which he must turn now, but there is coercion in opinions, fashions and fads. There is for him no inevitable purpose in the universe, but there are elaborate necessities, physical, political, economic. He does not feel himself to be an actor in a great and dramatic destiny, but he is subject to the massive powers of our civilization, forced to adopt their pace, bound to their routine, entangled in their conflicts. He can believe what he chooses about this civilization. He cannot, however, escape the compulsion of modern events. They compel his body and his senses as ruthlessly as ever did king or priest. They do not compel his mind. They have all the force of natural events, but not their majesty, all the tyrannical power of ancient institutions, but none of their moral certainty. Events are there, and they overpower him. But they do not convince him that they have that dignity which inheres in that which is necessary and in the nature of things.

In the old order the compulsions were often painful, but there was sense in the pain that was inflicted by the will of an all-knowing God. In the new order the compulsions are painful and, as it were, accidental, unnecessary, wanton, and full of mockery. The modern man does not make his peace with them. For in effect he has replaced natural piety with a grudging endurance of a series of unsanctified compulsions. When he believed that the unfolding of events was a manifestation of the will of God, he could say: Thy will be done. . . . In His will is our peace. But when he believes that events are determined by the votes of a majority, the orders of his bosses, the opinions of his neighbors, the laws of supply and demand, and the decisions of quite selfish men, he yields because he has to yield. He is conquered but unconvinced.

3. *Sorties and Retreats*

It might seem as if, in all this, men were merely going through once again what they have often gone through before. This is not the first age in which the orthodox religion has been in conflict with the science of the day. Plato was born into such an age. For two centuries the philosophers of Greece had been critical of Homer and of the popular gods, and when Socrates faced his accusers, his answer to the accusation of heresy must certainly have sounded unresponsive. "I do believe," he said, "that there are gods, and in a higher sense than that in which my accusers believe in them." That is all very well. But to believe in a "higher sense" is also to believe in a different sense.

There is nothing new in the fact that men have ceased to believe in the religion of their fathers. In the history of Catholic Christianity, there has always existed a tradition, extending from the author of the Fourth Gospel through Origen to the neo-Platonists of modern times, which rejects the popular idea of God as a power acting upon events, and of immortality as everlasting life, and translates the popular theology into a symbolic statement of a purely spiritual experience. In every civilized age there have been educated and discerning men who could not accept literally and simply the traditions of the ancient faith. We are told that during the Periclean Age "among educated men everything was in dispute: political sanctions, literary values, moral standards, religious convictions, even the possibility of reaching any truth about anything." When the educated classes of the Roman world accepted Christianity they had ceased to believe in the pagan gods, and were much too critical to accept the primitive Hebraic theories of the creation, the redemption, and the Messianic Kingdom which were so central in the popular religion. They had to do what Socrates had done; they had to take the popular theology in a "higher" and therefore in a different sense before they could use it. Indeed, it is so unusual to find an age of active-minded men in which the most highly educated are genuinely orthodox in the popular sense, that the Thirteenth Century, the age of Dante and St. Thomas Aquinas, when this phenomenon is reputed to have occurred, is regarded as a unique and wonderful period in the history of the world. It is not at all unlikely that there never was such an age in the history of civilized men.

And yet, the position of modern men who have broken with the religion of their fathers is in certain profound ways different from that of other men in other ages. This is the first age, I think, in the history of mankind when the circumstances of life have conspired with the intellectual habits of the time to render any fixed and authoritative belief incredible to large masses of men. The dissolution of the old modes of thought has gone so far, and is so cumulative in its effect, that the modern man is not able to sink back after a period of prophesying into a new but stable orthodoxy. The irreligion of the modern world is radical to a degree for which there is, I think, no counterpart. For always in the past it has been possible for new conventions to crystallize, and for men to find rest and surcease of effort in accepting them.

We often assume, therefore, that a period of dissolution will necessarily be followed by one of conformity, that the heterodoxy of one age will become the orthodoxy of the next, and that when this orthodoxy decays a new period of prophesying will begin. Thus we say that by the time of Hosea and Isaiah the religion of the Jews had become a system of rules for transacting business with Jehovah. The Prophets then revivified it by thundering against the conventional belief that religion was mere burnt offering and sacrifice. A few centuries passed and the religion based on the Law and the Prophets had in its turn become a set of mechanical rites manipulated by the Scribes and the Pharisees. As against this system Jesus and Paul preached a religion of grace, and against the "letter" of the synagogues the "spirit" of Christ. But the inner light which can perceive the spirit is rare, and so shortly after the death of Paul, the teaching gradually ceased to appeal to direct inspiration in the minds of the believers and became a body of dogma, a "sacred deposit" of the faith "once for all delivered to the saints." In the succeeding ages there appeared again many prophets who thought they had within them the revealing spirit. Though some of the prophets were burnt, much of the prophesying was absorbed into the canon. In Luther this sense of revelation appeared once more in a most confident form. He rejected the authority not only of the Pope and the clergy, but even of the Bible itself, except where in his opinion the Bible confirmed his faith. But in the establishment of a Lutheran Church the old difficulty reappeared: the inner light which had burned so fiercely in Luther did not burn brightly or steadily in all Lutherans, and so the right of private judgment, even in Luther's restricted use of the term, led to all kinds of heresies and abominations. Very soon there came to be an authoritative teaching backed by the power of the police. And in Calvinism the revolt of the Reformation became stabilized to the last degree. "Everything," said Calvin, "pertaining to the perfect rule of a good life the Lord has so comprehended in His law that there remains nothing for man to add to that summary."

Men fully as intelligent as the most emancipated among us once believed that, and I have no doubt that the successors of Mr. Darrow and Mr. Mencken would come to believe something very much like it if conditions permitted them to obey the instinct to retreat from the chaos of modernity into order and certainty. It is all very well to talk about being the captain of your soul. It is hard, and only a few heroes, saints, and geniuses have been the captains of their souls for any extended period of their lives. Most men, after a little freedom, have preferred authority with the consoling assurances and the economy of effort which it brings. "If, outside of Christ, you wish by your own thoughts to know your relation to God, you will break your neck. Thunder strikes him who examines." Thus spoke Martin Luther, and there is every reason to suppose that the German people thought he was talking the plainest common sense. "He who is gifted with the heavenly knowledge of faith," said the Council of Trent, "is free from an inquisitive curiosity." These words are rasping to our modern ears, but there is no occasion to doubt that the men who uttered them had made a shrewd appraisal of average human nature. The record of experience is one of sorties and retreats. The search for moral guidance which shall not depend upon external authority has invariably ended in the acknowledgment of some new authority.

4. *Deep Dissolution*

This same tendency manifests itself in the midst of our modern uneasiness. We have had a profusion of new cults, of revivals, and of essays in reconstruction. But there is reason for thinking that a new crystallization of an enduring and popular religion is unlikely in the modern world. For analogy drawn from the experience of the past is misleading.

When Luther, for example, rebelled against the authority of the Church, he did not suppose the way of life for the ordinary man would be radically altered. Luther supposed that men would continue to behave much as they had learned to behave under the Catholic discipline. The individual for whom he claimed the right of private judgment was one whose prejudgments had been well fixed in a Catholic society. The authority of the Pope was to be destroyed and certain evils abolished, but there was to remain that feeling for objective moral certainties which Catholicism had nurtured. When the Anabaptists carried the practice of his theory beyond this point, Luther denounced them violently. For what he believed in was Protestantism for good Catholics. The reformers of the Eighteenth Century made a similar assumption. They really believed in democracy for men who had an aristocratic training. Jefferson, for example, had an instinctive fear of the urban rabble, that most democratic part of the population. The society of free men which he dreamed about was composed of those who had the discipline, the standards of honor and the taste, without the privileges or the corruptions, that are to be found in a society of well-bred country gentlemen.

The more recent rebels frequently betray a somewhat similar inability to imagine the consequences of their own victories. For the smashing of idols is in itself such a preoccupation that it is almost impossible for the iconoclast to look clearly into a future when there will not be many idols left to smash. Yet that future is beginning to be our present, and it might be said that men are conscious of what modernity means insofar as they realize that they are confronted not so much with the necessity of promoting rebellion as of dealing with the consequences of it. The Nineteenth Century, roughly speaking the time between Voltaire and Mencken, was an age of terrific indictments and of feeble solutions. The Marxian indictment of capitalism is a case in point. The Nietzschean transvaluation of values is another; it is magnificent, but who can say, after he has shot his arrow of longing to the other shore, whether he will find Cæsar Borgia, Henry Ford, or Isadora Duncan? Who knows, having read Mr. Mencken and Mr. Sinclair Lewis, what kind of world will be left when all the boobs and yokels have crawled back in their holes and have died of shame?

The rebel, while he is making his attack, is not likely to feel the need to answer such questions. For he moves in an unreal environment, one might almost say a parasitic environment. He goes forth to destroy Cæsar, Mammon, George F. Babbitt, and Mrs. Grundy. As he wrestles with these demons, he leans upon them. By inversion they offer him much the same kind of support which the conformer enjoys. They provide him with an objective which enables him to know exactly what he thinks he wants to do. His energies are focussed by his indignation. He does not suffer from emptiness, doubt, and division of soul. These are the maladies which come later when the struggle is over. While the rebel is in conflict with the established nuisances he has an aim in life which absorbs all his passions. He has his own sense of righteousness and his own feeling of communion with a grand purpose. For in attacking idols there is a kind of piety, in overthrowing tyrants a kind of loyalty, in ridiculing stupidities

an imitation of wisdom.   In the heat of battle the rebel
is exalted by a whole-hearted tension which is easily mistaken for a taste of the freedom that is to come.   He is
under the spell of an illusion.   For what comes after the
struggle is not the exaltation of freedom but a letting
down of the tension that belongs solely to the struggle
itself.   The happiness of the rebel is as transient as the
iconoclasm which produced it.   When he has slain the
dragon and rescued the beautiful maiden, there is usually
nothing left for him to do but write his memoirs and
dream of a time when the world was young.

What most distinguishes the generation who have
approached maturity since the debacle of idealism at the
end of the War is not their rebellion against the religion
and the moral code of their parents, but their disillusionment with their own rebellion.   It is common for young
men and women to rebel, but that they should rebel sadly
and without faith in their own rebellion, that they should
distrust the new freedom no less than the old certainties—
that is something of a novelty.   As Mr. Canby once said,
at the age of seven they saw through their parents and
characterized them in a phrase.   At fourteen they saw
through education and dodged it.   At eighteen they saw
through morality and stepped over it.   At twenty they
lost respect for their home towns, and at twenty-one they
discovered that our social system is ridiculous.   At twenty-
three the autobiography ends because the author has run
through society to date and does not know what to do
next.   For, as Mr. Canby might have added, the idea of
reforming that society makes no appeal to them.   They
have seen through all that.   They cannot adopt any of

the synthetic religions of the Nineteenth Century. They
have seen through all of them.

They have seen through the religion of nature to which
the early romantics turned for consolation. They have
heard too much about the brutality of natural selection
to feel, as Wordsworth did, that pleasant landscapes are
divine. They have seen through the religion of beauty
because, for one thing, they are too much oppressed by
the ugliness of Main Street. They cannot take refuge in
an ivory tower because the modern apartment house, with
a radio loudspeaker on the floor above and on the floor
below and just across the courtyard, will not permit it.
They cannot, like Mazzini, make a religion of patriotism,
because they have just been demobilized. They cannot
make a religion of science like the post-Darwinians
because they do not understand modern science. They
never learned enough mathematics and physics. They do
not like Bernard Shaw's religion of creative evolution
because they have read enough to know that Mr. Shaw's
biology is literary and evangelical. As for the religion
of progress, that is preempted by George F. Babbitt and
the Rotary Club, and the religion of humanity is utterly
unacceptable to those who have to ride in the subways
during the rush hour.

Yet the current attempts to modernize religious creeds
are inspired by the hope that somehow it will be possible
to construct a form of belief which will fit into this
vacuum. It is evident that life soon becomes distracted
and tiresome if it is not illuminated by communion with
what William James called "a wider self through which
saving experiences come." The eager search for new reli-

gions, the hasty adherence to cults, and the urgent appeals
for a reconciliation between religion and science are con-
fessions that to the modern man his activity seems to
have no place in any rational order. His life seems mere
restlessness and compulsion, rather than conduct lighted
by luminous beliefs. He is possessed by a great deal of
excitement amidst which, as Mr. Santayana once remarked,
he redoubles his effort when he has forgotten his aim.

For in the modern age, at first imperceptibly with the
rise of the towns, and then catastrophically since the
mechanical revolution, there have gone into dissolution
not only the current orthodoxy, but the social order and
the ways of living which supported it. Thus rebellion
and emancipation have come to mean something far more
drastic than they have ever meant before. The earlier
rebels summoned men from one allegiance to another,
but the feeling for certainty in religion and for decorum
in society persisted. In the modern world it is this very
feeling of certainty itself which is dissolving. It is dissolving not merely for an educated minority but for every
one who comes within the orbit of modernity.

Yet there remain the wants which orthodoxy of some
sort satisfies. The natural man, when he is released from
restraints, and has no substitute for them, is at sixes and
sevens with himself and the world. For in the free play
of his uninhibited instincts he does not find any natural
substitute for those accumulated convictions which, however badly they did it, nevertheless organized his soul,
economized his effort, consoled him, and gave him dignity
in his own eyes because he was part of some greater whole.
The acids of modernity are so powerful that they do not

tolerate a crystallization of ideas which will serve as a new orthodoxy into which men can retreat. And so the modern world is haunted by a realization, which it becomes constantly less easy to ignore, that it is impossible to reconstruct an enduring orthodoxy, and impossible to live well without the satisfactions which an orthodoxy would provide.

CHAPTER II

GOD IN THE MODERN WORLD

1. *Imago Dei*

By the dissolution of their ancestral ways men have been deprived of their sense of certainty as to why they were born, why they must work, whom they must love, what they must honor, where they may turn in sorrow and defeat. They have left to them the ancient codes and the modern criticism of these codes, guesses, intuitions, inconclusive experiments, possibilities, probabilities, hypotheses. Below the level of reason, they may have unconscious prejudice, they may speak with a loud cocksureness, they may act with fanaticism. But there is gone that ineffable certainty which once made God and His Plan seem as real as the lamp-post.

I do not mean that modern men have ceased to believe in God. I do mean that they no longer believe in him simply and literally. I mean that they have defined and refined their ideas of him until they can no longer honestly say that he exists, as they would say that their neighbor exists. Search the writings of liberal churchmen, and when you come to the crucial passages which are intended to express their belief in God, you will find, I think, that at just this point their uncertainty is most evident.

The Reverend Harry Emerson Fosdick has written an essay, called "How Shall We Think of God?", which illustrates the difficulty. He begins by saying that "believing in God without considering how one shall picture him is deplorably unsatisfactory." Yet the old ways of picturing him are no longer credible. We cannot think of him as seated upon a throne, while around him are angels playing on harps and singing hymns. "God as a king on high—our fathers, living under monarchy, rejoiced in that image and found it meaningful. His throne, his crown, his scepter, his seraphic retinue, his laws, rewards, and punishments—how dominant that picture was and how persistent is the continuance of it in our hymns and prayers! It was always partly poetry, but it had a prose background: there really had been at first a celestial land above the clouds where God reigned and where his throne was in the heavens."

Having said that this picture is antiquated, Dr. Fosdick goes on to state that "the religious man must have imaginations of God, if God is to be real to him." He must "picture his dealing with the Divine in terms of personal relationship." But how? "The place where man vitally finds God . . . is within his own experience of goodness, truth, and beauty, and the truest images of God are therefore to be found in man's spiritual life." I should be the last to deny that a man may, if he chooses, think of God as the source of all that seems to him worthy in human experience. But certainly this is not the God of the ancient faith. This is not God the Father, the Lawgiver, the Judge. This is a highly sophisticated idea of God, employed by a modern man who would like to say, but cannot say with certainty, that there exists a personal God to whom men must accommodate themselves.

2. *An Indefinite God*

It may be that clear and unambiguous statements are
not now possible in our intellectual climate. But at least
we should not forget that the religions which have dominated human history have been founded on what the
faithful felt were undeniable facts. These facts were
mysterious only in the sense that they were uncommon,
like an eclipse of the sun, but not in the sense that they
were beyond human experience. No doubt there are passages in the Scriptures written by highly cultivated men
in which the Divine nature is called mysterious and
unknowable. But these passages are not the rock upon
which the popular churches are founded. No one, I
think, has truly observed the religious life of simple
people without understanding how plain, how literal,
how natural they take their supernatural personages to be.

The popular gods are not indefinite and unknowable.
They have a definite history and their favorite haunts,
and they have often been seen. They walk on earth, they
might appear to anyone, they are angered, they are
pleased, they weep and they rejoice, they eat and they
may fall in love. The modern man uses the word 'supernatural' to describe something that seems to him not quite
so credible as the things he calls natural. This is not
the supernaturalism of the devout. They do not distinguish two planes of reality and two orders of certainty.
For them Jesus Christ was born of a Virgin and was
raised from the dead as literally as Napoleon was Emperor
of the French and returned from Elba.

This is the kind of certainty one no longer finds in the

utterances of modern men. I might cite, for example, a typically modern assertion about the existence of God, made by Mr. W. C. Brownell, a critic who could not be reproached with insensitiveness to the value of traditional beliefs. He wrote that "the influence of the Holy Spirit, exquisitely called the Comforter, is a matter of actual experience, as solid a reality as that of electro-magnetism." I do not suppose that Mr. Brownell meant to admit the least possible doubt. But he was a modern man, and surreptitiously doubt invaded his certainty. For electro-magnetism is not an absolutely solid reality to a layman's mind. It has a questionable reality. I suspect that is why Mr. Brownell chose this metaphor; it would have seemed a little too blunt to his modern intelligence to say that his faith was founded not on electro-magnetism, but as men once believed, on a rock.

The attempts to reconstruct religious creeds are beset by the modern man's inability to convince himself that the constitution of the universe includes facts which in our skeptical jargon we call supernatural. Yet as William James once said, "religion, in her fullest exercise of function, is not a mere illumination of facts already elsewhere given, not a mere passion, like love, which views things in a rosier light. . . . It is something more, namely, a postulator of new *facts* as well." James himself was strongly disposed toward what he so candidly described as "overbeliefs"; he had sympathy with the beliefs of others which was as large and charitable as any man's can be. There was no trace of the intellectual snob in William James; he was in the other camp from those thin argumentative rationalists who find so much satisfaction in disproving what other men hold sacred. James loved cranks and naifs and sought them out for the wisdom they might have. But withal he was a modern man who lived toward the climax of the revolutionary period. He had the Will to Believe, he argued eloquently for the Right to Believe. But he did not wholly believe. The utmost that he could honestly believe was something which he confessed would "appear a sorry underbelief" to some of his readers. "Who knows," he said, "whether the faithfulness of individuals here below to their own poor overbeliefs may not actually help God in turn to be more effectively faithful to his own greater tasks?" Who knows? And on that question mark he paused and could say no more.

3. *God in More Senses Than One*

But even if there was some uncertainty as to the existence of the God whom William James described, he was at least the kind of God with whom human beings could commune. If they could jump the initial doubt they found themselves in an exciting world where they might live for a God who, like themselves, had work to do. James wrote the passage I have quoted in 1902. A quarter of a century later Alfred North Whitehead came to Harvard to deliver the Lowell Lectures. He undertook to define God for modern men.

Mr. Whitehead, like William James, is a compassionate man and on the side of the angels. But his is a wholly modernized mind in full command of all the conceptual instruments of scientific logic. By contrast with the austerity of Mr. Whitehead's thinking, James, with his chivalrous offer of fealty to God, seems like one of the last of the great romantics. There is a God in Mr. Whitehead's philosophy, and a very necessary God at that. Unhappily, I am not enough of a logician to say that I am quite sure I understand what it means to say that "God is not concrete, but He is the ground for concrete actuality." There have been moments when I imagined I had caught the meaning of this, but there have been more moments when I knew that I had not. I have never doubted, however, that the concept had meaning, and that I missed it because it was too deep for me. Why then, it may be asked, do I presume to discuss it? My answer is that a conception of God, which is incomprehensible to all who are not highly trained logicians, is a possible God for logicians alone. It is not presumptuous to say of Mr. Whitehead's God what he himself says of Aristotle's God: that it does "not lead him very far toward the production of a God available for religious purposes."

For while this God may satisfy a metaphysical need in the thinker, he does not satisfy the passions of the believer. This God does not govern the world like a king nor watch over his children like a father. He offers them no purposes to which they can consecrate themselves; he exhibits no image of holiness they can imitate. He does not chastise them in sin nor console them in sorrow. He is a principle with which to explain the facts, if you can understand the explanation. He is not himself a personality who deals with the facts. For the purposes of religion he is no God at all; his universe remains stonily unaware of man. Nothing has happened by accepting

Mr. Whitehead's definition which changes the inexorable character of that destiny which Bertrand Russell depicted when he wrote that

> we see, surrounding the narrow raft illumined by the flickering light of human comradeship, the dark ocean on whose rolling waves we toss for a brief hour; from the great night without, a chill blast breaks in upon our refuge; all the loneliness of humanity amid hostile forces is concentrated upon the individual soul, which must struggle alone, with what of courage it can command, against the whole weight of a universe that cares nothing for its hopes and fears.

It is a nice question whether the use of God's name is not misleading when it is applied by modernists to ideas so remote from the God men have worshiped. Plainly the modernist churchman does not believe in the God of Genesis who walked in the garden in the cool of the evening and called to Adam and his wife who had hidden themselves behind a tree; nor in the God of Exodus who appeared to Moses and Aaron and seventy of the Elders of Israel, standing with his feet upon a paved walk as if it were a sapphire stone; nor even in the God of the fifty-third chapter of Isaiah who in his compassion for the sheep who have gone astray, having turned everyone to his own way, laid on the Man of Sorrows the iniquity of us all.

This, as Kirsopp Lake says, is the God of most, if not all, the writings in the Bible. Yet "however much our inherited sentiments may shrink from the admission, the scientists are to-day almost unanimous in saying that the universe as they see it contains no evidence of the existence of any anthropomorphic God whatever. The experimentalist (*i.e.*, modernist) wholly agrees that this is so. Nevertheless he refuses as a rule, and I think rightly—to abandon the use of the word 'God.' " In justification of this refusal to abandon the word 'God,' although he has abandoned the accepted meaning of the word, Dr. Lake appeals to a tradition which reaches back at least to Origen who, as a Christian neo-platonist, used the word 'God' to mean, not the King and Father of creation, but the sum of all ideal values. It was this redefinition of the word 'God,' he says, which "made Christianity possible for the educated man of the third century." It is this same redefinition which still makes Christianity possible for educated churchmen like Dr. Lake and Dean Inge.

Dr. Lake admits that although this attractive bypath of tradition "is intellectually adorned by many princes of thought and lords of language" it is "ecclesiastically not free from reproach." He avows another reason for his use of the word 'God' which, if not more compelling, is certainly more worldly. "Atheist" has meant since Roman times an enemy of society; it gives a wholly false impression of the real state of mind of those who adhere to the platonic tradition. They have been wholly without the defiance which "atheism" connotes; on the contrary they have been a few individuals in each age who lived peaceably within the shelter of the church, worshiping a somewhat different God inwardly and in their own way, and often helping to refresh the more mundane spirit of the popular church. The term "agnostic" is almost as unavailable. It was invented to describe a tolerant unbelief in the anthropomorphic God. In popular usage it has come to mean about the same thing as atheist, for the instinct of the common man is sound in these matters. He feels that those who claim to be open-minded about God have for all practical purposes ceased to believe in him. The agnostic's reply that he would gladly believe if the evidence would confirm it, does not alter the fact that he does not now believe. And so Dr. Lake concludes that the modernist must use the word 'God' in his own sense, "endeavoring partly to preserve Origen's meaning of the word, and partly shrinking from any other policy as open to misconstruction."

I confess that the notion of adopting a policy about God somehow shocks me as intruding a rather worldly consideration which would seem to be wholly out of place. But this feeling is, I am sure, an injustice to Dr. Lake who is plainly and certainly not a worldling. He is moved, no doubt, by the conviction that in letting 'God' mean one thing to the mass of the devout and another to the educated minority, the loss of intellectual precision is more than compensated by the preservation of a community of feeling. This is not mere expediency. It may be the part of wisdom, which is profounder than mere reasoning, to wish that intellectual distinctions shall not divide men too sharply.

But if it is wisdom, it is an aristocratic wisdom. And in Dean Inge's writings this is frankly avowed. "The strength of Christianity," he says, "is in transforming the lives of individuals—of a small minority, certainly, as Christ clearly predicted, but a large number in the aggregate. To rescue a little flock, here and there, from materialism, selfishness, and hatred, is the task of the

Church of Christ in all ages alike, and there is no likelihood that it will ever be otherwise."

But in other ages, one thing was otherwise. And in this one thing lies the radical peculiarity of the modern difficulty. In other ages there was no acknowledged distinction between the ultimate beliefs of the educated and the uneducated. There were differences in learning, in religious genius, in the closeness of a chosen few to God and his angels. Inwardly there were even radical differences of meaning. But critical analysis had not made them overt and evident, and the common assumption was that there was one God for all, for the peasant who saw him dimly and could approach him only through his patron saint, and for the holy man who had seen God and talked with him face to face. It has remained for churchmen of our era to distinguish two or more different Gods, and openly to say that they are different. This may be a triumph of candor and of intelligence. But this very consciousness of what they are doing, these very honest admissions that the God of Dean Inge, for example, is only in name the God of millions of other protestants—that is an admission, when they understand it, which makes faith difficult for modern men.

4. *The Protest of the Fundamentalists*

Fundamentalism is a protest against all these definitions and attenuations which the modern man finds it necessary to make. It is avowedly a reaction within the Protestant communions against what the President of the World's Christian Fundamentalist Association rather accurately described as "that weasel method of sucking the meaning out of words, and then presenting the empty shells in an attempt to palm them off as giving the Christian faith a new and another interpretation." In actual practice this movement has become entangled with all sorts of bizarre and barbarous agitations, with the Ku Klux Klan, with fanatical prohibition, with the "anti-evolution laws," and with much persecution and intolerance. This in itself is significant. For it shows that the central truth, which the fundamentalists have grasped, no longer appeals to the best brains and the good sense of a modern community, and that the movement is recruited largely from the isolated, the inexperienced, and the uneducated.

Into the politics of the heated controversy between modernists and fundamentalists I do not propose here to enter. That it is not merely a dispute in the realm of the spirit is made evident by the President of the Fundamentalist Association when he avers that "nothing" holds modernists and fundamentalists together except "the billions of dollars invested. Nine out of ten of these dollars, if not ninety-nine out of every hundred of them, spent to construct the great denominational universities, colleges, schools of second grade, theological seminaries, great denominational mission stations, the multiplied hospitals that bear denominational names, the immense publication societies and the expensive societies were given by fundamentalists and filched by modernists. It took hundreds of years to collect this money and construct these institutions. It has taken only a quarter of a century for the liberal bandits to capture them. . . ."

Not all the fundamentalist argument, however, is pitched at this level. There is also a reasoned case against the modernists. Fortunately this case has been stated in a little book called *Christianity and Liberalism* by a man who is both a scholar and a gentleman. The author is Professor J. Gresham Machen of the Princeton Theological Seminary. It is an admirable book. For its acumen, for its saliency, and for its wit this cool and stringent defense of orthodox Protestantism is, I think, the best popular argument produced by either side in the current controversy. We shall do well to listen to Dr. Machen.

Modernism, he says, "is altogether in the imperative mood," while the traditional religion "begins with a triumphant indicative." I do not see how one can deny the force of this generalization. "From the beginning Christianity was certainly a way of life. *But how was the life to be produced?* Not by appealing to the human will, but by telling a story; not by exhortation, but by the narration of an event." Dr. Machen insists, rightly I think, that the historic influence of Christianity on the mass of men has depended upon their belief that an historic drama was enacted in Palestine nineteen hundred years ago during the reign of the Emperor Tiberius. The veracity of that story was fundamental to the Christian Church. For while all the ideal values may remain if you impugn the historic record set forth in the Gospels, these ideal values are not certified to the common man as inherent in the very nature of things. Once they are deprived of their root in historic fact, their poetry, their symbolism, their ethical significance depend for their sanction upon the temperament and experience of the individual believer. There is gone that deep, compulsive, organic faith in an external fact which is the essence of religion for all but that very small minority who can live within themselves in mystical communion or by the power of their understanding. For the great mass of men, if the history of religions is to be trusted, religious experience depends upon a complete belief in the concrete existence, one might almost say the materialization, of their God. The fundamentalist goes to the very heart of the matter, therefore, when he insists that you have destroyed the popular foundations of religion if you make your gospel a symbolic record of experience, and reject it as an actual record of events.

The liberals have yet to answer Dr. Machen when he says that "the Christian movement at its inception was not just a way of life in the modern sense, but a way of life founded upon a message. It was based, not upon mere feeling, not upon a mere program of work, but on an account of facts." It was based on the story of the birth, the life, the ministry, the death, and the resurrection of Jesus Christ. That story set forth the facts which certify the Christian experience. Modernism, which in varying degree casts doubt upon the truth of that story, may therefore be defined as an attempt to preserve selected parts of the experience after the facts which inspired it have been rejected. The orthodox believer may be mistaken as to the facts in which he believes. But he is not mistaken in thinking that you cannot, for the mass of men, have a faith of which the only foundation is their need and desire to believe. The historic churches, without any important exceptions, I think, have founded faith on clear statements about matters of fact, historic events, or physical manifestations. They have never been content with a symbolism which the believer knew was merely symbolic. Only the sophisticated in their private meditations and in esoteric writing have found satisfaction in symbolism as such.

Complete as was Dr. Machen's victory over the Protestant liberals, he did not long remain in possession of the field. There is a deeper fundamentalism than his, and it is based on a longer continuous experience. This is the teaching of the Roman Catholic Church. From a priest of that church, Father Riggs, has come the most searching criticism of Dr. Machen's case. Writing in the *Commonweal* Father Riggs points out that "the fundamentalists are well-nigh powerless. They are estopped, so to speak, from stemming the ravaging waters of agnosticism because they cannot, while remaining loyal to the (Protestant) reformers . . . set limits to destructive criticism of the Bible without making an un-Protestant appeal to tradition." Father Riggs, in other words, is asking the Protestant fundamentalists, like Dr. Machen, how they can be certain that they know these *facts* upon which they assert that the Christian religion is founded.

They must reply that they know them from reading the Bible. The reply is, however, unsatisfying. For obviously there are many ways of reading the Bible, and therefore the Protestant who demands the right of private judgment can never know with absolute certainty that his reading is the correct one. His position in a skeptical age is, therefore, as Father Riggs points out, a weak one, because a private judgment is, after all, only a private judgment. The history of Protestantism shows that the exercise of private judgment as to the meaning of Scripture leads not to universal and undeniable dogma, but to schism within schism and heresy within heresy. From the point of view, then, of the oldest fundamentalism of the western world the error of the modernists is that they deny the facts on which religious faith reposes; the error of the orthodox Protestants is that although they affirm the facts, they reject all authority which can verify them; the virtue of the Catholic system is that along with a dogmatic affirmation of the central facts, it provides a living authority in the Church which can ascertain and demonstrate and verify these facts.

5. *In Man's Image*

The long record of clerical opposition to certain kinds of scientific inquiry has a touch of dignity when it is realized that at the core of that opposition there is a very profound understanding of the religious needs of ordinary men. For once you weaken the belief that the central facts taught by the churches are facts in the most literal and absolute sense, the disintegration of the popular religion begins. We may confidently declare that Mr. Santayana is speaking not as a student of human nature, but as a cultivated unbeliever, when he writes that "the idea that religion contains a literal, not a symbolic, representation of truth and life is simply an impossible idea." The idea is impossible, no doubt, for the children of the great emancipation. But because it is impossible, religion itself, in the traditional popular meaning of the term, has become impossible for them.

If it is true that man creates God in his own image, it is no less true that for religious devotion he must remain unconscious of that fact. Once he knows that he has created the image of God, the reality of it vanishes like last night's dream. It may be that to anyone who is impregnated with the modern spirit it is almost self-evident that the truths of religion are truths of human experience. But this knowledge does not tolerate an abiding and absorbing faith. For when the truths of religion have lost their connection with a superhuman order, the cord of their life is cut. What remains is a somewhat archaic, a somewhat questionable, although a very touching, quaint medley of poetry, rhetoric, fable, exhortation, and insight into human travail. When Mr. Santayana says that "matters of religion should never be matters of controversy" because "we never argue with a lover about his taste, nor condemn him, if we are just, for knowing so human a passion," he expresses an ultimate unbelief.

For what would be the plight of a lover, if we told him that his passion was charming?—though, of course, there might be no such lady as the one he loved.

CHAPTER III

THE LOSS OF CERTAINTY

1. *Ways of Reading the Bible*

IT is important to an understanding of this matter that we should not confuse the modern practice of redefining God with the ancient use of allegory.

From the earliest days the words of the Bible have been embroidered with luxuriant and often fantastic meanings. In Leviticus it says, for example, that the meal offering may be baked in an oven, fried in a pan, or toasted on a plate. This passage, says Origen, proves that Scripture must have three meanings. It came to have any number of meanings. Thus St. Augustine explained that Eden meant the life of the blessed, and its four rivers the four virtues; farther on in the same chapter he declares that Eden is the Church, and that its four rivers are the four Gospels.

In the same manner Wyclif in a later age preached a sermon explaining the parable of the Good Samaritan. The man who went down from Jerusalem to Jericho represents Adam and Eve; the robbers are the fiends of hell; the priest and Levite who went by on the other side are the patriarchs, saints, and prophets who failed to bring salvation; the Good Samaritan is Jesus; the wine which he pours into his wounds is sharp words to prick men from sin, and the oil is hope. . . . Savonarola, we are told, preached during the whole of Lent, 1492, taking as his text Noah's Ark and "giving each day a different interpretation of the ten planks of which the Ark was composed."

By this method of interpretation the devout adapted the Bible to their own uses, smoothing away its contradictions and explaining away passages, like the command in Genesis to kill uncircumcised children, which, read literally, would have seemed to them barbarous and immoral. We must be careful, however, not to misunderstand this method of thought. When they said that the beautiful woman in the Song of Solomon was the Church, they were not conscious, as we are, that this is a figure of speech. There had not entered into their habits of thought the kind of analytical precision in which one thing can mean only one thing. It is no contradiction to say that the allegory was taken literally; certainly there was no sense of unreality about it, as there is for us. "These and similar allegorical interpretations may be suitably put . . ." says St. Augustine, speaking here to the educated minority, "without giving offense to anyone, while yet we believe the strict truth of the history confirmed by its circumstantial narrative of facts."

But at last men became too analytical and too self-conscious to accept the naive use of allegory. They realized that allegory was a loose method of interpretation which lent itself easily to the citing of scripture in order to justify heresy. If the ten planks in Noah's Ark could mean a different set of truths on each day in Lent, there was no telling what they might come to mean in the end. It was clear, therefore, that allegory was dangerous and might, as Luther said, "degenerate into a mere monkey game"; it was wanton, like "a sort of beautiful harlot who proves herself spiritually seductive to idle men."

This danger was a result of the general loosening of organic faith which was already evident in Luther's day. To men who had the unconscious certainties about God and his universe, allegory was a perfectly safe method of interpreting the Bible because all the interpretations, however fantastic, were inspired by the same prejudgments and tended therefore to confirm the same convictions. The allegories of simple men are like many-colored flowers in one garden, growing from the same soil, watered by the same rains, turning their faces toward the same sun. But as men became emancipated from their ancestral way of life, their convictions about God and destiny and human morality changed. Then the method of allegory ceased to be the merely exuberant expression of the same ancient truths, and became a confusing method of rationalizing all kinds of new experiments. It promoted heresy because men had become heretical, where once, while men were devout, it had only embroidered their devotions.

"To allegorize is to juggle with Scripture," said Luther. The Protestant Reformers could not tolerate that. For they lived in an age when faith was already disintegrating, and they had themselves destroyed the authority of an infallible source of religion. "We must," wrote Calvin, "entirely reject the allegories of Origen, and of others like him, which Satan, with the deepest subtlety, has endeavored to introduce into the Church, for the purpose of rendering the doctrine of Scripture ambiguous and destitute of all certainty and firmness."

The insistence of the Reformers on a literal interpretation of the Bible had, as Dr. Fosdick points out, two unforeseen results. It led to the so-called Higher Criticism which in substance is nothing but a scientific attempt to find out what the Bible did mean literally to those who wrote it. And this in turn made it practically impossible for modern men to believe all that the Bible literally says. When they read the Bible as allegory they found in it unending confirmation of what they already believed. But when they read it literally, as history, as astronomy, and biology, and as a code of laws, it contradicted at many crucial points the practical working convictions of their daily lives. "The consequence is," says Dr. Fosdick, "that we face the Biblical world made historically vivid over against the modern world presently experienced, and we cannot use the old method (*i.e.* allegory) of accommodating one to the other."

2. *Modernism: Immortality as an Example*

This predicament forced modern churchmen to seek what Dr. Fosdick calls "a new solution." They could not believe that the Bible was taken down, as John Donne put it, by "the Secretaries of the Holy Ghost." Yet they believed, as every sane man does, that the Bible contains wisdom which bears deeply upon the conduct of human life. Their problem was to find a way of picking and choosing passages in the Scriptures, and then of interpreting those which were chosen in such a way as to make them credible to modern men. They had to find some way of setting aside the story that God made Eve out of Adam's rib, that God commanded the massacre of whole populations, and that he enjoyed the slaughter of animals at the sacrifice; but they had at the same time to find a way of preserving for the use of modern men the lessons of the ministry of Jesus and the promise of life everlasting.

The method they employ is based on a theory. It is a theory that the Bible contains "abiding messages" placed in a "transient setting." The Bible, for example, is full of stories about devils and angels. Now, modern men do not believe in devils and angels. These are "categories" which they have outgrown. But what the devils and angels stood for are evils and blessings which modern men still encounter. We have, therefore, only to "decode" the Bible, and where it speaks of devils to see temptations, sin, disease, pain, and suffering, which have a psychic origin; where it speaks of angels to remember that sense of unseen friendliness which may help us at a crisis in our lives. The old wine is still good, but it needs to be put in new bottles. "The modern preacher's responsibility is thus to decode the abiding meanings of Scripture from outgrown phraseology."

This is not so difficult a thing to do for the devils and the angels. But a little reflection will show, I think, that in dealing with the major themes of religion, the solution is not so easy. The real difficulty appears when Dr. Fosdick attempts to decode the biblical promise of immortal life.

He begins by rejecting completely the resurrection of the flesh and any kind of immortality which is imagined as the survival of the physical person. Yet he believes in "the persistence of personality through death." For he maintains that without this belief the final victory of death would signify "the triumphant irrationality of existence"; not to believe in immortality is to submit to "mental confusion." Speaking quite frankly, however, he cannot easily imagine "a completely disembodied existence." Yet it is obviously not easy to imagine the persistence of personality through death once you have made up your mind not to imagine a concrete heaven inhabited by well-defined persons.

Modern churchmen, like Dean Inge for example, who have faced the difficulty more boldly than Dr. Fosdick does, arrive at an intelligible explanation of what they mean by immortality. But they mean something which is not only very difficult to understand, but extremely difficult for most men to enjoy when they have understood it. They inject intelligible meaning into the word "eternal" by employing it in a sense which is wholly different from that which the common man employs. By immortality he means life that goes on age after age without stopping. But the modern churchmen who have really clarified their minds are platonists. They apply the word "eternal" to that which is independent of time and existence. Between the two conceptions there is the profoundest difference, for in the commonsense of the worldling existence is so precious that he wishes it to continue for ever and ever. But to the platonist existence, or embodiment, is transient, accidental, irrational; only that is permanent which is timeless. Commonsense demands that if we are immortal we should meet our friend again later and continue our friendship; the platonist loves the memory of his friend after death as he loved an ideal image of him during his life. In communing with his memories and his ideals he knows himself to be in touch with eternal things. For not even the gods, says Homer, can undo the past; no accident of mortality can destroy anything which can be represented in the mind. Heroes die, but that such heroic deeds were done is a chapter forever, as Mr. Santayana says, in any complete history of the universe. The thinker dies, but his thoughts are beyond the reach of destruction. Men are mortal; but ideas are immortal.

I do not know whether I have known how to state clearly what is meant by this platonic view to which, in varying degrees of clarity, all emancipated minds turn when they talk of immortality. But, at least, it is clear that it is a conception which calls for a radically different adjustment to life than that to which the worldling is accustomed. He desires objects to love, goods and successes that are perishable, and he wishes them not to perish. Before he can enter the platonic world, before he can even attain to a hint of its meaning, he must abandon the very desires of which his hope of immortality is the expression. He must detach himself from his wish to acquire and possess objects that die; he must learn what it means to possess things not by holding them, but by understanding them, and to enjoy them as objects of reflection. He must not only cease to desire immortality as he conceives it, but the material embodiment of things as well. Then only, when he has renounced his love of existence, can he begin to love the forms of existence, and to live among imperishable ideas.

Then, and in this sense only, does he enter into eternal life.

The ordinary man, when he hears this doctrine expounded, is almost certain to say with the Indian sage: "the worship of the Impersonal laid no hold upon my heart." His heart is set on the enjoyment of worldly goods, and the doctrine, for all but a few exceptional spirits, requires a radical change of heart. It is forbidding except to the few in whom "the intellect (is) passionate and the passions cold." For it demands a conversion of their natural desire to possess tangible things into a passion to understand intangible and abstract things. This philosophy is ascetic, unworldly, and profoundly disinterested.

Now it can be argued that this is precisely what the Gospels teach as to the meaning of salvation. Excellent authority can be cited from the Gospel of St. John and the Epistles of St. Paul to justify this form of the Christian tradition: "Flesh and blood cannot inherit the kingdom of God" . . . "the things that are seen are temporal, but the things that are not seen are eternal" . . . "I see another law in my members, warring against the law of my mind." It can hardly be denied, as Dean Inge says, that "we are able to carry back to the fountain-head that Christian tradition" which may quite accurately be described as the religion of the spirit. But mixed with it in the Scripture, there is the other tradition, the popular tradition which may be called the religion of commonsense. Out of this latter have grown the institutions of the church and the faith of the mass of men. The religion of the spirit has been reserved for a few, "a succession of lives which have been sheltered rather than inspired by the machinery and statecraft of a mighty institution," and while the few who lived the life of the spirit have undoubtedly done much to inspire the popular religion with new insight, they have been, on the whole, a group apart.

Yet those who belonged to these two distinct traditions did use the same churches and the same symbolism. There was an even deeper bond of unity between them. Both believed that renunciation and self-discipline are the way of salvation—in the religion of the spirit as the way to enter now into love of eternal things; in the religion of commonsense as a rather heavy price paid to God in return for everlasting happiness after death. It may be argued, therefore, by churchmen like Dr. Fosdick, that the "abiding message" of the Bible about immortality is that men must renounce the world in order to win eternity. That some men mean by eternity a kind of perpetual motion and others a kind of abstraction is merely a difference in their habits of thought, and does not impair the validity or the importance of the central experience. If they will renounce their worldly passions, they will find what the idea of eternity has to give, no matter what they imagine it to mean.

But although Dr. Fosdick implies that this solves the difficulty, it can be shown, I believe, that it does not. What he has succeeded in doing is to disentangle from the Bible a meaning for immortality which has a noble tradition behind it and is at the same time intellectually possible for a modern man. But the history of religion ought to put us on guard against assuming too easily that a statement of the purest truth is in itself capable of affecting the lives of any considerable number of people. Dean Inge, who is a very much more clear-headed churchman, says quite frankly that "a religion succeeds, not because it is true, but because it suits the worshippers." Merely to tell men, however fervently, that they may conquer mortality by renouncing the flesh, will not go far toward persuading many of them to renounce the flesh. There must be, as there has been in all the historic religions, something more than a statement of the moral law. There must be a psychological machinery for enforcing the moral law.

For those who are suited to the religion of the spirit no machinery is needed. But for the mass of men who are not naturally suited to it, a machinery which compels this conversion is indispensable. Jesus in his time, and Gautama Buddha before him, taught a moral law which was addressed to those who could receive it. They were not many. Buddhism and Christianity became world religions centuries after the death of their founders, and only when there had been added to the central message a great organized method of teaching it.

The essence of such an organization is the title to say with apostolic certainty that the message is true. Churchmen like Dr. Fosdick can make no such claim about their message. They reject revelation. They reject the authority of any church to speak directly for God. They reject the literal inspiration of the Bible. They reject altogether many parts of the Bible as not only uninspired, but false and misleading. They do not believe in God as a lawgiver, judge, father, and spectator of human life.

When they say that this or that message in the Bible is
"permanently valid," they mean only that in their judgment, according to their reading of human experience,
it is a well-tested truth. To say this is not merely to
deny that the Bible is authoritative in astronomy and
biology; it is to deny equally that it is authoritative as
to what is good and bad for men. The Bible thus becomes
no more than a revered collection of hypotheses which
each man may reject or accept in the light of his own
knowledge.

The lessons may still be true. But they are robbed
of their certainty. Each man is thrown back upon his
own resources; he is denied the support which all popular
religion offers him, the conviction that outside himself
there is a power on which he can and must lean for
guidance. In the ancient faith a man said: "I believe
this on the authority of an all-wise God." In the new
faith he is in effect compelled to say: "I have examined
the alleged pronouncements of an all-knowing God; some
of them are obviously untrue, some are rather repulsive,
others, however, if they are properly restated, I find to be
exceedingly good."

Something quite fundamental is left out of the modernist creeds. At least something which has hitherto been
quite fundamental is left out. That something is the
most abiding of all the experiences of religion, namely,
the conviction that the religion comes from God. Suppose it were true, which it plainly is not, that Dr. Fosdick
by his process of selection and decoding has retained "precisely the thing at which the Bible was driving." Still
he would be without the thing on which popular religion

has been founded. For the Bible to our ancestors was not simply, as he implies, a book of wisdom. It was a book of wisdom backed by the power of God himself. That is not an inconsiderable difference. It is all the difference there is between a pious resolution and a moral law.

The Bible, as men formerly accepted it, contained wisdom *certified* by the powers that govern the universe. It did not merely contain many well-tested truths, similar in kind to those which are to be found in Plato, Aristotle, Montaigne, and Bernard Shaw. It contained truths which could not be doubted because they had been spoken by God through his prophets and his Son. They could not be wrong. But once it is allowed that each man may select from the Bible as he sees fit, judging each passage by his own notions of what is "abiding," you have stripped the Scriptures of their authority to command men's confidence and to compel their obedience. The Scriptures may still inspire respect. But they are disarmed.

3. *What Modernism Leaves Out*

Many reasons have been adduced to explain why people do not go to church as much as they once did. Surely the most important reason is that they are not so certain that they are going to meet God when they go to church. If they had that certainty they would go. If they really believed that they were being watched by a Supreme Being who is more powerful than all the kings of earth put together, if they really believed that not only their actions but their secret thoughts were known and would be remembered by the creator and ultimate judge of the

[48]

universe, there would be no complaint whatever about church attendance. The most worldly would be in the front pews, and preachers would not have to resort so often to their rather desperate expedients to attract an audience. If the conviction were there that the creed professed was invincibly true, the modern congregation would not come to church, as they usually do to-day, to hear the preacher and to listen to the music. They would come to worship God.

Religious professions will not work when they rest merely on a kind of passive assent; or on intricate reasoning, or on fierce exhortation, or on a good-natured conspiracy to be vague and highflown. A man cannot cheat about faith. Either he has it in the marrow of his bones, or in a crisis, when he is distracted and in sorrow, there is no conviction there to support him. Without complete certainty religion does not offer genuine consolation. It is without the strength to compensate our weakness. Nor can it sanction the rules of morality. Ethical codes cannot lay claim to unhesitating obedience when they are based upon the opinions of a majority, or on the notions of wise men, or on estimates of what is socially useful, or on an appeal to patriotism. For they depend then on the force which happens to range itself behind them at a particular time; or on their convenience for a moment. They are felt to be the outcome of human, and therefore quite fallible, decisions. They are no necessary part of the government of the universe. They were not given by God to Moses on Sinai. They are not the commandments of God speaking through his Infallible Church.

A human morality has no such sanction as a divine.

The sanction of a divine morality is the certainty of the believer that it originated with God. But if he has once come to think that the rule of conduct has a purely human, local, and temporal origin, its sanction is gone. His obedience is transformed, as ours has been by knowledge of that sort, from conviction to conformity or calculated expediency.

Without certainty there can be no profound sense that a man's own purpose has become part of the purpose of the whole creation. It is necessary to believe in a God who is active in the world before a man can feel himself to be, as St. Paul said, "a fellow laborer" with God. Yet this sense of partnership with a Person who transcends the individual's own life, his own ego, and his own capacities, is fundamental in all popular religion. It underlies all the other elements of religion. For in the certainty that he is enlisted with God, man finds not only comfort in defeat, not only an ideal of holiness which persuades him to renounce his immediate desires, but an ecstatic mobilizing of all his scattered energies in one triumphant sense of his own infinite importance.

CHAPTER IV

THE ACIDS OF MODERNITY

1. *The Kingly Pattern*

WHAT I have said thus far can be reduced to the statement that it is difficult for modern men to conceive a God whom they can worship. Yet it would be a crude misunderstanding of religious experience to assume that it depends upon a clear conception of God. In truly religious men the experience of God is much more intensely convincing than any definition of his nature which they can put into words. They do not insist on understanding that which they believe, for their belief gives them a consciousness of divinity which transcends any conviction they could reach by the understanding. They are not oppressed by the conflict between reason and faith because the testimony of faith is irresistible. It may become so irresistible that any attempt to understand is finally held, as it was by John Chrysostom, to be an impertinence.

St. Chrysostom, who is described by the *Catholic Encyclopedia* as the most prominent doctor of the Greek Church and the greatest preacher ever heard in a Christian pulpit, is a striking example of how in other ages a man who was both learned and devout was able to surmount the intellectual difficulties which to-day cause so much trouble for modernists and fundamentalists alike. Chrysostom was born at Antioch in the middle of the Fourth Century and grew up in a time when the intellectual foundations of Christianity were intensely disputed. The Catholic theology had not yet emerged victoriously, and Antioch was the theatre of fierce struggles between Pagans, Manichæans, Gnostics, Arians, Jews, and others. These struggles turned in considerable measure upon just such attempts to define and comprehend God as now confuse the teaching of the Protestant Church. Among the sectarians there were some who claimed that it was possible "to know God exactly" and it was against them that Chrysostom preached that "he insults God who seeks to apprehend His essential being." For "the difference between the being of God and the being of man is of such a kind that no word can express it and no thought can appraise it. . . . He dwells, says St. Paul, in an unapproachable light." Even the angels in heaven are stupefied by the glory and majesty of God: "Tell me," he says, "wherefore do they cover their faces and hide them with their wings? Why but that they cannot endure the dazzling radiance and its rays that pour from the Throne?"

Here in language so eloquent that the author became known as Chrysostom, "the golden-mouthed," we have the doctrine that "a comprehended God is no God," that "God is incomprehensible because He is blessed and blessed because He is incomprehensible." But if we look more closely at what Chrysostom actually says, it is apparent that he has a much clearer idea of God than he knows. He conceives of God as the creator, the ruler, and the judge of the universe. When he says that God is incomprehensible he means that it is impossible for a human being to imagine what it would be like to be God. But that does not prevent Chrysostom from knowing what it is like to be the creature of the incomprehensible God. He is very definitely on his knees before the throne of a divine king whose radiance is so dazzling that he cannot look his Lord in the face.

There is thus a very solid intellectual conception embedded in the faith of this great teacher who staked everything on the assertion that it is impossible to conceive God. The conception is there but it has not been isolated and realized. It is unconsciously assumed. We find the same thing in Luther when he said: "I venture to put my trust in the one God alone, the invisible and incomprehensible, who hath created Heaven and Earth and is alone above all creatures." For in spite of the fact that Luther calls God incomprehensible, he is able to make a number of extremely important statements about him. He is able to say that God is the only God, that he created the earth, that there is a heaven, that God created heaven, and that God alone is above all his creatures. To know that much about God is to comprehend the function of God if not his nature.

Now if we examine the religious difficulty of modern men, we find, I think, that they do not lack the sense of mystery, of majesty, of terror, and of wonder which overwhelm Chrysostom and Luther. The emotional disposition is there. But it is somehow inhibited from possessing them utterly. The will to believe is checked by something in their experience which Chrysostom did not have. That something is the sense that the testimony of faith is not wholly credible, that the feeling of sanctity is no assurance of the existence of sacred powers, that awe and

wonder and terror in the breast of the believer are not
guarantees that there exist real objects that are awful and
wonderful. The modern man is not incapable of faith,
but he has within him a contrary passion, as instinctive
and often as intense as faith, which makes incredible the
testimony of his faith.

It is that contrary passion, and not the thin argumenta-
tion of atheists and agnostics, which lies, I think, at the
root of what churchmen call modern irreligion. It is
that passion which they must understand if they are ever
to understand the modern religious difficulty. For just
as men could surmount any intellectual difficulty when
their passion to believe was whole-hearted, so to-day,
when the passion to disbelieve is so strong, they are unable
to believe no matter how perfectly their theological dilemmas are resolved.

We must ask ourselves, then, what there is in modern
men which makes the testimony of faith seem more or
less incredible to them. We have seen in the citations
from Chrysostom and Luther that the testimony of faith
really contains a large number of unconscious statements
of fact about the universe and how it is governed. It is
these statements of fact which we are no longer able to
assume unconsciously, and having become conscious of
them they are rather incredible. But why are they no
longer unconsciously assumed and why are they incredible? The answer is, I think, that they have ceased to
be consistent with our normal experience in ordinary
affairs.

The faith of Chrysostom and Luther is entangled with,
and supported upon, the assumption that the universe

was created and is governed by a father and king. They had projected upon the universe an imaginary picture which reflected their own daily experience of government among men. These pictures of how the universe is governed change with men's political experience. Thus it would not have been easy for an Asiatic people to imagine the divine government in any other way but as a despotism, and Yahveh, as he appears in many famous portraits in the Old Testament, is very evidently an Oriental monarch inclined to be somewhat moody and very vain. He governs as he chooses, constrained by no law, and often without mercy, justice, or righteousness. The God of mediæval Christianity, on the other hand, is more like a great feudal lord, supreme and yet bound by covenants to treat his vassals on earth according to a well-established system of reciprocal rights and duties. The God of the Enlightenment in the Eighteenth Century is a constitutional monarch who reigns but does not govern. And the God of Modernism, who is variously pictured as the *élan vital* within the evolutionary process, or as the sum total of the laws of nature, is really a kind of constitutionalism deified.

Provided that the picture is so consistent with experience that it is taken utterly for granted, it will serve as a background for the religious experience. But when daily experience for one reason or another provides no credible analogy by which men can imagine that the universe is governed by a supernatural king and father, then the disposition to believe, however strong it may be at the roots, is like a vine that reaches out and can find nothing solid upon which to grow. It cannot support itself. If faith is to flourish, there must be a conception of how the universe is governed to support it.

It is these supporting conceptions—the unconscious assumption that we are related to God as creatures to creator, as vassals to a king, as children to a father—that the acids of modernity have eaten away. The modern man's daily experience of modernity makes instinctively incredible to him these unconscious ideas which are at the core of the great traditional and popular religions. He does not wantonly reject belief, as so many churchmen assert. His predicament is much more serious. With the best will in the world, he finds himself not quite believing.

In the last four hundred years many influences have conspired to make incredible the idea that the universe is governed by a kingly person. An account of all of these influences would be a history of the growth of modern civilization. I am attempting nothing so comprehensive or so ambitious. I should like merely to note certain aspects of that revolutionary change which, as Lord Acton says, came "unheralded" and "founded a new order of things . . . sapping the ancient reign of continuity." For that new order of things has made it impossible for us to believe, as plainly and literally as our forefathers did, that the universe is a monarchy administered on this planet through divinely commissioned, and, therefore, unimpeachably authoritative ministers.

2. *Landmarks*

In a famous passage at the beginning of *Heretics*, Mr. Chesterton says that "nothing more strangely indicates the enormous and silent evil of modern society than the extraordinary use which is made nowadays of the word 'orthodox.' In former days the heretic was proud of not being a heretic. It was the kingdom of the world and the police and the judges who were heretics. He was orthodox. All the tortures born out of forgotten hells could not make him admit that he was heretical. But a few modern phrases have made him boast of it. He says with a conscious laugh, 'I suppose I am very heretical,' and looks around for applause. The word 'heresy' not only means no longer being wrong; it practically means being clear-headed and courageous."

Mr. Chesterton goes on to explain that this change of attitude has come about because "people care less for whether they are philosophically right than they used to care." It may be so. But if they cared as much or more, it would not help them. To be orthodox is to believe in the right doctrines and to follow the ancient rules of living deduced from a divine revelation. The modern man finds that the doctrines do not fit what he believes to be true, and that the rules do not show him how to conduct his life. For he is confronted at every turn with radical novelties about which his inherited dogma teaches him something which is plainly unworkable, or, as is even more often the case, teaches him nothing at all.

In the old world there were, of course, novelties, too. But the pace of change was so slow that it did not seem to cause radical change. There was ample time to make subtle and necessary revisions of the fundamental assumptions of right and wrong without seeming to challenge the distinction between right and wrong. Looking back at it in long perspective we can see now that there was a constant evolution of the Christian faith from the Apostles to the later councils of the Church. But in relation to the life of any individual the change was so slow that men could honestly believe that the Catholicism of Hildebrand was identical with the Christianity of Paul. Men had few means of reconstructing the past, and few ways of knowing how great was the variety of belief at any one time within the frontiers of Christendom. Within their horizon, change came too slowly to seem like change, because only that seems to move which moves rather fast.

For that reason the large changes which took place were not vividly realized. The small, quick changes, of which men were conscious, could therefore easily be made to seem, especially since men were not too exact and observant, as inevitable deductions from unchanging premises. Even in the great arguments over the nature of Christ, the rights of Church and Empire, the meaning of grace and transubstantiation, both sides appealed in theory to the same premises. Each side asserted that it was following the true revelation. And since ordinary men for the most part never heard the other side, except from their own priests and doctors, they had no reason for doubting that the side on which they happened to find themselves was absolutely right. They did not have to choose between competing creeds; they had merely to defend their creed, which was the true one, against the enemies of God. And so if they were disturbed by the quarrel, they were not disturbed much by doubt.

The grand adjustments were taken for granted, and within that framework men could make the minor adjustments patiently and elaborately, letting them become

really trust their God, they would trust laws, politicians, and policemen less. But because their whole field of consciousness is trembling with uncertainties they are in a state of fret and fuss; and their preaching is frousy, like the seductions of an old coquette.

3. *Barren Ground*

The American people, more than any other people, is composed of individuals who have lost association with their old landmarks. They have crossed an ocean, they have spread themselves across a new continent. The American who still lives in his grandfather's house feels almost as if he were living in a museum. There are few Americans who have not moved at least once since their childhood, and even if they have staid where they were born, the old landmarks themselves have been carted away to make room for progress. That, perhaps, is one reason why we have so much more Americanism than love of America. It takes time to learn to love the new gas station which stands where the wild honeysuckle grew. Moreover, the great majority of Americans have risen in the world. They have moved out of their class, lifting the old folks along with them perhaps, so that together they may sit by the steam pipes, and listen to the crooning of the radio. But more and more of them have moved not only out of their class, but out of their culture; and then they leave the old folks behind, and the continuity of life is broken. For faith grows well only as it is passed on from parents to their children amidst surroundings that bear witness, because nothing changes radically, to a deep permanence in the order of the world. It is true, no doubt, that in this great physical and psychic migration some of the old household gods are carefully packed up and put with the rest of the luggage, and then unpacked and set up on new altars in new places. But what can be taken along is at best no more than the tree which is above the ground. The roots remain in the soil where first they grew.

The sidewalks of a city would in any case be a stony soil in which to transplant religion. Throughout history, as Spengler points out, the large city has bred heresies, new cults, and irreligion. Now when we speak of modern civilization we mean a civilization dominated by the culture of the great metropolitan centers. Our own civilization in America is perhaps the most completely urbanized of all. For even the American farmers, though they live in the country, tend to be suburban rather than rural. I am aware of how dominating a role the population outside the great cities plays in American life. Yet it is in the large cities that the tempo of our civilization is determined, and the tendency of mechanical inventions as well as economic policy is to create an irresistible suction of the country towards the city.

The deep and abiding traditions of religion belong to the countryside. For it is there that man earns his daily bread by submitting to superhuman forces whose behavior he can only partially control. There is not much he can do when he has ploughed the ground and planted his seed except to wait hopefully for sun and rain from the sky. He is obviously part of a scheme that is greater than himself, subject to elements that transcend his powers and surpass his understanding. The city is an acid that dissolves this piety. How different it is from an ancient vineyard where men cultivate what their fathers have planted. In a modern city it is not easy to maintain that "reverent attachment to the sources of his being and the steadying of his life by that attachment." It is not natural to form reverent attachments to an apartment on a two-year lease, and an imitation mahogany desk on the thirty-second floor of an office building. In such an environment piety becomes absurd, a butt for the facetious, and the pious man looks like a picturesque yokel or a stuffy fool.

Yet without piety, without a patriotism of family and place, without an almost plant-like implication in unchangeable surroundings, there can be no disposition to believe in an external order of things. The omnipotence of God means something to men who submit daily to the cycles of the weather and the mysterious power of nature. But the city man puts his faith in furnaces to keep out the cold, is proudly aware of what bad sewage his ancestors endured, and of how ignorantly they believed that God, who made Adam at 9 A.M. on October 23 in the year 4004 B.C., was concerned with the behavior of Adam's children.

4. *Sophisticated Violence*

Much effort goes into finding substitutes for this radical loss of association. There is the Americanization movement, for example, which in some of its public manifestations has as much resemblance to patriotism as the rape of the Sabine women had to the love of Dante for Beatrice. There is the vociferous nationalism of the

hundred-percenters which is always most eloquent when
it is about to be most rowdy. There are the anxious outcries of the sectarians who in their efforts to revive the
religion of their fathers show the utmost contempt for
the aspirations of their sons. There is Mr. Henry Ford
hastily collecting American antiques before his cars
destroy the whole culture which produced them. There
is Mr. Lothrop Stoddard looking every man in the eye
to see whether it is Nordic blue. There are a thousand
and one patently artificial, sometimes earnest, often fantastic fundamentalist agitations. They are all attempts
to impose quickly by one kind of sophisticated violence
or another a posture of faith which can be genuine only
when it belongs to the unquestioned memories of the soul.
They are a shrill insistence that men ought to feel that
which no man can feel who does not already feel it in the
marrow of his bones.

Novelties crowd the consciousness of modern men.
The machinery of intelligence, the press, the radio, the
moving picture, have enormously multiplied the number
of unseen events and strange people and queer doings
with which he has to be concerned. They compel him
to pay attention to facts that are detached from their
backgrounds, their causes and their consequences, and are
only half known because they are not seen or touched
or actually heard. These experiences come to him having
no beginning, no middle, and no end, mere flashes of
publicity playing fitfully upon a dark tangle of circumstances. I pick up a newspaper at the start of the day
and I am depressed and rejoiced to learn that: anthracite
miners have struck in Pennsylvania; that a price boost

plot is charged; that Mr. Ziegfeld has imported a blonde from England who weighs 112 pounds and has pretty legs; that the Pope, on the other hand, has refused to receive women in low-necked dress and with their arms bare; that airplanes are flying to Hawaii; and that the Mayor says that the would-be Mayor is a liar. . . .

Now in an ordered universe there ought to be place for all human experiences. But it is not strange that the modern newspaper-reader finds it increasingly difficult to believe that through it all there is order, permanence, and connecting principle. Such experience as comes to him from the outside is a dissonance composed of a thousand noises. And amidst these noises he has for inner guidance only a conscience which consists, as he half-suspects, of the confused echoes of earlier tunes.

5. *Rulers*

He cannot look to his betters for guidance. The American social system is migratory, revolutionary, and protestant. It provides no recognized leaders and no clear standards of conduct. No one is recognized as the interpreter of morals and the arbiter of taste. There is no social hierarchy, there is no acknowledged ruling class, no well-known system of rights and duties, no code of manners. There are smart sets, first families, and successful people, to whom a good deal of deference is paid and a certain tribute of imitation. But these leaders have no real authority in morals or in matters of taste because they themselves have few standards that are not the fashions of a season. They exercise, therefore, an almost autocratic power over deportment at the country club.

But what they believe about God, salvation, or the destiny of America nobody knows, not even they themselves.

There have been perhaps three ruling classes in America, the Puritan merchants, the Knickerbocker gentry, and the Cavalier planters of the South. Each presided for a few generations over an ordered civilization. But the New Englanders uprooted themselves and went west, and those who have been left behind are marooned in a flood of aliens. The Knickerbocker squirearchy dissolved in the commercial greatness of New York, and the southern aristocracy was overthrown and ruined by a social revolution which culminated in the Civil War. They have left no successors, and unless and until American society becomes stabilized once more somewhere for a few generations, they are not likely to have any successors.

Our rulers to-day consist of random collections of successful men and their wives. They are to be found in the inner circles of banks and corporations, in the best clubs, in the dominant cliques of trade unions, among the political churchmen, the higher manipulating bosses, the leading professional Catholics, Baptists, Methodists, Irish, Germans, Jews, and the grand panjandrums of the secret societies. They give orders. They have to be consulted. They can more or less effectively speak for, and lead some part of, the population. But none of them is seated on an assured throne, and all of them are forever concerned as to how they may keep from being toppled off. They do not know how they happen to be where they are, although they often explain what are the secrets of success. They have been educated to achieve success; few of them have been educated to exercise power. Nor do they count with any confidence upon retaining their power, nor of handing it on to their sons. They live, therefore, from day to day, and they govern by ear. Their impromptu statements of policy may be obeyed, but nobody seriously regards them as having authority.

CHAPTER V

THE BREAKDOWN OF AUTHORITY

1. *God's Government*

THE dissolution of the ancestral order is still under way, and much of our current controversy is between those who hope to stay the dissolution and those who would like to hasten it. The prime fact about modernity, as it presents itself to us, is that it not merely denies the central ideas of our forefathers but dissolves the disposition to believe in them. The ancestral tradition still lives in many corners of the world. But it no longer represents for us, as it did for Dante and for St. Thomas Aquinas seven hundred years ago, the triumphant wisdom of the age. A child born in a modern city may still learn to use the images of the theological drama, but more or less consciously he is made to feel that in using them he is not speaking of things that are literally and exactly true.

Its dogma, as Mr. Santayana once said, is insensibly understood to be nothing but myth, its miracles nothing but legend, its sacraments mere symbols, its bible pure literature, its liturgy just poetry, its hierarchy an administrative convenience, its ethics an historical accident, and its whole function simply to lend a warm mystical aureole to human culture and ignorance. The modern man does not take his religion as a real account of the constitution, the government, the history, and the actual destiny of the universe. With rare exceptions his ancestors did. They believed that all their activities on this earth had a sequel in other activities hereafter, and that they themselves in their own persons would be alive through all the stretches of infinite time to experience this fulfilment. The sense of actuality has gone out of this tremendous conception of life; only the echoes of it persist, and in our memories they create a world apart from the world in which we do our work, a noble world perhaps in which it is refreshing to dwell now and then, and in anxiety to take refuge. But the spaces between the stars are so great; the earth is now so small a planet in the skies; man is so close, as St. Francis said, to his brother the ass, that in the daylight he does not believe that a great cosmic story is being unfolded of which his every thought and act is a significant part. The universe may have a conscious purpose, but he does not believe he knows just what it is; humanity may be acting out a divine drama, but he is not certain that he knows the plot.

There has gone out of modern life a working conviction that we are living under the dominion of one supreme ideal, the attainment of eternal happiness by obedience to God's will on earth. This conviction found its most perfect expression in the period which begins with St. Augustine's *City of God* and culminates in the *Divine Comedy* of Dante. But the underlying intuitions are to be found in nearly all popular religion; they are the creature's feeling of dependence upon his creator, a sense that his destiny is fixed by a being greater than himself. At the bottom of it there is a conviction that the universe is governed by superhuman persons, that the daily visible

life of the world is constitutionally subject to the laws
and the will of an invisible government. What the
thinkers of the Middle Ages did was to work out in
elaborate detail and in grandiose style the constitutional
system under which supernatural government operates. It
is not fanciful, and I hope not irreverent, to suggest that
the great debates about the nature of the Trinity and the
Godhead were attempts to work out a theory of divine
sovereignty; that the debates about election and predesti-
nation and grace are attempts to work out a theory of
citizenship in a divine society. The essential idea which
dominates the whole speculation is man's relation to a
heavenly king.

As this idea was finally worked out by the legists and
canonists and scholastics

> every ordering of a human community must appear as a
> component part of that ordering of the world which exists
> because God exists, and every earthly group must appear
> as an organic member of that *Civitas Dei,* that God-State,
> which comprehends the heavens and the earth. Then, on
> the other hand, the eternal and other-worldly aim and
> object of every individual man must, in a directer or an
> indirecter fashion, determine the aim and object of every
> group into which he enters.
>
> But as there must, of necessity, be connection between
> the various groups, and as all of them must be connected
> with the divinely ordered Universe, we come by the further
> notion of a divinely instituted Harmony which pervades the
> Universal Whole and every part thereof. To every Being
> is assigned its place in that whole, and to every link between
> Beings corresponds a divine decree. . . .

There is no need to suppose that everyone in the Middle
Ages understood the theory, as Gierke describes it here,

in all its architectural grandeur. Nevertheless, the theory is implicit in the feeling of simple men. It is the logical elaboration of the fundamental belief that the God who governs the world is no mere abstraction made up of hazy nouns and a vague adoration, but that, as Henry Adams says, he is the feudal seigneur to whom Roland, when he was dying, could proffer "his right-hand glove" as a last act of homage, such as he might have made to Charlemagne, and could pray:

> O God the Father who has never lied,
> Who raised up Saint Lazarus from death,
> And Daniel from the lions saved,
> Save my soul from all the perils
> For the sins that in my life I did!

2. *The Doctrine of the Keys*

The theory of divine government has always presented some difficulties to human reason, as we can see even in St. Augustine, who never clearly made up his mind whether the City of God was the actual church presided over by the Bishop of Rome or whether it was an ideal and invisible congregation of the saved. But we may be sure that to plainer minds it was necessary to believe that God governs mankind through the agency of the visible church. The unsophisticated man may not be realistic, but he is literal; he would be quite incapable, we may be sure, of understanding what St. Thomas meant when he asked "why should not the same sacred letter . . . contain several senses founded on the literal?" He would accept all the senses but he would accept them all literally. And taking them literally he would have to believe that if God governs the world, he governs it, not in some obscure meaning of the term, but that he actually governs it, as a king who is mightier than Charlemagne, but not essentially unlike Charlemagne.

The disposition to believe in the rule of God depended, therefore, upon the capacity to believe in a visible church upon earth which holds its commission from God. In some form or other all simple people look to a priestly caste who make visible the divine power. Without some such actualization the human imagination falters and becomes vagrant. The Catholic Church by its splendor and its power and its universality during the Middle Ages must have made easily credible the conception of God the Ruler. It was a government exercising jurisdiction over the known world, powerful enough to depose princes, and at its head was the Pope who could prove by the evidence of Scripture that he was the successor to Peter and was the Vice-gerent of God. To ask whether this grandiose claim was in fact true is, from the point of view of this argument, to miss the point. It was believed to be true in the Middle Ages. Because it was believed, the Church flourished. Because the Church flourished, it was ever so much easier to be certain that the claim was true. When men said that God ruled the world, they had evidence as convincing as we have when we say that the President is head of the United States Government; they were convinced because they came into daily contact with God's appointees administering God's laws.

It is this concrete sense of divine government which modern men have lost, and it may well be that this is where the Reformation has exercised its most revolutionary effect. What Luther did was to destroy the pretensions not only of the Roman Catholic Church, but of any church and of any priestly class to administer God's government on earth. The Protestant reformers may not have intended to destroy as deeply as they did; the theocracies established by Calvin and Knox imply as much. But, nevertheless, when Luther succeeded in defying the Holy See by rejecting its claim that it was the exclusive agent of God, he made it impossible for any other church to set up the same claim and sustain it for any length of time.

> Now Christ says that not alone in the Church is there forgiveness of sins, but that where two or three are gathered together in His name, they shall have the right and the liberty to proclaim and promise to each other comfort and the forgiveness of sins. . . . We are not only kings and the freest of all men, but also priests forever, a dignity far higher than kingship, because by that priesthood we are worthy to appear before God, to pray for others, and to teach one another mutually the things which are of God.

This denial of the special function of the priesthood did not, of course, originate with Luther. Its historical antecedents go back to the primitive Christians; there is quotable authority for it in St. Augustine. It was anticipated by Wyclif and Huss and by many of the mystics of the Middle Ages. But Luther, possibly because the times were ripe for it, translated the denial of the authority of the priesthood into a political revolution which divided Christendom. When the Reformation was an accomplished fact, men looked out upon the world and no longer saw a single Catholic Apostolic Church as the visible embodiment of God's government. A large part of

mankind, and that an economically and politically powerful part, no longer believed that Christ gave to Simon
Peter and his successors at the Roman See the Keys of the
Kingdom of Heaven with the promise that "whatsoever
thou shalt bind on earth shall be bound in heaven: and
whatsoever thou shalt loose on earth shall be loosed in
heaven."

3. *The Logic of Toleration*

As a result of the great religious wars the governing
classes were forced to realize that unless they consented
to the policy of toleration they would be ruined. There
is no reason to suppose that except among a few idealists
toleration has ever been much admired as a principle. It
was originally, and in large measure it still is, nothing but
a practical necessity. For in its interior life no church can
wholly admit that its rivals may provide an equally good
vehicle of salvation.

Martin Luther certainly had none of the modern notion
that one church is about as good as the next. To be sure
he appealed to the right of private judgment, but he made
it plain nevertheless that in his opinion "pagans or Turks
or Jews or fake Christians" would "remain under eternal
wrath and an everlasting damnation." John Calvin let it
be known in no uncertain tone that he did not wish any
new sects in Geneva. Milton, writing his beautiful essay
on liberty, drew the line at Papists. And in our own day
the *Catholic Encyclopedia* says in the course of an eloquent argument for practical civic toleration that "as the
true God can tolerate no strange gods, the true Church
of Christ can tolerate no strange churches beside herself,

or, what amounts to the same, she can recognize none as theoretically justified." This is the ancient dogma that outside the church there is no salvation—*extra ecclesiam nulla salus*. Like many another dogma of the Roman church, it is not even in theory absolutely unbending. Thus it appears from the allocution of Pope Pius IX, *Singulari quadam* (1854), that "those who are ignorant of the true religion, if their ignorance is invincible (which means, if they have never had a chance to know the true religion) are not, in this matter, guilty of any fault in the sight of God."

As a consequence of the modern theory of religious freedom the churches find themselves in an anomalous position. Inwardly, to their communicants, they continue to assert that they possess the only complete version of the truth. But outwardly, in their civic relations with other churches and with the civil power, they preach and practice toleration. The separation of church and state involves more than a mere logical difficulty for the churchman. It involves a deep psychological difficulty for the members of the congregation. As communicants they are expected to believe without reservation that their church is the only true means of salvation; otherwise the multitude of separate sects would be meaningless. But as citizens they are expected to maintain a neutral indifference to the claims of all the sects, and to resist encroachments by any one sect upon the religious practices of the others. This is the best compromise which human wisdom has as yet devised, but it has one inevitable consequence which the superficial advocates of toleration often overlook. It is difficult to remain warmly convinced that the authority of any one sect is divine, when as a matter of daily experience all sects have to be treated alike.

The human soul is not so divided in compartments that a man can be indifferent in one part of his soul and firmly believing in another. The existence of rival sects, the visible demonstration that none has a monopoly, the habit of neutrality, cannot but dispose men against an unquestioning acceptance of the authority of one sect. So many faiths, so many loyalties, are offered to the modern man that at last none seems to him wholly inevitable and fixed in the order of the universe. The existence of many churches in one community weakens the foundation of all of them. And that is why every church in the heyday of its power proclaims itself to be catholic and intolerant.

But when there are many churches in the same community, none can make wholly good the claim that it is catholic. None has that power to discipline the individual which a universal church exercises. For, as Dr. Figgis puts it, when many churches are tolerated, "excommunication has ceased to be tyrannical by becoming futile."

4. *A Working Compromise*

If the rival churches were not compelled to tolerate one other, they could not, consistently with their own teaching, accept the prevailing theory of the public school. Under that theory the schools are silent about matters of faith, and teachers are supposed to be neutral on the issues of history and science which bear upon religion. The churches permit this because they cannot agree on the dogma they would wish to have taught. The Catholics would rather have no dogma in the schools than

Protestant dogma; the fundamentalists would rather have none than have modernist. This situation is held to be a good one. But that is only because all the alternatives are so much worse. No church can sincerely subscribe to the theory that questions of faith do not enter into the education of children.

Wherever churches are rich enough to establish their own schools, or powerful enough to control the public school, they make short work of the "godless" school. Either they establish religious schools of their own, as the Catholics and Lutherans have done, or they impose their views on the public schools as the fundamentalists have done wherever they have the necessary voting strength. The last fight of Mr. Bryan's life was made on behalf of the theory that if a majority of voters in Tennessee were fundamentalists then they had the right to make public education in Tennessee fundamentalist too. One of the standing grievances of the Catholic Church in America is that Catholics are taxed to support schools to which they cannot conscientiously send their children.

As a matter of fact non-sectarianism is a useful political phrase rather than an accurate description of what goes on in the schools. If there is teaching of science, that teaching is by implication almost always agnostic. The fundamentalists point this out, and they are quite right. The teaching of history, under a so-called non-sectarian policy, is usually, in this country, a rather diluted Protestant version of history. The Catholics are quite right when they point this out. Occasionally, it may be, a teacher of science appears who has managed to assimilate his science to his theology; now and then a Catholic history-teacher will depart from the standard textbooks to give the Catholic version of disputed events during the last few hundred years. But the chief effect of the non-sectarian policy is to weaken sectarian attachment, to wean the child from the faith of his fathers by making him feel that patriotism somehow demands that he shall not press his convictions too far, that commonsense and good-fellowship mean that he must not be too absolute. The leaders of the churches are aware of this peril. Every once in a while they make an effort to combat it. Committees composed of parsons, priests, and rabbis appear before the school boards and petition that a non-sectarian God be worshiped and the non-controversial passages of the Bible be read. They always agree that the present godless system of education diminishes the sanctions of morality and the attendance at their respective churches. But they disagree when they try to agree on the nature of a neutral God, and they have been known to dispute fiercely about a non-controversial text of the Ten Commandments. So, if the sects are evenly balanced, the practical sense of the community turns in the end against the reform.

5. *The Effect of Patriotism*

Modern governments are not merely neutral as between rival churches. They draw to themselves much of the loyalty which once was given to the churches. In fact it has been said with some truth that patriotism has many of the characteristics of an authoritative religion. Certainly it is true that during the last few hundred years there has been transferred to government a considerable part of the devotion which once sustained the churches.

In the older world the priest was a divinely commissioned agent and the prince a divinely tolerated power. But by the Sixteenth Century Melanchthon, a friend of Luther's, had denied that the church could make laws binding the conscience. Only the prince, he said, could do that. Out of this view developed the much-misunderstood but essentially modern doctrine of the divine right of kings. In its original historic setting this doctrine was a way of asserting that the civil authority, embodied in the king, derived its power not from the Pope, as God's viceroy on earth, but by direct appointment from God himself. The divine right of kings was a declaration of independence as against the authority of the church. This heresy was challenged not only by the Pope, but by the Presbyterians as well. And it was to combat the Presbyterian preachers who insisted on trying to dictate to the government that King James I wrote his *True Law of Free Monarchy*, asserting the whole doctrine of the Divine Right of Kings.

In the Religious Peace of Augsburg an even more destructive blow was struck at the ancient claim of the church that it is a universal power. It was agreed that the citizen of a state must adopt the religion of his king. *Cuius regio ejus religio.* This was not religious liberty as we understand it, but it was a supreme assertion of the civil power. Where once the church had administered religion for the multitude, and had exercised the right to depose an heretical king, it now became the prerogative

of the king to determine the religious duties of his subjects. The way was open for the modern absolute state,
a conception which would have been entirely incomprehensible to men who lived in the ages of faith.

We must here avoid using words ambiguously. When
I speak of the absolute state, I do not refer to the constitutional arrangement of powers within the state. It is
of no importance in this connection whether the absolute
power of the state is exercised by a king, a landed aristocracy, bankers and manufacturers, professional politicians, soldiers, or a random majority of voters. It does
not matter whether the right to govern is hereditary or
obtained with the consent of the governed. A state is
absolute in the sense which I have in mind when it claims
the right to a monopoly of all the force within the community, to make war, to make peace, to conscript life,
to tax, to establish and disestablish property, to define
crime, to punish disobedience, to control education, to
supervise the family, to regulate personal habits, and to
censor opinions. The modern state claims all these
powers, and in the matter of theory there is no real difference in the size of the claim between communists,
fascists, and democrats. There are lingering traces in the
American constitutional system of the older theory that
there are inalienable rights which government may not
absorb. But these rights are really not inalienable because
they can be taken away by constitutional amendment.
There is no theoretical limit upon the power of the ultimate majorities which create civil government. There
are only practical limits. They are restrained by inertia,
and by prudence, even by good will. But ultimately

and theoretically they claim absolute authority as against all foreign states, as against all churches, associations, and persons within their jurisdiction.

The victory of the civil power was not achieved everywhere at the same time. Spasmodically, with occasional setbacks, but in the long run irresistibly, the state has attained supremacy. In the feudal age the monarch was at no time sovereign. The Pope was the universal lawgiver, not only in what we should call matters of faith, but in matters of business and politics as well. As late as the beginning of the Seventeenth Century, Pope Paul V insisted that the Doge of the Venetian Republic had no right to arrest a canon of the church on the charge of flagrant immorality. When, nevertheless, the canon was arrested, the Pope laid Venice under an interdict and excommunicated the Doge and the Senate. But the Venetian Government answered that it was founded on Divine Right; its title to govern did not come from the church. In the end the Pope gave way, and "the reign of the Pope," says Dr. Figgis, "as King of Kings was over."

It was as a result of the loss of its civil power that the Roman Church evolved the modern doctrine of infallibility. This claim, as Dr. Figgis points out, is not the culmination but the (implicit) surrender of the notions embodied in the famous papal bull, *Unam Sanctam*. The Pope could no longer claim the political sovereignty of the world; he then asserted supreme rights as the religious teacher of the Catholic communion. "The Pope, from being the Lord of Lords, has become the Doctor of Doctors. From being the mother of states, the Curia has become the authoritative organ of a teaching society."

6. *The Dissolution of a Sovereignty*

Thus there has gradually been dissolving the conception that the government of human affairs is a subordinate part of a divine government presided over by God the King. In place of one church which is sovereign over all men, there are now many rival churches, rival states, voluntary associations, and detached individuals. God is no longer believed to be a universal king in the full meaning of the word king, and religious obedience is no longer the central loyalty from which all other obligations are derived. Religion has become for most modern men one phase in a varied experience; it no longer regulates their civic duties, their economic activities, their family life, and their opinions. It has ceased to have universal dominion, and is now held to be supreme only within its own domain. But there is much uncertainty as to what that domain is. In actual affairs, the religious obligations of modern men are often weaker than their social interests and generally weaker than the fiercer claims of patriotism. The conduct of the churches and of churchmen during the War demonstrated that fact overwhelmingly. They submitted willingly or unwillingly to the overwhelming force of the civil power. Against this force many men claim the right of revolution, or at least the right of passive resistance and conscientious objection. Sometimes they base their claims upon a religious precept which they hold sacred. But even in their disobedience to Caesar they are forced to acknowledge that loyalty in the modern world is complex, that it has become divided and uncertain, and that the age of faith which was absolute is gone for them. However reverent they may be when they are in their churches, they no longer feel wholly assured when they listen to the teaching that these are the words of the ministers of a heavenly king.

CHAPTER VI

LOST PROVINCES

1. *Business*

IN any scheme of things where the churches, as agents of God, assert the right to speak with authority about the conduct of life they should be able to lay down rules about the way business shall be carried on. The churches once did just that. In some degree they still attempt to do it. But the attempts have grown feebler and feebler. In the last six hundred years the churches have fought a losing battle against the emancipation of business from religious control.

The early Christian writers looked upon business as a peril to the soul. Although the church was in itself, among other things, a large business corporation, they did not countenance business enterprise. Money-making they called avarice and money-lending usury, just as they spoke of lust when they meant sexual desire. They had sound reasons of their own for this attitude. They knew from observation, perhaps even from introspection, that the desire for riches is so strong a passion that men possessed by it will devote only their odd moments to God. The objection to a business career was like the objection to fornication; it diverted the energies of the soul.

There were, no doubt, worldly reasons as well which account for the long resistance of the mediæval Church to what we now regard as the highest form of capitalistic endeavor. The Church belonged to the feudal system. The Pope and his bishops were in fact great feudal lords. They thrived best in a social order where men lived upon the land. They had a premonition that the rise of capitalism, with its large cities, its financiers, merchants, and proletarian workers, was bound to weaken the secular authority of the church and to dissolve the influence of religion in men's lives. They failed in their resistance, but surely one can hardly say that their vision was not prophetic. The drastic legislation of the church against business was enacted in the early days of capitalism; it was inspired, like the English corn laws and many another agrarian measure, by a determination to preserve a landed order of society. Thus in discussing whether money might properly be loaned out at interest Pope Innocent IV argued that if this were permitted "men would not give thought to the cultivation of their land, except when they could do naught else . . . even if they could get land to cultivate, they would not be able to get the beasts and implements for cultivating it, since the poor themselves would not have them, and the rich, both for the sake of profit and security, would put their money into usury rather than into smaller and more risky investments." The argument is the same as that which the American farmer makes when he complains that the bankers in Wall Street prefer to lend money to business men and to speculators rather than to farmers.

But the solid reasons which once inspired the church's opposition to business do not concern us here. The opposition was unsuccessful, the reasons were forgotten, and the old pronouncements against usury were looked upon as quaint and unworldly. For the new economic order which displaced feudalism, the Catholic Church, at least, had no program. It did not adapt itself readily to the spirit of commercial enterprise which captured the active minds of Northern Europe. The Protestant churches did adapt themselves and contrived to preach a gospel which encouraged, where Roman Catholicism had discouraged, the enterprising business man. They preached the divine duty of labor. "At the day of doom," said John Bunyan, "men shall be judged according to their fruits. It will not be said then, Did you Believe? But, were you Doers, or Talkers only?" As this preaching became more concrete, to be a doer meant to do work and make money. Baxter in his *Christian Directory* wrote that "if God show you a way in which you may lawfully get more than in another way (without wrong to your soul or to any other), if you refuse this, and choose the less gainful way, you cross one of the ends of your calling, and you refuse to be God's steward." Richard Steele in *The Tradesman's Calling* pointed out that the virtues enjoined on Christians—diligence, moderation, sobriety, and thrift—are the very qualities which are most needed for commercial success. For "godly wisdom . . . comes in and puts due bounds" to his expenses, "and teaches the tradesman to live rather somewhat below than at all above his income."

However edifying such doctrine may have been, it was clearly an abandonment of the right, once so eloquently asserted by the church, that it had the authority to regulate business in the interest of man's spiritual welfare. That right is still sometimes asserted. Sermons are still preached about business ethics; there are programs of Christian socialism and Christian capitalism. Churchmen still interest themselves, often very effectively, to reform some flagrant industrial abuse like the sweating of women and children. But the modern efforts to moralize business and to subordinate profit-seeking to humane ends are radically different from those of the mediæval church. They are admittedly experimental—that is to say, debatable—since they do not derive their authority from revelation. And they are presented as an appeal to reason, to conscience, to generosity, not as the commandments of God. The Council of Vienna in 1312 declared that any ruler or magistrate who sanctioned usury and compelled debtors to observe usurious contracts would be excommunicated; all laws which sanctioned money-lending at interest were to be repealed within three months. The churches do not speak in that tone of voice to-day.

Thus if an organization like the Federal Council of Churches of Christ is distressed by, let us say, the labor policy of a great corporation, it inquires courteously of the president's secretary whether it would not be possible for him to confer with a delegation about the matter. If the churchmen are granted an interview, which is never altogether certain, they have to argue with the business man on secular grounds. Were they to say that the eight-hour day was the will of God, he would conclude they were cranks, he would surreptitiously press the buzzer under his desk, and in a few moments his secretary would appear summoning him to an important board meeting. They have to argue with him, if they are to obtain a hearing, about the effect on health, efficiency, turnover, and other such matters which are worked up for them by economists. As churchmen they have kindly impulses, but there is no longer a body of doctrine in the churches which enables them to speak with authority.

The emancipation of business from religious control is perhaps even more threatening to the authority of the churches than the rivalry of sects or the rise of the civil power. Business is a daily occupation; government meets the eye of the ordinary men only now and then. That the main interest in the waking life of most people should be carried on wholly separated from the faith they profess means that the churches have lost one of the great provinces of the human soul. The sponsors of the Broadway Temple in New York City put the matter in a thoroughly modern, even if it was a rather coarse, way when they proclaimed a campaign to sell bonds as "a five percent investment in your Fellow Man's Salvation—Broadway Temple is to be a combination of Church and Skyscraper, Religion and Revenue, Salvation and 5 Percent—and the 5 percent is based on ethical Christian grounds." The five per cent, they hastened to add, was also based on a gilt-edged real-estate mortgage; the salvation, however, was, we may suppose, a speculative profit.

2. The Family

The family is the inner citadel of religious authority and there the churches have taken their most determined stand. Long after they had abandoned politics to Caesar and business to Mammon, they continued to insist upon their authority to fix the ideal of sexual relations. But here, too, the dissolution of their authority has proceeded inexorably. They have lost their exclusive right to preside over marriages. They have not been able to maintain the dogma that marriage is indissoluble. They are not able to prevent the remarriage of divorced persons. Although in many jurisdictions fornication and adultery are still crimes, there is no longer any serious attempt to enforce the statutes. The churches have failed in their insistence that sexual intercourse by married persons is a sin unless it is validated by the willingness to beget a child. Except to the poorest and most ignorant the means of preventing conception are available to all. There is no longer any compulsion to regard the sexual life as within the jurisdiction of the commissioners of the Lord.

Religious teachers knew long ago what modern psychologists have somewhat excitedly rediscovered: that there is a very intimate connection between the sexual life and the religious life. Only men living in a time when religion has lost so much of its inward vitality could be shocked at this simple truth, for the churches, when their inspiration was fresh, have always known it. That is why they have laid such tremendous emphasis upon the religious control of sexual experience, have extolled chastity, have preached continence after marriage except where parenthood was in view, have inveighed against fornication, adultery, divorce, and all unprocreative indulgence, have insisted that marriages be celebrated within the communion, have upheld the parental authority over children. They were not prudish. That is a state of mind which marks the decay of vigorous determination to control the sexual life. The early teachers did not avert their eyes. They did not mince their words. For they knew what they were doing.

Men like St. Paul and St. Augustine knew in the most direct way what sexual desire can do to distract the religious life; how if it is not sternly regulated, and if it is allowed to run wild, it intoxicates the whole personality to the exclusion of spiritual interests. They knew, too, although perhaps not quite so explicitly, that these same passions, if they are repressed and redirected, may come forth as an ecstasy of religious devotion. They were not reformers. They did not think of progress. They did not suppose that the animal in man could somehow be refined until it was no longer animal. When Paul spoke of the law of his members warring against the law of his mind, and bringing him into captivity to the law of sin, he had made a realistic observation which any candid person can verify out of his own experience. There was no vague finical nonsense about this war of the members against the inward man seeking delight in the law of God.

If the sexual impulse were not deeply related to the religious life, the preoccupation of churchmen with it throughout the ages would be absurd. They have not been preoccupied in any comparable degree with the other physiological functions of the body. They have concerned themselves somewhat with eating and drinking, for gluttony and drunkenness can also distract men from religion. But hunger and thirst are minor passions, far more easily satisfied than lust, and in no way so pervasive and imperious. The world, the flesh, and the devil may usually be taken to mean sexual desire. Around it, then, the churches have built up a ritual, to dominate it lest they be dominated by it. Tenaciously and with good reason they have fought against surrendering their authority.

With equally great insight they have kept the closest possible association with family life especially during the childhood of the offspring. Here again they anticipated by many long ages the discoveries of modern psychologists. They have always known that it is in the earliest years, before puberty, that tradition is transmitted. Much is learned after puberty, but in childhood education is more than mere learning. There education is the growth of the disposition, the fixing of the prejudices to which all later experience is cumulative. In childhood men acquire the forms of their seeing, the prototypes of their feeling, the style of their character. There presumably the very pattern of authority itself is implanted by habit, fitted to the model presented by the child's parents. There the assumption is fixed that there are wiser and stronger beings whom, in the nature of things, one must obey. There the need to obey is fixed. There the whole drift of experience is such as to make credible the idea that above the child there is the father, above the father a king and the wise men, above them all a heavenly Father and King.

It is plain that any change which disturbs the constitution of the home will tend profoundly to alter the child's sense of what he may expect the constitution of the universe to be. There are many disturbing changes of which none is more important surely than the emancipation of women. The God of popular religion has usually been an elderly male. There have been some female divinities worshipped in different parts of the world as there have been matriarchal societies. But by and large the imagination of men has conceived God as a father. They have magnified to a cosmic scale what they had seen at home. It was the male who created the child. It was his seed that the mother cherished in her womb. It was the male who provided for the needs of the family, even if the woman did the hard work. It was the male who fended off enemies. It was the male who laid down the law. It was the name of the male parent which was preserved and passed on from generation to generation. Everything conspired to fix the belief that the true order of life was a hierarchy with a man at the apex.

This general notion becomes less and less credible as women assert themselves. The child of the modern household is soon made to see that there are at least two persons who can give him orders, and that they do not always give him the same ones. This does not educate him to believe that there is one certain guide to conduct in the universe. There are likely to be two guides to conduct in his universe, as women insist that they are independent personalities with minds of their own. This insistence, moreover, tends rather to disarrange the notion that the father is the creator of the child. An observant youngster, especially in these days of frank talk about sex, soon becomes aware of the fact that the role of the male in procreation is a relatively minor one. But most disturbing of all is the very modern household in which the woman earns her own living. For here the child is deprived of the opportunity, which is so conducive to belief in authority, of seeing daily that even his mother is dependent upon a greater person for the good things in life.

Although women, by and large, are by no means able to earn as much money as men, the fact which counts is that they can earn enough to support themselves. They may not actually support themselves. But the knowledge that they could, as it becomes an accepted idea in society, has revolutionary consequences. In former times the woman was dependent upon her husband for bed, board, shelter, and clothing. Her whole existence was determined by her mating; her sexual experience was an integral part of her livelihood and her social position. But once it had become established that a woman could live without a husband, the intimate connection between her sex and her career began to dissolve.

The invention of dependable methods of preventing conception has carried this dissolution much further. Birth control has separated the sexual act from the whole series of social consequences which were once probable if not inevitable. For with the discovery that children need be born only when they are wanted, the sexual experience has become increasingly a personal and private affair. It was once an institutional affair—for the woman. For the man, from time immemorial, there have been two sorts of sexual experience—one which had no public consequences, and one which entailed the responsibilities of a family. The effect of the modern changes, particularly of woman's economic independence and of birth control, is to equalize the freedom and the obligations of men and women.

That the sexual life has become separated from parenthood and that therefore it is no longer subject to external regulation, is evident. While the desires of men and women for each other were links in a chain which included the family and the household and children, authority, and by that token religious authority, could hope to fix the sex-

ual ideal. When the chain broke, and love had no consequences which were not too subtle for the outsider to
measure, the ideal of love was fixed not by the church
in the name of God, but by prudence, convention, the
prevailing rules of hygiene, by taste, circumstances, and
personal sensibility.

3. *Art*

(*a*) *The Disappearance of Religious Painting*

To walk through a museum of Western European art is
to behold a peculiarly vivid record of how the great
themes of popular religion have ceased to inspire the imagination of modern men. One can visualize there the whole
story of the dissolution of the ancestral order and of our
present bewilderment. One can see how toward the close
of the Fifteenth Century the great themes illustrating the
reign of a heavenly king and of the drama of man's salvation had ceased to be naively believed; how at the close
of the next century which witnessed the Reformation and
the Counter-Reformation, the beginnings of modern
science, the growth of cities, and the rise of capitalism,
religious painting ceased to be the concern of the best
painters; and finally how in the last hundred years
painters have illustrated by feverish experimentation the
modern man's effort to find an adequate substitute for the
organizing principle of the religion which he has lost.

It has been said by way of explanation that painters
must sell their work, and they must, therefore, paint what
the rich and powerful will buy. Thus it is pointed out that
in the Middle Ages they worked under the patronage of
the Church; in the Renaissance their patrons were pagan-

ized princes and popes, and artists made pictures which, even when the theme was religious, were no longer Christian in spirit. Later in the north of Europe the bourgeoisie acquired money and station, and the Dutch painters did their portraits, and made faithful representations of their kitchens and their parlors. A little later French painters at the Court of Versailles made pictures for courtiers, and in our time John Sargent painted the wives of millionaires. To say all this is to say that the ruling classes in the modern world are no longer interested in pictures which illustrate or are inspired by the religion they profess.

This attempt at an explanation in terms of supply and demand may or may not be sound for the ordinary run of painters. It leaves out of account, however, those very painters who are the most significant and interesting. It leaves out of account the painters who, by heroic refusal to supply the existing market, deserve universal respect, and in many cases have won an ultimate public vindication. These men do not fit into the theory of supply and demand, for they endured poverty and derision in order to paint what they most wanted to paint. They are not of the tribe, which Mr. Walter Pach calls Ananias, who betray the truth that is in them. But for that truth they did not draw upon the themes nor the sense of life which almost all of them must have been taught when they were children. They did not paint religious pictures. They painted landscapes, streets, interiors, still life, heads, persons, nudes. Whatever else they perceived and tried to express, they did not see their objects in the perspective of human destiny and divine government. There is no reason, then, to say that religious painting, even in the broadest sense of the term, has disappeared because there is no effective demand for it. Obviously it has disappeared because the will to produce it has disappeared.

(b) The Loss of a Heritage

In setting the religious tradition aside as something with which they are not concerned when they are at work, artists are merely behaving like modern men. It is plain that the religious tradition has become progressively less relevant to anyone who as painter or sculptor is engaged in making images. This is a direct result of that increasing sophistication of religious thought which was signalized in Europe by the iconoclasm of the Protestant reformers and the puritanism of the Catholic Counter-Reformation. Before the acids of modernity had begun to dissolve the organic reality of the ancient faith, there was no difficulty about picturing God the Father as a patriarch and the Virgin Mary as a young blonde Tuscan mother. There was no disposition to disbelieve, and so the imagination was at once nourished by a great heritage of ideas and yet free to elaborate it. But when the authority of the old beliefs was challenged, a great literature of controversy and definition was let loose upon the world. And from the point of view of the artist the chief effect of this effort to argue and to state exactly, to defend and to rebut, was to substitute concepts for pictorial ideas. When the nature of God became a matter of definition, it was obviously crude and illiterate to represent him as a benign old man. Thus the more the theologians refined the dogmas of their religion the more impossible they made it for painters to express its significance. No painter who ever lived could make a picture which expressed the religion of the Rev. Harry Emerson Fosdick. There is nothing there which the visual imagination can use.

Painters have, therefore, a rather better reason than most men for having turned their backs upon the religious tradition. They can say with a clear conscience that the contemporary churches have removed from that tradition those very qualities which once made it an inexhaustible source of artistic inspiration. They need only point to modern religious writing in their own support: at its best it has the qualities of an impassioned argument and more often it is intolerably flat and vague because in our intellectual climate skepticism dissolves the concreteness of the imagery and leaves behind sonorous adjectives and opaque nouns.

The full effects of this separation of the artist from the ancient traditions of Christendom have been felt only in the last two or three generations. It is no doubt true that the modern disbelief had its beginnings many generations ago, perhaps in the Fifteenth Century, but the momentum of the ancient faith was so great that it took a long time, even after corrosive doubt had started, before its influence came to an end. The artists of the Seventeenth and Eighteenth Centuries may not have been devout, but they lived in a society in which the forms of the old order, the hierarchy of classes, the sense of authority, and the general fund of ideas about human destiny, still had vast prestige. But in the Nineteenth Century that old order was almost completely dissolved and the prestige of its ideas destroyed. The artist of the last two or three generations has confronted the world without any accepted understanding of human life. He has had to improvise his own understanding of life. That is a new thing in the experience of artists.

(c) The Artist Formerly

In 787 the Second Council of Nicæa laid down the rule which for nearly five hundred years was binding upon the artists of Christendom:

> The substance of religious scenes is not left to the initiative of the artists: it derives from the principles laid down by the Catholic Church and religious tradition. . . . His art alone belongs to the painter, its organization and arrangement belong to the clergy.

This was a reasonable rule, since the Church and not the individual was held to be the guardian of those sacred truths upon which depended the salvation of souls and the safety of society. The notion had occurred to nobody that the artist was divinely inspired and knew more than the doctors of the church. Therefore, the artist was given careful specifications as to what he was to represent.

Thus when the Church of St. Urban of Troyes decided to order a set of tapestries illustrating the story of St. Valerian and of his wife, St. Cecilia, a learned priest was deputed to draw up the contract for the artist. In it he wrote among other specifications that: "there shall be portrayed a place and a tabernacle in the manner of a beautiful room, in which there shall be St. Cecilia, humbly on her knees with her hands joined, praying to God. And beside her shall be Valerian expressing great admiration and watching an angel which, being above their heads, should be holding two crowns made of lilies and of roses,

which he will be placing the one on the head of St. Cecilia
and the other on the head of Valerian, her husband. . . ."

The rest, one might suppose, was left to the artist's
imagination. But it was not. Having been given his subject matter and his theme, he was bound further by strict
conventions as to how sacred subjects were to be depicted.
Jesus on the Cross had to be shown with his mother on
the right and St. John on the left. The centurion pierced
his left side. His nimbus contained a cross, as the mark
of divinity, whereas the saints had the nimbus without a
cross. Only God, the angels, Jesus Christ, and the Apostles
could be represented with bare feet; it was heretical to depict the Virgin or the Saints with bare feet. The purpose
of these conventions was to help the spectator identify the
figures in the picture. Thus St. Peter was given a short
beard and a tonsure; St. Paul was bald and had a long
beard. It is possible that these conventions, which were
immensely intricate, were actually codified in manuals
which were passed on from master to apprentice in the
workshops.

As a general rule the ecclesiastics who drew up specifications did not invent the themes. Thus the learned priest
who drafted the contract for the tapestry of St. Cecilia drew
his material from the encyclopedia of Vincent de Beau-
vais. This was a compendium of universal knowledge
covering the whole of history from Creation to the Last
Judgment. It was a source book to which any man could
turn in order to find the truth he happened to need. It
contained all of human knowledge and the answer to all
human problems. By the Thirteenth Century there were
a number of these encyclopedias, of which the greatest was

the *Summa* of St. Thomas Aquinas. From these books churchmen took the themes which they employed their artists to embellish. The artist himself had no concern as to what he would paint, nor even as to how he would paint it. That was given, and his energies could be employed without the travail of intellectual invention, upon the task of expressing a clear conception in well-established forms.

It must not be supposed, of course, that either doctrines, lore, or symbolism were uniformly standardized and exactly enforced. In an age of faith, contradictions and discrepancies are not evident; they are merely variations on the same theme. Thus, while it may be true that en-thusiastic mediævalists like M. Mâle have exaggerated the order and symmetry of the mediæval tradition, they are right, surely, on the main point, which is that the or-ganic character of the popular religion provided a con-sensus of feeling about human destiny which, in conjunc-tion with the resources of the popular lore, sustained and organized the imagination of mediæval artists. Because religious faith was simple and genuine, it could absorb and master almost anything. Thus the clergy ruled the artists with a relatively light hand, and they were not disturbed if, in illuminating the pages of a Book of Hours, the artist adorned the margins with a picture of Bacchus or the love of Pyramus and Thisbe.

It was only when the clergy had been made self-con-scious by the controversies which raged around the Refor-mation that they began in any strict and literally-minded modern sense to enforce the rule laid down at Nicæa in 787. At the Council of Trent in 1563 the great liberty of the artist within the Christian tradition came to an end:

The Holy Council forbids the placing in a church of any image which calls to mind an erroneous dogma which might mislead the simple-minded. It desires that all impurity be avoided, that provocative qualities be not given to images. In order to insure respect for its decisions, the Holy Council forbids anyone to place or to have placed anywhere, and even in churches which are not open to the public, any unusual image unless the bishop has approved it.

In theory this decree at Trent is not far removed from the decree at Nicæa nearly one thousand years earlier. But in fact it is a whole world removed from it. For the dogmas at Nicæa rested upon naive faith and the dogmas at Trent rested upon definition. The outcome showed the difference, for within a generation Catholic scholars made a critical survey of the lore which mediæval art had employed, and on grounds of taste, doctrine, and the like, condemned the greater part of it. After that, as M. Mâle says, there might still be artists who were Christians but there was no longer a Christian art.

(d) The Artist as Prophet

Whether the necessity of creating his own tradition is a good or a bad thing for the artist, there can be no doubt that it is a novel thing and a burdensome one. Artists have responded to it by proclaiming one of two theories: they have said that the artist, being a genius, was a prophet; when they did not say that, they said that religion, morality, and philosophy were irrelevant, and that art should be practiced for art's sake. Both theories are obviously attempts to find some personal substitute for those traditions upon which artists in all other ages have been dependent.

The theory of the artist as prophet has this serious defect: there is practically no evidence to support it. Why should there be? What connection is there between the capacity to make beautiful objects and the capacity to discover truth? Surely experience shows that it is something of a marvel when a great artist appears who, like Leonardo or Goethe, is also an original and important thinker. Indeed, it is reasonable to ask whether the analysis and abstraction which thinking involves are not radically different psychological processes from the painter's passionate appreciation of the appearance of things. Certainly to think as physicists think is to strip objects of all their secondary characters, not alone of their emotional significance, but of their color, their texture, their fragrance, and even of their superficial forms. The world as we know it through our senses has completely disappeared before the physicist begins to think about it. And in its place there is a collection of concepts which have no pictorial value whatsoever. These concepts are by definition incapable of being visualized, and when as a concession to human weakness, his own or his pupil's, the scientist constructs a mechanical model to illustrate an idea, this model is at best a crude analogy, and in no real sense the portrait of that idea.

Thus when Shelley made Earth say:

> I spin beneath my pyramid of night,
> Which points into the heavens . . .

he borrowed an image from astronomy. But this image, which is, I think, superb poetry, radically alters the original scientific idea, for it introduces into a realm of purely physical relations the notion of a gigantic spectator with a vastly magnified human eye. There are, no doubt, many other concepts in science which, if poets knew more science, would lend themselves to translation into equally noble images. But these images would not state the scientific truth.

The current belief that artists are prophets is an inheritance from the time when science had no critical method of its own, and poets, being reflective persons, had at least as good a chance as anyone else of stumbling upon truths which were subsequently verified. It is due in some measure also to the human tendency to remember the happy guesses of poets and to forget their unhappy ones, a tendency which has gone far to sustain the reputations of fortune-tellers, oracles, and stockbrokers. But above all, the reputation of the artist as one who must have wisdom is sustained by a rather genial fallacy: he finds expression for the feelings of the spectator, and the spectator rather quickly assumes that the artist has found an explanation for the world.

Yet unless I am greatly mistaken the modern painter has ceased not only to depict any theory of destiny but has ceased to express any important human mood in the presence of destiny. One goes to a museum and comes out feeling that one has beheld an odd assortment of nude bodies, copper kettles, oranges, tomatoes, and zinnias, babies, street corners, apple trees, bathing-beaches, bankers, and fashionable ladies. I do not say that this person or that may not find a picture immensely significant to him. But the general impression for anyone, I think, is of a chaos of anecdotes, perceptions, fantasies, and little commentaries, which may be all very well in their way, but are not sustaining and could readily be dispensed with.

The conclusive answer to the romantic theory of the artist as prophet is a visit to a collection of modern paintings.

(e) Art for Art's Sake

This brings us to the other theory, which is that art has nothing to do with prophecy, wisdom, and the meaning of life, but has to do only with art. This theory must command an altogether different kind of respect than the sentimental theory of the artist as prophet. This indeed is the theory which most artists now hold. "I am convinced," says Mr. R. H. Wilenski in his book *The Modern Movement in Art,* "that all the most intelligent artists of Western Europe in recent centuries have been tormented by this search for a justification of their work and a criterion of its value; and that almost all such artists have attempted to solve the problem by some consciously-held idea of art; or in other words that in place of art justified by service to a religion they have sought to evolve an art justified by service to an idea of art itself."

The instinct of artists in this matter is, I think, much sounder than the rationalizations which they have constructed. As working artists they do not think of themselves as seers, philosophers, or moralists. They do not wish to be judged as thinkers, but as painters, and they are justifiably impatient with the Philistines who are interested primarily in the subject matter and its human significance. The painter knows quite well that in the

broadly human sense he has no special qualifications as
story-teller or wise man. What he is driving at, therefore, in his expression of contel t for the subject matter
of art is the wish that he might again be in the position
of the mediæval artist who did not have to concern himself
as artist with the significance of his themes. The intuition behind the theory of art for art's sake is the artist's
wish to be free of a responsibility which he has never
before had put upon him. The peculiar circumstances of
modernity have thrust upon him, much against his will
and regardless of his aptitudes, the intolerably heavy burden of doing for himself what in other ages was done
for him by tradition and authority.

The philosophy which he has invented is an attempt to
prove that no philosophy is necessary. Carried to its conclusion, this theory eventuates in the belief that painting
must become an arrangement of forms and colors which
have no human connotation whatsoever for the artist or
the spectator. These arrangements represent nothing in
the real world. They signify nothing. They are an
esthetic artifice in the same sense that the more esoteric
geometries are logical artifices. This much can at least
be said of them: they are a consistent effort to practice
the arts in a world where there is no human tradition
upon which the representative arts can draw.

This absolute estheticism is not, however, art without
philosophy. Some sort of philosophy is implied in all
human activity. The artist who says that it is delightful
above all other things to realize the pure form of objects,
regardless of whether this object is a saint, a lovely
woman, or a dish of fruit, has made a very important

statement about life. He has said that the ordinary meanings which men attach to objects are of no consequence, that their order of moral values is ultimately a delusion, that all facts are equally good and equally bad, and that to contemplate anything, it does not matter what, under the aspect of its esthetic form, is to realize all that the artist can give.

This, too, is a philosophy and a very radical philosophy at that. It is in fact just the philosophy which men were bound to construct for themselves in an age when the traditional theory of the purpose of life had lost its meaning for them. For they are saying that experience has no meaning beyond that which each man can find in the intense realization of each passing moment. He must fail, they would feel, if he attempts to connect these passing moments into a coherent story of his whole experience, let alone the whole experience of the human race. For experience has no underlying significance, man himself has no station in the universe, and the universe has no plan which is more than a drift of circumstances, illuminated here and there by flashes of self-consciousness.

(f) The Burden of Originality

As a matter of fact this doctrine is merely the esthetic version of the rather crude mechanistic materialism which our grandfathers thought was the final conclusion of science. The connection is made evident in the famous Conclusions to The Renaissance which Walter Pater wrote in 1868, and then omitted from the second edition because "it might possibly mislead some of those young men into whose hands it might fall." In this essay there was the startling, though it is now hackneyed, assertion that "to burn always with this hard, gem-like flame, to maintain this ecstasy, is success in life," and that "of this wisdom, the poetic passion, the desire of beauty, the love of art for art's sake, has most; for art comes to you professing frankly to give nothing but the highest quality to your moments as they pass, and simply for those moments' sake." What is never quoted, and is apparently forgotten, is the reasoning by which Pater arrived at the conclusion that momentary ecstasy is the end and aim of life. It is, if we turn back a few pages, that scientific analysis has reduced everything to a mere swarm of whirling atoms, upon which consciousness discerns impressions that are "unstable, flickering, inconsistent." It was out of this misunderstanding of the nature of scientific concepts that Pater developed his theory of art for the moment's sake.

I dwell upon this only in order to show that what appeared to be an estheticism divorced from all human concern was really a somewhat casual by-product of a fashionable misunderstanding at the time Pater was writing. We should find that to-day equally far-reaching conclusions are arrived at by half-understood popularizations of Bergson or Freud. I venture to believe that any theory of art is inevitably implicated in some philosophy of life, and that the only question is whether the artist is conscious or unconscious of the theory he is acting upon. For unless the artist deals with purely logical essences, provided he observes and perceives anything in the outer world, no matter how he represents it or symbolizes it or comments upon it, there must be implicit in it some attitude toward the meaning of existence. If his conclusion is that human existence has no meaning, that, too, is an attitude toward the meaning of existence. The mediæval artist worked on much less tangled premises. He painted pictures which illustrated the great hopes and fears of Christendom. But he did not himself attempt to formulate those hopes and fears. He accepted them more or less ready-made, understanding them and believing in them because, as a child of his age, they were his hopes and fears. But because they existed and were there for him to work upon, he could put his whole energy into realizing them passionately. The modern artist would like to have the same freedom from preoccupation, but he cannot have it. He has first to decide what it is that he shall passionately realize.

In effect the mediæval artist was reproducing a story that had often been told before. But the modern artist has to undergo a whole preliminary labor of inventing, creating, formulating, for which there was almost no counterpart in the life of a mediæval artist. The modern artist has to be original. That is to say, he has to seize experience, pick it over, and drag from it his theme. It is a very exhausting task, as anyone can testify who has tried it.

That surely is why we hear so much of the storm and stress in the soul of a modern artist. The craftsman does not go through agonies over the choice of words, images, and rhythms. The agony of the modern artist lies in the effort to give birth to the idea, to bring some intuition of order out of the chaos of experience, to create the idea with which his art can deal. We assume, quite falsely I think, that this act of 'creation' is an inherent part of the artist's task. But if we refrain from using words loosely, and reserve the word creation to mean the finding of the original intuition and idea, then creation is plainly not a necessary part of the artist's equipment. Creation is an obligation which the artist has had thrust upon him as a result of the dissolution of the great accepted themes. He is compelled to be creative because his world is chaotic.

This labor of creation has no connection with his gifts as a painter. There is no more reason why a painter should be able to extemporize a satisfactory interpretation of life than that he should be able to govern a city or write a treatise on chemistry. Giotto surely was as profoundly original a painter as the world is likely to see; it has been said of him by Mr. Berenson, who has full title to speak, that he had "a thoroughgoing sense for the significant in the visible world." But with all his genius, what would have been Giotto's plight if, in addition to exercising his sense of the significant, he had had to create for himself all his standards of significance? For Giotto those standards existed in the Catholic Christianity of the Thirteenth Century, and it was by the measure of these standards, within the framework of a great accepted tradition, that he followed his own personal sense of the significant. But the modern artist, though he had Giotto's gifts, would not have Giotto's freedom to use them. A very large part of his energies, consciously or unconsciously, would have to be spent in devising some sort of substitute for the traditional view of life which Giotto took for granted. For there is no longer an accepted view of life organized in stories which all men know and understand.

There is instead a profusion of creeds and philosophies, fads and intellectual experiments among which the modern painter, like every other modern man, finds himself trying to choose a philosophy of life. Everybody is somewhat dithered by these choices: the business of being a Shavian one year, a Nietzschean the next, a Bergsonian the third, then of being a patriot for the duration of the war, and after that a Freudian, is not conducive to the serene exercise of a painter's talents. For these various philosophies which the artist picks up here and there, or by which he is oftener than not picked up and carried along, are immensely in dispute. They are not clear. They are rather personal and somewhat accidental visions of the world. They are essentially unpictorial because they originate in science and are incomplete, abstracted reachings for the meaning of things. As a result the art in which they are implicit is often uninteresting, and usually unintelligible, to those who do not happen to belong to the same cult.

The painter can hardly expect to invent for himself a view of life which will bring order out of the chaos of modernity. Yet he is compelled to try, for he is engaged in setting down a vision of the world, and every vision of the world implies some sort of philosophy. The effects of the modern emancipation are more clearly evident in the history of painting during the last hundred years than in almost any other activity, because in the galleries hang in frames the successive attempts of men, who are deeply immersed in the modern scene, to set down their statements about life. Mr. Wilenski, who is an astute and well-informed critic, has estimated that during the last hundred years in Paris a new movement in painting has been inaugurated every ten years. That would correspond fairly accurately to the birth and death of new philosophies in the advanced and most emancipated circles.

What was happening to painting is precisely what has happened to all the other separated activities of men. Each activity has its own ideal, indeed a succession of ideals, for with the dissolution of the supreme ideal of service to God, there is no ideal which unites them all, and sets them in order. Each ideal is supreme within a sphere of its own. There is no point of reference outside which can determine the relative value of competing ideals. The modern man desires health, he desires money, he desires power, beauty, love, truth, but which he shall desire the most since he cannot pursue them all to their logical conclusions, he no longer has any means of deciding. His impulses are no longer parts of one attitude toward life; his ideals are no longer in a hierarchy under one lordly ideal. They have become differentiated. They are free and they are incommensurable.

The religious synthesis has dissolved. The modern man no longer holds a belief about the universe which sustains a pervasive emotion about his destiny; he no longer believes genuinely in any idea which organizes his interests within the framework of a cosmic order.

CHAPTER VII

THE DRAMA OF DESTINY

1. *The Soul in the Modern World*

THE effect of modernity, then, is to specialize and thus to intensify our separated activities. Once all things were phases of a single destiny: the church, the state, the family, the school were means to the same end; the rights and duties of the individual in society, the rules of morality, the themes of art, and the teachings of science were all of them ways of revealing, of celebrating, of applying the laws laid down in the divine constitution of the universe. In the modern world institutions are more or less independent, each serving its own proximate purpose, and our culture is really a collection of separate interests each sovereign within its own realm. We do not put shrines in our workshops, and we think it unseemly to talk business in the vestibule of a church. We dislike politics in the pulpit and preaching from politicians. We do not look upon our scholars as priests or upon our priests as learned men. We do not expect science to sustain theology, nor religion to dominate art. On the contrary we insist with much fervor on the separation of church and state, of religion and science, of politics and historical research, of morality and art, of business and love. This separation of activities has its counterpart in a separation of selves; the life of a modern man is not so much the history of a single soul; it is rather a play of many characters within a single body.

That may be why the modern autobiographical novel usually runs to two volumes; the author requires more space to explain how his various personalities came to be what they were at each little crisis of adolescence and of middle age than St. Augustine, St. Thomas à Kempis, and St. Francis put together needed in order to describe their whole destiny in this world and the next. No doubt we are rather long-winded and tiresome about the complexities of our souls. But from the knowledge that we are complex there is no escape.

The modern man is unable any longer to think of himself as a single personality approaching an everlasting judgment. He is one man to-day and another to-morrow, one person here and another there. He does not feel he knows himself. He is sure that no one else knows him at all. His motives are intricate, and not wholly what they seem. He is moved by impulses which he feels but cannot describe. There are dark depths in his nature which no one has ever explored. There are splendors which are unreleased. He has become greatly interested in his moods. The precise nuances of his likes and dislikes have become very important. There is no telling just what he is or what he may become, but there is a certain breathless interest in having one of his selves watch and comment upon the mischief and the frustrations of his other selves. The problems of his character have become dissociated from any feeling that they involve his immortal destiny. They have become dissociated from the feeling that they deeply matter. From the feeling that they are deeply his own. From the feeling that there is any personality to own them. There they are: his inferiority complex and mine, your sadistic impulse and Tom Jones's, Anna's father fixation, and little Willie's pyromania.

The thoroughly modern man has really ceased to believe that there is an immortal essence presiding like a king over his appetites. The word 'soul' has become a figure of speech, which he uses loosely, sometimes to mean his tenderer aspirations, sometimes to mean the whole collection of his impulses, sometimes, when he is in a hurry, to mean nothing at all. It is certainly not the fashion any longer to think of the soul as a little lord ruling the turbulent rabble of his carnal passions; the constitutional form in popular psychology to-day is republican. Each impulse may invoke the Bill of Rights, and have its way if the others will let it. As Bertrand Russell has put it: "A single desire is no better and no worse, considered in isolation, than any other; but a group of desires is better than another group if all of the first group can be satisfied, while in the second group some are inconsistent with others," but since, unhappily as is usually the case, desires are extremely inconsistent, the uttermost that the modern man can say is that the victory must go to the strongest desires. Morality thus becomes a traffic code designed to keep as many desires as possible moving together without too many violent collisions. When men insist that morality is more than that, they are quickly denounced, in general correctly, as Meddlesome Matties, as enemies of human liberty, or as schemers trying to get the better of their fellow men. Morality, conceived as a discipline to fit men for heaven, is resented; morality, conceived as a discipline for happiness, is understood by very few. The objective moral certitudes have dissolved, and in the liberal philosophy there is nothing to take their place.

2. *The Great Scenario*

The modern world is like a stage on which a stupendous play has just been presented. Many who were in the audience are still spellbound, and as they pass out into the street, the scenario of the drama still seems to them the very clue and plan of life. In the prologue the earth was without form and void, and darkness was upon the face of the deep. Then at the command of God the sun, the moon, the stars, the earth, its plants and its animals, then man, and after him woman, were created. And in the epilogue the blessed were living in the New Jerusalem, a city of pure gold like clear glass, with walls laid on foundations of precious stones. Between the darkness that preceded creation and the glory of this heavenly city which had no need of the sun, a plot was unfolded which constitutes the history of mankind. In the beginning man was perfect. But the devil tempted him to eat the forbidden fruit, and as a punishment God banished him from paradise, and laid upon him and his descendants the curse of labor and of death.

But in meting out this punishment, God in his mercy promised ultimately to redeem the children of Adam. From among them he chose one tribe who were to be the custodians of this promise. And then in due time he sent his Son, born of a Virgin, to teach the gospel of salvation, and to expiate the sin of Adam upon a cross.

Those who believed in this gospel and followed its commandments, would at the final day of reckoning enter into the heavenly Jerusalem; the rest would be consigned to the devil and his everlasting torments.

Into this marvelous story the whole of human history and of human knowledge could be fitted, and only in accordance with it could they be understood. This was the key to existence, the answer to doubt, the solace for pain, and the guarantee of happiness. But to many who were in the audience it is now evident that they have seen a play, a magnificent play, one of the most sublime ever created by the human imagination, but nevertheless a play, and not a literal account of human destiny. They know it was a play. They have lingered long enough to see the scene-shifters at work. The painted drop is half rolled up; some of the turrets of the celestial city can still be seen, and part of the choir of angels. But behind them, plainly visible, are the struts and gears which held in place what under a gentler light looked like the boundaries of the universe. They are only human fears and human hopes, and bits of antique science and half-forgotten history, and symbols here and there of experiences through which some in each generation pass.

Conceivably men might once again imagine another drama which was as great as the epic of the Christian Bible. But like *Paradise Lost* or *Faust,* it would remain a work of the imagination. While the intellectual climate in which we live is what it is, while we continue to be as conscious as we are of how our own minds work, we could not again accept naively such a gorgeous fable of our destiny. Yet only five hundred years ago the whole of Christendom believed that this story was literally and objectively true. God was not another name for the evolutionary process, or for the sum total of the laws of nature, or for a compendium of all noble things, as he is in modernist accounts of him; he was the ruler of the universe, an omnipotent, magical King, who felt, who thought, who remembered and issued his commands. And because there was such a God, whose plan was clearly revealed in all its essentials, human life had a definite meaning, morality had a certain foundation, men felt themselves to be living within the framework of a universe which they called divine because it corresponded with their deepest desires.

If we ask ourselves why it is impossible for us to sum up the meaning of existence in a great personal drama, we have to begin by remembering that every great story of this kind must assume that the universe is governed by forces which are essentially of the same order as the promptings of the human heart. Otherwise it would not greatly interest us. A story, however plausible, about beings who had no human qualities, a plot which unfolded itself as utterly indifferent to our own personal fate, would not serve as a substitute for the Christian epic. This is the trouble with the so-called religion of creative evolution: even if it is true, which is far from certain, it is so profoundly indifferent to our individual fate, that it leaves most men cold. For there are very few who are so mystical as to be able to sink themselves wholly in the hidden purposes of an unconscious natural force. This, too, as the Catholic Church has always insisted, is the trouble with pantheistic religion, for if everything is divine, then nothing is peculiarly divine, and all the distinctions of good and evil are meaningless.

The story must not only assume that human ideals inspire the whole creation, but it must contain guarantees that this is so. There must be no doubt about it. Science must confirm the moral assumptions; the highest and most certain available knowledge must clinch the conviction that the story unfolded is the secret of life.

3. *Earmarks of Truth*

Religious teachers who were close to the people have always understood that they must perform wonders if they were to make their God convincing and their own title to speak for him valid. The writer of Exodus, for example, was quite clear in his mind about this:

> And Moses answered and said, But, behold, they will not believe me, nor hearken unto my voice: for they will say, The Lord hath not appeared unto thee.
>
> And the Lord said unto him, What is that in thine hand? And he said, A rod.
>
> And he said, Cast it on the ground. And he cast it on the ground, and it became a serpent; and Moses fled from before it.
>
> And the Lord said unto Moses, Put forth thine hand, and take it by the tail. And he put forth his hand, and caught it, and it became a rod in his hand:
>
> That they may believe that the Lord God of their fathers, the God of Abraham, the God of Isaac, and the God of Jacob, hath appeared unto thee.

Even in the wildest flights of his fancy the common man is almost always primarily interested in the prosaic consequences. If he believes in fairies he is not likely to imagine them as spirits inhabiting a world apart, but as little people who do things which affect his own affairs. The common man is an unconscious pragmatist: he believes because he is satisfied that his beliefs change the course of events. He would not be inspired to worship a god who merely contemplates the universe, or a god who created it once, and then rested, while its destiny unfolds itself inexorably. To the plain people religion is not disinterested speculation but a very practical matter. It is concerned with their well-being in this world and in an equally concrete world hereafter. They have wanted to know the will of God because they had to know it if they were to put themselves right with the king of creation.

Those who professed to know God's will had to demonstrate that they knew it. This was the function of miracles. They were tangible evidence that the religious teacher had a true commission. "Then those men, when they had seen the miracle (of the loaves and the fishes) that Jesus did, said, This is of a truth that prophet that should come into the world." When Jesus raised the dead man at the gate of the city of Nain, "there came a fear on all: and they glorified God, saying, That a great prophet is risen up among us; and, That God hath visited his people." The most authoritative Catholic theologians teach that miracles "are not wrought to show the internal truth of the doctrines, but only to give *manifest* reasons why we should accept the doctrines." They are "essentially an appeal to knowledge," demonstrations, one might almost say divine experiments, by which men are enabled to know the glory and the providence of God.

The Catholic apologists maintain that God can be known by the exercise of reason, but the miracle helps, as it were, to clinch the conviction. The persistent attachment of the Catholic Church to miracles is significant. It has a longer unbroken experience with human nature than any other institution in the western world. It has adapted itself to many circumstances, and under the profession of an unalterable creed it has abandoned and then added much. But it has never ceased to insist upon the need of a physical manifestation of the divine power. For with an unerring instinct for realities, Catholic churchmen have understood that there is a residuum of prosaic matter-of-factness, of a need to touch and to see, which verbal proofs can never quite satisfy. They have resolutely responded to that need. They have not preached God merely by praising him; they have brought God near to men by revealing him to the senses, as one who is great enough and good enough and sufficiently interested in them to heal the sick and to make the floods recede.

But to-day scientists are ever so much superior to churchmen at this kind of demonstration. The miracles which are recounted from the pulpit were, after all, few and far between. There are even theologians who teach that miracles ceased with the death of the Apostles. But the miracles of science seem to be inexhaustible. It is not surprising, then, that men of science should have acquired much of the intellectual authority which churchmen once exercised. Scientists do not, of course, speak of their discoveries as miracles. But to the common man they have much the same character as miracles. They are wonderful, they are inexplicable, they are manifestations of a great power over the forces of nature.

It cannot be said, I think, that the people at large, even the moderately educated minority, understand the difference between scientific method and revelation, or that they have decided upon reflection to trust science. There is at least as much mystery in science for the common man as there ever was in religion; in a sense there is more mystery, for the logic of science is still altogether beyond his understanding, whereas the logic of revelation is the logic of his own feelings. But if men at large do not understand the method of science, they can appreciate some of its more tangible results. And these results are so impressive that scientific men are often embarrassed by the unbounded popular expectations which they have so unintentionally aroused.

Their authority in the realm of knowledge has become virtually irresistible. And so when scientists teach one theory and the Bible another, the scientists invariably carry the greater conviction.

4. *On Reconciling Religion and Science*

The conflicts between scientists and churchmen are sometimes ascribed to a misunderstanding on both sides. But when we examine the proposals for peace, it is plain, I think, that they are in effect proposals for a truce. There is, for example, the suggestion first put out, I believe, in the Seventeenth Century that God made the universe like a clock, and that having started it running he will let it alone till it runs down. By this ingenious metaphor, which can be neither proved nor disproved, it was possible to reconcile for a time the scientific notion of natural law with the older notion of God as creator and as judge. The religious conception was held to be true for the beginning of the world and for the end, the scientific conception was true in between. Later, when the theatre of the difficulty was transferred from physics and astronomy to biology and history, a variation was propounded. God, it was said, created the world and governs it; the way he creates and governs is the way described by scientists as 'evolution.'

Attempts at reconciliations like these are based on a theory that it is feasible somewhere in the field of knowledge to draw a line and say that on one side the methods of science shall prevail, on the other the methods of traditional religion. It is acknowledged that where experiment and observation are possible, the field belongs to the scientists; but it is argued that there is a vast field of great interest to mankind which is beyond the reach of practical scientific inquiry, and that here, touching questions like the ultimate destiny of man, the purpose of life, and immortality, the older method of revelation, inspired and verified by intuition, is still reliable.

In any truce of this sort there is bound to be aggression from both sides. For it is a working policy rather than an inwardly accepted conviction. Scientists cannot really believe that there are fields of possible knowledge which they can never enter. They are bound to enter all fields and to explore everything. And even if they fail, they cannot believe that other scientists must always fail. Their essays, moreover, create disturbance and doubt which orthodox churchmen are forced to resent. For in any division of authority, there must be some ultimate authority to settle questions of jurisdiction. Shall scientists determine what belongs to science, or shall churchmen? The question is insoluble as long as both claim that they have the right to expound the nature of existence.

And so while the policy of toleration may be temporarily workable, it is inherently unstable. Therefore, among men who are at once devoted to the method of science and sensitive to the human need of religion, the hope has arisen that something better can be worked out than a purely diplomatic division of the mind into spheres of influence. Mr. Whitehead, for example, in his book called *Science and the Modern World,* argues "there are wider truths and finer perspectives within which a reconciliation of a deeper religion and a more subtle science will be found." He illustrates what he means in this fashion. Galileo said the earth moves and the sun is fixed; the Inquisition said the earth is fixed and the sun moves; the Newtonian astronomers said that both the sun and the earth move. "But now we say that any one of these three statements is equally true, provided you have fixed your sense of 'rest' and 'motion' in the way required by the statement adopted. At the date of Galileo's controversy with the Inquisition, Galileo's way of stating the facts was beyond question the fruitful procedure for the sake of scientific research. But at that time the concepts of relative motion were in nobody's mind; so that the statements were made in ignorance of the qualifications required for the more perfect truth. . . . All sides had got hold of important truths. . . .

[123]

But with the knowledge of those times, the truths appeared to be inconsistent."

This is reconciliation through a higher synthesis. But I cannot help feeling that the scientist has here produced the synthesis, and that the churchmen have merely provided one of the ideas which are to be synthesized. Mr. Whitehead argues in effect that a subtler science would confirm many ideas that were once taken on faith. But he holds unswervingly to the belief of the scientist that his method contains the criterion of truth. In his illustration the reconciliation between Galileo, the Inquisition, and the Newtonian physicists is reached if all three parties accept "the modern concept of relative motion." But the modern concept of relative motion was reached by scientific thought, and not by apostolic revelation. To Mr. Whitehead, therefore, the ultimate arbiter is science, and what he means by reconciliation is a scientific view of the universe sufficiently wide and sufficiently subtle to justify many of the important, but hitherto unverified, claims of traditional religion. Mr. Whitehead, it happens, is an Englishman as well as a great logician, and it is difficult to resist the suspicion that he conceives the church of the future as enjoying the dignities of an Indian Maharajah, with a resident scientist behind the altar.

A reconciliation of this kind may soften the conflict for a while. But it cannot for long disguise the fact that it is based on a denial of the premises of faith. If the method of science has the last word, then revelation is reduced from a means of arriving at absolute certainty to a flash of insight which can be trusted if and when it is verified by science. Under such terms of peace, the religious experiences of mankind become merely one of the instruments of knowledge, like the microscope and the binomial theorem, usable now and then, but subject to correction, and provisional. They no longer yield complete, ultimate, invincible truths. They yield an hypothesis. But the religious life of most men has not, until this day at least, been founded upon hypotheses which, when accurately stated, included a coefficient of probable error.

5. *Gospels of Science*

Because its prestige is so great, science has been acclaimed as a new revelation. Cults have attached themselves to scientific hypotheses as fortune-tellers to a circus. A whole series of pseudo-religions have been hastily constructed upon such dogmas as the laws of nature, mechanism, Darwinian evolution, Lamarckian evolution, and psychoanalysis. Each of these cults has had its own Decalogue of Science founded at last, it was said, upon certain knowledge.

These cults are an attempt to fit the working theories of science to the ordinary man's desire for personal salvation. They do violence to the integrity of scientific thought and they cannot satisfy the layman's need to believe. For the essence of the scientific method is a determination to investigate phenomena without conceding anything to naive human prejudices. Therefore, genuine men of science shrink from the attempts of poets, prophets, and popular lecturers to translate the current scientific theory into the broad and passionate dogmas of popular faith. As a matter of common honesty they know that no theory has the kind of absolute verity which popular faith would attribute to it. As a matter of prudence they fear these popular cults, knowing quite well that freedom of inquiry is endangered when men become passionately loyal to an idea, and stake their personal pride and hope of happiness upon its vindication. In the light of human experience, men of science have learned what happens when investigators are not free to discard any theory without breaking some dear old lady's heart. Their theories are not the kind of revelation which the old lady is seeking, and their beliefs are relative and provisional to a degree which must seem utterly alien and bewildering to her.

Here, for example, is the conclusion of some lectures by one of the greatest living astronomers. I have italicized the words which the dear old lady would not be likely to hear in a sermon:

> I have dealt mainly with two salient points—the problem of the source of a star's energy, and the change of mass which must occur if there is any evolution of faint stars from bright stars. I have shown how these *appear* to meet in the *hypothesis* of the annihilation of matter. I *do not hold this as a secure conclusion. I hesitate even to advocate it as probable,* because there are many details which seem to me to throw *considerable doubt* on it, and I have formed a strong impression that there must be *some essential point which has not yet been grasped*. I *simply* tell it you as the *clue* which at the moment we are *trying* to follow up—*not knowing whether it is false scent or true*. I should have liked to have closed these lectures by leading up to some great climax. But perhaps it is more in accordance with the true conditions of scientific progress that they should *fizzle out* with a glimpse of the *obscurity* which marks the frontiers of present knowledge. I do not apologize for the

lameness of the conclusion, *for it is not a conclusion.* I *wish I could feel confident that it is even a beginning.*

This great climax, to which Dr. Eddington was unable to lead up, is what the layman is looking for. We know quite well what the nature of that great climax would be: it would be a statement of fact which related the destiny of each individual to the destiny of the universe. That is the kind of truth which is found in revelation. It is the kind of truth which men would like to find in science. But it is the kind of truth which science does not afford. The difficulty is deeper than the provisional character of scientific hypothesis; it is not due merely to the inability of the scientist to say that his conclusion is absolutely secure. The layman in search of a dogma upon which to organize his destiny might be willing to grant that the conclusions of science to-day are as yet provisional. What he tends to misunderstand is that even if the conclusions were guaranteed by all investigators now and for all time to come, those conclusions would still fail to provide him with a conception of the world of which the great climax was a prophecy of the fate of creation in terms of his hopes and fears.

The radical novelty of modern science lies precisely in the rejection of the belief, which is at the heart of all popular religion, that the forces which move the stars and atoms are contingent upon the preferences of the human heart. The science of Aristotle and of the Schoolmen, on the other hand, was a truly popular science. It was in its inspiration the instinctive science of the unscientific man. "They read into the cause and goal of the universe," as Dr. Randall has said, "that which alone justifies it for man, its service of the good." They provided a conception of the universe which was available for the religious needs of ordinary men, and in the *Divine Comedy* we can see the supreme example of what science must be like if it is to satisfy the human need to believe. The purpose of the whole poem, said Dante himself, "is to remove those who are living in this life from the state of wretchedness, and to lead them to the state of blessedness." Mediæval science, which follows the logic of human desire, was such that Dante could without violence either to its substance or its spirit say at the summit of Paradise:

> To the high fantasy here power failed; but already my desire and will were rolled—even as a wheel that moveth equally—by the Love that moves the sun and the other stars.

This is the great climax which men instinctively expect: the ability to say with perfect assurance that when the truth is fully evident it will be seen that their desire and will are rolled by the love that moves the sun and the other stars. They hope not only to find the will of God in the universe but to know that his will is fundamentally like their own. Only if they could believe that on the basis of scientific investigation would they really feel that science had 'explained' the world.

Explanation, in this sense, cannot come from modern science because it is not in this sense that modern science attempts to explain the universe. It is wholly misleading to say, for example, that the scientific picture of the world is mechanical. All that can properly be said is that many scientists have found it satisfying to think about the universe as if it were built on a mechanical model. "If I can make a mechanical model," said Lord Kelvin, "I can understand it. As long as I cannot make a mechanical model all the way through, I cannot understand it." But what does the scientist mean by "understanding it"? He means, says Professor Bridgman, that he has "reduced a situation to elements with which we are so familiar that we accept them as a matter of course, so that our curiosity rests." Modern men are familiar with machines. They can take them apart and put them together, so that even though we should all be a little flustered if we had to tell just what we mean by a machine, our curiosity tends to be satisfied if we hear that the phenomenon, say, of electricity or of human behavior, is like a machine.

The place at which curiosity rests is not a fixed point called 'the truth.' The unscientific man, like the Schoolmen of the Middle Ages, really means by the truth an explanation of the universe in terms of human desire. What modern science means by the truth has been stated most clearly perhaps by the late Charles S. Peirce when he said that "the opinion which is fated to be ultimately agreed to by all those who investigate, is what we mean by the truth, and the object represented in this opinion is the real." When we say that something has been 'explained' by science, we really mean only that our own curiosity is satisfied. Another man, whose mind was more critical, who commanded a greater field of experience, might not be satisfied at all. Thus "the savage is satisfied by explaining the thunderstorm as the capricious act of an angry God. . . . (But) even if the physicist believed in the existence of the angry god, he would not be satisfied with this explanation of the thunderstorm because he is not so well acquainted with angry gods as to be able to predict when anger is followed by a storm. He would have to know why the god had become angry, and why making a thunderstorm eased his ire." But even carrying the explanation to this point would not be carrying it to its limit. For there is no formal limit. The next scientist might wish to know what a god was and what anger is. And when he had been told what their elements are, the next man might be dissatisfied until he had found the elements of these elements.

The man who says that the world is a machine has really advanced no further than to say that he is so well satisfied with this analogy that he is through with searching any further. That is his business, as long as he does not insist that he has reached a clear and ultimate picture of the universe. For obviously he has not. A machine is something in which the parts push and pull each other. But why are they pushing and pulling, and how do *they* work? Do they push and pull because of the action of the electrons in their orbits within the atoms? If that is true, then how does an electron work? Is it, too, a machine? Or is it something quite different from a machine? Shall we attempt to explain machines electrically, or shall we attempt to explain electricity mechanically?

It becomes plain, therefore, that scientific explanation is altogether unlike the explanations to which the common man is accustomed. It does not yield a certain picture of anything which can be taken naively as a representation of reality. And therefore the philosophies which have grown up about science, like mechanism or creative evolution, are in no way guaranteed by science as the account of creation in Genesis is guaranteed by the authority of Scripture. They are nothing but provisional dramatizations which are soon dissolved by the progress of science itself.

That is why nothing is so dead as the scientific religion of yesterday. It is far more completely dead than any revealed religion, because the revealed religion, whatever may be the defects of its cosmology or its history, has some human experience at its core which we can recognize and to which we may respond. But a religion like scientific materialism has nothing in it, except the pretension that it is a true account of the world. Once that pretension is exploded, it is wholly valueless as a religion. It has become a collection of discarded concepts.

6. *The Deeper Conflict*

It follows from the very nature of scientific explanation, then, that it cannot give men such a clue to a plan of existence as they find in popular religion. For that plan must suppose that existence is explained in terms of human destiny. Now conceivably existence might again be explained, as it was in the Middle Ages, as the drama of human destiny. It does not seem probable to us; yet we cannot say that it is impossible. But even if science worked out such an explanation, it would still be radically different from the explanations which popular religion employs.

For if it were honestly stated, it would be necessary to say first, that it is tentative, and subject to disproof by further experiment; second, that it is relative, in that the same facts seen from some other point and with some other purpose in mind could be explained quite differently; third, that it is not a picture of the world, as God would see it, and as all men must see it, but that it is simply one among many possible creations of the mind into which most of the data of experience can be fitted. When the scientist had finished setting down his qualifications, the essence of the matter as a simple, devout man sees it, would have evaporated. Certainty, as the devout desire it, would be gone; verity, as they understand it, would be gone; objectivity, as they imagine it, would be gone. What would remain would be a highly abstracted, logical fiction, suited to disinterested inquiry, but utterly unsuited to be the vehicle of his salvation.

The difficulty of reconciling popular religion with science is far deeper than that of reconciling Genesis with Darwin, or any statement of fact in the Bible with any discovery by scientists. It is the difficulty of reconciling the human desire for a certain kind of universe with a method of explaining the world which is absolutely neutral in its intention. One can by twisting language sufficiently "reconcile" Genesis with "evolution." But what no one can do is to guarantee that science will not destroy the doctrine of evolution the day after it has been triumphantly proved that Genesis is compatible with the theory of evolution. As a matter of fact, just that has happened. The Darwinian theory, which theologians are busily accepting, is so greatly modified already by science that some of it is almost as obsolete as the Babylonian myth in Genesis. The reconciliation which theologians are attempting is an impossible one, because one of the factors which has to be reconciled—namely, the scientific theory, changes so rapidly that the layman is never sure at any one moment what the theory is which he has to reconcile with religious dogma.

Yet the purpose of these attempts at reconciliation is evident enough. It is to find a solid foundation for human ideals in the facts of existence. Authority based on revelation once provided that foundation. It gave an account of how the world began, of how it is governed, and of how it will end, which made pain and joy, hope and fear, desire and the denial of desire the central motives in the cosmic drama. This account no longer satisfies our curiosity as to the nature of things; the authority which certifies it no longer commands our complete allegiance. The prestige, which once adhered to those who spoke by revelation, has passed to scientists. But science, though it is the most reliable method of knowledge we now possess, does not provide an account of the world in which human destiny is the central theme. Therefore, science, though it has displaced revelation, is not a substitute for it. It yields a radically different kind of knowledge. It explains the facts. But it does not pretend to justify the ways of God to man. It enables us to realize some of our hopes. But it offers no guarantees that they can be fulfilled.

7. *Theocracy and Humanism*

There is a revolution here in the realm of the spirit. We may describe it briefly by saying that whereas men once felt they were living under the eye of an all-powerful spectator, to-day they are watched only by their neighbors and their own consciences. A few, perhaps, act as if posterity were aware of them; the great number feel themselves accountable only to their own consciences or to the opinion of the society in which they live. Once men believed that they would be judged at the throne of God. They believed that he saw not only their deeds but their motives; there was no hole deep enough into which a man could crawl to hide himself from the sight of God; there was no mood, however fleeting, which escaped his notice.

The moral problem for each man, therefore, was to make his will conform to the will of God. There were differences of opinion as to how this could be done. There were differing conceptions of the nature of God, and of what he most desired. But there was no difference of opinion on the main point that it was imperative to obey him. Whether they thought they could serve God best by burnt offerings or a contrite heart, by slaying the infidel or by loving their neighbors, by vows of poverty or by the magnificence of their altars, they never doubted that the chief duty of man, and his ultimate chance of happiness, was to discover and then to cultivate a right relationship to a supreme being.

This was the major premise upon which all human choices hinged. There followed from it certain necessary conclusions. In determining what was a right relationship to God, the test of rightness lay in a revelation of the putative experience of God and not in the actual experience of His creatures. It was God alone, therefore, who really understood the reasons for righteousness and its nature. "The procedure of Divine Justice," said

Calvin, "is too high to be scanned by human measure or comprehended by the feebleness of human intellect." That was good which man understood was good in the eyes of God, regardless of how it seemed to men.

Thus the distinction between good and evil, including not only all rules of personal conduct but the whole arrangement of rights and duties in society, were laws established not by the consent of the governed, but by a king in heaven. They were his commandments. By obedience men could obtain happiness. But they obtained it not because virtue is the cause of happiness but because God rewarded with happiness those who obeyed his commandments. Men did not really know why God preferred certain kinds of conduct; they merely professed to know what kind of conduct he preferred. They could not really ask themselves what the difference was between good and evil. That was a secret locked in the nature of a being whose choices were ultimately inscrutable. The only question was what he willed. Even Job had to be content without fathoming his reasons.

The moral commandments based upon divine authority were, in the nature of things, rather broad generalizations. Obviously there could not be special revelation as to the unique aspects of each human difficulty. The divine law, like our ordinary human law, was addressed to typical rather than to individual cases. Nevertheless, for much the greater part of recorded history men have accepted such law without questioning its validity. They could not have done so if the rules of morality had not, at least in some rough way, worked. It is not difficult to see why they worked. They were broad rules of conduct imposed upon people living close to the soil, upon people, therefore, whose ways of living changed little in the course of generations. The same situations were so nearly and so often repeated that a typical solution would on the whole be satisfactory.

These typical solutions, such as we find in the Mosaic law or the code of Hammurabi, were no doubt the deposits of custom. They had, therefore, become perfected in practice, and were solidly based upon human experience. In the society in which they originated, there was nothing arbitrary or alien about them. When, therefore, the lawgiver carried these immemorial usages up with him on to Sinai, and brought them down again graven on tablets of stone, the rationality of the revelation was self-evident. It appeared to be arbitrary only when a radical change in the way of life dissolved the premises and the usages upon which the authoritative code was established.

That dissolution has proceeded to great lengths within the centuries which we call modern. The crisis was reached, it seems, during the Eighteenth Century, and in the teaching of Immanuel Kant it was made manifest to the educated classes of the western world. Kant argued in the *Critique of Pure Reason* that the existence of God cannot be demonstrated. He then insisted that without belief in God, freedom, and immortality, there was no valid and true morality. So he insisted that God must exist to justify morality. This highly sophisticated doctrine marks the end of simple theism in modern thought. For Kant's proof of the existence of God was nothing but a plea that God ought to exist, and the whole temper of the modern intellect is to deny that what ought to be true necessarily is true.

Insofar as men have now lost their belief in a heavenly king, they have to find some other ground for their moral choices than the revelation of his will. It follows necessarily that they must find the tests of righteousness wholly within human experience. The difference between good and evil must be a difference which men themselves recognize and understand. Happiness cannot be the reward of virtue; it must be the intelligible consequence of it. It follows, too, that virtue cannot be commanded; it must be willed out of personal conviction and desire. Such a morality may properly be called humanism, for it is centered not in superhuman but in human nature. When men can no longer be theists, they must, if they are civilized, become humanists. They must live by the premise that whatever is righteous is inherently desirable because experience will demonstrate its desirability. They must live, therefore, in the belief that the duty of man is not to make his will conform to the will of God but to the surest knowledge of the conditions of human happiness.

It is evident that a morality of humanism presents far greater difficulties than a morality premised on theism. For one thing, it is put immediately to a much severer test. When Kant, for example, argued that theism was necessary to morality, his chief reason was that since the good man is often defeated on earth, he must be permitted to believe in a superhuman power which is "able to connect happiness and morality in exact harmony with each other." Humanism is not provided with such reserves of moral credit; it cannot claim all eternity in which its promises may be fulfilled. Unless its wisdom in any sphere of life is demonstrated within a reasonable time in actual experience, there is nothing to commend it.

A morality of humanism labors under even greater difficulties. It appears in a complex and changing society; it is an attitude toward life to which rational men necessarily turn whenever their circumstances have rendered a theistic view incredible. It is just because the simpler rules no longer work that the subtler choices of humanism present themselves. These choices have to be made under conditions, like those which prevail in modern urban societies, where the extreme complexity of rapidly changing human relations makes it very difficult to foresee all the consequences of any moral decision. The men who must make their decisions are skeptical by habit and unsettled amidst the novelties of their surroundings.

The teachers of a theistic morality, when the audience is devout, have only to fortify the impression that the rules of conduct are certified by God the invisible King. The ethical problem for the common man is to recognize the well-known credentials of his teachers. In practice he has merely to decide whether the priest, the prince, and the elders, are what they claim to be. When he has done that, there are no radical questions to be asked. But the teachers of humanism have no credentials. Their teaching is not certified. They have to prove their case by the test of mundane experience. They speak with no authority, which can be scrutinized once and for all, and then forever accepted. They can proclaim no rule of conduct with certainty, for they have no inherent personal authority and they cannot be altogether sure they are right. They cannot command. They cannot truly exhort. They can only inquire, infer, and persuade. They have only human insight to guide them and those to whom they speak must in the end themselves accept the full responsibility for the consequences of any advice they choose to accept.

Yet with all its difficulties, it is to a morality of humanism that men must turn when the ancient order of things dissolves. When they find that they no longer believe seriously and deeply that they are governed from heaven, there is anarchy in their souls until by conscious effort they find ways of governing themselves.

PART II

THE FOUNDATIONS OF HUMANISM

The stone which the builders rejected,
The same is become the head of the corner.

LUKE XX, 17.

INTRODUCTION

THE upshot of the discussion to this point is that modernity destroys the disposition to believe that behind the visible world of physical objects and human institutions there is a supernatural kingdom from which ultimately all laws, all judgments, all rewards, all punishments, and all compensations are derived. To those who believe that this kingdom exists the modern spirit is nothing less than treason to God.

The popular religion rests on the belief that the kingdom is an objective fact, as certain, as definite, and as real, in spite of its invisibility, as the British Empire; it holds that this faith is justified by overwhelming evidence supplied by revelation, unimpeachable testimony, and incontrovertible signs. To the modern spirit, on the other hand, the belief in this kingdom must necessarily seem a grandiose fiction projected by human needs and desires. The humanistic view is that the popular faith does not prove the existence of its objects, but only the presence of a desire that such objects should exist. The popular religion, in short, rests on a theory which, if true, is an extension of physics and of history; the humanistic view rests on human psychology and an interpretation of human experience.

It follows, then, that in exploring the modern problem it is necessary consciously and clearly to make a choice between these diametrically opposite points of view. The choice is fundamental and exclusive, and it determines all the conclusions which follow. For obviously to one who believes that the world is a theocracy, the problem is how to bring the strayed and rebellious masses of mankind back to their obedience, how to restore the lost provinces of God the invisible King. But to one who takes the humanistic view the problem is how mankind, deprived of the great fictions, is to come to terms with the needs which created those fictions.

In this book I take the humanistic view because, in the kind of world I happen to live in, I can do no other.

CHAPTER VIII

GOLDEN MEMORIES

It will be granted, I suppose, that there would be no need for certainty about the plan and government of the universe if, as a matter of course, all our desires were regularly fulfilled. In a world where no man desired what he could not have, there would be no need to regulate human conduct and therefore no need for morality. In a world where each man could have what he desired, there would be no need for consolation and for reassuring guarantees that justice, mercy, and love will ultimately prevail. In a world where there was perfect adjustment between human desires and their environment, there would be no problem of evil: we should not know the meaning of sin, sorrow, crime, fear, frustration, pain, and emptiness. We do not live in such a well-ordered world. But we can imagine it by making either of two assumptions: that we have ceased to desire anything which causes evil, or that omnipotence fulfills all our desires. The first of these assumptions leads to the Nirvana of the Buddhists, where all craving has ceased and there is perfect peace. The second leads to the heaven of all popular religions, to some paradise like that of Mohammed perhaps where, as Mr. Santayana says, men may "sit in well-watered gardens, clad in green silks, drinking delicious sherbets, and transfixed by the gazelle-like glance of some young girl, all innocence and fire."

Among educated men it has always been difficult to imagine a heaven of fulfilled desires. For since no two persons have exactly the same desires, one man's imagination of heaven may not suit another man's. In general, the attempts which have been made to picture the Christian heaven reflect the temperaments of highly contemplative spirits, and it is customary nowadays to say that this heaven would be a most uninteresting place. No doubt it would be to those who are not contemplative. But the objectors have missed the main point, which is that no one is supposed to pass through the pearly gates who is not suited to dwell in Paradise. That is what St. Peter is there for, to see that the unfit do not enter; the other places, Purgatory and the Inferno, are available to those spirits who could not be happy in Heaven. There are, by definition, no uncongenial spirits in Heaven. There were once, but Satan and his followers were thrown out headlong, and they now live in places which are suited to their temperaments. A devout man may quite properly, therefore, advise those who do not think they would enjoy Heaven to go to Hell.

The attempt to imagine a heaven is an attempt to conceive a world in which the disorders of human desire no longer exist. Now it is in their prayers that men have sought to come to terms with their disorders, and their prayers reveal most concretely how much the hunger for certainty and for help is a hunger for the fulfillment of desire. For prayer, says Father Wynne, is "the expression of our desires to God whether for ourselves or for others." In the higher reaches of religion "the expression is not intended to instruct or direct God what to do, but to appeal to His goodness for the things we need; and the appeal is necessary, not because He is ignorant of our needs or sentiments, but to give definite form to our desires, to concentrate our whole attention on what we have to recommend to Him, to help us appreciate our close personal relation with Him." But in order to know what to pray for, we need grace, that is to say, God Himself must teach us what to ask Him for. We can be sure that we should pray for salvation, but in particular we need guidance from God "to know the special means that will most help us in any particular need." But besides the spiritual objects of prayer "we are to ask also for temporal things, our daily bread and all that it implies, health, strength, and other worldly or temporal goods . . ."; we are to pray also for escape from evils, "the penalty of our sins, the dangers of temptation, and every manner of physical or spiritual affliction."

There has, however, always been a logical difficulty about offering petitions to an all-wise and all-powerful Providence. Thus in the *Dialogue of Dives and Pauper,* which was published in 1493, the question is put: "Why pray we to God with oure mouth sithe he knowyth alle oure thoughte, all our desire, al our wyl and what us nedeth?" To this question the only answer which was not evasive came from the mystics who led a life of contemplation. Prayer, they said, is not mere petition; it is communion with God. It is not because prayer gives a man what he wants, but because it "ones the soul to God," that it is rational and necessary. This, too, is the conception of prayer held by a liberal pastor like Dr. Fosdick who looks with scorn upon "clamorous petition to an

anthropomorphic God" and says that "true prayer . . .
is to assimilate . . . (the) spirit which is God (that)
. . . surrounds our lives." The same idea, stated in somewhat more precise language, is set down by Mr. Santayana when he says that "in rational prayer the soul may
be said to accomplish three things important to its welfare:
it withdraws within itself and defines its good, it accommodates itself to destiny, and it grows like the ideal which
it conceives."

But, of course, this is not the way the common man
through the ages has conceived prayer. In fact he must
have prayed before he had any clear conception of what a
prayer is or of whom it is addressed to. Thus we are
told that in Arcadia the girls invoked Hera by the title
of "Hera the Girl," the married women prayed to "Hera
the Married One," and the widows prayed to "Hera the
Widow." Sometimes the prayer is a spontaneous expression of sorrow or of delight, a lyrical cry which has no
ulterior purpose and is addressed to no one. Sometimes
prayer is a magical formula which compels the deity to
listen and to obey. The subject is both complicated and
obscure. But this much at least is clear: along with elements which can be described only as spontaneous and
lyrical, with traces of magic, and at times with a purely
disinterested desire to commune with God, simple people
have looked upon prayer as "an instrument for applying
God's illimitable power to daily life."

Popular discussion of prayer has often been extremely
practical: "How can prayer be made most efficient? Is it
by ordinary Masses or by other offices? Is it by the elaboration or the multiplication of services?" Lady Alice

West who died in 1395 ordered 4400 Masses "in the m̃
haste that it may be do, withynne xiiii nyght next aft
my deces." Thomas Walwayn who died in 1415 le
orders for 10,000 Masses "with oute pompe whyche may
not profyt myn soule." John Plot, however, wished his
Masses said "with solempne seruise that ys for to sayn
wyth Belle Ryngyng." There was debate as to whether
prayers were most effective if said in Rome or in the Holy
Land . . . by certain priests rather than by others . . .
by the friars rather than by the priests . . . whether there
were more potent prayers than the *Pater* . . . whether
prayers should be addressed to the Father, the Son, or to
St. Mary . . . whether St. Mary could be approached best
through her mother, St. Anne. . . .

It is not necessary to dogmatize by saying that prayer
is magic, or soliloquy, or communion, or petition for this
and that, in order to see that it is the expression of a human need. The quality of the need varies. It may be
anything from a desire for rain to a desire for friendship
with unseen spirits, but always it illustrates the saying that
"all men stand in need of God."

If we ask ourselves what we mean by 'need,' we must
answer, I suppose, that the resources of our own natures
and the power we are able to exercise over events are insufficient to satisfy the cravings of our natures. We must
eat, but we cannot be sure that drought will not destroy
the crops. We are beset by enemies, and we are not sure
we can conquer them. We are threatened by earthquake,
storm, and disease against which we cannot wholly protect
ourselves. We become deeply attached to other persons.
But they must die and we must die, and we cannot stay

the doom. In brief, we find ourselves in a world in which our hopes are defeated.

Somehow we are so constituted that we demand the impossible. There is in us somewhere an intimation that we ought not to be defeated. But where did this intimation come from? How is it that we are not born satisfied with our mortality, content with our fate? Why is it that the normal fate of man seems to us abnormal? What is there in the back of our heads which keeps telling us that life as we find it is not what it ought to be?

The biologist might answer, I suppose, that this craving for a different kind of world is simply our own consciousness of that blind push of natural forces which create the variations on which natural selection works to produce the survival of the fittest. Nature, he might say, is wholly indifferent to the outcries of the individual; this vast process of which each of us is so insignificant a part, keeps going because there is in all the parts a superabundant urging to go on. There is no human economy in it and no human order. Man, for example, has far more sexual desire than is needed for the rational propagation of the species. But there is no rational plan in nature. It works here, and everywhere, on the principle that by having too much there will surely be enough; the seeds which do not germinate, the seedlings which perish, the desires which are left over, are no concern of nature's. For nature has no concern. There is no concern except that which we ourselves feel, and that is a mere flicker on the stream of time, and will soon go out.

While there is no way of gainsaying that this explanation is true, it is true only if we look at life from the particular point of view which the biologist adopts. If, how-

ever, we look inwardly upon ourselves, instead of surveying our species from the outside, we find, I think, that this
sense that the world ought not to be what it is seems to
originate in a kind of dim memory that it once was what
we feel it ought to be. Indeed, so vivid is this memory
that for ages men took it to be an account of historical
events; in absolute good faith they constituted for themselves the picture of a Golden Age which existed before
evil came into the world. Hope was, therefore, a kind of
memory; the ideal was to achieve something which had
been lost. The memory of an age of innocence has
haunted the whole of mankind. It has been a light behind
their present experience which cast shadows upon it, and
made it seem insubstantial and not inevitable. Before
this life, there had been another which was happier. And
so they reasoned that what once was possible must somehow be possible again. Having once known the good, it
was unbelievable that evil should be final.

Even after criticism has dissolved the beautiful legends
in which it was embodied, this memory of a Golden Age
persists. It persists as an intimation of our own inward
experience, and like an uneasy spirit it intrudes itself upon
our most realistic efforts to accept the world as we find it.
For it takes many shapes, which sometimes deceive us,
appearing then not as the memory of a happiness we have
lost, but as the anticipation of utopia to come.

It is an intimation that man is entitled to live in the
land of heart's desire. It is a deep conviction that happiness is possible, and all inquiry into the foundations of
morals turns ultimately upon whether man can achieve
this happiness by pursuing his desires, or whether he must
first learn to desire the kind of happiness which is possible.

CHAPTER IX

THE INSIGHT OF HUMANISM

1. *The Two Approaches to Life*

THE land of heart's desire is a place in which no man desires what he cannot have and each man can have what he desires. There have been great differences of opinion among men as to how they could best enter this happy land.

If they thought their natural impulses were by way of being lecherous, greedy, and cruel, they have accepted some form of the classical and Christian doctrine that man must subdue his naive impulses, and by reason, grace, or renunciation, transform his will. If they thought that man was naturally innocent and good, they have accepted some one of the many variants of liberalism, and concerned themselves not with the reform of desire but with the provision of opportunities for its fulfilment.

There are differences of emphasis among liberals, but they all accept the same premise, which is that if only external circumstances are favorable the internal life of man will adjust itself successfully. So completely does this theory of human nature dominate the field of contemporary thought that modern men are rarely reminded, and then only by those whom it is the fashion to ignore, that they are challenging the testimony not merely of their maiden aunts, but of all the greatest teachers of wisdom.

Yet if the modern man is an optimist on the subject of his impulses, the reason is to be found less in his own self-confidence than in his distrust of men and in his intoxication over things.

Owing to the dissolution of the ancestral order he has learned to distrust those who exercise authority. Owing to the progress of science he has acquired an unbounded confidence in his capacity to create desirable objects. He is so rebellious and so constructive that he has still to ask himself whether the free and naive pursuit of desirable objects can really produce a desirable world. Yet in all the books of wisdom that is the question which confronts him. There it is written in many languages and in the idiom of many different cultures that if man is to find happiness, he must reconstruct not merely his world, but, first of all, himself.

Is this wisdom dead and done with, or has it a bearing upon the deep uneasiness of the modern man? The answer depends upon what we must conceive to be the nature of man.

2. Freedom and Restraint

It is significant that fashions in human nature are continually changing. There are, as it were, two extremes: at the one is the belief that our naive passions are evil, at the other that they are good, and between these two poles, the prevailing opinion oscillates. One might suppose that somewhere, perhaps near the center, there would be a point which was the truth, and that on that point men would reach an agreement. But experience shows that there is no agreement, and that there is no known point where the two views are perfectly balanced. The fact is that the prevailing view is invariably a rebound from the excesses of the other, and one can understand it only by knowing what it is a reaction from.

It is impossible, for example, to do justice to Rousseau and the romantics without understanding the dead classicism, the conventionalities, and the tyrannies of the Eighteenth Century. It is equally impossible to do justice to the Eighteenth Century without understanding the licentiousness of the High Renaissance and the political disorders resulting from the Reformation. These in their turn become intelligible only when we have understood the later consequences of the mediæval view of life. No particular view endures. When human nature is wholly distrusted and severely repressed, sooner or later it asserts itself and bursts its bonds; and when it is naively trusted, it produces so much disorder and corruption that men once again idealize order and restraint.

We happen to be living in an age when there is a severe reaction against the distrust and repression practiced by those whom it is customary to describe as Puritans. It is, in fact, a reaction against a degenerate form of Puritanism which manifested itself as a disposition to be prim, prudish, and pedantic. For latter-day Puritanism had become a rather second-rate notion that less obvious things are more noble than grosser ones and that spirituality is the pursuit of rarefied sensations. It had embraced the idea that a man had advanced in the realm of the spirit in proportion to his concern with abstractions, and cults of grimly spiritual persons devoted themselves to the worship of sonorous generalities. All this associated itself with a rather preposterous idealism which insisted that maidens should be wan and easily frightened, that draperies and decorations should conceal the essential forms of objects, and that the good life had something to do with expurgated speech, with pale colors, and shadows and silhouettes, with the thin music of harps and soprano voices, with fig leaves and a general conspiracy to tell lies to children, with philosophies that denied the reality of evil, and with all manner of affectation and self-deception.

Yet in these many attempts to grow wings and take off from the things that are of the earth earthy, it is impossible not to recognize a resemblance, somewhat in the nature of a caricature, to the teaching of the sages. There is no doubt that in one form or another, Socrates and Buddha, Jesus and St. Paul, Plotinus and Spinoza, taught that the good life is impossible without asceticism, that without renunciation of many of the ordinary appetites, no man can really live well. Prejudice against the human body and a tendency to be disgusted with its habits, a contempt for the ordinary concerns of daily experience is to be found in all of them, and it is not surprising that men, living in an age of moral confusion like that associated with the name of the good Queen Victoria, should have come to believe that if only they covered up their passions they had conquered them. It was a rather ludicrous mistake as the satirists of the anti-Victorian era have so copiously pointed out. But at least there was a dim recognition in this cult of the genteel that the good life does involve some kind of conquest of the carnal passions.

That conception of the good life has become so repulsive to the present generation that it is almost incapable of understanding and appreciating the original insight of which the works of Dr. Bowdler and Mrs. Grundy are a caricature. Yet it is a fact, and a most arresting one, that in all the great religions, and in all the great moral philosophies from Aristotle to Bernard Shaw, it is taught that one of the conditions of happiness is to renounce some of the satisfactions which men normally crave. This tradition as to what constitutes the wisdom of life is supported by testimony from so many independent sources that it cannot be dismissed lightly. With minor variations it is a common theme in the teaching of an Athenian aristocrat like Plato, an Indian nobleman like Buddha, and a humble Jew like Spinoza; in fact, wherever men have thought at all carefully about the problem of evil and of what constitutes a good life, they have concluded that an essential element in any human philosophy is renunciation. They cannot all have been so foolish as Anthony Comstock. They must have had some insight into experience which led them to that conclusion.

If asceticism in all its forms were as stupid and cruel as it is now the fashion to think it is, then the traditions of saintliness and of heroism are monstrously misleading. For in the legends of heroes, of sages, of explorers, inventors and discoverers, of pioneers and patriots, there is almost invariably this same underlying theme of sacrifice and unworldliness. They are poor. They live dangerously. By ordinary standards they are extremely uncomfortable. They give up ease, property, pleasure, pride, place, and power to attain things which are transcendent and rare. They live for ends which seem to yield them no profit, and they are ready to die, if need be, for that which the dead can no longer enjoy. And yet, though there is nothing in our current morality to justify their unworldliness, we continue to admire them greatly.

In saying all this I am not trying to clinch an argument by appealing to great names. There is much in the teaching of all the spiritual leaders of the past which is wholly obsolete to-day, and there is no compulsive authority in any part of their teaching. They may have been as mistaken in their insight into the human soul as they usually were in their notions of physics and history. To say, then, that there is an ascetic element in all the great philosophies of the past is not proof that there must be one in modern philosophy. But it creates a presumption, I think, which cannot be ignored, for we must remember that the least perishable part of the literature and thought of the past is that which deals with human nature. Scientific method and historical scholarship have enormously increased our competence in the whole field of physics and history. But for an understanding of human nature we are still very largely dependent, as they were, upon introspection, general observation, and intuition. There has been no revolutionary advance here since the Hellenic philosophers. That is why Aristotle's ethics is still as fresh for anyone who accustoms himself to the idiom as Nietzsche, or Freud, or Bertrand Russell, whereas Aristotle's physics, his biology, or his zoology is of interest only to antiquarians.

It is, then, as an insight into human nature, and not as a rule authoritatively imposed or highly sanctioned by the prestige of great men, that I propose now to inquire what meaning there is for us in the fact that men in the past have so persistently associated the good life with some form of ascetic discipline and renunciation. The modern world, as it has emancipated itself from its ancestral regime, has assumed almost as a matter of course that the human passions, if thoroughly liberated from all tyrannies and distortions, would by their fulfilment achieve happiness. All those who teach asceticism, deny this major premise of modernity, and the result is that the prevailing philosophy is at odds on the most fundamental of all issues with the wisdom of the past.

3. *The Ascetic Principle*

The average man to-day, when he hears the word asceticism, is likely to think of St. Simeon Stylites who sat on top of a pillar, of hermits living in caves, of hair-shirts, of long fasts, chastity, strange vigils, and even of tattooing, self-mutilation, and flagellation. Or if he does not think of such examples, which the modern man regards as pathological and for the psychiatrist to explain, the word asceticism may connote some such attitude of mind as Herbert Asbury has recorded in the biography of his kinsman, Bishop Asbury, the founder of American Methodism, of whom a friend, who knew him well, wrote: "I never saw him indulge in even innocent pleasantry. His was the solemnity of an apostle; it was so interwoven with his conduct that he could not put off the gravity of the bishop either in the parlour or the dining-room. He was a rigid enemy to ease; hence the pleasures of study and the charms of recreation he alike sacrificed to the more sublime work of saving souls. . . . He knew nothing about pleasing the flesh at the expense of duty; flesh and blood were enemies with whom he never took counsel."

If asceticism meant only this sort of thing, it might be interesting only as a curiosity. But apart from the asceticism of primitive peoples and of the pathological, there is a sane and civilized asceticism which presents a quite different face. There is, for example, the argument of Socrates in the *Phædo* that the body is a nuisance to a philosopher in search of truth. It is, he says, "a source of endless trouble to us by reason of the mere requirement of food; and is liable also to diseases which overtake and impede us in the search after true being: it fills us full of loves, and lusts, and fears, and fancies of all kinds, and endless foolery, and in fact, as men say, takes away from us the power of thinking at all. Whence come wars, and fightings, and factions? Whence but from the body and the lusts of the body? Wars are occasioned by the love of money, and money has to be acquired for the sake and in the service of the body; and by reason of all these impediments we have no time to give to philosophy; and, last and worst of all, even if we are at leisure and betake ourselves to some speculation, the body is always breaking in upon us, causing us turmoil and confusion in our inquiries, and so amazing us that we are prevented from seeing the truth."

Plato, in pursuing the argument in this particular dialogue, concludes that because the body is such a nuisance the only pure philosopher is a dead one. It is, perhaps, a logical conclusion. But in other places, particularly in the *Republic,* Plato described a system of education which he thought would produce philosophers: the neophytes were put through a stern discipline of hard living and gymnastics and learning, were compelled to live in tents, to own nothing which they could call their own, and to cut themselves off from all family ties.

When the description of this regime provokes Adeimantus to remark that "you are not making the men of this class particularly happy," Socrates is made to reply that while it is not his object to make any class particularly happy, yet it would not surprise him if in the given circumstances even this class were very happy. When we look further for his meaning, we find it to be that the guardians are trained by their ascetic discipline to abandon all private aims and to find their happiness in an appreciation of a perfectly ordered commonwealth. If we understand this we shall, I believe, understand what civilized asceticism means. We shall have come back to the original meaning of the word itself, which is derived from the Greek ἀσκέω, "I practice," and "embodies a metaphor taken from the ancient wrestling place or palæstra, where victory rewarded those who had best trained their bodies." An ascetic in the original meaning of the term is an athlete; and it was in this spirit that the early Christians trained themselves deliberately as "athletes of Christ" to bear without flinching the tortures of their martyrdom.

When asceticism is irrational, it is a form of totemism or fetich worship and derives from a belief that certain things are tabu or that evil spirits can be placated by human suffering. Or without any coherent belief whatsoever asceticism may be merely a perversion arising out of that ambivalence of the human passions which often makes pain, inflicted on others or self-inflicted, an exquisite pleasure. But when asceticism is rational, it is a discipline of the mind and body to fit men for the service of an ideal. Its purpose is to harden and to purify, to suppress contrary passions, and thus to intensify the passion for the ideal. "I chastise my body," said St. Paul, "and bring it into subjection." The Church, especially in the earlier centuries, was compelled to fight continually against irrational asceticism, and as late as the Middle Ages, the Inquisition pursued sects which regarded marriage as the "greater adultery" and practiced self-emasculation. The rational view was the view of St. Jerome: "Be on your guard when you begin to mortify your body by abstinence and fasting, lest you imagine yourself to be perfect and a saint; for perfection does not consist in this virtue. It is only a help; a disposition; a means, though a fitting one, for the attainment of true perfection."

Now when St. Paul said that he had to bring his body into subjection, when Aristotle defined the barbarians' ideal as "the living as one likes," when Plato made Socrates say that the soul is infected by the body, when Buddha preached the extinction of all craving, when Spinoza wrote that because we rejoice in virtue we are able to control our lusts, they accepted a view of human nature which is quite diametrically opposed to one which has had wide currency in our civilization since the Renaissance.

This contrary view was undoubtedly provoked by the evils which came from the attempt to put the ascetic principle extensively into practice. Rabelais is by all odds the most convincing of the moderns who revolted, for

Rabelais not only talked about the natural man but actually knew him and delighted in him.   Thus when Villers writes to Madame de Staël that in her work "primitive, incorruptible, naive, passionate nature" is "in conflict with the barriers and shackles of conventional life," we feel, I think, that neither Villers nor the lady would really have cared very much for primitive nature in all its naivete. The natural man that they were talking about lived in Arcady and his passions were as violent as those of a lapdog; throughout the romantic movement, with rare exceptions, the talk about passion and impulse and instinct has this air of unreality and of neurotic confusion.   There is not in it, as there is in Rabelais, for example, an honest gusto for the passions that are to be liberated from the restraints imposed by that "rabble of squint-minded fellows, dissembling and counterfeit saints, demure lookers, hypocrites, pretended zealots, tough friars, buskin-monks, and other such sects of men, who disguise themselves like masquers to deceive the world."

Rabelais advised his readers that if they desired to become good Pantagruelists, "that is to say, to live in peace, joy, health, making yourself always merry—never trust those men that always peep out through a little hole." And in establishing the Abbey of Theleme, Gargantua furnished it magnificently and barred the gates against bigots, hypocrites, dissemblers, attorneys, barristers, usurers, drunkards, and cannibals; he invited in all noble blades and brisk and handsome people, faithful expounders of the Scripture, and lovely ladies, proper, fair, and mirthful.   "Their life," he says, "was spent not in laws, statutes, or rules, but at their own free will and pleasure.

They rose from bed when they thought good, drank, ate, worked, slept, when the desire came to them. None did awaken them, none constrained them either to drink or eat, nor to do any other thing: for so had Gargantua established it. The Rule of their order had but one clause: *Do What Thou Wilt.*"

But there was a catch in this rule. Not only had drunkards and cannibals been excluded in the first place, but Rabelais assures us that those who were admitted, because they were "free, well born, well educated, and accustomed to good company, have by nature an instinct and spur which prompts them to virtuous acts and withdraws them from vice. This they call honor." And in another passage Rabelais limits the propensities of the natural man even more radically when he speaks of "a certain gaiety of spirit *cured* in contempt of chance and fortune."

There is always a catch in any doctrine of the natural goodness of man. For mere passive obedience to impulse as it comes and goes, without effort to check it or direct it, ends in something like Alfred de Musset's Rolla, of whom it was said:

> It was not Rolla who ruled his life,
> It was his passions; he let them go
> As a drowsy shepherd watches the water flow.

So even Dora Russell at the crisis of her assault upon the Christian tradition advises us to "live by instinct *and* intelligence," which must mean, if it means anything, that intelligence is to be in some respects the master as well as the servant of instinct. That this is what Mrs. Russell means is abundantly plain by her fury at capitalists, imperialists, conservatives, and churchmen, whose instincts lead them to do things of which she does not approve. For like her distinguished husband she trusts those impulses which are creative and beneficent, and distrusts those which are possessive and destructive. That is to say, like every other moralist, she trusts those parts of human nature which she trusts.

4. *Oscillation between Two Principles*

These cycles of action and reaction are disastrous to the establishment of a stable humanism. A theocratic culture depends upon an assured view of the way in which God governs the universe, and as long as that view suits the typical needs of a society made stable by custom, the theocratic culture is stable. But humanism arises in complex and changing societies, and if it is to have any power to make life coherent and orderly, it must hold an assured view of how man can govern himself. If he oscillates aimlessly between the belief that he must distrust his impulses and the belief that he may naively obey them, it is impossible for him to fix any point of reference for the development of his moral code, his educational plans, his human relationships, his politics, and his personal ideals.

It is not hard to see, I think, why he oscillates in this fashion between trust and distrust. He cannot obey every impulse, for he has conflicting impulses within himself. There are also his neighbors with their impulses. They cannot all be satisfied, for the very simple reason that the sum of their demands far outruns the available supply of satisfactions. There is not room enough, there are not objects enough in the world to fulfill all human desires. Desires are, for all practical purposes, unlimited and insatiable, and therefore any ethics which does not recognize the necessity of putting restraint upon naive desire is inherently absurd. On the other hand, it is impossible to distrust every impulse, for the only conclusion then is to commit suicide. Buddha did, to be sure, teach that craving was the source of all misery, and that it must be wholly extinguished. But it is evident from an examination of what he actually advised his disciples to renounce, that while they were to be poor, chaste, unworldly, and incurious about the nature of things, they were to be rewarded with the highest of all satisfactions, and were to be "like the broad earth, unvexed; like the pillar of the city gate, unmoved; like a pellucid lake, unruffled." For Nirvana meant, as Rhys Davids says, the extinction of a sinful, grasping condition of mind.

Confronted by two opposed views of human nature, neither of which can be taken unreservedly, moralists have had to pick and choose, deciding how much or how little they would trust the different impulses. But there is no measure by which they could decide how much of an impulse is virtuous, how much more is intemperate, and how much more than that is utterly sinful. The attempts to regulate the sexual impulse illustrate the difficulty. Shall the moralist call the complete absence of all conscious sexual desire virtue? Then he disobeys the commandment to be fruitful and multiply and replenish the earth. Shall he then limit virtuous desire to that which is felt for a lawful mate? That implies that man and woman must mate with the first person for whom they feel any sexual desire.

But this cannot always be arranged. The first person may be otherwise engaged. It becomes necessary then to permit a certain amount of promiscuous, though unfulfilled, sexual desire in the process of sexual selection. And then having somehow gotten past that difficulty, and with two persons safely mated, a whole new series of problems arise out of the question of how far sexual satisfaction depends for its virtue upon its being the successful means to, or more subtly still, the intended means to, procreation. I shall not pursue the matter further. The attempt to measure the degree in which impulse is to be permitted to express itself is obviously full of difficulties.

The moral problem remains utterly insoluble as long as men regard it as an attempt to separate their good impulses from their bad ones, and to decide how much their good impulses are to be encouraged. Morality, if it is not fixed by custom and authority, becomes a mere matter of taste determined by the idiosyncrasies of the moralist.

5. The Golden Mean and Its Difficulties

Aristotle faced this fundamental difficulty of humanism in the *Ethics*. He had expounded the theory that happiness is due to virtue, and that virtue is a mean between two extremes. There must, he said, be neither defect nor excess of any quality. We must, in brief, go so far but no further in obedience to our impulses. Thus between rashness and cowardice the mean is courage; between prodigality and niggardliness it is liberality; between incontinence and total abstinence it is temperateness; between ostentation and meanness it is magnificence; between empty boasting and little-mindedness it is magnanimity; between

flattery and moroseness it is friendliness; between bash-
fulness and impudence it is modesty; between arrogance
and false modesty, it is truthfulness.

So runs the Aristotelian catalogue, and probably no code
ever described so well the ideal of a gentleman. But having laid down his general precepts, Aristotle, unlike most
moralists, faced the difficulty of applying them. He recognized that it is one thing to accept the theory of a golden
mean, and quite another to know where that mean lies.
"For in each case it is difficult to find the mean . . . thus
it is easy, and in every man's power to be angry, and to
give and spend money; but to determine the person to
whom, and the quantity, and the time, and the motive,
and the manner, is no longer in every man's power, nor is
it easy; therefore excellence is rare, and praiseworthy and
honorable." For while the mean between excess and
defect is excellent, "it is easy to miss a mark, but difficult
to hit it."

If we look at the matter more closely in order to find out
why moral codes are, as Aristotle says, so hit and miss, we
must, I think, come to the conclusion that there is an undetected fallacy in most moral thinking which renders moral
insight abortive. It is that fallacy which I now propose to
examine.

A moral code like Aristotle's, which we may fairly regard as the rational prototype of all humanistic codes, consists of an inventory of good and bad appetites and of good
and bad satisfactions. All conventional moralizing, which
does not rest on the sheer fiat of public opinion, custom,
or God, assumes the existence of some such inventory of
permissible desires and permissible fulfilments. But what

does the making of such inventories mean? It means that good and evil are believed to be objective qualities of the natural world like weight, dimension, and motion, that certain desires are inherently good, certain others are inherently bad, and that the same is true of the different objects of desire. But this is nothing but what is known as the pathetic fallacy. For surely each desire and each object as such, taken separately without relation to anything else, is as innocent and as neutral as the forces that move the planets.

The categories of good and evil would not apply if there were no sentient being to experience good and evil. In such a world no object would be any better or any worse than any other object; nobody talks about good and bad electrons. All electrons are morally alike because no sentient being can tell them apart. Nor would the categories of good and evil apply to a world in which each impulse was in a vacuum of its own. In such a world all our impulses would be like our digestive tracts on a day when we do not know we have a stomach. If our impulses did not impinge upon each other and upon objects there would be no problem of good and evil. Therefore the quality of good and evil lies not in impulses as such, nor in objects as such, but in the relationship between impulses and objects. Therefore the making of inventories is fundamentally misleading.

There is another fallacy which is closely associated with this one. We make lists of our impulses. A standard list which is much used comprises the following: flight, repulsion, curiosity, pugnacity, self-abasement, self-assertion, parental, reproductive, gregarious, acquisitive, constructive. Whether this is a good list or not is neither here nor there. Through the ages men have been making such lists in the fond belief that they were analyzing the human character. No doubt these terms describe something; we all recognize that these words are the names of impulses that move us. But if we consider them further, we must also recognize that these impulses do not move all persons the same way, nor any one person the same way at all times in his life and under all circumstances.

It is hardly necessary, I am sure, to labor the point very much. There is the instinct to be curious: it disposes one man to measure the diameter of Betelgeuse when he is forty years old; when he was a child it disposed him to find out whether he could hang up a cat by its tail; that curious child's companion in the experiment on the cat was disposed, when he grew up, to take much trouble in finding out how much income tax his neighbor paid and whether his employer was faithful to his wife. The parental instinct of one man is to launch his child on the world as an independent human being; in another man the instinct manifests itself as a determination to have children who will depend upon him and cater to him all his days long. So when we make lists of our impulses we really do not know enough about them to pass judgment. For desires are complex, and their greatest complexity lies in the fact that they change.

The objects of desire are no less complex. Take, for example, a jade goddess. To a Chinese coolie it is an object with mysterious powers, a part of the mechanism which governs the universe. But the jade goddess is now in a Fifth Avenue shop window, and a policeman on his beat sees it. It is a green stone figure to him. The dealer inside knows that it is rare and is worth a thousand dollars. The collector could enjoy it immensely if he possessed it. The connoisseur finds intricate pleasure in it as a work of art and an elaborate interest in it as a memento of a whole culture. The objects of desire, then, are not simple things. We help to create them. We say that this man desires that woman. But what, in fact, does he desire? A few moments of ecstasy from her body, something which a thousand women could give him equally well, or an intimate union with so much of her whole being that for that very reason she is unique to him? The quality of his passion and the character of his mistress will depend in a very large degree on how much of her being he takes into account. It depends also, I hasten to add, on how much there is to take into account.

At any moment in our lives we desire only those objects which we are then capable of desiring and in the way we are then capable of desiring them. But our desires do not remain fixed from the cradle to the grave. They change. And as they change the desirability of objects about us changes too. It is impossible, then, to make lists of good and evil desires and of good and evil objects. For good and evil are qualities in the relationship between variable desires and variable objects of desire.

The attempt to construct moral codes on the basis of an inventory is an attempt to understand something which is always in process of change by treating it as a still life and taking snapshots of it. That is what moralists have almost always attempted to do. They have tried to capture the essence of a changing thing in a collection of fixed concepts. It cannot be done. The reality of human nature is bound to elude us if we look only at a momentary cross-section of it. To understand it, therefore, for the purposes of moralizing, we have to revise our intellectual apparatus, and learn to look upon each moment of behavior not as the manifestation of certain fixed elements in human nature, but as a stage in the evolution of human nature. We grow up, mature, and decline; being endowed with memory and the capacity to form habits, our conduct is cumulative. We drag our past along with us and it pushes us on. We do not make a new approach to each new experience. We approach new experiences with the expectations and habits developed by previous experience, and under the impact of novelty these expectations and habits become modified.

6. *The Matrix of Humanism*

The conception of human nature as developing behavior is, of course, accepted by all modern psychologists. If they study the child they are bound to consider him as potentially an adult. If they study the adult they are bound to regard him as originally a child. Abnormal psychology makes sense only insofar as it can be understood as an abnormal development of the personality, regardless of whether that abnormality is traceable to prenatal variations, to organic disease, or to functional disturbance. Folk psychology, whether or not one accepts the interesting but speculative hypothesis that there is a parallel between the development of the individual and the development of the race, is another mode of investigating the evolution of behavior. The concept of development is thoroughly established in psychology as the major clue to the understanding of human nature.

The moralist, since he is concerned with human nature, is compelled to employ this concept. But he employs it somewhat differently than the scientist. Being a moralist, he is interested in understanding the principles of behavior in order that he may understand the principles of right behavior. The psychologist, as such, is interested in the development of behavior, regardless of whether that development leads to misery or to happiness. He studies the various processes no matter where they lead. For in science the concept of development implies no judgment as to whether there is a good or a bad development. The development of an idiot and of a genius are on the same footing, and are theoretically of equal interest. But to the moralist the study of development is focussed on the effort to discover those processes of development which can be made to produce right relationships between the individual and his environment, and by a right relationship he is bound to mean one in which there is an harmonious adjustment between desires and the objects of desire. How often, and how nearly, it is possible for human beings to approximate such perfection is an unanswerable question. The proof of that pudding lies in the eating of it, and it is not the function of the moralist under humanism to guarantee the outcome. His function is to point out as clearly as it is possible to do so the path which presumably leads toward the good life.

In describing that path he is bound to depend upon the best available insight into the processes by which good and bad adjustments are made. In the present state of our knowledge this means that he must rely to a very large degree upon his own intuitions, commonsense, and sense of life. Great progress has been made in scientific psychology within the last generation, enough progress, I think, to supplement in important ways our own unanalyzed and intuitive wisdom about life. But it would be idle to suppose that the science of psychology is in a stage where it can be used as a substitute for experienced and penetrating imaginative insight. We can be confident that on the whole a good meteorologist can tell us more about the weather than even the most weather-wise old sea captain. But we cannot have that kind of confidence in even the best of psychologists. Indeed, an acquaintance with psychologists will, I think, compel anyone to admit that, if they are good psychologists, they are almost certain to possess a gift of insight which is unaccounted for by their technical apparatus. Doubtless it is true that in all the sciences the difference between a good scientist and a poor one comes down at last, after all the technical and theoretical procedure has been learned, to some sort of residual flair for the realities of that subject. But in the study of human nature that residual flair, which seems to be composed of intuition, commonsense, and unconsciously deposited experience, plays a much greater role than it does in the more advanced sciences.

The uses of psychology to the moralist are, therefore, in confirming and correcting, in broadening and organizing, his insight into human nature. He is confronted, of course, with a great deal of confusion. There is, to begin with, no agreed terminology, and therefore it is often almost impossible to know whether two psychologists using the same word mean the same thing. Anyone who has stumbled about amidst words like instinct, impulse, consciousness, the unconscious, will know how confusing it all is. Psychologists are still using a literary language in which the connotations of words tend to overwhelm their precise signification. To make the confusion greater there is the elaborate system-making, the headstrong generalizing, and the fierce dogmatism which have produced the psychological sects. But all of this is characteristic of a young science, and if that is borne in mind, there is nothing disconcerting about it. The Eighteenth Century in dealing with the Newtonian physics, and the Nineteenth in dealing with the Darwinian biology, went through a hullabaloo similar to that which we are now going through in connection with behaviorism, psychoanalysis, and the so-called *gestalt-theorie*. Our only concern here is to ask whether underneath all the controversy there is not some trustworthy common ground on which the moralist can stand.

I have already said that there was common ground in the concept of development. We can go further than that, however, and say, I think, that with the help of psychology we are in position now to construct reliable and useful pictures, which confirm and correct our own intuitive understanding, of the infantile and of the mature approach to experience. We can, as it were, fix these two poles and regard the history of each soul as the history of its progress from infantilism to maturity. We are by no means able as yet to describe all the phases of development between these two poles; we know that progress is often temporarily interrupted, often completely arrested, and sometimes turned into a rout. But insofar as we are able to realize clearly what a fully matured character is like, the word progress has a meaning because we know what we mean by the goal of moral effort. That goal is maturity. If we knew all the stages in the development to maturity, and how to control them, we should have an adequate science of education, we could deal successfully with functional disorders, we should have a very great mastery of the art of life. For the problems of education are at bottom problems in how to lead the child from one stage of development to another until at last he becomes an harmonious and autonomous personality; the functional disorders of the character are problems in the fixations and repressions on the path to maturity; the art of living is to pass gracefully from youth to old age, and, at last, as Montaigne said, to learn to die.

It is this progress which we have to understand and imaginatively to conceive. For in conceiving it we conceive the matrix of humanism. In this conception is to be found, I believe, the substitute for that conception of divine government which gives shape and form to the theocratic culture. To replace the conception of man as the subject of a heavenly king, which dominates the whole ancestral order of life, humanism takes as its dominant pattern the progress of the individual from helpless infancy to self-governing maturity.

7. *The Career of the Soul*

If our scientific knowledge of human nature were adequate, we could achieve in the humanistic culture that which all theologies have tried to achieve: we could found

our morality on tested truths. They would be truths about
the development of human nature, and not, as in the
popular religions, truth of physics and of history. But
our knowledge of human nature is inadequate, and therefore, like the teachers of popular religion, we have in place
of exact knowledge to invent imaginative fictions in the
hope that the progress of science will confirm and correct,
but will not utterly contradict, our hypotheses. We can
claim no more than this: for our understanding of human
nature we are compelled to use our insight and the best
available psychological science of our age, exactly as
Dante, for his understanding of the divine constitution of
the universe, had to use the accepted astronomy of his
day. If our psychology turns out to be wrong, the only
difference will be that we shall have to discard an hypothesis whereas our forefathers had to discard a revealed
dogma.

The sketch which I am about to make of the progress
from infancy to maturity is to be taken, then, not as tested
scientific truth, but as an imaginative construction. It will
be, if you like, a modern fable which symbolizes rather
than describes, as the·primitive legends of the sun god
symbolized, rather than described, the observed facts. Because it is an imaginative construction, the same meaning
might be expressed in other ways and with many variations of detail. But though the fiction itself is of no consequence, the meaning it conveys is of the highest consequence, and it is confirmed, as I shall attempt to show,
not only by ordinary insight but by the deepest wisdom
of the greatest teachers.

Freud, in a famous paper, has described the passage

from infancy to maturity as a transition from the dominion of momentary pleasure and pain to the dominion of reality. This theory is not peculiar to psychoanalysis in any of its several schools, and it does not depend upon the controverted points of doctrine. It is, in fact, more or less of a commonplace in psychological thought. I am employing it here because a distinguished colleague of Freud's, Dr. S. Ferenczi of Budapest, has made an attempt to indicate the chief stages in the development between these two poles of experience. It is a most useful bit of speculation, and while I believe it could be duplicated in terms either of behaviorism or of the *gestalt-theorie,* I do not happen to have come across any portrait of the idea which is as vivid as Dr. Ferenczi's.

The first stage of human development, says Ferenczi, takes place in the womb where the embryo lives as a parasite of the mother's body. An outer world exists for it only in a very restricted degree; all it needs for protection, warmth, and nourishment is assured by the mother. Because everything is there which is necessary for the satisfaction of the instincts, Ferenczi calls this the Period of Unconditional Omnipotence.

It is, therefore, rather disagreeable and perhaps terrifying to be born, for with the detachment from the mother and the "rude disturbance of the wish-less tranquillity he had enjoyed in the womb," the trouble of living begins, and evokes feelings which might perhaps be described as a longing to recover the perfect pre-natal adjustment. Nurses instinctively recognize this longing, says Ferenczi, and as soon as the infant expresses his discomfort by struggling and crying, they deliberately create a situation which resembles as closely as possible the one he has just left. They lay him down by the warm body of the mother, or wrap him up in soft, warm coverings, shield his eyes from the light and his ears from noise. The illusion is more or less complete, for, of course, the infant is unaware of the activities of the nurse. For all he knows "his wishes are realized simply by imagining the satisfaction of them." Ferenczi calls this the Period of Magical-Hallucinatory Omnipotence.

But this period does not last very long, since the nurse is unable to anticipate every desire that the growing infant feels. "The hallucinatory representation of the wish-fulfilment soon proves inadequate to bring about any longer a real wish-fulfilment." So the infant has to give signals, and the more complicated his wishes become the more signals he has to give. He begins to use a gesture-language, and if there is a willing nurse always at hand without too many newfangled notions, the child gets what he wants for the mere trouble of expressing his wants. Ferenczi calls this the Period of Omnipotence by the Help of Magic Gestures.

But as time goes on and as the number of his wants increases these gestures lose some of their magic. The number of the conditions increase to which he has to submit. "The outstretched hand must often be drawn back empty. . . . Indeed, an invincible hostile power may forcibly oppose itself to this gesture and compel the hand to resume its former position." At this point his sense of reality begins; the sense, that is to say, of something outside himself which does not submit to his wishes. "Till now the 'all-powerful' being has been able to feel himself one with the world that obliged him and followed his every nod, but gradually there appears a painful discordance in his experiences." Because all experiences are no longer incorporated in the ego, Ferenczi calls this the Projection Phase.

But though the child has now begun to discern the existence of reality, his sense of that reality is still quite imperfect. At first, perhaps, he regards this outer world, though it opposes his wishes, as having qualities like his own. Ferenczi calls this the Animistic Period. The child then begins to talk and to substitute for gestures actual statements of what he desires. Provided he lives in a household bent on fulfilling his wants as soon as possible, he retains to a very great degree the illusion that his wishes are sovereign. Ferenczi calls this the Period of Magic Thoughts and Magic Words.

Finally, if he matures successfully, he passes into the last period where he is no longer under the domination of the pleasure-principle: the feeling of omnipotence gives way to the full appreciation of the force of circumstances. Now unfortunately neither Freud nor Ferenczi, nor, so far as I know, any other psychoanalyst, devotes much attention to this last phase of maturity in which the sense of reality has become perfected. They are preoccupied with pathology; that is to say, with the problems which arise out of a failure to attain this last stage in which the adult makes a complete adjustment with his world because his wishes are matured to accept the conditions which reality imposes.

Yet it is this last stage which plainly constitutes the goal of moral effort, for here alone the adult once again recovers that harmony between himself and his environment which he lost in that period of infancy when he first discovered that his wishes were no longer sovereign. It is the memory of that earliest harmony which he carries with him all his days. This is his memory of a golden age, his intimation, as Wordsworth says, of immortality. But insofar as he expects by an infantile philosophy to recover that heaven which lay about him in his infancy, he is doomed to disappointment. In the womb, and for a few years of his childhood, happiness was the gratification of his naive desires. His family arranged the world to suit his wishes. But as he grows up, and begins to be an independent personality, this providence ministering to his wishes disappears. He can then no longer hope that the world will be adjusted to his wishes, and he is compelled by a long and difficult process of learning and training to adjust his wishes to the world. If he succeeds he is mature. If he is mature, he is once again harmonious with the nature of things. He has virtue. And he is happy.

The process of maturing consists then of a revision of his desires in the light of an understanding of reality. When he is completely infantile there is nothing in the world but his wishes. Therefore, he does not need and does not have an understanding of the outer world. It exists for him merely as gratification or denial. But as he begins to learn that the universe is not composed of his wishes, he begins to see his wishes in a context and in perspective. He begins to acquire a sense of space and to learn how much there is beyond his reach, until at last he realizes how small a figure he is on this earth, and how small a part of the universe is the solar system of which

ours is one of the smaller planets. He has learned a
from the days when he put out his hand and reached for
the moon. He begins, also, to acquire a sense of time and
to realize that the moment in which he feels the intense
desire to seize something is an instant in a lifetime, an
infinitesimal point in the history of the race. He acquires
a sense of birth and decay and death, a knowledge that
that which he craves, his craving itself, and he himself
who feels that craving, did not have this craving yesterday
and will no longer have it to-morrow. He acquires a
sense of cause and effect, a knowledge, that is to say, that
the sequences of events are not to be interrupted by his
preferences. He begins to discern the existence of other
beings besides himself, and to understand that they too
have their preferences and their wishes, that these wishes
are often contrary to his own, and that there is not room
enough in the world, nor are there things enough, to
gratify all the wishes of everybody.

Thus to learn the lessons of experience is to undergo
a transvaluation of the values we bring with us from the
womb and to transmute our naive impulses. The breakdown of the infantile adjustment in which providential
powers ministered to every wish compels us either to flee
from reality or to understand it. And by understanding
it we create new objects of desire. For when we know a
good deal about a thing, know how it originated, how
it is likely to behave, what it is made of, and what is its
place amidst other things, we are dealing with something
quite different from the simple object naively apprehended.

The understanding creates a new environment. The
more subtle and discriminating, the more informed and

sympathetic the understanding is, the more complex and yet ordered do the things about us become. To most of us, as Mr. Santayana once said, music is a pleasant noise which produces a drowsy revery relieved by nervous thrills. But the trained musician hears what we do not hear at all; he hears the form, the structure, the pattern, and the significance of an ideal world. A naturalist out of doors perceives a whole universe of related life which the rest of us do not even see. A world which is ordinarily unseen has become visible through the understanding. When the mind has fetched it out of the flux of dumb sensations, defined it and fixed it, this unseen world becomes more real than the dumb sensations it supplants. When the understanding is at work, it is as if circumstance had ceased to mutter strange sounds and had begun to speak our language. When experience is understood, it is no longer what it is wholly to the infant, very largely to youth, and in great measure to most men, a succession of desirable objects at which they instinctively grasp, interspersed with undesirable ones from which they instinctively shrink. If objects are seen in their context, in the light of their origin and destiny, with sympathy for their own logic and their own purposes, they become interesting in themselves, and are no longer blind stimuli to pleasant and unpleasant sensations.

For when our desires come into contact with the world created by the understanding, their character is altered. They are confronted by a much more complex stimulus which evokes a much more complex response. Instead of the naive and imperious lust of our infantile natures which is to seize, to have and to hold, our lusts are offset by other lusts and a balance between them is set up. That is to say, they are made rational by the ordered variety with which the understanding confronts them. We learn that there are more things in heaven and earth than we dreamed of in our immature philosophy, that there are many choices and that none is absolute, that beyond the mountains, as the Chinese say, there are people also. The obviously pleasant or unpleasant thus becomes less obviously what we felt it was before our knowledge of it became complicated by anticipation and memory. The immediately desirable seems not quite so desirable and the undesirable less intolerable. Delight is perhaps not so intense nor pain so poignant as youth and the romantics would have them. They are absorbed into a larger experience in which the rewards are a sustained and more even enjoyment, and serenity in the presence of inescapable evil. In place of a world, where like children we are ministered to by a solicitous mother, the understanding introduces us into a world where delight is reserved for those who can appreciate the meaning and purpose of things outside ourselves, and can make these meanings and purposes their own.

8. *The Passage into Maturity*

The critical phase of human experience, then, is the passage from childhood to maturity; the critical question is whether childish habits and expectations are to persist or to be transformed. We grow older. But it is by no means certain that we shall grow up. The human character is a complicated thing, and its elements do not necessarily march in step. It is possible to be a sage in some things and a child in others, to be at once precocious and retarded, to be shrewd and foolish, serene and irritable. For some parts of our personalities may well be more mature than others; not infrequently we participate in the enterprises of an adult with the mood and manners of a child.

The successful passage into maturity depends, therefore, on a breaking-up and reconstruction of those habits which were appropriate only to our earliest experience.

In a certain larger sense this is the essence of education. For unless a man has acquired the character of an adult, he is a lost soul no matter how good his technical equipment. The world unhappily contains many such lost souls. They are often in high places, men trained to manipulate the machinery of civilization, but utterly incapable of handling their own purposes in any civilized fashion. For their purposes are merely the relics of an infancy when their wishes were law, and they knew neither necessity nor change.

When a childish disposition is carried over into an adult environment the result is a radically false valuation of that environment. The symptoms are fairly evident. They may appear as a disposition to feel that everything which happens to a man has an intentional relation to himself; life becomes a kind of conspiracy to make him happy or to make him miserable. In either case it is thought to be deeply concerned with his destiny. The childish pattern appears also as a deep sense that life owes him something, that somehow it is the duty of the universe to look after him, and to listen sharply when he speaks to it. The notion that the universe is full of purposes utterly unknown to him, utterly indifferent to him, is as outrageous to one who is imperfectly matured as would be the conduct of a mother who forgot to give a hungry child its lunch. The childish pattern appears also as a disposition to believe that he may reach out for anything in sight and take it, and that having gotten it nobody must ever under any circumstances take it away. Death and decay are, therefore, almost an insult, a kind of mischief in the nature of things, which ought not to be there, and would not be there, if everything only behaved as good little boys believe it should. There is indeed authority for the belief that we are all being punished for the naughtiness of our first grandmother; that work and trouble and death would not really be there to plague us but for her unhappy transgression; that by rights we ought to live in paradise and have everything we want for ever and ever.

Here, too, is the source of that common complaint of the world-weary that they are tired of their pleasures. They have what they yearned for; yet having it they are depressed at finding that they do not care. Their inability to enjoy what they can have is the obverse of the desire to possess the unattainable: both are due to carrying over the expectations of youth into adult life. They find themselves in a world unlike the world of their youth; they themselves are no longer youths. But they retain the criteria of youth, and with them measure the world and their own deserts.

Here, too, is the origin of the apparent paradox that as men grow older they grow wiser but sadder. It is not a paradox at all if we remember that this wisdom which makes them sadder is, after all, an incomplete wisdom. They have grown wiser as to the character of the world, wiser too about their own powers, but they remain naive as to what they may expect of the world and themselves. The expectations which they formed in their youth persist as deeply ingrained habits to worry them in their maturity. They are only partially matured; they have become only partially wise. They have acquired skill and information, but the parts of them which are adult are embedded in other parts of their natures which are childish. For men do not necessarily mature altogether and in unison; they learn to do this and that more easily than they learn what to like and what to reject. Intelligence is often more completely educated than desire; our outward behavior has an appearance of being grown up which our inner vanities and hopes, our dim but powerful cravings, often belie. In a word, we learn the arts and the sciences long before we learn philosophy.

If we ask ourselves what is this wisdom which experience forces upon us, the answer must be that we discover the world is not constituted as we had supposed it to be. It is not that we learn more about its physical elements, or its geography, or the variety of its inhabitants, or the ways in which human society is governed. Knowledge of this sort can be taught to a child without in any fundamental way disturbing his childishness. In fact, all of us are aware that we once knew a great many things which we have since forgotten. The essential discovery of maturity has little if anything to do with information about the names, the locations, and the sequences of facts; it is the acquiring of a different sense of life, a different kind of intuition about the nature of things.

A boy can take you into the open at night and show you the stars; he might tell you no end of things about them, conceivably all that an astronomer could teach. But until and unless he feels the vast indifference of the universe to his own fate, and has placed himself in the perspective of cold and illimitable space, he has not looked maturely at the heavens. Until he has felt this, and unless he can endure this, he remains a child, and in his childishness he will resent the heavens when they are not accommodating. He will demand sunshine when he wishes to play, and rain when the ground is dry, and he will look upon storms as anger directed at him, and the thunder as a personal threat.

The discovery that our wishes have little or no authority in the world brings with it experience of the necessity that is in the nature of things. The lesson of this experience is one from which we shrink and to which few ever wholly accommodate themselves. The world of the child is a kind of enchanted island. The labor that went into procuring his food, his clothes, his toys, is wholly invisible at first. His earliest expectations are, therefore, that somehow the Lord will provide. Only gradually does the truth come home to him how much effort it costs to satisfy his wants. It takes even longer for him to understand that not only does he not get what he wants by asking for it but he cannot be sure to get what he wants by working for it. It is not easy to accept the knowledge that desire, that prayer, that effort can be and often are frustrated, that in the nature of things there is much fumbling, trial and error, deadlock and defeat.

The sense of evil is acquired late; by many persons it is never acquired at all. Children suffer, and childhood is by no means so unreservedly happy as some make it out to be. But childish suffering is not inherently tragic. It is not stamped with the irrevocability which the adult feels to be part of the essence of evil. Evil for the child is something which can be explained away, made up for, done away with. Pretentious philosophies have been built on this fancy purporting somehow to absorb the evil of the world in an all-embracing goodness, as a child's tears are dried by its mother's kisses. The discovery that there is evil which is as genuine as goodness, that there is ugliness and violence which are no less real than joy and love, is one of those discoveries that the adult is forced somehow to accept in his valuation of experience.

And then there is the knowledge, which only experience can give, that everything changes and that everything comes to an end. It is possible to tell a child about mortality, but to realize it he must live long enough to experience it. This knowledge does not come from words; it comes in feeling, in the feeling that he himself is older, in the death of kin and friends, in seeing well-known objects wear out, in discarding old things, in awakening to the sense that there is a whole new generation in the world which looks upon him as old. There is an intimation of immortality in our youth because we have not yet had experience of mortality. The persons and the things which surround us seem eternal because we have known them too briefly to realize that they change. We have seen neither their beginning nor their end.

In the last analysis we have no right to say that the world of youth is an illusion. For the child it is a true picture of the world in that it corresponds to, and is justified in, his experience. If he did not have to grow older, it would be quite sufficient because nothing in his experience would contradict it. Our sense of life as we mature is quite different, but there is no reason to think that it has any absolute finality. Perhaps if we lived several hundred years we should acquire a wholly different sense of life, compared with which all our adult philosophy would seem quite callow.

The child's sense of life can be called an illusion only if it is carried over into manhood, for then it ceases to fit his experience and to be justified by events. The habits formed in a childish environment become progressively unworkable and contradictory as the youth is thrust out from the protection of his family into an adult environment. Then the infantile conviction that his wants will somehow be met collides with the fact that he must provide for himself. The world begins to seem out of joint. The child's notion that things are to be had for the asking becomes a vast confusion in which words are treated as laws, and rhetoric as action. The childish belief that each of us is the center of an adoring and solicitous universe becomes the source of endless disappointments because we cannot reconcile what we feel is due us with what we must resign ourselves to. The sense of the unreality of evil, which our earliest experience seemed to justify, becomes a deep preference for not knowing the truth, an habitual desire to think of the world as we should prefer it to be; out of this rebellion against truth, out of this determination that the facts shall conform to our wishes, are born all manner of bigotry and uncharitableness. The child's sense that things do not end, that they are there forever, becomes, once it is carried over into maturity, a vain and anxious effort to possess things forever. The incapacity to realize that the objects of desire will last only a little while makes us put an extravagant value upon them, and to care for them, not as they are and for what they can actually give us, but for what we foolishly insist they ought to be and ought always to give us.

The child's philosophy rests upon the assumption that the world outside is in gear with his own appetites. For this reason an adult with a childish character will ascribe an authority to his appetites which may easily land him in fanaticism or frustration, in a crazy indulgence or a miserable starvation. And to the environment he will ascribe a willingness to conform to him, a capacity to be owned by him, which land him in all sorts of delusions of grandeur. Only the extreme cases are in the asylums. The world is full of semi-adult persons who secretly nurse the notion that they are, or that by rights they ought to be, Don Juan, Crœsus, Napoleon, or the Messiah.

They have brought with them the notion that they are still as intimately attached to nature and to society as the child is to its household. The adult has to break this attachment to persons and things. His world does not permit him to remain fused with it, but compels him to stand away from things. For things no longer obey his wishes. And therefore he cannot let his wishes become too deeply involved in things. He can no longer count on possessing whatever he may happen to want. And therefore he must learn to want what he can possess. He can no longer hold forever the things at which he grasps; for they change, and slip away. And therefore he must learn to hold on to things which do not slip away and change, to hold on to things not by grasping them, but by understanding them and by remembering them. Then he is wholly an adult. Then he has conquered mortality in the only way mortal men can conquer it. For he has ceased to expect anything of the world which it cannot give, and he has learned to love it under the only aspect in which it is eternal.

9. The Function of High Religion

In the light of this conception of maturity as the ultimate phase in the development of the human personality, we are, I think, in a position to understand the riddle which we set ourselves at the beginning of this chapter. I asked what significance there was for us in the fact that men have so persistently associated the good life with some form of ascetic discipline and renunciation. The answer is that asceticism is an effort to overcome immaturity. When men do not outgrow their childish desires, they seek to repress them. The ascetic discipline, if it is successful, is a form of education; if it is unsuccessful, it is an agonized conflict due to an imperfect education or an incapacity to grow up. By the same token, moral regulations imposed on others, insofar as they are at all rational, and not methods of exploitation or expressions of jealousy, are attempts to curb the social disorders which result from the activities of grown-up children.

It follows that asceticisms and moralities are at best means to an end; they are more or less inadequate substitutes for the educational process and the natural growth of wisdom. They are often confused with virtue, but they are not virtue. For virtue is the quality of mature desire, and when desire is mature the tortures of renunciations and of prohibitions have ceased to be necessary. "Blessedness," says Spinoza, "is not the reward of virtue, but virtue itself; nor should we rejoice in it for that we restrain our lusts, but, on the contrary, because we rejoice therein we can restrain our lusts." The mature character may be attained by growth and experience and insight, or by ascetic discipline, or by that process of being reborn which is called conversion; when it is attained, the moral problem of whether to yield to impulse or to check it, and how much to check it and how much to yield, has disappeared. A mature desire is innocent. This, I think, is the final teaching of the great sages. "To him who has finished the Path, and passed beyond sorrow, who has freed himself on all sides, and thrown away every fetter, there is no more fever of grief," says a Buddhist writer.

The Master said,
"At fifteen I had my mind bent on learning.
"At thirty, I stood firm.
"At forty, I had no doubts.
"At fifty, I knew the decrees of Heaven.
"At sixty, my ear was an obedient organ for the reception of truth.
"At seventy, I could follow what my heart desired, without transgressing what was right."

To be able, as Confucius indicates, to follow wh[...]
heart desires without coming into collision with the[...]
born facts of life is the privilege of the utterly inn[...]
and of the utterly wise. It is the privilege of the infant
and of the sage who stand at the two poles of experience;
of the infant because the world ministers to his heart's
desire and of the sage because he has learned what to
desire. Perhaps this is what Jesus meant when he told
his followers that they must become like little children.

If this is what he meant, and if this is what Buddha,
Confucius, and Spinoza meant, then we have here the
clue to the function of high religion in human affairs.
I venture, at least, to suggest that the function of high
religion is to reveal to men the quality of mature experience, that high religion is a prophecy and an anticipation
of what life is like when desire is in perfect harmony with
reality. It announces the discovery that men can enter into
the realm of the spirit when they have outgrown all childishness.

CHAPTER X

HIGH RELIGION AND THE MODERN WORLD

1. *Popular Religion and the Great Teachers*

IN popular thought it is taken for granted that to be religious is to accept in some form or other the theocratic view that God governs the universe. If that assumption is correct then the orthodox who inveigh against the godlessness of contemporary thought and the militant atheists who rejoice in this godlessness are both right when they insist that religion is disappearing. Insofar as religion is identical with a belief in theocracy, it has indeed lost much of its reality for modern men.

There is little doubt, I think, that popular religion has been always and everywhere theocratic in principle. If, then, we are to define as religion that which the overwhelming majority of mankind have cherished, it would be necessary to concede at once that the dissolution of the belief in a supernatural government of human affairs is a dissolution of religion itself. But if that is conceded, then it is necessary to concede also that many whom the world recognizes as its greatest religious teachers were not themselves religious men. For it could be demonstrated, I think, that in the central intuition of Aristotle, of the author of the Fourth Gospel, of Buddha, of Spinoza, to name only originating minds, the theocratic principle is irrelevant. No one of these teachers held the belief,

which is at the heart of theocratic religion, that the relationship between God and man is somehow analogous
with that of a king to his subjects, that the relationship
is in any sense a transaction between personalities involving, however subtly, a quid pro quo, that God's will and
the human will are interacting forces.

In place of the popular conception of religion as a matter of commandments and obedience, reward and punishment, in a word, as a form of government, these great
teachers placed their emphasis upon the conversion, the
education, and the discipline of the human will. Such
beliefs as they had about God were not in the nature of
oaths of allegiance to a superior; their concern was not
to placate the will of God but to alter the will of man.
This alteration of the human will they conceived as good
not because God commands it, but because it is intrinsi-
cally good for man, because by the test of experience it
yields happiness, serenity, whole-heartedness. Belief is
not, as it is in popular religion, an act which by creating
a claim upon divinity insures man's salvation; the force
of belief, as Mr. Whitehead has put it, is in "cleansing
the inward parts." Thus religion becomes "the art and
the theory of the internal life of man, so far as it depends
on the man himself and on what is permanent in the
nature of things."

The difference between religion conceived as the art
and theory of the internal life of man and religion conceived as cosmic government is the great difference
between the religion of these great sages and the religion
of the multitude. Though in matters of this kind the
distinction is not always absolutely clear in every case,

on the whole it cannot be disputed, I believe, that the difference is real and of fundamental importance. If we observe popular religions as they are administered by ecclesiastical establishments, it is overwhelmingly plain that their main appeal rests upon the belief that through their offices the devout are able to obtain eternal salvation, and even earthly favors, from an invisible king. But if we observe truly, I think, we shall see also that side by side with the popular religion, sometimes in open conflict with it, sometimes in outward conformity with it, there is generally to be found in cultivated communities a minority to whom religion is primarily a reconditioning of their own souls. They may be mystics like Eckhart, they may be platonists like Origen or Dean Inge, they may be protestants like St. Augustine and Luther in certain phases of their thought, they may be humanists like Erasmus and Montaigne; as of Confucius, it may be said of them that "the subjects on which the Master did not talk were: extraordinary things, feats of strength, disorder, and spiritual beings." They may be inside the churches or outside them, but in intention, in the inner meaning of their religion, they are wholly at variance with the popular creeds. For in one form or another they reject the idea of attaining salvation by placating God; in one form or another they regard salvation as a condition of the soul which is reached only by some kind of self-discipline.

It must be obvious that religion, conceived in this way, "as the art and theory of the internal life of man," is not dissolved by what I have been calling the acids of modernity. It is the popular religion which is dissolved.

But just because this vast dissolution is destroying the disposition to believe in a theocratic government of the universe, just because men no longer find it wholly credible that their affairs are subject to the ordinances of a heavenly king, just because they no longer vividly believe in an invisible power which regulates their lives, judges them, and sustains them, their only hope of salvation lies in a religion which provides an internal discipline.

The real effect of modernity upon religion, therefore, is to make the religion which was once the possession of an aristocracy of the spirit the only possible kind of religion for all modern men.

2. *The Aristocratic Principle*

To those who want salvation cheap, and most men do, there is very little comfort to be had out of the great teachers. Spinoza might have been speaking for all of them when he said:

> If the way which I have pointed out . . . seems exceedingly hard, it may nevertheless be discovered. Needs must it be hard, since it is so seldom found. How would it be possible, if salvation were ready to our hand, and could without great labor be found, that it should be by almost all men neglected? But all things excellent are as difficult as they are rare.

But why, we may ask, is salvation by almost all men neglected? The answer is that they do not desire that which they have never learned to desire. "One cannot," as Voltaire said, "desire that which one does not know." Can a man love good wine when he has drunk nothing but ginger beer? Did we have naturally and instinctively a taste for that which constitutes the happiness of the saved, we should already be saved, and their happiness would be ours. We lack the taste, which is, I suppose, another way of saying what the theologians meant when they spoke of original sin. To be saved, in the sense which the sages had in mind, is by conversion, education, and self-discipline to have achieved a certain quality and harmony of the passions. Then the good life is possible. But although men have often heard this said, and have read about it, unless in some measure they already desire it, the whole teaching remains mere words and abstractions which are high, cold, and remote. As long as they feel that the way to happiness is through a will other than their own, and that somehow events can in this fashion be made to yield to their unregenerate wishes, in this world or another, the wisdom of the sages will not touch their hearts, and the way which is pointed out will be neglected.

Wisdom will seem inhuman. In a sense it is inhuman, for it is so uncommon. Those who have it speak a strange language, of which the words perhaps have a familiar sound, but the meaning is too high and abstract; their delights are strange delights, and unfathomable, like a passion which we have never known. And if we encounter them in their lives or in their writings, they seem to us a mixture of grandeur and queerness. For they are at once more deeply at home in the world than the transients who make up most of mankind; yet, because of the quality of their passions, they are not wholly of the world as the worldling understands it. But unless the worldling is entirely without the capacity to transcend himself, he is bound in such an encounter to catch a glimpse now and then of an experience where there is a serenity he himself has never known, a peace that passes his understanding, an ecstasy exquisite and without regret, and happiness so clarified that it seems like brilliant and kindly light.

Yet no teacher has ever appeared in the world who was wise enough to know how to teach his wisdom to all mankind. In fact, the great teachers have attempted nothing so utopian. They were quite well aware how difficult for most men is wisdom, and they have confessed frankly that the perfect life was for a select few. It is arguable, in fact, that the very idea of teaching the highest wisdom to all men is the recent notion of a humanitarian and romantically democratic age, and that it is quite foreign to the thought of the greatest teachers. Gautama Buddha, for example, abolished caste within the religious order which he founded, and declared that the path to Nirvana was open to the lowest outcast as well as to the proudest Brahman. But it was necessary to enter the order and submit to its stringent discipline. It is obvious that Buddha never believed that very many could or would do that. Jesus, whom we are accustomed to think of as wholly catholic in his sympathies, spoke the bitter words: "Give not what is holy to the dogs and cast not your pearls before swine." In Mohammedanism that which is mystical is esoteric: "all those emotions are meant only for a small number of chosen ones . . . even some of the noblest minds in Islam restrict true religious life to an aristocracy, and accept the ignorance of the multitude as an irremediable evil."

There is an aristocratic principle in all the religions

which have attained wide acceptance. It is significant that Jesus was content to leave the governance of the mass of men to Caesar, and that he created no organization during his lifetime beyond the appointment of the Apostles. It is significant, because it shows how much more he was concerned with the few who could be saved than with arranging the affairs of the mass of mankind. Plato, who was a more systematic teacher than either Jesus or Buddha, did work out an elaborate social order which took account not only of the philosophers, but of all the citizens of the state. But in that very attempt he rested upon the premise that most men will not attain the good life, and that for them it is necessary to institute the laws. "The worthy disciples of philosophy will be but a small remnant," he said, ". . . the guardian . . . must be required to take the longer circuit, and toil at learning as well as at gymnastics, or he will never reach the highest knowledge of all which is his proper calling."

Perhaps because they looked upon the attempts as hopeless, perhaps because they did not know how to go about it, perhaps because they were so wise, the greatest teachers have never offered their full wisdom to the multitude. Like Mr. Valiant-for-truth in *The Pilgrim's Progress* they said: "My sword I give to him that shall succeed me in my pilgrimage, and my courage and skill to him that can get it."

3. *The Peculiarity of the Modern Situation*

But because the teaching of the sages was incomprehensible, the multitude, impressed but also bewildered, ignored them as teachers and worshipped them as gods.

In their wisdom the people were not interested, but in legends of their power, which rumor created, there was something understandable. And thus, the religions which have been organized around the names of great spiritual teachers have been popular in proportion, one might almost say, to the degree in which the original insight into the necessity for conversion and self-discipline has been reduced to a system of commands and promises which the common man can understand.

For popular religion is suited to the capacities of the unconverted. The adherents of a popular religion necessarily include an enormous number of people who are too young, or too feeble, too dull or too violent, too unstable or too incurious, to have any comprehension whatsoever of anything but the simplest scheme of rewards and punishments. An organized religion cannot neglect them if it has any pretensions to being universal. The great ecclesiastical establishments have often sheltered spiritual lives, and drawn new vitality from them. But fundamentally the great churches are secular institutions; they are governments preoccupied inevitably with the regulation of the unregenerate appetites of mankind. In their scriptures there is to be found the teaching that true salvation depends upon internal reform of desire. But since this reform is so very difficult, in practice the churches have devoted themselves not so much to making real conversions, as to governing the dispositions of the unconverted multitude.

They are immensely engaged by the task of administering their moral codes, persuading their congregations with promises, and threatening them with punishments

if they do not keep their childish lusts within bounds.
The fact that they use rewards and punishments, and
appeal even to Caesar, is evidence enough that they are
dealing with the unconverted. The fact that they invoke
authority is in itself evidence that they are speaking to
the naive. The fact that they pretend to have certain
knowledge about the constitution of the universe is evidence that they are interested in those who are not wise
enough to understand the limitations of knowledge. For
to the few who are converted, goodness is pleasant, and
needs no sanctions. It needs no authority, for it has been
verified by experience. But when men have to be coerced
into goodness, it is plain that they do not care for it.

Now although the great teachers saw clearly enough
the difference between the popular religion and their own
insight, they were under no great compulsion to try and
overcome it. They accepted the fact that the true
religion was esoteric and for the few. They saw that it
demanded the re-education of desire, but they had no
systematic and tested knowledge of how new habits can
be formed. Invincible as was their insight into the principle of happiness, they were compelled to depend upon
introspection, and to generalize from a limited observation. They understood that the good life was in some
degree an acquired disposition; they were aware that it
is not easily or naively acquired.

For those who somehow had the disposition, the
teachers instituted stern disciplines which were really
primitive experiments in the re-education of desire. But
there was no very urgent practical need which impelled
them to search for ways of making disciplines more

widely available. Those who submitted to them were in general individuals who were already out of the ordinary. The mass of mankind lived solidly within the framework of custom and the psychological compulsions of theocracy. There was no pressing reason, as there is to-day, now that this ancestral order is dissolved, why anyone should seek to formulate a mode of life by which ordinary men, thrown upon their own resources, can find their way without supernatural rules, commands, punishments, and compensations. In the past there were a few men here and there who had somehow, for reasons which we do not understand, outgrown the ancestral society in which they lived. But the society itself remained. It sheltered them. And it ruled the many.

The peculiarity of our modern situation is that multitudes, instead of a few, are compelled to make radical and original adjustments. These multitudes, though they have lost the ancient certainties, have not outgrown the needs to which they ministered. They need to believe, but they cannot. They need to be commanded, but they cannot find a commander. They need support, and there is none. Their situation is adult, but their dispositions are not. The religion of the spirit would suit their needs, but it would seem to be beyond their powers.

4. *The Stone Which the Builders Rejected*

The way of life which I have called high religion has in all ages seemed so unapproachably high that it has been reserved for a voluntary aristocracy of the spirit. It has, in fact, been looked upon not only as a kind of splendid idiosyncrasy of a few men here and there, but as incompatible, in essence, with the practical conditions under which life is lived. It is for these reasons, no doubt, that the practice of high religion has almost invariably been associated either with a solitary asceticism or with a specially organized life in monastic establishments. High religion has been regarded as something separate from the main concerns of mankind.

It is not difficult to see why this was so if we realize that the insight into the value of disinterestedness, which is the core of high religion, was not a sudden discovery nor a complete one, anywhere or any time. Like all other things associated with evolutionary man, this insight must have had very crude beginnings; it would be possible to show, I think, that there have been many tentative and partial perceptions of it which, under the clarifying power of men of genius, have at times become coherent. When we remember that we are dealing with an insight into the qualities of a matured personality, there is no reason to suppose that the full significance of this insight has ever been completely exhausted. It seems far more likely that the sages demonstrated the existence of the realm of the spirit, but that it still remains to be thoroughly explored.

If that is true then the attempt to live by these partial insights must necessarily have presented inordinate practical difficulties. Pythagoras, for example, seems to have grasped the idea that the disinterested study of mathematics and music was cleansing to the passions and also that in order to be disinterested it was necessary to have purity of mind. So when he established his society in Southern Italy he evidently attempted to combine the serious pursuit of science with an ascetic discipline. But the pursuit of science was too much for the mass of the faithful who assumed that "to follow Pythagoras meant to go barefoot and to abstain from animal flesh and beans." And this in turn was too much for the dignity of the learned who proceeded to dissociate themselves from the disciplinary aspect of the Pythagorean teaching. It is a fair conclusion, I think, that the breakdown of this early experiment must have been due fundamentally to the fact that Pythagoras could not have known any well-tested method of equipping his followers to appreciate science or anything besides a crude asceticism as a means of moral discipline. If this is true, then the reason for the failure lay in the fact that though the original insight was marvelously good, it was not implemented with the necessary technical knowledge for applying it. Only a few, we may suppose, who were already by the accidents of nature and nurture suited to the Pythagorean ideal, can ever have successfully applied it.

In the Christian pursuit of the higher religious life the practical difficulties presented themselves in a different way. In its beginning Christianity was a sect of obscure men and women who were out of touch with the intellectual interests of the Roman world. They were persecuted aliens both in Palestine and elsewhere, and they came to the conclusion that the Roman Empire and all its concerns was the Kingdom of Satan. This, together with the widespread belief in the Second Coming of Christ, dissociated the Christian life at the outset from the life of the world. Later on, when Christianity became the official religion of the Empire, and the Church a great secular institution which concerned itself with government and property and diplomacy and war, those who wished to live as nearly as possible according to the original meaning of the Gospels were quite evidently compelled to withdraw and live a separated life. "If any man love the world, the love of the Father is not in him. For all that is in the world, the lust of the flesh, and the lust of the eyes, and the pride of life, is not of the Father, but is of the world. And the world passeth away, and the lust thereof: but he that doeth the will of God abideth forever."

Although for some centuries the monasteries were the centers of what learning there was, the impression left by monasticism on mankind seems to have been that the highest type of religious life is not disinterested in human affairs, but uninterested; that it requires not merely the renunciation of worldly desires, but of the world itself. The insight was imperfect, and therefore as an example to mankind the practice was abortive and confusing. Yet only an uncomprehending person can fail to see that the vows of poverty, chastity, and obedience proceeded from a profound, if partial, understanding of human nature and its most perfect harmony. Plainly all manner of disorder both in society and in the individual result from greed, uncontrollable sexual desire, arrogance, and imperiousness. That was so plain to the early Christians, and on the other hand it was so little plain how those powerful passions could be civilized, that the monastics in effect gave up and attempted to excise them entirely from their natures. In this they did not succeed.

Had they known any way of curing the fever of human

passion except by attempting to excise it, the insight of high religion would have had some practicable meaning for those who did not withdraw from the world. But no way was known, and therefore the practice of high religion had to mean separation from human society and violence to human nature. But why was there no other way known of overcoming the chaos of the passions? Was it because there is no other way? If that were so then the world is as hopeless as the early Christians thought it was; indeed it is more hopeless because it does not show any signs, as they believed, of coming to an end. Was it because the early Christian Fathers were not wise enough to discover a way? It is always a good rule, I think, to discard any idea based on the premise that the best minds of another age were congenitally inferior to our own. My conviction is that necessity is the mother of discovery and invention, and that the reason why the insight of high religion and the methods of practicing it were so imperfectly developed, is that there was no practical necessity for developing them.

The mass of men lived in an ancestral order which was regulated by custom and authority, and made endurable by usage and compensatory consolations. The organic quality of that society into which they fitted took care of their passions; those who had outgrown such a society, or were so constituted that they did not fit it, were the exceptions. From them came the insight of high religion; for them a separated life was a possible solution of their personal problems. There was nothing in the nature of things to compel men to work out a way of life, I won't say for all men, but at least for many men, by which they could govern their own natures. Behind any such effort there would almost certainly have to be an urgent need. For the inertia of the human race is immense.

It is my thesis that because the acids of modernity have dissolved the adjustments of the ancestral order, there exists to-day on a scale never before experienced by mankind and of an urgency without a parallel, the need for that philosophy of life of which the insight of high religion is a prophecy. For it is immature and unregenerate desire which creates the disorders and the frustrations that confound us. The preoccupation of the popular religion has been to find a way of governing these disorders and of compensating for their frustrations. The preoccupation of high religion is with the regeneration of the passions that create the disorders and the frustrations. Insofar as modernity has dissolved the power of the popular religion to govern and to compensate, the need for a high religion which regenerates becomes imperative, and what was once a kind of spiritual luxury of the few has, under modern conditions, become an urgent necessity of the many. The insight of high religion which has hitherto indicated a kind of bypath into rare experiences is now a trail which the leaders of mankind are compelled to take.

There is implied in this a radical displacement in the field of morals. The main interest of the practical moralist in the past has been to interpret, administer, and enforce a moral code. He knew what was right. The populace acknowledged that he knew what was right. His task was to persuade and compel them to do what was right. There was a tacit assumption, which was quite correct, that very often the populace and even the moralist himself would much rather have done what was wrong. Very often they did it. Then they were punished in this world or in the next. But to-day the moralist finds himself in a different position. He is no longer absolutely sure that he knows what is right. The populace, even if it respects him, is disinclined to believe that a thing is right simply because he says it is. The populace continues very frequently to prefer what was once regarded as wrong. It no longer knows whether it is right or wrong, and of course it gives itself the benefit of the doubt. The result is that there no longer exists a moral code which the moralist can interpret, administer, and enforce. The effect of that is moral anarchy within and without. Since there is no principle under modern conditions which authorizes the re-establishment of a moral code, the moralist, unless he revises his premises, becomes entirely ineffectual. To revise his premises can, under the circumstances, mean only one thing: that he occupies himself with the problem of how to encourage that growth into maturity, that outgrowing of naive desire, that cultivation of disinterestedness, which render passion innocent and an authoritative morality unnecessary.

The novelty of all this lies in the fact that the guardians of morality among the people are compelled at last to take seriously what the teachers of wisdom have taught. The insight of high religion may be said, then, to be a discovery in the field of human experience comparable with those prophetic conceptions in the natural sciences which, after being looked upon for long periods as a curiosity, are at last, because circumstances are ripe, seen to be the clue to otherwise insoluble perplexities. The concept of evolution was discovered by sheer insight innumerable times before the time of Darwin. Not much came of it until the rapid evolution of human affairs after the industrial revolution had somehow brought this neglected insight into focus with men's interests. There are many conceptions in the science of the Greeks which are true intimations of what modern physicists have found. But an insight of this sort comes into its own only when circumstances conspire to make it inevitably appropriate. It is my contention that in the field of morals circumstances are producing a somewhat analogous condition: that the insight of the sages into the value of disinterestedness has become the clue to otherwise insoluble perplexities.

PART III

THE GENIUS OF MODERNITY

Where is the way where light dwelleth?

JOB 38:19.

CHAPTER XI

THE CURE OF SOULS

1. *The Problem of Evil*

THE greatest of all perplexities in theology has been to reconcile the infinite goodness of God with his omnipotence. Nothing puts a greater strain upon the faith of the common man than the existence of utterly irrational suffering in the universe, and the problem which tormented Job still troubles every devout and thoughtful man who beholds the monstrous injustices of nature. If there were no pain in the world except that which was felt by responsible beings who had knowingly transgressed some law of conduct, there would, of course, be no problem of evil. Pain would be nothing but a rational punishment. But the pain which is suffered by those who according to all human standards are innocent, by children and by animals, for example, cannot be fitted into any rational theory of reward and punishment. It never has been. The classic attempts to solve the problem of evil invariably falsify the premises. This falsification may for a time satisfy the inquirer, but it does not settle the problem. That is why the problem is forever presenting itself again.

The solutions which have been proposed neglect one or the other of the attributes of God: tacitly or otherwise either his infinite power or his infinite love is denied.

In the Old Testament, at least in the older parts of it, the power of God is exalted at the expense of his goodness. For it is simply impossible by any human standard and within any intelligible meaning of the words to regard Yahveh as wholly good. His cruelty is notorious and his capriciousness is that of an Oriental despot. It is admitted, I believe, by all but the most literally-minded of the fundamentalists that there are innumerable incidents in the Old Testament which have to be expurgated if the Bible is to be used as a source book of conduct for impressionable children. Now for the ancient Hebrews who conceived God in their fashion, the problem of evil did not exist because it had not occurred to them that a ruler should be just and good as well as great and powerful.

As men came to believe that God must be just, beneficent, and loving, the problem soon presented itself. And in the Book of Job, which is supposed to date from the Fifth or Fourth Century B.C., we have a poignant effort to solve it. Job's conclusion is that the goodness of Jehovah is among the "things too wonderful for me." He accepts the judgments of God, and acknowledges their goodness by attributing to God a kind of goodness which is unlike the human conception of goodness. He holds fast to the premise that God is omnipotent—"I know that thou canst do all things"—and the other premise that God is beneficent he redefines. Job's mind was satisfied, and it is reported that he prospered greatly thereafter. What had really happened was that Job gave up the attempt to prove that God was like Job, that the world was as Job wished it to be, and so piously and with his mind at rest he made the best of things, and went about his affairs.

In Job the solution is reached by claiming that what seems evil to us would really be recognized as goodness if our minds were not so limited. To the naive this is no solution at all, for it depends upon using the word 'good' in two senses; actually it was a perfect solution, for Job had resigned himself to the fact that God and the universe in which he was manifest are not controlled by human desires. Those who refused to accept this solution involved themselves in intricate theorizing. Some of them argued that evil is an illusion. This theory has been widely held, though it is rather difficult to see how, if evil is an illusion, good is not also an illusion. The one seems as vividly real as the other. It has also been argued by some that evil is not important. This, of course, does not solve the theoretical problem. In fact it ignores the problem and is really a piece of advice as to how men ought to conduct themselves in the presence of God. Many have argued, also, that evil exists in the world to test human character, that by bearing it and conquering it men prove their worth. There is a core of truth in this observation as there is in the theory that many things are not so bad as they seem. But it does not explain why a good and all-powerful Deity chose to make men go through a school of suffering to achieve goodness, when he might have created them good in the first place.

These theoretical difficulties have furnished the material for endless debate. I shall not pursue the matter in all its intricacies, but I venture to point out that what is attempted in all these solutions is ultimately to make plain why the ruler of the universe does not order things as we should order them if we had his power. Once we confess, as Job finally did, that the plan of the universe is not what we naively wish it would be, there is no problem of evil. For the whole difficulty arises because of our desire to impute to the universe itself, or to the god who rules it, purposes like our own; failing to find them, we are disappointed, and are plunged into elaborate and interminable debate.

The final insight of Job, though it seems to be consistent with the orthodox popular religion, is really wholly inconsistent with the inwardness of popular religion. The God of the Book of Job does not minister to human desires, and the story of Job is really the story of a man's renunciation of the belief in such a God. It is the story of how a man learned to accept life maturely. The God whose ways Job finally acknowledges is no longer a projection of Job's desires. He is like the God of Spinoza who cannot be cajoled into returning the love of his worshipper. He is, in short, the God of an impersonal reality.

Whether God is conceived as a creator of that reality, who administers it inexorably, or whether he is identified with reality and is conceived as the sum total of its laws, or whether, as in the language of modern science, the name of God is not employed at all, is a matter of metaphysical taste. The great divide lies between those who think their wishes are of more than human significance and those who do not. For these latter the problem of evil does not arise out of the difficulty of reconciling the existence of evil with their assumptions. They do not assume that reality must conform to human desire. The problem for them is wholly practical. It is the problem of how to remove evil and of how to bear the evil which cannot be removed.

Thus from the attempt to explain the ways of God in the world as it now is, nature and human nature being what they are, the center of interest is shifted to an attempt to discover ways of equipping man to conquer evil. This displacement has in fact taken place in the modern world. In their actual practice men do not try to account for evil in order that they may accept it; they do not deny evil in order that they may not have to account for it; they explain it in order that they may deal with it.

2. *Superstition and Self-Consciousness*

This change of attitude toward evil is not, as at first perhaps it may seem, merely a new way of talking about the same thing. It alters radically the nature of evil itself. For evil is not a quality of things as such. It is a quality of our relation to them. A dissonance in music is unpleasant only to a musical ear. Pain is an evil only if someone suffers, and there are those to whom pain is pleasure and most men's evil their good. For things are neutral and evil is a certain way of experiencing them.

To realize this is to destroy the awfulness of evil. I use the word 'awful' in its exact sense, and I mean that in abandoning the notion that evil has to be reconciled with a theory of how the world is governed, we rob it of universal significance. We deflate it. The psychological consequences are enormous, for a very great part of all human suffering lies not in the pain itself, but in the anxiety contributed by the meaning which we attach to it. Lucretius understood this quite well, and in his superb argument against the fear of death he reasoned that death has no terror because nothing can be terrible to those who no longer exist. Before we were born, he says, "we felt no distress when the Poeni from all sides came together to do battle. . . . For he whom evil is to befall, must in his own person exist at the very time it comes, if the misery and suffering are haply to have any place at all." St. Thomas defines superstition as the vice of excess in religion, and in this sense of the word it may be said that the effect of the modern approach is to take evils out of the context of superstition.

They cease to be signs and portents symbolizing the whole of human destiny and become specific and distinguishable situations which have to be dealt with. The effect of this is not only to limit drastically the meaning, and therefore the dreadfulness, of any evil, but to substitute for a general sense of evil an analytical estimate of particular evils. They are then seen to be of long duration and of short, preventable, curable, or inevitable. As long as all evils are believed somehow to fit into a divine, if mysterious, plan, the effort to eradicate them must seem on the whole futile, and even impious. The history of medical progress offers innumerable instances of how men have resisted the introduction of sanitary measures because they dreaded to interfere with the providence of God. It is still felt, I believe, in many quarters, even in medical circles, that to mitigate the labor pains in childbirth is to blaspheme against the commandment that in pain children shall be brought forth. An aura of dread surrounds evil as long as evil situations remain entangled with a theory of divine government.

The realization that evil exists only because we feel it to be painful helps us not only to dissociate it from this aura of dread but to dissociate ourselves from our own feelings about it. This is a momentous achievement in the inner life of man. To be able to observe our own feelings as if they were objective facts, to detach ourselves from our own fears, hates, and lusts, to examine them, name them, identify them, understand their origin, and finally to judge them, is somehow to rob them of their imperiousness. They are no longer the same feelings. They no longer dominate the whole field of consciousness. They seem no longer to command the whole energy of our being. By becoming conscious of them we in some fashion or other destroy their concentration and diffuse their energy into other channels. We cease to be possessed by one passion; contrary passions retain their vitality, and an equilibrium tends to establish itself.

Just what the psychological mechanism of all this is I do not pretend to say. It is something to which psychologists are giving increasing attention. But since Hellenic times the phenomenon which I have been describing has been well known. It was undoubtedly what the Sophists meant by the injunction: know thyself. It was in large measure to achieve control through detachment that Socrates elaborated his dialectic, for the Socratic dialectic is an instrument for making men self-conscious, and therefore the masters of their motives. Spinoza grasped this principle with great clarity. "An emotion," he says, "which is a passion ceases to be a passion as soon as we form a clear and distinct idea of it." He goes on to say that "insofar as the mind understands all things as necessary, it has more power over the emotions, or is less passive to them."

The more recent discoveries in the field of psychoanalysis are an elaboration of this principle. They are based on the discovery of Freud and Breuer at the close of the last century that a catharsis of emotion is often obtained if the patient can be made to recall, and thus to relive by describing it, the emotional situation which troubles him. The release of the psychic poison is known technically as an abreaction. Where the new psychology supplements the insights of the Sophists, of Socrates, and Spinoza, is in the demonstration that there are powerful passions affecting our lives of which it is impossible by ordinary effort of memory "to form a clear and distinct idea." They are said to be unconscious, or more accurately, I suppose, they are out of the reach of the normal consciousness. Freud and his school have invented an elaborate technic by which the analyst is able frequently to help the patient thread his way back through a chain of associations to the buried passion and fetch it into consciousness.

The special technic of psychoanalysis can be tested only by scientific experience. The therapeutic claims made by psychoanalysts, and their theories of the functional disorders, lie outside the realm of this discussion. But the essential principle is not a technical matter. Anyone can confirm it out of his own experience. It has been discovered and rediscovered by shrewd observers of human nature for at least two thousand years. To become detached from one's passions and to understand them consciously is to render them disinterested. A disinterested mind is harmonious with itself and with reality.

This is the principle by which a humanistic culture becomes bearable. If the principle of a theocratic culture is dependence, obedience, conformity in the presence of a superhuman power which administers reality, the principle of humanism is detachment, understanding, and disinterestedness in the presence of reality itself.

3. *Virtue*

It can be shown, I think, that those qualities which civilized men, regardless of their theologies and their allegiances, have agreed to call virtues, have disinterestedness as their inner principle. I am not talking now about the eccentric virtues which at some time or other have been held in great esteem. I am not talking about the virtue of not playing cards, or of not drinking wine, or of not eating beef, or of not eating pork, or of not admitting that women have legs. These little virtues are historical accidents which may or may not once have had a rational origin. I am talking about the central virtues which are esteemed by every civilized people. I am talking about such virtues as courage, honor, faithfulness, veracity, justice, temperance, magnanimity, and love.

They would not be called virtues and held in high esteem if there were no difficulty about them. There are innumerable dispositions which are essential to living that no one takes the trouble to praise. Thus it is not accounted a virtue if a man eats when he is hungry or goes to bed when he is ill. He can be depended upon to take care of his immediate wants. It is only those actions which he cannot be depended upon to do, and yet are highly desirable, that men call virtuous. They recognize that a premium has to be put upon certain qualities if men are to make the effort which is required to transcend their ordinary impulses. The premium consists in describing these desirable and rarer qualities as virtues. For virtue is that kind of conduct which is esteemed by God, or public opinion, or that less immediate part of a man's personality which he calls his conscience.

To transcend the ordinary impulses is, therefore, the common element in all virtue. Courage, for example, is the willingness to face situations from which it would be more or less natural to run away. No one thinks it is courageous to run risks unwittingly. The drunken driver of an automobile, the boy playing with a stick of dynamite, the man drinking water which he does not know is polluted, all take risks as great as those of the most renowned heroes. But the fact that they do not know the risks, and do not, therefore, have to conquer the fear they would feel if they did know them, robs their conduct of all courage. The test is not the uselessness or even the undesirability of their acts. It is useless to go over Niagara Falls in a barrel. But it is brave, assuming the performer to be in his right mind. It is a wicked thing to assassinate a king. But if it is not done from ambush, it is brave, however wicked and however useless.

Because courage consists in transcending normal fears, the highest kind of courage is cold courage; that is to say, courage in which the danger has been fully realized and there is no emotional excitement to conceal the danger. The world instantly recognized this in Colonel Lindbergh's flight to Paris. He flew alone; he was not an impetuous fool, but a man of the utmost sobriety of judgment. He had no companion to keep his courage screwed up; he knew exactly what he was doing, yet apparently he did not realize the rewards which were in store for him. The world understood that here was somebody who was altogether braver than the average sensual man. For Colonel Lindbergh did not merely conquer the Atlantic Ocean; he conquered those things in himself which the rest of us would have found unconquerable.

The cold courage of a man like Noguchi who, though in failing health, went into one of the unhealthiest parts of Africa to study a deadly disease, could come only from a nature which was overwhelmingly interested in objects outside itself. Noguchi must have known exactly how dangerous it was for him to go to Africa, and exactly how horrible was the disease to which he exposed himself. To have gone anyway is really to have cared for science in a way which very few care for anything so remote and impersonal. But even courage like Lindbergh's and Noguchi's is more comprehensible than the kind of courage which anonymous men have displayed. I am thinking of the four soldiers at the Walter Reed Hospital who let themselves be used for the study of yellow fever. They did not even have Lindbergh's interest in performing a great feat or Noguchi's interest in science to buoy them up and carry them past the point where they might have faltered. Their courage was as near to absolute courage as it is possible to imagine, and I who think this cannot even recall their names.

To understand the inwardness of courage would be, I

think, to have understood almost all the other important virtues. It is "not only the chiefest virtue and most dignifies the haver," but it embodies the principle of all virtue, which is to transcend the immediacy of desire and to live for ends which are transpersonal. Virtuous action is conduct which responds to situations that are more extensive, more complicated, and take longer to reach their fulfilment, than the situations to which we instinctively respond. An infant knows neither vice nor virtue because it can respond only to what touches it immediately. A man has virtue insofar as he can respond to a larger situation.

He has honor if he holds himself to an ideal of conduct though it is inconvenient, unprofitable, or dangerous to do so. He has veracity if he says and believes what he thinks is true though it would be easier to deceive others or himself. He is just if he acknowledges the interests of all concerned in a transaction and not merely his own apparent interest. He is temperate if, in the presence of temptation, he can still prefer Philip sober to Philip drunk. He is magnanimous if, as Aristotle says, he cares "more for truth than for opinion," speaks and acts openly, will not live at the will of another, except it be a friend, does not recollect injuries, does not care that he should be praised or that others should be blamed, does not complain or ask for help in unavoidable or trifling calamities. For such a man, as the word 'magnanimous' itself implies, is "conversant with great matters."

A man who has these virtues has somehow overcome the inertia of his impulses. Their disposition is to respond to the immediate situation, and not merely to the situation

at the moment, but to the most obvious fragment of it, and
not only to the most obvious fragment, but to that aspect
which promises instant pleasure or pain. To have virtue
is to respond to larger situations and to longer stretches
of time and without much interest in their immediate
result in convenience and pleasure. It is to overcome the
impulses of immaturity, to detach one's self from the objects that preoccupy it and from one's own preoccupations.
There are many virtues in the catalogues of the moralists,
and they have many different names. But they have a
common principle, which is detachment from that which
is apparently pleasant or unpleasant, and they have a
common quality, which is disinterestedness, and they
spring from a common source, which is maturity of
character.

Few men, if any, possess virtue in all its varieties
because few men are wholly matured to the core of their
being. We are for the most part like fruit which is partly
ripened: there is sourness and sweetness in our natures.
This may be due to the casualness of our upbringing; it
may be due to unknown congenital causes; it may be due
to functional and organic disease, to partial inferiorities of
mind and body. But it is due also to the fact that we can
give our full attention only to a few phases of our experience. With the equipment at our disposal we are forced
to specialize and to neglect very much. Hence the mature
scientist with petty ambitions and ignoble timidities.
Hence the realistic statesman who is a peevish husband.
Hence the man who manages his affairs in masterly
fashion and bungles every personal relationship when he
is away from his office. Hence the loyal friend who is a

crooked politician, the kind father who is a merciless employer, the champion of mankind who is an intolerable companion. If any of these could carry over into all their relationships the qualities which have made them distinguished in some, they would be wholly adult and wholly good. It would not be necessary to imagine the ideal character, for he would already exist.

It is out of these practical virtues that our conception of virtue has been formed. We may be sure that no quality is likely to have become esteemed as a virtue which did not somewhere and sometime produce at least the appearance of happiness. The virtues are grounded in experience; they are not idle suggestions inadvertently adopted because somebody took it into his head one fine day to proclaim a new ideal. There are, to be sure, certain residual and obsolete virtues which no longer correspond to anything in our own experience and now seem utterly arbitrary and capricious. But the cardinal virtues correspond to an experience so long and so nearly universal among men of our civilization, that when they are understood they are seen to contain a deposited wisdom of the race.

4. From Clue to Practice

The wisdom deposited in our moral ideals is heavily obscured at the present time. We continue to use the language of morality, having no other which we can use. But the words are so hackneyed that their meanings are concealed, and it is very hard, especially for young people, to realize that virtue is really good and really relevant.

Morality has become so stereotyped, so thin and verbal, so encrusted with pious fraud, it has been so much monopolized by the tender-minded and the sentimental, and made so odious by the outcries of foolish men and sour old women, that our generation has almost forgotten that virtue was not invented in Sunday schools but derives originally from a profound realization of the character of human life.

This sense of unreality is, I believe, due directly to the widespread loss of genuine belief in the premises of popular religion. Virtue is a product of human experience: men acquired their knowledge of the value of courage, honor, temperance, veracity, faithfulness, and love, because these qualities were necessary to their survival and to the attainment of happiness. But this human justification of virtue does not carry conviction to the immature, and would not of itself break up the inertia of their naive impulses. Therefore, virtue which derives from human insight has to be imposed on the immature by authority; what was obtained on Sinai was not the revelation of the moral law but divine authority to teach it.

Now the very thing which made moral wisdom convincing to our ancestors makes it unconvincing to modern men. We do not live in a patriarchal society. We do not live in a world which disposes us to a belief in theocratic government. And therefore insofar as moral wisdom is entangled with the premises of theocracy it is unreal to us. The very thing which gave authority to moral insight for our forefathers obscures moral insight for us. They lived in the kind of world which disposed them to practice virtue if it came to them as a divine commandment. A thoroughly modernized young man to-day distrusts moral wisdom precisely because it is commanded.

It is often said that this distrust is merely an aspect of the normal rebellion of youth. I do not believe it. This distrust is due to a much more fundamental cause. It is due not to a rebellion against authority but to an unbelief in it. This unbelief is the result of that dissolution of the ancient order out of which modern civilization is emerging, and unless we understand the radical character of this unbelief we shall never understand the moral confusion of this age. We shall fail to see that morals taught with authority are pervaded with a sense of unreality because the sense of authority is no longer real. Men will not feel that wisdom is authentic if they are asked to believe that it derives from something which does not seem authentic.

We may be quite certain, therefore, that we shall not succeed in making the traditional morality convincingly authentic to modern men. The whole tendency of the age is to make it seem less and less authentic. The effort to impose it, nevertheless, merely deepens the confusion by converting the discussion of morals from an examination of experience into a dispute over its metaphysical sanctions. The consequence of this dispute is to drive men, especially the most sensitive and courageous, further away from insight into virtue and deeper and deeper into mere negation and rebellion. What they are actually rebelling against is the theocratic system in which they do not believe. But because that system appears to them to claim a vested interest in morality they empty out the baby with the bath, and lose all sense of the inwardness of deposited wisdom.

For that reason the recovery of moral insight depends upon disentangling virtue from its traditional sanctions and the metaphysical framework which has hitherto supported it. It will be said, I know, that this would rob virtue of its popular prestige. My answer is that in those communities which are deeply under modern influences the loss of belief in these very traditional sanctions and this very metaphysical framework has robbed virtue of its relevance. I should readily grant that for communities and for individuals which are outside the orbit of modernity, it is neither necessary nor desirable to disentangle morality from its ancient associations. It is also impossible to do so, for when the ancestral order is genuinely alive, there is no problem of unbelief. But where the problem exists, when the ancient premises of morality have faded into mere verbal acknowledgments, then these ancient premises obscure vision. They have ceased to be the sanctions of virtue and have become obstructions to moral insight. Only by deliberately thinking their way past these obstructions can modern men recover that innocence of the eye, that fresh, authentic sense of the good in human relations on which a living morality depends.

I have tried in these pages to do that for myself. I am under no illusion as to the present value of the conceptions arrived at. I regard them simply as a probable clue to the understanding of modernity. If the clue is indicative, the more we explore the modern world the more coherence it will give to our understanding of it. A true insight is fruitful; it multiplies insight, until at last it not only illuminates a situation but provides a practical guide to conduct. I believe the insight of high religion into the value of disinterestedness will, if pursued resolutely, untangle the moral confusion of the age and make plain, as it is not now plain, what we are really driving at in our manifold activity, what we are compelled to want, what, rather dimly now, we do want, and how to proceed about achieving it. To say that is to say that I believe in the hypothesis. I do believe in it. I believe that this valuation of human life, which was once the possession of an élite, now conforms to the premises of a whole civilization.

The proof of that must lie in a detailed and searching examination of the facts all about us. If the ideal of human character which is prophesied in high religion is really suitable and necessary in modern civilization, then an examination ought to show that events themselves are pregnant with it. If they are not, then all this is moonshine and cobwebs and castles in the air. Unless circumstance and necessity are behind it, the insight of high religion is still, as it has always been hitherto, a noble eccentricity of the soul. For men will not take it seriously, they will not devote themselves to the discovery and invention of ways of cultivating maturity, detachment, and disinterestedness unless events conspire to drive them to it.

The realization of this ideal is plainly a process of education in the most inclusive sense of that term. But it will not do much good to tell mothers that they should lead their children away from their childishness; an actual mother, even if she understood so abstruse a bit of advice, and did not reject it out of hand as a reflection upon the glory of childhood, would insist upon being told very concretely what this good advice means and how with a bawling infant in the cradle you go about cultivating his capacity to be disinterested. It is not much better to offer the advice to school-teachers; they will wish to know what they must not do that they now do, and what they must do that they leave undone. But the answers to these questions are no more to be had from the original concept than are rules for breeding fine cattle to be had from the theory of evolution and Mendel's law. By the use of the concept, psychologists and educators may, if the concept is correct and if they are properly encouraged, thread their way by dialectic and by experiment to practical knowledge which is actually usable as a method of education and as a personal discipline.

If they are to do that they will have to see quite clearly just how and in what sense the ideal of disinterestedness is inherent and inevitable in the modern world. The remaining chapters of this book are an attempt to do that by demonstrating that in three great phases of human interest, in business, in government, and in sexual relations, the ideal is now implicit and necessary.

CHAPTER XII

THE BUSINESS OF THE GREAT SOCIETY

1. *The Invention of Invention*

ONE of the characteristics of the age we live in is that we are forever trying to explain it. We feel that if we understood it better we should know better how to live in it, and should cease to be aliens who do not know the landmarks of a strange country. There is, however, a school of philosophic historians who argue that this sense of novelty in the modern world is an illusion, and that as a matter of fact mankind has passed before through the same phase of the same inexorable cycle. The boldest of them, like Oswald Spengler, cite chapter and verse to show that there have been several of these great cycles of development from incubation through maturity to decay, and that our western civilization which began about 900 A.D. is now in the phase which corresponds with the century after Pericles in the classical world.

That the analogy is striking no reader of Spengler will deny who can endure Spengler's procrustean determination to make the evidence fit the theory. We can see the growth of towns at the expense of the farms, the rise of capitalism, the growth of international trade and finance, a development of nationalism, of democracy, attempts at the abolition of war through international organization, and with it all a dissolution of the popular religion, of the traditional morality, and vast and searching inquiry into the meaning of life. There is little doubt that the speculation of the Greek philosophers seems extraordinarily fresh to us, because they were confronted with a situation in many respects remarkably like our own.

But however nicely such analogies are worked out they are superficial and misleading. There is something radically new in the modern world, something for which there is no parallel in any other civilization. This new thing is usually described as power-driven machinery. Thus Mr. Charles A. Beard says that "what is called Western or modern civilization by way of contrast with the civilization of the Orient or Mediæval times is at bottom a civilization that rests upon machinery and science as distinguished from one founded on agriculture or handicraft commerce. It is in reality a technological civilization . . . and . . . it threatens to overcome and transform the whole globe." By way of illustrating how deeply machinery affects human life, Mr. Beard says that because they are untouched by this machine civilization "there are more fundamental resemblances between the culture of a peasant in a remote village in Spain and that of a peasant in a remote village in Japan than between the culture of a Christian priest of the upper Pyrenees and that of a Baptist clergyman in a thriving manufacturing town in Illinois."

Mr. H. G. Wells uses much the same argument to show that in spite of the apparent similarities there is an essential difference between our civilization and the later phases of the classical. "The essential difference," he says, "between the amassing of riches, the extinction of small farmers and small business men, and the phase of big finance in the latter centuries of the Roman republic on the one hand, and the very similar concentration of capital in the eighteenth and nineteenth centuries on the other, lies in the profound difference in the character of labor that the mechanical revolution was bringing about. The power of the old world was human power; everything depended ultimately upon the driving power of human muscle, the muscle of ignorant and subjugated men. A little animal muscle, supplied by draft oxen, horse traction, and the like contributed. Where a weight had to be lifted, men lifted it; where a rock had to be quarried, men chipped it out; where a field had to be ploughed, men and oxen ploughed it; the Roman equivalent of the steamship was the galley with its banks of sweating rowers. . . . The Roman civilization was built upon cheap and degraded human beings; modern civilization is being rebuilt upon cheap mechanical power."

These differences are genuine enough, and yet it is doubtful whether Mr. Wells has described the really "new thing in human experience." After all a great deal of cheap man power is still used in conjunction with cheap mechanical power; it is somewhat of an idealization to talk as if the machine had supplanted the drudge. What Mr. Wells has in mind, of course, is that in the Roman world a vast proportion of mankind were doomed to "purely mechanical drudgery" whereas in the modern world there is tangible hope that they will be released from it. They are not yet released from it, however, and their hope of release rests upon the really new element in human experience.

The various mechanical inventions from James Watt's

steam engine to the electric dishwasher and vacuum cleaner are not this new element. All these inventions, singly or collectively, though they have revolutionized the manner of human life, are not the ultimate reason why men put such hope in machines. Their hope is not based on the machines we possess. They are obviously a mixed blessing. Their hope is based on the machines that are yet to be made, and they have reason to hope because a really new thing has come into the world. That thing is the invention of invention.

Men have not merely invented the modern machines. There have been machines invented since the earliest days, incalculably important, like the wheel, like sailing ships, like the windmill and the watermill. But in modern times men have invented a method of inventing, they have discovered a method of discovery. Mechanical progress has ceased to be casual and accidental and has become systematic and cumulative. We know, as no other people ever knew before, that we shall make more and more perfect machines. When Mr. Beard says that "the machine civilization differs from all others in that it is highly dynamic, containing within itself the seeds of constant reconstruction," he is, I take it, referring to this supreme discovery which is the art of discovery itself.

2. *The Creative Principle in Modernity*

Although the disposition to scientific thought may be said to have originated in remote antiquity, it was not until the Sixteenth Century of our era that it ceased to appear spasmodically and as if by chance. The Greeks had their schools on the shores of the Ægean, in Sicily, and in Alexandria, and in them some of the conclusions and much of the spirit of scientific inquiry was imaginatively anticipated. But the conscious organized effort to relate "general principles to irreducible and stubborn facts," as Mr. Whitehead puts it, began about three hundred years ago. The first society chiefly devoted to science seems to have been founded by della Porta at Naples in 1560, but it was closed by the ecclesiastical authorities. Forty years later the *Accademia dei Lincei* was founded at Rome with Galileo among its early members. The Royal Society of London was chartered in 1662. The French Academy of Sciences began its meetings in 1666, the Berlin Academy in 1700, the American Philosophical Association was proposed by Benjamin Franklin in 1743 and organized in 1769.

The active pursuit of science is a matter, then, of only a few hundred years. The practical consequences in the form of useful inventions are still more recent. Newcomen's air-and-steam engine dates from 1705, but it was not until 1764 that James Watt produced a practicable steam engine. It was not until the beginning of the Nineteenth Century that invention really got under way and began to transform the structure of civilization. It was not until about 1850 that the importance of invention had impressed itself upon the English people, yet they were the first to experience the effects of the mechanical revolution. They had seen the first railway, the first steamboat, the illumination of towns by gas, and the application of power-driven machinery to manufacture. Professor Bury fixes the Exhibition of London in 1851 as the event which marks the public recognition of the role of science in modern civilization. The Prince Consort who originated the Exhibition said in his opening speech that it was designed "to give us a true test and a living picture of the point of development at which the whole of mankind has arrived in this great task, and a new starting-point from which the nations will be able to direct their further exertions."

But this public recognition was at first rather sentimental and gaping. The full realization of the place of science in modern life came slowly, and only in our generation can it be said that political rulers, captains of industry, and leaders of thought have actually begun to appreciate how central is science in our civilization, and to act upon that realization. In our time governments have begun to take science seriously and to promote research and invention not only in the art of war, but in the interest of trade, agriculture, and public hygiene. Great corporations have established laboratories of their own, not merely for the perfecting of their own processes, but for the promotion of pure research. Money has become available in great quantities for scientific work in the universities, and the educational curriculum down to the lowest grades has begun to be reorganized not only in order to train a minority of the population for research and invention, but to train the great majority to understand and use the machines and the processes which are available.

The motives and the habits of mind which are thus brought into play at the very heart of modern civilization are mature and disinterested. That may not be the primary intention, but it is the inevitable result. No doubt governments encourage research in order to have powerful weapons with which to overawe their neighbors; no doubt industries encourage research because it pays; no doubt scientists and inventors are in some measure moved by the desire for wealth and fame; no doubt the general public approves of science because of the pleasures and conveniences it provides; no doubt there is an intuitive sense in modern communities that the prospects of survival both for nations and for individuals are somehow related to their command of scientific knowledge. But nevertheless, whatever the motives which cause men to endow laboratories, to work patiently in laboratories or to buy the products, the fact remains that inside the laboratory, at the heart of this whole business, the habit of disinterested realism in dealing with the data is the indispensable habit of mind. Unless this habit of mind exists in the actual research, all the endowments and honorary degrees and prize awards will not produce the results desired. This is an original and tremendous fact in human experience: that a whole civilization should be dependent upon technology, that this technology should be dependent upon pure science, and that this pure science should be dependent upon a race of men who consciously refuse, as Mr. Bertrand Russell has said, to regard their "own desires, tastes, and interests as affording a key to the understanding of the world."

When I say that the refusal is conscious I do not mean merely that scientists tell themselves that they must ignore their prejudices. They have developed an elaborate method for detecting and discounting their prejudices. It consists of instruments of precision, an accurate vocabulary, controlled experiment, and the submission not only of their results but of their processes to the judgment of their peers. This method provides a body in which the spirit of disinterestedness can live, and it might be said that modern science, not in its crude consequences but in its inward principle, not, that is to say, as manifested in automobiles, electric refrigerators, and rayon silk, but in the behavior of the men who invent and perfect these things, is the actual realization in a practicable mode of conduct which can be learned and practiced, of the insight of high religion. The scientific discipline is one way in which this insight, hitherto lyrical and personal and apart, is brought down to earth and into direct and decisive contact with the concerns of mankind.

It is no exaggeration to say that pure science is high religion incarnate. No doubt the science we have is not the whole incarnation, but as far as it goes it translates into a usable procedure what in the teaching of the sages has been an esoteric insight. Scientific method can be learned. The learning of it matures the human character. Its value can be demonstrated in concrete results. Its importance in human life is indisputable. But the insight of high religion as such could be appreciated only by those who were already mature; it corresponded to nothing in the experience and the necessities of the ordinary man. It could be talked about but not taught; it could inspire only the few who were somehow already inspired. With the discovery of scientific method the insight has ceased to be an intangible and somewhat formless idea and has become an organized effort which moves mankind more profoundly than anything else in human affairs. Therefore, what was once a personal attitude on the part of a few who were somewhat withdrawn and disregarded has become the central principle in the careers of innumerable, immensely influential, men.

Because the scientific discipline is, in fact, the creative element in that which is distinctively modern, circumstances conspire to enhance its prestige and to extend its acceptance. It is the ultimate source of profit and of power, and therefore it is assured of protection and encouragement by those who rule the modern state. They cannot afford not to cultivate the scientific spirit: the nation which does not cultivate it cannot hold its place among the nations, the corporation which ignores it will be destroyed by its competitors. The training of an ever increasing number of pure scientists, of inventors, and of men who can operate and repair machinery is, therefore, a sheer practical necessity. The scientific discipline has become, as Mr. Graham Wallas would say, an essential part of our social heritage. For the machine technology requires a population which in some measure partakes of the spirit which created it.

Naturally enough, however, the influence of the scientific spirit becomes more and more diluted the further one goes from the work of the men who actually conceive, discover, invent, and perfect the modern machines. From Faraday, Maxwell, and Hertz who did the chief work which made possible the wireless it is a long way to the broker who sells radio stock or the householder with his six-tube set. I have not been supposing that these latter partake in any way of the original spirit which made the radio possible. But it is a fact of enormous consequences, cumulative in its effect upon the education of succeeding generations, that the radio, and all the other contrivances around which modern civilization is constructed, should be possible only by the increasing use of a scientific discipline.

3. *Naive Capitalism*

The application of science to the daily affairs of men was acclaimed at first with more enthusiasm than understanding. "That early people," said Buffon, speaking of the Babylonians, "was very happy, because it was very scientific." Entranced with the success of the Newtonian physics and by the dazzling effect of inventions, the intellectuals of the Eighteenth Century persuaded themselves that science was a messianic force which would liberate mankind from pain, drudgery, and error. It was believed that science would somewhat mysteriously endow mankind with invincible power over the forces of nature, and that men, if they were released from the bondage of religious custom and belief, could employ the power of science to their own consummate happiness. The mechanical revolution, in short, was inaugurated on the theory that the natural man must be liberated from moral conventions and that nature must be subjugated by mechanical instruments.

There are intelligible historical reasons why our great-grandfathers adopted this view. They found themselves in a world regulated by the customs and beliefs of a landed society. They could not operate their factories successfully in such a society, and they rebelled fiercely against the customs which restricted them. That rebellion was rationalized in the philosophy of *laissez-faire* which meant in essence that machine industry must not be interfered with by landlords and peasants who had feudal rights, nor by governments which protected those rights. On the positive side this rebellion expressed itself in declarations of the rights of man. These declarations were a denial of the vested rights of men under the old landed order and an assertion of the rights of men, particularly the new middle-class men, who proposed to make the most of the new industrial and mechanical order. By the rights of men they meant primarily freedom of contract, freedom of trade, freedom of occupation—those freedoms, that is to say, which made it possible for the new employer to buy and sell, to hire and fire without being accountable to anyone.

The prophet of this new dispensation was Adam Smith. In the *Wealth of Nations* he wrote that

> All systems either of preference or of restraint . . . being thus completely taken away, the obvious and simple system of natural liberty establishes itself of its own accord. Every man, as long as he does not violate the laws of justice, is left perfectly free to pursue his own interest his own way, and to bring both his industry and capital into competition with those of any other man, or order of men.

The employing class in the early days of capitalism honestly believed, and indeed its less enlightened members still believe to this very day, that somehow the general welfare will be served by trusting naively to the acquisitive instincts of the employing capitalist. Thus at the outset the machine technology was applied under the direction of men who scorned as sentimental, when they did not regard as subversive, that disinterestedness which alone makes possible the machine technology itself. They did not understand science. They merely exploited certain of the inventions which scientists produced. What they believed, insofar as they had any philosophy, was that there exists a preestablished harmony in the universe—an "obvious and simple system of natural liberty," in Adam Smith's language, "which establishes itself of its own accord"—by which if each man naively pursued his primitive impulse to have and to hold in competition with other men, peace, prosperity, and happiness would ensue.

They did not ensue. And the social history of the last seventy-five years has in large measure been concerned with the birth pains of an industrial philosophy that will really suit the machine technology and the nature of man. For the notion that an intricate and delicately poised industrial mechanism could be operated by uneducated men snatching competitively at profits was soon exposed as a simple-minded delusion.

It was discovered that if each banker was permitted to do what seemed to him immediately most profitable, the result was a succession of disastrous inflations and deflations of credit; that if natural resources in oil, coal, lumber, and the like were subjected to the competitive principle, the result was a shocking waste of irreplaceable wealth; that if the hiring and firing of labor were carried on under absolute freedom of contract, a whole chain of social evils in the form of child labor, unsuitable labor for women, sweating, unemployment, and the importation of cheap and unassimilable labor resulted; that if business men were left to their own devices the consumer of necessary goods was helpless when he was confronted with industries in which there was an element of monopoly. There is no need here to recount the well-known story of how in every modern community the theory of free competition has in the course of the last generation been modified by legislation, by organized labor, by organized business itself. So little has *laissez-faire* worked under actual experience that all the powers of the government have actually had to be invoked to preserve a certain amount of compulsory "free competition." For the industrial machine, as soon as it passes out of the early phase of rough exploitation in virgin territory, becomes unmanageable by naively competitive and acquisitive men.

4. *The Credo of Old-Style Business*

It was frequently pointed out by moralists like Ruskin and William Morris, and by churchmen as well, that this "obvious and simple system of natural liberty" by which "every man was left perfectly free to pursue his own interest his own way," was not only contrary to the dogmas of the popular religion but irreconcilable with moral wisdom. The credo of the unregenerate business man was utterly atheistical in its premises, for it displaced the notion that there is any higher will than his own to which the employer is accountable. It was more than atheistical, however; it was, in Aristotle's sense of the word, barbarous in that it implied "the living as one likes" with virtually complete acquiescence in the supremacy of the acquisitive instinct.

There is no reason to suppose that such theoretical comments on the credo of naive capitalism did more than rub off a little of its unction. Capitalism may be, as Mr. Maynard Keynes has said, "absolutely irreligious . . . often, though not always, a mere congeries of possessors and pursuers." Were the credo workable in practice, some way would have been found of anointing it with attractive phrases. The real reason for the gradual abandonment of the credo, proclaimed by Adam Smith and repeated so steadily since his day, is that the credo of naive capitalism is deeply at variance with the real character of modern industry. It rests upon false premises, is therefore contradicted by experience, and has proved to be unworkable.

The system of natural liberty assumes that if each man pursues his own interest his own way, each man will promote his interest. There is an unanalyzed fallacy in this theory which makes it utterly meaningless. It is assumed that each man knows his own interest and can therefore pursue it. But that is precisely what no man is certain to know, and what few men can possibly know if they consult only their own impulses. There is nothing in the natural equipment of man which enables him to know intuitively whether it will be profitable to increase his output or reduce it, to enter a new line of business, to buy or to sell, or to make any of the other thousand and one decisions on which the conduct of business depends. Since he is not born with this wisdom, since he does not automatically absorb it from the air, to pursue his own interest his own way is a fairly certain way to disaster.

The fallacy of the theory of natural liberty is undetected in a bonanza period of industrial development. Where the business man has unexhausted natural resources to

draw upon, where there is a surplus of customers competing for his goods, he can with naive and furious energy
pursue his own interests his own way and reap enormous
profits. There is no real resistance from the outside; there
are no stubborn and irreducible facts to which he must
adjust himself. He can proceed with an infantile philosophy to achieve success. But this bonanza period when
the omnipotence of the capitalist is unthwarted, and his
omniscience therefore assumed, soon comes to an end. In
advanced communities the mere multiplication of industries produces such a complicated environment that the
business man is compelled to substitute considered policies
for his intuitions, objective surveys for his guesses, and
conferences world without end for his natural liberties.

What has upset the idea of the old-style business man
that he knows what's what is that the relevant facts are
no longer visible. The owner of a primitive factory
might have known all his working men and all his customers; the keeper of a little neighborhood shop may still,
to a certain extent, know personally his whole business.
But for most men to-day the facts which matter vitally to
them are out of sight, beyond their personal control, intricate, subject to more or less unpredictable changes, and
even with highly technical reporting and analysis almost
unintelligible to the average man.

It is, of course, the machine process itself which has
created these complications. Men are forced to buy and
sell in markets that for many commodities are world-wide:
they do not buy and sell in one market but in many markets, in markets for raw materials, in markets for semi-
finished goods, in wholesale and retail markets, in labor

markets, in the money market. They employ and are employed in corporate organizations which are owned here, there, and everywhere. They compete not only with their obvious competitors in the same line of business, but with competitors in wholly different lines of business, automobiles with railroads, railroads with ships, cotton goods with silk and silk with artificial silk, pianos with furs and cigarettes with chewing-gum. The modern environment is invisible, complex, without settled plan, subtly and swiftly changing, offering innumerable choices, demanding great knowledge and imaginative effort to comprehend it.

It is not a social order at all as the Greek city state or the feudal society was a social order. It is rather a field for careers, an arena of talents, an ordeal by trial and error, and a risky speculation. No man has an established position in the modern world. There is no system of rights and duties to which he is clearly subject. He moves among these complexities which are shrouded in obscurity, making the best he can out of what little it is possible for him to know.

5. *Old-Style Reform and Revolution*

Naive capitalism—that is to say, the theory of each for himself according to such light as he might happen to possess—produced such monstrous evils the world over that an anti-capitalist reaction was the inevitable result. What had happened was that the most intricate and consequential technology which man has ever employed on this planet was given over to the direction of a class of enterprising, acquisitive, uneducated, and undisciplined men. No doubt it could not have been otherwise. The only discipline that was known was the discipline of custom in a society of farmers, hand-workers, and traders. The only education available was one based on the premises of the past. The revolution in human affairs produced by the machine began slowly, and no one could have anticipated its course. It would be absurd, therefore, to complain in retrospect over the fact that no one was prepared for the industrial changes which took place. The only absurdity, and it is still a prevalent one, is to go on supposing that the political philosophy and the "economic laws" which were extemporized to justify the behavior of the first bewildered capitalists have any real bearing upon modern industry.

But it is almost equally absurd to take too seriously the "reforms" and "solutions" which were devised by kind-hearted men to alleviate the pains suffered by those who were hurt by the results of this early capitalist control of the machine. These proposals, when they are examined, turn out almost invariably to have been proposals for coercing or for abolishing the then masters of industry. I do not mean to deny the utility of the long series of legislative enactments which began about the middle of the Nineteenth Century and are still being elaborated. The factory acts, the regulatory laws, the measures designed to protect the consumers against fraud were, looked at singly, good, bad, or indifferent. As a whole they were a necessary attempt to police those who had been left free to pursue their own interest their own way. But when it has been said that they were necessary, and that they are still necessary, it is important to realize just what they imply. They imply that the masters of industry are unregenerate and will remain unregenerate. The whole effort to police capitalism assumes that the capitalist can be civilized only by means of the police. The trouble with this theory is that there is no way to make sure that the policemen will themselves be civilized. It presupposes that somehow politicians and office-holders will be wise enough and disinterested enough to make business men do what they would not otherwise do. The fundamental problem, which is to find a way of directing industry wisely, is not solved. It is merely deposited on the doorsteps of the politician.

The revolutionary programs sponsored by the socialists in the half-century before the Great War were based on the notion that it is impossible to police the capitalist employers and that, therefore, they should be abolished. In their place functionaries were to be installed. The theory was that these functionaries, being hired by the state and being deprived of all incentive for personal profit, would administer the industrial machine disinterestedly. The trouble with this theory is in its assumption that the removal of one kind of temptation, namely, the possibility of direct personal pecuniary profit—will make the functionaries mature and disinterested men.

This is nothing but a new variant of the ascetic principle that it is possible to shut off an undesirable impulse by thwarting it. Human nature does not work that way. The mere frustration of an impulse like acquisitiveness produces either some new expression of that impulse or disorders due to its frustration. It produces, that is to say, either corruption or the lethargy, the pedantry, and the officiousness which are the diseases of bureaucracy the world over. The socialists are right, as the early Christians were right, in their profound distrust of the acquisitive instinct as the dominant motive in society. But they are wrong in supposing that by transferring the command of industry from business men to socialist officials they can in any fundamental sense alter the acquisitive instinct. That can be done only by refining the human character through a better understanding of the environment. I do not mean to say that a revolution like the Russian does not sweep away a vast amount of accumulated rubbish. I am talking not about the salutary destruction which may accompany a revolution, but of the problem which confronts the successful revolutionists when they have to carry on the necessary affairs of men.

When that time comes they are bound to find that the administration of industry under socialism no less than under capitalism depends upon the character of the administrators. Corrupt, stupid, grasping functionaries will make at least as big a muddle of socialism as stupid, selfish, and acquisitive employers can make of capitalism. There is no escape from this elementary truth, and all social policies which attempt to ignore it must come to grief. They are essentially utopian. The early doctrine of *laissez-faire* was utopian because it assumed that unregenerate men were destined somehow to muddle their way to a harmonious result. The early socialism was utopian because it assumed that these same unregenerate men, once the laws of property had been altered, would somehow muddle their way to a harmonious result. Both ignored the chief lesson of human experience, which is the insight of high religion, that unregenerate men can only muddle into muddle.

A dim recognition of this truth has helped to inspire the procedure of the two most recent manifestations of the revolutionary spirit. I refer to bolshevism and to fascism. It is proper, I believe, to talk of them as one phenomenon, for their fundamental similarities, as most everyone but the bolshevists and the fascists themselves has noted, are much greater than their superficial differences. They were attempts to cure the evils resulting from the breakdown of a somewhat primitive form of capitalism. In neither Russia nor Italy had modern industrialism passed beyond its adolescent phase. In both countries the prevailing social order for the great mass of people was still pre-machine and pre-industrial. In both countries the acids of modernity had not yet eaten deeply into the religious disposition of the people. In both countries the natural pattern of all government was still the primitive pattern of the hierarchy with an absolute sovereign at the top. The bolshevik dictatorship and the fascist dictatorship, underneath all their modernist labels and theories, are feudal military organizations attempting to subdue and administer the machine technology.

The theorists of the two dictatorships are, however, men educated under modern influences, and the result is that their theories are an attempt to explain the primitive behavior of the two dictatorships in terms which are consistent with modern ideas. The formula reached in both instances is the same one. The dictatorships are said to be temporary. Their purpose, we are told, is to put the new social order into effect, and to keep it going long enough by dictation from on top to give time for a new generation to grow up which will be purged of those vices which would make the new order unworkable. The bolshevists and fascists regard themselves as ever so much more realistic than the old democratic socialists and the *laissez-faire* liberals whom they have executed, exiled, or dosed with castor oil. In an important sense they are more realistic. They have recognized that a substitute for primitive capitalism cannot be inaugurated or administered by a generation which has been schooled in the ways of primitive capitalism. And therefore the oligarchy of dictators, as a conscious, enlightened, superior, and heavily armed minority, propose to administer the industrial machine as trustees until there is a generation ready to accept the responsibilities.

It would be idle to predict that they will not succeed. But it is reasonable, I believe, to predict that if they succeed it will be because they are administering relatively simple industrial arrangements. It is precisely because the economic system of Russia is still fundamentally pre-capitalist and pre-mechanical that the feudal organization of the bolshevists is most likely to survive. Because the economic system of Italy is more modern than Russia's, the future of the fascist dictatorship is much less assured. For insofar as the machine technology is advanced, it becomes complex, delicate, and difficult to manage by commands from the top.

6. *The Diffusion of the Acquisitive Instinct*
While both the bolshevists and the fascists look upon

themselves as pathfinders of progress, it is fairly clear, I think, that they are, in the literal meaning of the term, reactionary. They have won their victories among the people to whom modern large-scale industrial organization is still an unnatural and alien thing. It is no accident that fascism or bolshevism took root in Italy and Spain, but not in Germany and England, in Hungary but not in Austria, in Poland but not in Czechoslovakia, in Russia but not in Scandinavia, in China but not in Japan, in Central America but not in Canada or the United States. Dictatorship, based on a military hierarchy, administering the affairs of the community on behalf of the "nation" or of the "proletariat," is nothing but a return to the natural organization of society in the pre-machine age. Some countries, like Russia, Mexico, and China, for example, are still living in the pre-machine age. Others, like Italy, had become only partially industrialized when they were subjected to such strains by the War that they reverted to the feudal pattern of behavior. Unable to master the industrial process by methods which are appropriate to it, the fascists and the bolshevists are attempting to master it by methods which antedate it. That is why military dictatorship in a country like Mexico may be looked upon as the normal type of social control, whereas in Italy it is regressive and neurotic. Feudal habits are appropriate to a feudal society; in a semi-industrialized nation they are a social disease. It is the disease of frightened and despairing men who, having failed to adjust themselves to the reality of the industrial process, try, by main force and awkwardness, to adjust the machine process to a pre-machine mentality.

The more primitive the machine process is—that is, the more nearly it resembles the petty handicrafts of earlier days—the better are the chances for survival of a bolshevist or fascist dictatorship. Where the machine technology is really established and advanced it is simply unmanageable by militarized functionaries. For when the process has become infinitely complicated, the sub-division of function is carried so far, the internal adjust-ments are so numerous and so varied that no collection of oligarchs in a capital city, however much they may look like supermen, can possibly direct the industrial system. In its advanced stages, as it now exists in England, Ger-many, or the United States, nobody comprehends the sys-tem as a whole. One has only to glance over the financial pages of an American newspaper, to look at the list of corporations doing business, to try and imagine the myriad daily decisions at a thousand points which their business involves, in order to realize the bewildering complexity of modern industrial society. To suppose that all that can be administered, or even directed, from any central point by any human brain, by any cabinet of office holders or cabal of revolutionists, is simply to have failed to take it in. Here is the essential reason why bolshevism and fascism are, as we say, un-American. They are no less un-Belgian, un-German, un-English. For they are unin-dustrial.

The same reasons which make dictatorship unworkable are rapidly rendering obsolete the attempts to reform industry by policing it. Every year as the machine tech-nology becomes more elaborated, the legislative control for which the pre-war progressives fought becomes less effective. It becomes more and more difficult for legislatures to make laws to protect the workers which really fit the rapidly changing conditions of work. Hence the tendency to put the real lawmaking power in the hands of administrative officials and judges who can adjust the general purpose of the law to the unclassifiable facts of industry. The whole attempt to regulate public utilities in the interest of the consumer is chaotic, for these organizations, by their intricacies, their scale, and their constant revolutions in technology, tend to escape the jurisdiction of officials exercising a local jurisdiction. The current outcry against the multiplication of laws and the meddling of legislatures is in part, but not wholly, the outcry of old-fashioned business men demanding their old natural liberty to pursue their own interest their own way. The outcry is due no less to a recognition that the industrial process is becoming too subtly organized to be policed successfully by the wholesale, uninformed enactments of legislatures.

Yet the very thing which makes an advanced industrial organization too complex to be directed by a dictatorship, or to be policed by democratic politicians, is forcing the leaders of industry to evolve forms of self-control. When I say that they are being forced to do this I am not referring to those ostentatiously benevolent things which are done now and then as sops to Cerberus. There is a certain amount of reform undertaken voluntarily by men who profess to fear 'bolshevism,' and if not bolshevism, then Congress. That is relatively unimportant. So also is the discovery that it pays to cultivate the good will of the public. What I am referring to is the fact that the sheer complexity of the industrial system would make it unmanageable to business men, no less than to politicians or dictators, if business men were not learning to organize its control.

It is the necessity of stabilizing their own business, of directing technical processes which are beyond the understanding of stockholders, of adjusting the supply and demand of the multitudinous elements they deal in, which is the compelling force behind that divorce between management and ownership, that growing use of experts and of statistical measurements, and that development of trade associations, of conferences, committees, and councils, with which modern industry is honeycombed. The captain of industry in the romantic sense tends to disappear in highly evolved industrial organizations. His thundering commands are replaced by the decisions of executives who consult with representatives of the interests involved and check their opinions by the findings of experts. The greater the corporation the more the shareholders and the directors lose the actual direction of the institution. They cannot direct the corporation because they do not really know what it is and what it is doing. That knowledge is subdivided among the executives and bureau chiefs and consultants, all of them on salary; each of them is so relatively small a factor in the whole that his personal success is in very large degree bound up with the success of the institution. A certain amount of jealousy, intrigue, and destructive pushing, of office politics, in short, naturally prevails, men being what they are. But as compared with the old-style business man, the ordinary executive in a great corporation is something quite strange. He is so little the monarch of all he surveys, his experience is so continually with stubborn and irreducible facts, he is so much compelled to adjust his own preferences to the preferences of others, that he becomes a relatively disinterested person. The more clearly he realizes the nature of his position in industry, the more he tends to submit his desires to the discipline of objective information. And the more he does this the less dominated he is by the acquisitiveness of immaturity. He may on the side gamble acquisitively in the stock market or at the race track, but in relation to his business his acquisitive instinct tends to become diffused and to be absorbed in the job itself.

7. *Ideals*

It is my impression that when machine industry reaches a certain scale of complexity it exerts such pressure upon the men who run it that they cannot help socializing it. They are subject to a kind of economic selection under which only those men survive who are capable of taking a somewhat disinterested view of their work. A mature industry, because it is too subtly organized to be run by naively passionate men, puts a premium upon men whose characters are sufficiently matured to make them respect reality and to discount their own prejudices.

When the machine technology is really advanced, that is to say when it has drawn great masses of men within the orbit of its influence, when a corporation has become really great, the old distinction between public and private interest becomes very dim. I think it is destined largely to disappear. It is difficult even to-day to say whether the great railways, the General Electric Company, the United States Steel Corporation, the bigger insurance companies and banks are public or private institutions. When institutions reach a point where the legal owners are virtually disfranchised, when the direction is in the hands of salaried executives, technicians, and experts who hold themselves more or less accountable in standards of conduct to their fellow professionals, when the ultimate control is looked upon by the directors not as "business" but as a trust, it is not fanciful to say, as Mr. Keynes has said, that "the battle of socialism against unlimited private profit is being won in detail hour by hour."

Insofar as industry itself evolves its own control, it will regain its liberty from external interference. To say that is to say simply that the "natural liberty" of the early business man was unworkable because the early business man was unregenerate: he was immature, and he was therefore acquisitive. The only kind of liberty which is workable in the real world is the liberty of the disinterested man, of the man who has transformed his passions by an understanding of necessity. He can, as Confucius said, follow what his heart desires without transgressing what is right. For he has learned to desire what is right.

The more perfectly we understand the implications of the machine technology upon which our civilization is based, the easier it will be for us to live with it. We shall discern the ideals of our industry in the necessities of industry itself. They are the direction in which it must evolve if it is to fulfill itself. That is what ideals are. They are not hallucinations. They are not a collection of pretty and casual preferences. Ideals are an imaginative understanding of that which is desirable in that which is possible. As we discern the ideals of the machine technology we can consciously pursue them, knowing that we are not vainly trying to impose our casual prejudices, but that we are in harmony with the age we live in.

CHAPTER XIII

GOVERNMENT IN THE GREAT SOCIETY

1. *Loyalty*

THE difficulty of discovering an industrial philosophy which fits machine industry on a large scale has proved less trying than the discovery of a political philosophy which fits the modern state. I do not know why this should be so unless it be that, as compared with politicians, business men have had a closer opportunity to observe and more pressing reasons for trying to understand the transformation wrought by machinery and scientific invention. Certainly even the best political thinking is notably inferior in realism and in pertinence to the economic thinking which now plays so important a part in the direction of industry. To a very considerable degree the writer on politics to-day is about where the economist was when all economic theory began and for all practical purposes seemed to end with Robinson Crusoe and his man Friday. Nobody takes political science very seriously, for nobody is convinced that it is a science or that it has any important bearing on politics.

In very considerable measure political theory in the modern world is sterilized by its own ideas. There have been passed down from generation to generation a collection of concepts which are so hallowed and so dense that their only use is to excite emotions and to obscure insight.

How many of us really know what we are talking about when we use words like the state, sovereignty, independence, democracy, representative government, national honor, liberty, and loyalty? Very few of us, I think, could define any of these terms under cross-examination, though we are prepared to shed blood, or at least ink, in their behalf. These terms have ceased to be intellectual instruments for apprehending the facts we have to deal with and have become push buttons which touch off emotional reflexes.

As good a way as any to raise the temperature of political debate is to talk about loyalty. Everybody regards himself as loyal and resents any imputation upon his loyalty, yet even a cursory inspection of this term will show, I think, that it may mean any number of different things. It is clearest when used in a military sense. A loyal soldier is one who obeys his superior officer. A loyal officer is one who obeys his commander-in-chief. But just exactly what is a loyal commander-in-chief cannot be told so easily. He is loyal to the nation. He is loyal to the best interests of the nation. But what those best interests may be, whether they mean making peace or carrying the war into the enemy's country, is an exceedingly debatable question. When the citizen's loyalty is in question the whole matter becomes immensely subtle. Must he be loyal to every law and every command issued by the established authorities, kings, legislators, and aldermen? There are many who would say that this is the definition of civic loyalty, to obey the law without qualifications while it is a law. But such definition puts the taint of disloyalty on almost all citizens of the modern state. For the fact is that all the laws on the books are not even known, and that a considerable portion are entirely disregarded, and many it is impossible to obey. The definition, moreover, places outside the pale many who rank as great patriots, men who defied the law out of loyalty to some principle which the lawmakers have rejected. But what makes matters even more complicated is the fact that in modern communities the principle is accepted that the commands of the established authorities not only may be criticized but that they ought to be.

At this stage of political development the military element in loyalty has virtually disappeared. The idea of toleration, of freedom of speech, and above all the idea of organized opposition, alters radically the attributes of the sovereign. For a sovereign who has to be obeyed but not believed in, whose decisions are legitimate matters of dispute, who may be displaced by his bitterest opponents, has lost all semblance of omnipotence and omniscience. "He has sovereignty," wrote Jean Bodin, "who, after God, acknowledges no one greater than himself." Our governors command only for the time being—and within strict limits. Their authority is only such as they can win and hold. Political loyalty under these conditions, whatever else it may be, is certainly not unqualified allegiance to those who hold office, to the policies they pursue, or even to the laws they enact. Neither the government as it exists, nor its conduct, nor even the constitution by which it operates, exercises any ultimate claim upon the loyalty of the citizen. The most one can say, I think, is that the loyal citizen is one who loves his country and regards the status quo as an arrangement which he is at liberty to modify only by argument, according to well-understood rules, without violence, and with due regard for the interests and opinions of his fellow men. If he is loyal to this ideal of political conduct he is as loyal as the modern state can force him to be, or as it is desirable that he should be.

2. *The Evolution of Loyalty*

Broadly speaking, the evolution of political loyalty passes through three phases. In the earliest, the most primitive, and for almost all men the most natural, loyalty is allegiance to a chieftain; in the middle phase it tends to become allegiance to an institution—that is to say, to a corporate, rather than to a human, personality; and in the last phase it becomes allegiance to a pattern of conduct. The kind of government which any community is capable of operating is very largely determined by the kind of loyalty of which its members are capable.

It is plain, for example, that among a people who are capable only of loyalty to another human being the political system is bound to take the shape of a hierarchy, in which each man is loyal to his superior, and the man at the top is loyal to God alone. Such a society will be feudal, military, theocratic. If it is successfully organized it will be an ordered despotism, culminating, as the feudal system did, in God's Vice-gerent on earth. If it is unsuccessfully organized, as for example, in the more backward countries of Central America to-day, the system of personal allegiances will produce little factions each with its chief, all of them contending for, without quite achieving, absolute power. This type of organization is so fundamentally human that it prevails even in communities which think they have outgrown it. Thus it appears in what Americans call a political machine, which is nothing but a hierarchy of professional politicians held together by profitable personal loyalties. The political boss is a demilitarized chieftain in the direct line of descent from his prototypes.

The modern world has come to regard organization on the basis of human allegiances as alien and dangerous. Yet the political machine exists even in the most advanced communities. The reason for that is obvious. With the enfranchisement of virtually the whole adult population, political power has passed into the hands of a great mass of people most of whom are altogether incapable of loyalty to institutions, much less to ideas. They do not understand them. For these voters the only kind of political behavior is through allegiance to a human superior, and modern democracies are considered fortunate if the political leaders and bosses on whom these human allegiances converge are relatively loyal to the institutions of the country. This, for example, is the meaning of the dramatic speech in which President Calles on September 1, 1928, voluntarily renounced the continuation of his own dictatorship. "For the first time in Mexican history," he said, "the Republic faces a situation (owing to the assassination of General Obregon) whose dominant note is the lack of a military leader, which is going to make it finally possible for us to direct the policy of the country into truly institutional channels, striving to pass once for all from our historical condition of one-man rule to the higher, more dignified, more useful, and more civilized condition of a nation of laws and institutions." It is hardly to be supposed that President Calles thought that the Mexican people as a whole could pass once for all from their historical condition of one-man rule. What he meant was that the political chieftains to whom the people were loyal ought thereafter to arrange the succession and to exercise power not as seemed desirable to them, or as they might imagine that God had privately commanded them, but in accordance with objective rules of political conduct.

The conceptions of sovereignty which we inherit are derived from the primitive system of personal allegiances. That is why the conception of sovereignty has become increasingly confused as modern civilization has become more complex. In the Middle Ages the theory reached its symmetrical perfection. Mankind was conceived as a great organism in which the spiritual and temporal hierarchies were united as the soul is united with the body in "an inseverable connection and an unbroken interaction which must display itself in every part and also throughout the whole." But of course even in the Middle Ages the symmetry of this conception was marred by the fierce disputes between the Emperors and the Popes. After the Sixteenth Century the whole conception began to disintegrate. There appeared a congeries of monarchs each claiming to rule in his territory by divine right. But obviously when there are many agents of the Lord ruling men, and when they do not agree, the theory of sovereignty in its moral aspects is in grave difficulties.

As time went on, limitations of all kinds began to be imposed upon sovereigns. The existence at the same time of many sovereigns produced the need of international law, for obviously there could have been no international law in a world where all of mankind, barring infidels who did not have to be considered, were under one sovereign power. The limitations imposed by international law from without were accompanied by limitations imposed from within.

These limitations from within were based on quite practical considerations. There grew up slowly in the Middle Ages the idea that the State originated "in a contract of Subjection made between People and Ruler." The first modern writer to argue effectively that government was based not on a warrant from the Lord, but on a "social compact" is said to have been Richard Hooker, a clergyman of the Established Church, who held, in 1594, that the royal authority was derived from a contract between the king and the people. This idea soon became popular, for it suited the needs of all those who did not participate in the privileges of the absolute monarchy. It suited not only the Church of England, when as in Hooker's time it was assailed, but also the dissenting churches, and then the rising middle class whose ambitions were frustrated by the landed nobles with the king at their head. The doctrine of the social compact was expounded in many different forms in the Seventeenth and Eighteenth Centuries by men like Milton, Spinoza, Hobbes, Locke, and Rousseau.

As an historical theory to explain the origin of human society it is of course demonstrably false, but as a weapon for breaking up the concentration of sovereign power and distributing it, the idea has played a mighty role in history. It is almost certain to appear wherever there is an absolutism which men feel the need of checking. But the theory of the social compact disappears when power has become so widely diffused that no one can any longer locate the sovereign. That is what is happening in the advanced modern communities. The sovereign, whom it was once desirable to put under contract, has become so anonymous and diffuse that his very existence to-day is a legal fiction rather than a political fact. And loyalty by the same token is no longer provided with a personal superior of indubitable prestige to which it can be attached.

3. *Pluralism*

The relationship between lord and vassals in which each man attaches himself for better or worse to some superior person tends gradually to disappear in the modern world. Its passing was somewhat prematurely announced by the Declaration of the Rights of Man; it did not wholly disappear by the dissolution of the bonds which bound one man to another, for the psychological bonds are stronger than the legal. Nevertheless the effect of modern civilization is to dissolve these psychological bonds, to break up clannishness and personal dependence. Men and women alike tend to become more or less independent persons rather than to remain members of a social organism.

The reason for this lies in the diversification of their interests. Life in the ancestral order was not only simpler and contained within narrower limits than it is to-day, but there was a far greater unity in the activity of each individual. Working the land, fighting, raising a family, worshipping, were so closely related that they could be governed by a very simple allegiance to the chief of the tribe or the lord of the manor. In the modern world this synthesis has disintegrated and the activities of a man cannot be directed by a simple allegiance. Each man finds himself the center of a complex of loyalties. He is loyal to his government, he is loyal to his state, he is loyal to his village, he is loyal to his neighborhood. He has his own family. He has his wife's family. His wife has her family. He has his church. His wife may have a different church. He may be an employer of thousands of men. He may be an employee. He must be loyal to his corporation, to his trade union, or his professional society. He is a buyer in many different markets. He is a seller in many different markets. He is a creditor and a debtor. He owns shares in several industries. He belongs to a political party, to clubs, to a social set. The multiplicity of his interests makes it impossible for him to give his whole allegiance to any person or to any institution.

It may be, in fact for most men it must be, that in each of these associations he follows a leader. In any considerable number of people it is certain that they will group themselves in hierarchical form. In every club, in every social circle, in every trade union, in every stockholders' meeting there are leaders and their lieutenants and the led. But these allegiances are partial. Because a man has so many loyalties each loyalty commands only a segment of himself. They are not, therefore, wholehearted loyalties like that of a good soldier to his captain. They are qualified, calculated, debatable, and they are sanctioned not by inherent authority but by expediency or inertia.

The outward manifestation of these complex loyalties of the modern man is the multitude of institutions through which the affairs of mankind are directed. Now since each of these corporate entities represents only a part of any man's interest, except perhaps in the case of the paid executive secretary, none of these institutions can count to the bitter end upon the undivided loyalty of all its members. The conflicts between institutions are in considerable measure conflicts of interest within the same individuals. There is a point where the activity of a man's trade union may so seriously affect the value of the securities he owns that he does not know which way his interest lies. The criss-crossing of loyalties is so great in an advanced community that no grouping is self-contained. No grouping, therefore, can maintain a military discipline or a military character. For when men strive too fiercely as members of any one group they soon find that they are at war with themselves as members of another group.

The statement that modern society is pluralistic cannot, then, be dismissed as a newfangled notion invented by theorists. It is a sober description of the actual facts. Each man has countless interests through which he is attached to a very complex social situation. The complexity of his allegiance cannot fail to be reflected in his political conduct.

4. *Live and Let Live*

One of the inevitable effects of being attached to many different, somewhat conflicting, interdependent groupings is to blunt the edges of partisanship. It is possible to be fiercely partisan only as against those who are wholly alien. It is a fair generalization to say that the fiercest Democrats are to be found where there are the fewest Republicans, the most bloodthirsty patriots in the safest swivel chairs. Where men are personally entangled with the groups that are in potential conflict, where Democrats and Republicans belong to the same country club and where Protestants and Catholics marry each other, it is psychologically impossible to be sharply intolerant. That is why astute directors of corporations adopt the policy of distributing their securities as widely as they can; they know quite well that even the most modest shareholder is in some measure insulated against anti-corporate agitation. It is inherent in the complex pluralism of the modern world that men should behave moderately, and experience amply confirms this conclusion.

There is little doubt that in the great metropolitan centers there exists a disposition to live and let live, to give and take, to agree and to agree to differ, which is not to be found in simple homogeneous communities. In complex communities life quickly becomes intolerable if men are intolerant. For they are in daily contact with almost everybody and everything they could conceivably wish to persecute. Their victims would be their customers, their employees, their landlords, their tenants and perhaps their wives' relations. But in a simple community a kind of pastoral intolerance for everything alien adds a quaint flavor to living. For the most part it vents itself in the open air. The terrible indictments drawn up in a Mississippi village against the Pope in Rome, the Russian nation, the vices of Paris, and the enormities of New York are in the main quite lyrical. The Pope may never even know what the Mississippi preacher thinks of him and New York continues to go to, but never apparently to reach, hell.

When an agitator wishes to start a crusade, a religious revival, an inquisition, or some sort of jingo excitement, the further he goes from the centers of modern civilization the more following he can attract. It is in the backwoods and in the hill country, in kitchens and in old men's clubs, that fanaticism can be kindled. The urban crowd, if it has been urban for any length of time and has become used to its environment, may be fickle, faddish, nervous, unstable, but it lacks the concentration of energy to become fiercely excited for any length of time about anything. At its worst it is a raging mob, but it is not persistently fanatical. There are too many things to attract its attention for it to remain preoccupied for long with any one thing.

To responsible men of affairs the complexity of modern civilization is a daily lesson in the necessity of not pressing any claim too far, of understanding opposing points of view, of seeking to reconcile them, of conducting matters so that there is some kind of harmony in a plural society. This accounts, I think, for the increasing use of political devices which are wholly unknown in simpler societies. There is, for example, the ideal of a civil service. It is wholly modern and it is quite revolutionary. For it assumes that a great deal of the business of the state can and must be carried on by a class of men who have no personal and no party allegiance, who are in fact neutral in politics and concerned only with the execution of a task. I know how imperfectly the civil service works, but that it should exist at all, and that the ideal it embodies should be generally acknowledged, is profound testimony as to how inherent in the modern situation is the concept of disinterestedness. The theory of an independent judiciary arises out of the same need for disinterested judgment. Even more significant, perhaps, is the use in all political debates of the evidence of technicians, experts, and neutral investigators. The statesman who imagined he had thought up a solution for a social problem while he was in his bath would be a good deal of a joke; even if he had stumbled on a good idea, he would not dare to commit himself to it without elaborate preliminary surveys, investigations, hearings, conferences, and the like.

Men occupying responsible posts in the Great Society have become aware, in short, that their guesses and their prejudices are untrustworthy, and that successful decisions can be made only in a neutral spirit by comparing their hypotheses with their understanding of reality.

5. *Government in the People*

It has been the cause of considerable wonder to many persons that the most complex modern communities, where the old loyalties are most completely dissolved, where authority has so little prestige, where moral codes are held in such small esteem, should nevertheless have proved to be far more impervious to the strain of war and revolution than the older and simpler types of civilization. It has been Russia, China, Poland, Italy, Spain, rather than England, Germany, Belgium, and the United States which have been most disorderly in the post-war period. The contrary might have been expected. It might well have been anticipated that the highly organized, delicately poised social mechanisms would disintegrate the most easily.

Yet it is now evident why modern civilization is so durable. Its strength lies in its sensitiveness. The effect of bad decisions is so quickly felt, the consequences are so inescapably serious, that corrective action is almost immediately set in motion. A simple society like Russia can let its railroads go gradually to wrack and ruin, but a complex society like London or New York is instantly disorganized if the railroads do not run on schedule. So many persons are at once affected in so many vitally important ways that remedies have to be found immediately. This does not mean that modern states are governed as wisely as they should be, or that they do not neglect much that they cannot really afford to neglect. They blunder along badly enough in all conscience. There is nevertheless a minimum of order and of necessary services which they have to provide for themselves. They have to keep going. They cannot afford the luxury of prolonged disorder or of a general paralysis. Their own necessities are dependent on such fragile structures, and everyone is so much affected, that when a modern state is in trouble it can draw upon incomparable reserves of public spirit.

"I made ninety-one local committees in ninety-one local communities to look after the Mississippi flood," Mr. Hoover once explained, "that's what I principally did. . . . You say: 'a couple of thousand refugees are coming. They've got to have accommodations. Huts.

Water-mains. Sewers. Streets. Dining-halls. Meals. Doctors. Everything.' . . . So you go away and they go ahead and just simply do it. Of all those ninety-one committees there was just one that fell down." Mr. Hard, who reports these remarks, goes on to make Mr. Hoover say that: "No other Main Street in the world could have done what the American Main Street did in the Mississippi flood; and Europe may jeer as it pleases at our mass production and our mass organization and our mass education. The safety of the United States is its multitudinous mass leadership." Allowing for the fact that these remarks appeared in a campaign biography at a time when Mr. Hoover's friends were rather concerned about demonstrating the intensity of his patriotism, there is nevertheless substantial truth in them. I am inclined to believe that "multitudinous mass leadership" will be found wherever industrial society is firmly established, that is to say, wherever a people has lived with the machine process long enough to acquire the aptitudes that it calls for. This capacity to organize, to administer affairs, to deal realistically with necessity, can hardly be due to some congenital superiority in the American people. They are, after all only transplanted Europeans. That their aptitudes may be somewhat more highly developed is not, however, inconceivable: the new civilization may have developed more freely in a land where it did not have to contend with the institutions of a military, feudal, and clerical society.

The essential point is that as the machine technology makes social relations complex, it dissolves the habits of obedience and dependence; it disintegrates the centralization of power and of leadership; it diffuses the experience of responsible decision throughout the population, compelling each man to acquire the habit of making judgments instead of looking for orders, of adjusting his will to the wills of others instead of trusting to custom and organic loyalties. The real law under which modern society is administered is neither the accumulated precedents of tradition nor a set of commands originating on high which are imposed like orders in an army upon the rank and file below. The real law in the modern state is the multitude of little decisions made daily by millions of men.

Because this is so, the character of government is changing radically. This change is obscured for us in our theorizing by the fact that our political ideas derive from a different kind of social experience. We think of governing as the act of a person; for the actual king we have tried to substitute a corporate king, which we call the nation, the people, the majority, public opinion, or the general will. But none of these entities has the attributes of a king, and the failure of political thinking to lay the ghosts of monarchy leads to endless misunderstanding. The crucial difference between modern politics and that to which mankind has been accustomed is that the power to act and to compel obedience is almost never sufficiently centralized nowadays to be exercised by one will. The power is distributed and qualified so that power is exerted not by command but by interaction.

The prime business of government, therefore, is not to direct the affairs of the community, but to harmonize the direction which the community gives to its affairs.

The Congress of the United States, for example, does not consult the conscience and its God and then decree a tariff law. It enacts the kind of tariff which at the moment represents the most stable compromise among the interests which have made themselves heard. The law may be outrageously unfair. But if it is, that is because those whose interests are neglected did not at that time have the power to make themselves felt. If the law favors manufacturers rather than farmers, it is because the manufacturers at that time have greater weight in the social equilibrium than the farmers. That may sound hard. But it is doubtful whether a modern legislature can make laws effective if those laws are not the formal expression of what the persons actually affected can and wish to do.

The amount of law is relatively small which a modern legislature can successfully impose. The reason for this is that unless the enforcement of the law is taken in hand by the citizenry, the officials as such are quite helpless. It is possible to enforce the law of contracts, because the injured party will sue; it is possible to enforce the law against burglary, because almost everybody will report a burglary to the police. But it is not possible to enforce the old-fashioned speed laws on the highways because the police are too few and far between, the pedestrians are uninterested, and motorists like to speed. There is here a very fundamental principle of modern lawmaking: insofar as a law depends upon the initiative of officials in detecting violations and in prosecuting, that law will almost certainly be difficult to enforce. If a considerable part of the population is hostile to the law, and if the majority has only a platonic belief in it, the law will surely break down. For what gives law reality is not that it is commanded by the sovereign but that it brings the organized force of the state to the aid of those citizens who believe in the law.

What the government really does is not to rule men, but to add overwhelming force to men when they rule their affairs. The passage of a law is in effect a promise that the police, the courts, and the officials will defend and enforce certain rights when citizens choose to exercise them. For all practical purposes this is just as true when what was once a private wrong to be redressed by private action in law courts on proof of specific injury has been made by statute a public wrong which is preventable and punishable by administrative action. When the citizens are no longer interested in preventing or punishing specific instances of what the statute declares is a public wrong, the statute becomes a dead letter. The principle is most obviously true in the case of a sumptuary law like prohibition. The reason prohibition is unenforceable in the great cities is that the citizens will not report the names and addresses of their bootleggers to the prohibition officials. But the principle is no less true in less obvious cases, as, for example, in tariffs or laws to regulate railroads. Thus it is difficult to enforce the tariff law on jewels, for they are easily smuggled. Insofar as the law is enforced it is because jewelers find it profitable to maintain an organization which detects smuggling. Because they know the ins and outs of the trade, and have men in all the jewelry markets of the world who have an interest in catching smugglers, it is possible for the United

States Government to make a fair showing in administering the law. The government cannot from hour to hour inspect all the transactions of its people, and any law which rests on the premise that government can do this is a foolish law. The railroad laws are enforced because shippers are vigilant. The criminal laws depend upon how earnestly citizens object to certain kinds of crime. In fact it may be said that laws which make certain kinds of conduct illicit are effective insofar as the breach of these laws arouses the citizenry to call in the police and to take the trouble to help the police. It is not enough that the mass of the population should be law-abiding. A minority can stultify the law if the population as a whole is not also law-enforcing.

This is the real sense in which it can be said that power in the modern state resides not in the government but in the people. As that phrase is usually employed it alleges that 'the people,' as articulated by elected officials, can govern by command as the monarch or tribal chieftain once governed. In this sense government by the people is a delusion. What we have among advanced communities is something that might perhaps be described as government in the people. The naively democratic theory was that out of the mass of the voters there arose a cloud of wills which ascended to heaven, condensed into a thunderbolt, and then smote the people. It was supposed that the opinion of masses of persons somehow became the opinion of a corporate person called The People, and that this corporate person then directed human affairs like a monarch. But that is not what happens. Government is in the people and stays there. Government is their multitudinous decisions in concrete situations, and what officials do is to assist and facilitate this process of governing. Effective laws may be said to register an understanding among those concerned by which the law-abiding know what to expect and what is expected of them; they are insured with all the force that the state commands against the disruption of this understanding by the recalcitrant minority. In the modern state a law which does not register the inward assent of most of those who are affected will have very little force as against the breakers of that law. For it is only by that inward assent that power becomes mobilized to enforce the law. The government in the person of its officials, its paltry inspectors and policemen, has relatively little power of its own. It derives its power from the people in amounts which vary with the circumstances of each law. That is why the same government may act with invincible majesty in one place and with ludicrous futility in another.

6. *Politicians and Statesmen*

The role of the leader would be easier to define if it were agreed to give separate meanings to two very common words. I mean the words "politician" and "statesman." In popular usage a vague distinction is recognized: to call a man a statesman is eulogy, to call him a politician is to be, however faintly, disparaging. The dictionary, in fact, defines a politician as one who seeks to subserve the interests of a political party *merely;* as an afterthought it defines him as one skilled in political science: a statesman. And in defining a statesman the dictionary says that he is a political leader of distinguished ability.

These definitions can, I think, be improved upon by clarifying the meanings which are vaguely intended in popular usage. When we think offhand of a politician we think of a man who works for a partial interest. At the worst it is his own pocket. At the best it may be his party, his class, or an institution with which he is identified. We never feel that he can or will take into account all the interests concerned, and because bias and partisanship are the qualities of his conduct, we feel, unless we are naively afflicted with the same bias, that he is not to be trusted too far. Now the word 'statesman,' when it is not mere pomposity, connotes a man whose mind is elevated sufficiently above the conflict of contending parties to enable him to adopt a course of action which takes into account a greater number of interests in the perspective of a longer period of time. It is some such conception as this that Edmund Burke had in mind when he wrote that the state "ought not to be considered as nothing better than a partnership in a trade of pepper and coffee, calico or tobacco, or some other such low concern, to be taken up for a little temporary interest and to be dissolved by the fancy of the parties. . . . It is a partnership in a higher and more permanent sense— a partnership in all science; a partnership in all art; a partnership in every virtue and in all perfection. As the ends of such a partnership cannot be obtained in many generations it becomes a partnership not only between those who are living, but between those who are dead and those who are to be born."

The politician, then, is a man who seeks to attain the special objects of particular interests. If he is the leader of a political party he will try either to purchase the support of particular interests by specific pledges, or if that is impracticable, he will employ some form of deception. I include under the term 'deception' the whole art of propaganda, whether it consists of half-truths, lies, ambiguities, evasions, calculated silence, red herrings, unresponsiveness, slogans, catchwords, showmanship, bathos, hokum, and buncombe. They are, one and all, methods of preventing a disinterested inquiry into the situation. I do not say that any one can be elected to office without employing deception, though I am inclined to think that there is a new school of political reporters in the land who with a kind of beautiful cruelty are making it rather embarrassing for politicians to employ their old tricks. A man may have to be a politician to be elected when there is adult suffrage, and it may be that statesmanship, in the sense in which I am using the term, cannot occupy the whole attention of any public man. It is true at least that it never does.

The reason for this is that in order to hold office a man must array in his support a varied assortment of persons with all sorts of confused and conflicting purposes. When then, it may be asked, does he begin to be a statesman? He begins whenever he stops trying merely to satisfy or to obfuscate the momentary wishes of his constituents, and sets out to make them realize and assent to those hidden interests of theirs which are permanent because they fit the facts and can be harmonized with the interests of their neighbors. The politician says: "I will give you what you want." The statesman says: "What you think you want is this. What it is possible for you to get is that. What you really want, therefore, is the following." The politician stirs up a following; the statesman leads it. The politician, in brief, accepts unregenerate desire at its face value and either fulfills it or perpetrates a fraud; the statesman reeducates desire by confronting it with the reality, and so makes possible an enduring adjustment of interests within the community.

The chief element in the art of statesmanship under modern conditions is the ability to elucidate the confused and clamorous interests which converge upon the seat of government. It is an ability to penetrate from the naive self-interest of each group to its permanent and real interest. It is a difficult art which requires great courage, deep sympathy, and a vast amount of information. That is why it is so rare. But when a statesman is successful in converting his constituents from a childlike pursuit of what seems interesting to a realistic view of their interests, he receives a kind of support which the ordinary glib politician can never hope for. Candor is a bitter pill when first it is tasted but it is full of health, and once a man becomes established in the public mind as a person who deals habitually and successfully with real things, he acquires an eminence of a wholly different quality from that of even the most celebrated caterer to the popular favor. His hold on the people is enduring because he promises nothing which he cannot achieve; he proposes nothing which turns out to be a fake. Sooner or later the politician, because he deals in unrealities, is found out. Then he either goes to jail, or he is tolerated cynically as a picturesque and amiable scoundrel; or he retires and ceases to meddle with the destinies of men. The words of a statesman prove to have value because they express not the desires of the moment but the conditions under which desires can actually be adjusted to reality. His projects are policies which lay down an ordered plan of action in which all the elements affected will, after they have had some experience of it, find it profitable to co-operate. His laws register what the people really desire when they have clarified their wants. His laws have force because they mobilize the energies which alone can make laws effective.

It is not necessary, nor is it probable, that a statesman-like policy will win such assent when it is first proposed. Nor is it necessary for the statesman to wait until he has won complete assent. There are many things which people cannot understand until they have lived with them for a while. Often, therefore, the great statesman is bound to act boldly in advance of his constituents. When he does this he stakes his judgment as to what the people will in the end find to be good against what the people happen ardently to desire. This capacity to act upon the hidden realities of a situation in spite of appearances is the essence of statesmanship. It consists in giving the people not what they want but what they will learn to want. It requires the courage which is possible only in a mind that is detached from the agitations of the moment. It requires the insight which comes only from an objective and discerning knowledge of the facts, and a high and imperturbable disinterestedness.

CHAPTER XIV

LOVE IN THE GREAT SOCIETY

1. *The External Control of Sexual Conduct*

WHILE the changes which modernity implies affect the premises of all human conduct, the problem as a whole engages the attention of relatively few persons. The larger number of men and women living within the orbit of the Great Society are no doubt aware that their inherited beliefs about religion, politics, business, and sex do not square entirely with the actual beliefs upon which they feel compelled to act. But the fundamental alterations in political and economic ideals which the machine technology is inducing come home to each man only indirectly and partially. The consequences are subtle, delayed, and what is even more important, they are outside the scope of the ordinary man's personal decision. There is little that is urgent, immediate, or decisive which he can do, even if he understands them, about the changes in the structure and purpose of industry and the state. Most men can manage, therefore, to live without ever attempting to decide for themselves any fundamental question about business or politics. But they can neither ignore changes in sexual relations nor do they wish to. It is possible for a man to be a socialist or an individualist without ever having to make one responsible decision in which his theories play any part. But what he thinks

[284]

about divorce and contraception, continence and license, monogamy, prostitution, and sexual experience outside of marriage, are matters that are bound at some point in his life to affect his own happiness immediately and directly. It is possible to be hypocritical about sex. But it is not possible for any adult who is not anæsthetic to be indifferent. The affairs of state may be regulated by leaders. But the affairs of a man and a woman are inescapably their own.

That obviously is the reason why in the popular mind it is immediately assumed that when morals are discussed it is sexual morals that are meant. The morals of the politician and the voter, of the shareholder and executive and employee, are only moderately interesting to the general public: thus they almost never supply the main theme of popular fiction. But the relation between boy and girl, man and woman, husband and wife, mistress and lover, parents and children, are themes which no amount of repetition makes stale. The explanation is obvious. The modern audience is composed of persons among whom only a comparatively negligible few are serenely happy in their personal lives. Popular fiction responds to their longings: to the unappeased it offers some measure of vicarious satisfaction, to the prurient an indulgence, to the worried, if not a way out, then at least the comfort of knowing that their secret despair is a common, and not a unique, experience.

Yet in spite of this immense preoccupation with sex it is extraordinarily difficult to arrive at any reliable knowledge of what actual change in human behavior it reflects. This is not surprising. In fact this is the very essence of the matter. The reason it is difficult to know the actual facts about sexual behavior in modern society is that sexual behavior eludes observation and control. We know that the old conventions have lost most of their authority because we cannot know about, and therefore can no longer regulate, the sexual behavior of others. It may be that there is, as some optimists believe, a fine but candid restraint practiced among modern men and women. It may be that incredible licentiousness exists all about us, as the gloomier prophets insist. It may be that there is just about as much unconventional conduct and no more than there has always been. Nobody, I think, really knows. Nobody knows whether the conversation about sex reflects more promiscuity or less hypocrisy. But what everybody must know is that sexual conduct, whatever it may be, is regulated personally and not publicly in modern society. If there is restraint it is, in the last analysis, voluntary; if there is promiscuity, it can be quite secret.

The circumstances which have wrought this change are inherent in modern ways of living. Until quite recently the main conventions of sex were enforced first by the parents and then by the husband through their control over the life of the woman. The main conventions were: first, that she must not encourage or display any amorous inclinations except where there was practical certainty that the young man's intentions were serious; second, that when she was married to the young man she submitted to his embraces only because the Lord somehow failed to contrive a less vile method of perpetuating the species. All the minor conventions were subsidiary to these; the whole system was organized on the premise that procreation was the woman's only sanction for sexual intercourse. Such control as was exercised over the conduct of men was subordinate to this control over the conduct of women. The chastity of women before marriage was guarded; that meant that seduction was a crime, but that relations with "lost" or unchaste women were tolerated. The virtuous man, by popular standards, was one who before his marriage did not have sexual relations with a virtuous woman. There is ample testimony in the outcries of moralists that even in the olden days these conventions were not perfectly administered. But they were sufficiently well administered to remain the accepted conventions, honored even in the breach. It was possible, because of the way people lived, to administer them.

The woman lived a sheltered life. That is another way of saying that she lived under the constant inspection of her family. She lived at home. She worked at home. She met young men under the zealous chaperonage of practically the whole community. No doubt, couples slipped away occasionally and more went on than was known or acknowledged. But even then there was a very powerful deterrent against an illicit relationship. This deterrent was the fear of pregnancy. That in the end made it almost certain that if a secret affair were consummated it could not be kept secret and that terrible penalties would be exacted. In the modern world effective chaperonage has become impracticable and the fear of pregnancy has been virtually eliminated by the very general knowledge of contraceptive methods.

The whole revolution in the field of sexual morals turns upon the fact that external control of the chastity of women is becoming impossible.

2. *Birth Control*

The Biblical account of how Jehovah slew Onan for disobeying his father's commandment to go to his brother's widow, Tamar, and "perform the duty of an husband's brother," shows that the deliberate prevention of conception is not a new discovery. Mr. Harold Cox must be right when he says "it is fairly certain that in all ages and in all countries men and women have practiced various devices to prevent conception while continuing to indulge in sexual intercourse." For while I know of no positive evidence to support this, it appears to be self-evident that the human race within historical times has not multiplied up to the limits of human fecundity. Since it is hardly probable that this has been due to the continence of husbands, nor wholly to infanticide, abortion, infant mortality, and postponement of marriage, it is safe to conclude that birth control is an ancient practice.

Nevertheless, it was not until the Nineteenth Century that the practice of contraception began to be publicly advocated on grounds of public policy. Until the industrial age the weight of opinion was overwhelmingly in favor of very large families. Kings and nobles needed soldiers and retainers: "As arrows in the hand of a mighty man, so are the children of youth. Happy is the man that hath his quiver full of them. They shall not be ashamed, but they shall speak with the enemies in the gate." Fathers of families desired many sons. The early factory-owners could use abundant cheap labor. There had been men from Plato's time who had their doubts about the value of an indefinitely growing population. But the substantial opinion down to the end of the Eighteenth Century was Adam Smith's that: "the most decisive mark of the prosperity of any country is the increase of the number of its inhabitants."

Apparently it was the sinister character of the early factory system, and the ominous unrest which pervaded Europe after the French Revolution, which rather suddenly changed into pessimism this bland optimism about an ever growing population. Malthus published the first edition of his *Essay on Population* in 1798. This book is undoubtedly one of the great landmarks of human culture, for it focussed the attention of Europe on the necessity of regulating the growth of population. Malthus himself, it seems, hoped that this regulation could be achieved by the postponement of marriage and by continence. It is not clear whether he disapproved of what is now called neo-Malthusianism, or whether he did not regard it as practicable. Nevertheless, within less than twenty-five years James Mill in the *Encyclopædia Britannica* had in guarded fashion put forward the neo-Malthusian principle, and shortly thereafter, that is in 1823, an active public propaganda was set on foot, most probably by Francis Place, by means of what were known as the "diabolical handbills." These leaflets were addressed to the working classes and contained descriptions of methods for preventing conception. Some of them were sent to a good lady named Mrs. Fildes, who indignantly, but mistakenly from her point of view, assisted the nefarious propaganda by exposing it in the public prints. Fifty years later Mr. Bradlaugh and Mrs. Besant had themselves indicted and tried for selling an illustrated edition of Knowlton's *Fruits of Philosophy*. After that advertisement, neo-Malthusian principles and practices were known and were, therefore, available to all but the poorest and most illiterate.

No propaganda so threatening to the established moral order ever encountered such an ineffective opposition. I do not know how much money has been spent on the propaganda nor how many martyrs have had to coerce reluctant judges to try them. But it is evident that once it was known that fairly dependable methods of contraception exist, the people took the matter into their own hands. For the public reasons by which neo-Malthusianism was justified were also private reasons. The social philosopher said that population must be adjusted to the means of subsistence. Man and wife said that they must have only as many children as they could afford to rear. The eugenist said that certain stocks ought not to multiply. Individual women decided that too many children, or even any children, were bad for their health. But these were not the only reasons which explain the demand for neo-Malthusian knowledge. There was also the very plain demand due to a desire to enjoy sexual intercourse without social consequences.

On this aspect of birth control the liberal reformers have, I think, been until recently more than a little disingenuous. They have been arguing for the removal of the prohibitory laws, and they have built their case on two main theses. They have argued, first, that the limitation of births was sound public policy for economic and eugenic reasons; and second, that it was necessary to the happiness of families, the health of mothers, and the welfare of children. All these reasons may be unimpeachable. I think they are. But it was idle to pretend that the dissemination of this knowledge, even if legally confined to the instruction of married women by licensed physicians, could be kept from the rest of the adult population. Obviously that which all married couples are permitted to know every one is bound to know. Human curiosity will make that certain. Now this is what the Christian churches, especially the Roman Catholic, which oppose contraception on principle, instantly recognized. They were quite right. They were quite right, too, in recognizing that whether or not birth control is eugenic, hygienic, and economic, it is the most revolutionary practice in the history of sexual morals.

For when conception could be prevented, there was an end to the theory that woman submits to the embrace of the male only for purposes of procreation. She had to be persuaded to cooperate, and no possible reason could be advanced except that the pleasure was reciprocal. She had to understand and inwardly assent to the principle that it is proper to have sexual intercourse with her husband and to prevent conception. She had, therefore, to give up the whole traditional theory which she may have only half-believed anyway, that sexual intercourse was an impure means to a noble end. She could no longer believe that procreation alone mitigated the vileness of cohabiting with a man, and so she had to change her valuation and accept it as inherently delightful. Thus by an inevitable process the practice of contraception led husbands and wives to the conviction that they need not be in the least ashamed of their desires for each other.

But this transvaluation of values within the sanctity of the marital chamber could hardly be kept a secret. What had happened was that married couples were indulging in the pleasures of sex because they had learned how to isolate them from the responsibilities of parenthood. When we talk about the unconventional theories of the younger generation we might in all honesty take this fact into account. They have had it demonstrated to them by their own parents, by those in whom the administering of the conventions is vested, that under certain circumstances it is legitimate and proper to gratify sexual desire apart from any obligation to the family or to the race. They have been taught that it is possible to do this, and that it may be proper. Therefore, the older generation could no longer argue that sexual intercourse as such was evil. It could no longer argue that it was obviously dangerous. It could only maintain that the psychological consequences are serious if sexual gratification is not made incidental to the enduring partnership of marriage and a home. That may be, in fact, I think it can be shown to be, the real wisdom of the matter. Yet if it is the wisdom of the matter, it is a kind of wisdom which men and women can acquire by experience alone. They do not have it instinctively. They cannot be compelled to adopt it. They can only learn to believe it.

That is a very different thing from submitting to a convention upheld by all human and divine authority.

3. *The Logic of Birth Control*

With contraception established as a more or less legitimate idea in modern society, a vast discussion has ensued
as to how the practice of it can be rationalized.   In this
discussion the pace is set by those who accept the apparent
logic of contraception and are prepared boldly to revise
the sexual conventions accordingly.   They take as their
major premise the obvious fact that by contraception it
is possible to dissociate procreation from gratification, and
therefore to pursue independently what Mr. Havelock
Ellis calls the primary and secondary objects of the sexual
impulse.   They propose, therefore, to sanction two distinct sets of conventions: one designed to protect the
interests of the offspring by promoting intelligent, secure,
and cheerful parenthood; the other designed to permit
the freest and fullest expression of the erotic personality.
They propose, in other words, to distinguish between
parenthood as a vocation involving public responsibility,
and love as an art, pursued privately for the sake of
happiness.

As a preparation for the vocation of parenthood it is
proposed to educate both men and women in the care, both
physical and psychological, of children.   It is proposed
further that mating for parenthood shall become an altogether deliberate and voluntary choice: the argument here
is that the duties of parenthood cannot be successfully fulfilled except where both parents cheerfully and knowingly
assume them.   Therefore, it is proposed, in order to avert
the dangers of love at first sight and of mating under the
blind compulsion of instinct, that a period of free experi-

mentation be allowed to precede the solemn engagement to produce and rear children. This engagement is regarded as so much a public responsibility that it is even proposed, and to some extent has been embodied in the law of certain jurisdictions, that marriages for parenthood must be sanctioned by medical authority. In order, too, that no compulsive considerations may determine what ought to be a free and intelligent choice, it is argued that women should be economically independent before and during marriage. As this may not be possible for women without property of their own during the years when they are bearing and rearing children, it is proposed in some form or other to endow motherhood. This endowment may take the form of a legal claim upon the earnings of the father, or it may mean a subsidy from the state through mothers' pensions, free medical attention, day nurseries, and kindergartens. The principle that successful parenthood must be voluntary is maintained as consistently as possible. Therefore, among those who follow the logic of their idea, it is proposed that even marriages deliberately entered into for procreation shall be dissoluble at the will of either party, the state intervening only to insure the economic security of the offspring. It is proposed, furthermore, that where women find the vocation of motherhood impracticable for one reason or another, they may be relieved of the duty of rearing their children.

Not all of the advanced reformers adopt the whole of this program, but the whole of this program is logically inherent in the conception of parenthood as a vocation deliberately undertaken, publicly pursued, and motivated solely by the parental instincts.

The separate set of conventions which it is proposed to adopt for the development of love as an art have a logic of their own. Their function is not to protect the welfare of the child but the happiness of lovers. It is very easy to misunderstand this conception. Mr. Havelock Ellis, in fact, describes it as a "divine and elusive mystery," a description which threatens to provide a rather elusive standard by which to fix a new set of sexual conventions. But baffling as this sounds, it is not wholly inscrutable, and a sufficient understanding of what is meant can be attained by clearing up the dangerous ambiguity in the phrase "love as an art."

There are two arts of love and it makes a considerable difference which one is meant. There is the art of love as Casanova, for example, practiced it. It is the art of seduction, courtship, and sexual gratification: it is an art which culminates in the sexual act. It can be repeated with the same lover and with other lovers, but it exhausts itself in the moment of ecstasy. When that moment is reached, the work of art is done, and the lover as artist "after an interval, perhaps of stupor and vital recuperation" must start all over again, until at last the rhythm is so stale it is a weariness to start at all; or the lover must find new lovers and new resistances to conquer. The aftermath of romantic love—that is, of love that is consummated in sexual ecstasy—is either tedium in middle age or the compulsive adventurousness of the libertine.

Now this is not what Mr. Ellis means when he talks about love as an art. "The act of intercourse," he says, "is only an incident, and not an essential in love." Incident to what? His answer is that it is an incident to an "exquisitely and variously and harmoniously blended" activity of "all the finer activities of the organism, physical and psychic." I take this to mean that when a man and woman are successfully in love, their whole activity is energized and victorious. They walk better, their digestion improves, they think more clearly, their secret worries drop away, the world is fresh and interesting, and they can do more than they dreamed that they could do. In love of this kind sexual intimacy is not the dead end of desire as it is in romantic or promiscuous love, but periodic affirmation of the inward delight of desire pervading an active life. Love of this sort can grow: it is not, like youth itself, a moment that comes and is gone and remains only a memory of something which cannot be recovered. It can grow because it has something to grow upon and to grow with; it is not contracted and stale because it has for its object, not the mere relief of physical tension, but all the objects with which the two lovers are concerned. They desire their worlds in each other, and therefore their love is as interesting as their worlds and their worlds are as interesting as their love.

It is to promote unions of this sort that the older liberals are proposing a new set of sexual conventions. There are, however, reformers in the field who take a much less exalted view of the sexual act, who regard it, indeed, not only as without biological or social significance, but also as without any very impressive psychological significance. "The practice of birth control," says Mr. C. E. M. Joad, for example, "will profoundly modify our sexual habits. It will enable the pleasures of sex to be tasted without its penalties, and it will remove the most formidable deterrent to irregular intercourse." For birth control "offers to the young . . . the prospect of shameless, harmless, and unlimited pleasure." But whether the reformers agree with Mr. Ellis that sexual intimacy is, as he says, a sacrament signifying some great spiritual reality, or with Mr. Joad that it is a harmless pleasure, they are agreed that the sexual conventions should be revised to permit such unions without penalties and without any sense of shame.

They ask public opinion to sanction what contraception has made feasible. They point out that "a large number of the men and women of to-day form sexual relationships outside marriage—whether or not they ultimately lead to marriage—which they conceal or seek to conceal from the world." These relationships, says Mr. Ellis, differ from the extra-marital manifestations of the sexual life of the past in that they do not derive from prostitution or seduction. Both of these ancient practices, he adds, are diminishing, for prostitution is becoming less attractive and, with the education of women, seduction is becoming less possible. The novelty of these new relations, the prevalence of which is conceded though it cannot be measured, lies in the fact that they are entered into voluntarily, have no obvious social consequences, and are altogether beyond the power of law or opinion to control. The argument, therefore, is that they should be approved, the chief point made being that by removing all stigma from such unions, they will become candid, wholesome, and delightful. The objection of the reformers to the existing conventions is that the sense of sin poisons the spontaneous goodness of such relationships.

The actual proposals go by a great variety of fancy names such as free love, trial marriage, companionate marriage. When these proposals are examined it is evident they all take birth control as their major premise, and then deduce from it some part or all of the logical consequences. Companionate marriage, for example, is from the point of view of the law, whatever it may be subjectively, nothing but a somewhat roundabout way of saying that childless couples may be divorced by mutual consent. It is a proposal, if not to control, then at least to register, publicly all sexual unions, the theory being that this public registration will abolish shame and furtiveness and give them a certain permanence. Companionate marriage is frankly an attempt at a compromise between marriages that are difficult to dissolve and clandestine relationships which have no sanction whatever.

The uncompromising logic of birth control has been stated more clearly, I think, by Mr. Bertrand Russell than by anyone else. Writing to Judge Lindsey during the uproar about companionate marriage, Mr. Russell said:

> I go further than you do: the things which your enemies say about you would be largely true of me. My own view is that the state and the law should take no notice of sexual relations apart from children, and that no marriage ceremony should be valid unless accompanied by a medical certificate of the woman's pregnancy. But when once there are children, I think that divorce should be avoided except for very grave cause. I should not regard physical infidelity as a very grave cause and should teach people that it is to be expected and tolerated, but should not involve the begetting of illegitimate children—not because illegitimacy is bad in

itself, but because a home with two parents is best for children. I do not feel that the main thing in marriage is the feeling of the parents for each other; the main thing is cooperation in bearing children.

In this admirably clear statement there is set forth a plan for that complete separation between the primary and secondary function of sexual intercourse which contraception makes possible.

4. *The Use of Convention*

It is one thing, however, to recognize the full logic of birth control and quite another thing to say that convention ought to be determined by that logic. One might as well argue that because automobiles can be driven at a hundred miles an hour the laws should sanction driving at the rate of a hundred miles an hour. Birth control is a device like the automobile, and its inherent possibilities do not fix the best uses to be made of it.

What an understanding of the logic of birth control does is to set before us the limits of coercive control of sexual relations. The law can, for example, make divorce very difficult where there are children. It could, as Mr. Bertrand Russell suggests, refuse divorce on the ground of infidelity. On the other hand the law cannot effectively prohibit infidelity, and as a matter of fact does not do so to-day. It cannot effectively prohibit fornication though there are statutes against it. Therefore, what Mr. Russell has done is to describe accurately enough the actual limits of effective legal control.

But sexual conventions are not statutes, and it is important to define quite clearly just what they are. In the older world they were rules of conduct enforceable by the family and the community through habit, coercion, and authority. In this sense of the word, convention tends to lose force and effect in modern civilization. Yet a convention is essentially a theory of conduct and all human conduct implies some theory of conduct. Therefore, although it may be that no convention is any longer coercive, conventions remain, are adopted, revised, and debated. They embody the considered results of experience: perhaps the experience of a lonely pioneer or perhaps the collective experience of the dominant members of a community. In any event they are as necessary to a society which recognizes no authority as to one which does. For the inexperienced must be offered some kind of hypothesis when they are confronted with the necessity of making choices: they cannot be so utterly open-minded that they stand inert until something collides with them. In the modern world, therefore, the function of conventions is to declare the meaning of experience. A good convention is one which will most probably show the inexperienced the way to happy experience.

Just because the rule of sexual conduct by authority is dissolving, the need of conventions which will guide conduct is increasing. That, in fact, is the reason for the immense and urgent discussion of sex throughout the modern world. It is an attempt to attain an understanding of the bewilderingly new experiences to which few men or women know how to adjust themselves. The true business of the moralist in the midst of all this is not to denounce this and to advocate that, but to see as clearly as he can into the meaning of it, so that out of the chaos of pain and happiness and worry he may help to deliver a usable insight.

It is, I think, to the separation of parenthood as a vocation from love as an end in itself that the moralist must address himself. For this is the heart of the problem: to determine whether this separation, which birth control has made feasible and which law can no longer prevent, is in harmony with the conditions of human happiness.

5. *The New Hedonism*

Among those who hold that the separation of the primary and secondary functions of the sexual impulse is good and should constitute the major premise of modern sexual conventions, there are, as I have already pointed out, two schools of thought. There are the transcendentalists who believe with Mr. Havelock Ellis that "sexual pleasure, wisely used and not abused, may prove the stimulus and liberator of our finest and most exalted activities," and there are the unpretentious hedonists who believe that sexual pleasure is pleasure and not the stimulus or liberator of anything important. Both are, as we say, emancipated: neither recognizes the legitimacy of objective control unless a child is born, and both reject as an evil the traditional subjective control exercised by the sense of sin. Where they differ is in their valuation of love.

Hedonism as an attitude toward life is, of course, not a new thing in the world, but it has never before been tested out under such favorable conditions. To be a successful hedonist a man must have the opportunity to seek his pleasures without fear of any kind. Theodorus of Cyrene, who taught about 310 B.C., saw that clearly, and therefore to release men from fear openly denied the Olympian gods. But the newest hedonism has had an even better prospect than the classical: it finds men emancipated not only of all fear of divine authority and human custom but of physical and social consequences as well. If the pursuit of pleasure by carefree men were the way to happiness, hedonism ought, then, to be proving itself triumphantly in the modern world. Possibly it is too early to judge, but the fact is nevertheless highly significant, I think, that the new hedonists should already have arrived at the same conclusion as the later hedonists in the classical world. Hegesias, for example, wrote when hedonism had already had a great vogue: he was called, rather significantly, the "persuader to die." For having started from the premise that pleasure is the end of life, he concluded that, since life affords at least as much pain as pleasure, the end of life cannot be realized. There is now a generation in the world which is approaching middle age. They have exercised the privileges which were won by the iconoclasts who attacked what was usually called the Puritan or Victorian tradition. They have exercised the privileges without external restraint and without inhibition. Their conclusions are reported in the latest works of fiction. Do they report that they have found happiness in their freedom? Well, hardly. Instead of the gladness which they were promised, they seem, like Hegesias, to have found the wasteland.

"If love has come to be less often a sin," says that very discerning critic of life and letters, Mr. Joseph Wood Krutch, "it has come also to be less often a supreme privilege. If one turns to the smarter of those novelists who describe the doings of the more advanced set of those who are experimenting with life—to, for example, Mr. Aldous Huxley or Mr. Ernest Hemingway,—one will discover in their tragic farces the picture of a society which is at bottom in despair because, though it is more completely absorbed in the pursuit of love than in anything else, it has lost the sense of any ultimate importance inherent in the experience which preoccupies it; and if one turns to the graver of the intellectual writers,—to, for example, Mr. D. H. Lawrence, Mr. T. S. Eliot, or Mr. James Joyce,—one will find both explicitly and implicitly a similar sense that the transcendental value of love has become somehow attenuated, and that, to take a perfectly concrete example, a conclusion which does no more than bring a man and woman into complete possession of one another is a mere bathos which does nothing except legitimately provoke the comment, 'Well, what of it?' One can hardly imagine them concerned with what used to be called, in a phrase which they have helped to make faintly ridiculous, 'the right to love.' Individual freedom they have inherited and assumed as a right, but they are concerned with something which their more restricted forefathers assumed— with, that is to say, the value of love itself. No inhibitions either within or without restrain them, but they are asking themselves, 'What is it worth?' and they are certainly no longer feeling that it is obviously and in itself something which makes life worth the living.

"To Huxley and Hemingway—I take them as the most conspicuous exemplars of a whole school—love is at times only a sort of obscene joke. The former in particular has delighted to mock sentiment with physiology, to place the emotions of the lover in comic juxtaposition with quaint biological lore, and to picture a romantic pair 'quietly sweating palm to palm.' But the joke is one which turns quickly bitter upon the tongue, for a great and gratifying illusion has passed away, leaving the need for it still there. His characters still feel the psychological urge, and, since they have no sense of sin in connection with it, they yield easily and continually to that urge; but they have also the human need to respect their chief preoccupation, and it is the capacity to do this that they have lost. Absorbed in the pursuit of sexual satisfaction, they never find love and they are scarcely aware that they are seeking it, but they are far from content with themselves. In a generally devaluated world they are eagerly endeavoring to get what they can in the pursuit of satisfactions which are sufficiently instinctive to retain inevitably a modicum of animal pleasure, but they cannot transmute that simple animal pleasure into anything else. They themselves not infrequently share the contempt with which their creator regards them, and nothing could be less seductive, because nothing could be less glamorous, than the description of the debaucheries born of nothing except a sense of the emptiness of life."

This "generally devaluated world," of which Mr. Krutch speaks, what is it after all, but a world in which nothing connects itself very much with anything else? If you start with the belief that love is the pleasure of a moment, is it really surprising that it yields only a momentary pleasure? For it is the most ironical of all illusions to suppose that one is free of illusions in contracting any human desire to its primary physiological satisfaction. Does a man dine well because he ingests the requisite number of calories? Is he freer from illusions about his appetite than the man who creates an interesting dinner party out of the underlying fact that his guests and he have the need to fill their stomachs? Would it really be a mark of enlightenment if each of them filled his stomach in the solitary and solemn conviction that good conversation and pleasant companionship are one thing and nutrition is another?

This much the transcendentalists understand well enough. They do not wish to isolate the satisfaction of desire from our "finest and most exalted activities." They would make it "the stimulus and the liberator" of these activities. They would use it to arouse to "wholesome activity all the complex and interrelated systems of the organism." But what are these finest and most exalted activities which are to be stimulated and liberated? The discovery of truth, the making of works of art, meditation and insight? Mr. Ellis does not specify. If these are the activities that are meant, then the discussion applies to a very few of the men and women on earth. For the activities of most of them are necessarily concerned with earning a living and managing a household and rearing children and finding recreation. If the art of love is to stimulate and liberate activities, it is these prosaic activities which it must stimulate and liberate. But if you idealize the logic of birth control, make parenthood a separate vocation, isolate love from work and the hard realities of living, and say that it must be spontaneous and carefree, what have you done? You have separated

it from all the important activities which it might stimulate and liberate. You have made love spontaneous but
empty, and you have made home-building and parenthood
efficient, responsible, and dull.

What has happened, I believe, is what so often happens
in the first enthusiasm for a revolutionary invention. Its
possibilities are so dazzling that men forget that inventions belong to man and not man to his inventions. In
the discussion which has ensued since birth control became
generally feasible, the central confusion has been that the
reformers have tried to fix their sexual ideals in accordance with the logic of birth control instead of the logic of
human nature. Birth control does make feasible this
dissociation of interests which were once organically
united. There are undoubtedly the best of reasons for
dissociating them up to a point. But how completely it
is wise to dissociate them is a matter to be determined not
by saying how completely it is possible to dissociate them,
but how much it is desirable to dissociate them.

All the varieties of the modern doctrine that man is a
collection of separate impulses, each of which can attain
its private satisfaction, are in fundamental contradiction
not only with the traditional body of human wisdom but
with the modern conception of the human character. Thus
in one breath it is said in advanced circles that love is a
series of casual episodes, and in the next it transpires that
the speaker is in process of having himself elaborately
psychoanalyzed in order to disengage his soul from the
effects of apparently trivial episodes in his childhood. On
the one hand it is asserted that sex pervades everything
and on the other that sexual behavior is inconsequential.

It is taught that experience is cumulative, that we are what our past has made us and shall be what we are making of ourselves now, and then with bland indifference to the significance of this we are told that all experiences are free, equal, and independent.

6. *Marriage and Affinity*

It is not hard to see why those who are concerned in revising sexual conventions should have taken the logic of birth control rather than knowledge of human nature as their major premise. Birth control is an immensely beneficent invention which can and does relieve men and women of some of the most tragic sorrows which afflict them: the tragedies of the unwanted child, the tragedies of insupportable economic burdens, the tragedies of excessive child-bearing and the destruction of youth and the necessity of living in an unrelenting series of pregnancies. It offers them freedom from intolerable mismating, from sterile virtue, from withering denials of happiness. These are the facts which the reformers saw, and in birth control they saw the instrument by which such freedom could be obtained.

The sexual conventions which they have proposed are really designed to cure notorious evils. They do not define the good life in sex; they point out ways of escape from the bad life. Thus companionate marriage is proposed by Judge Lindsey not as a type of union which is inherently desirable, but as an avenue of escape from corrupt marriages on the one hand and furtive promiscuity on the other. The movement for free divorce comes down to this: it is necessary because so many marriages are a failure. The whole theory that love is separate from parenthood and home-building is supported by the evidence in those cases where married couples are not lovers. It is the pathology of sexual relations which inspires the reformers of sexual conventions.

There is no need to quarrel with them because they insist upon remedies for manifest evils. Deep confusion results when they forget that these remedies are only remedies, and go on to institute them as ideals. It is better, without any doubt, that incompatible couples should be divorced and that each should then be free to find a mate who is compatible. But the frequency with which men and women have to resort to divorce because they are incompatible will be greatly influenced by the notions they have before and during marriage of what compatibility is, and what it involves. The remedies for failure are important. But what is central is the conception of sexual relations by which they expect to live successfully.

They cannot—I am, of course, speaking broadly—expect to live successfully by the conception that the primary and secondary functions of sex are in separate compartments of the soul. I have indicated why this conception is self-defeating and why, since human nature is organic and experience cumulative, our activities must, so to speak, engage and imply each other. Mates who are not lovers will not really cooperate, as Mr. Bertrand Russell thinks they should, in bearing children; they will be distracted, insufficient, and worst of all they will be merely dutiful. Lovers who have nothing to do but love each other are not really to be envied; love and nothing else very soon is nothing else. The emotion of love, in spite of the romantics, is not self-sustaining; it endures only when the lovers love many things together, and not merely each other. It is this understanding that love cannot successfully be isolated from the business of living which is the enduring wisdom of the institution of marriage. Let the law be what it may be as to what constitutes a marriage contract and how and when it may be dissolved. Let public opinion be as tolerant as it can be toward any and every kind of irregular and experimental relationship. When all the criticisms have been made, when all supernatural sanctions have been discarded, all subjective inhibitions erased, all compulsions abolished, the convention of marriage still remains to be considered as an interpretation of human experience. It is by the test of how genuinely it interprets human experience that the convention of marriage will ultimately be judged.

The wisdom of marriage rests upon an extremely unsentimental view of lovers and their passions. Its assumptions, when they are frankly exposed, are horrifying to those who have been brought up in the popular romantic tradition of the Nineteenth Century. These assumptions are that, given an initial attraction, a common social background, common responsibilities, and the conviction that the relationship is permanent, compatibility in marriage can normally be achieved. It is precisely this that the prevailing sentimentality about love denies. It assumes that marriages are made in heaven, that compatibility is instinctive, a mere coincidence, that happy unions are, in the last analysis, lucky accidents in which two people who happen to suit each other happen to have met. The convention of marriage rests on an interpretation of human nature which does not confuse the subjective feeling of the lovers that their passion is unique, with the brutal but objective fact that, had they never met, each of them would in all probability have found a lover who was just as unique. "Love," says Mr. Santayana, "is indeed much less exacting than it thinks itself. Nine-tenths of its cause are in the lover, for one-tenth that may be in the object. Were the latter not accidentally at hand, an almost identical passion would probably have been felt for some one else; for, although with acquaintance the quality of an attachment naturally adapts itself to the person loved, and makes that person its standard and ideal, the first assault and mysterious glow of the passion is much the same for every object."

This is the reason why the popular conception of romantic love as the meeting of two affinities produces so much unhappiness. The mysterious glow of passion is accepted as a sign that the great coincidence has occurred; there is a wedding and soon, as the glow of passion cools, it is discovered that no instinctive and preordained affinity is present. At this point the wisdom of popular romantic marriage is exhausted. For it proceeds on the assumption that love is a mysterious visitation. There is nothing left, then, but to grin and bear a miserably dull and nagging fate, or to break off and try again. The deep fallacy of the conception is in the failure to realize that compatibility is a process and not an accident, that it depends upon the maturing of instinctive desire by adaptation to the whole nature of the other person and to the common concerns of the pair of lovers.

The romantic theory of affinities rests upon an immature

theory of desire. It springs from an infantile belief that the success of love is in the satisfactions which the other person provides. What this really means is that in child-like fashion the lover expects his mistress to supply him with happiness. But in the adult world that expectation is false. Because nine-tenths of the cause, as Mr. Santayana says, are in the lover for one-tenth that may be in the object, it is what the lover does about that nine-tenths which is decisive for his happiness. It is the claim, there-fore, of those who uphold the ideal of marriage as a full partnership, and reject the ideal which would separate love as an art from parenthood as a vocation, that in the home made by a couple who propose to see it through, there are provided the essential conditions under which the pas-sions of men and women are most likely to become mature, and therefore harmonious and disinterested.

7. *The Schooling of Desire*

They need not deny, indeed it would be foolish as well as cruel for them to underestimate, the enormous difficulty of achieving successful marriages under modern condi-tions. For with the dissolution of authority and compul-sion, a successful marriage depends wholly upon the capacity of the man and the woman to make it successful. They have to accomplish wholly by understanding and sympathy and disinterestedness of purpose what was once in a very large measure achieved by habit, necessity, and the absence of any practicable alternative. It takes two persons to make a successful marriage in the modern world, and that fact more than doubles its difficulty. For these reasons alone the modern state ought to do what it would none the less be compelled to do: it ought to provide decent ways of retreat in case of failure.

But if it is the truth that the convention of marriage correctly interprets human experience, whereas the separatist conventions are self-defeating, then the convention of marriage will prove to be the conclusion which emerges out of all this immense experimenting. It will survive not as a rule of law imposed by force, for that is now, I think, become impossible. It will not survive as a moral commandment with which the elderly can threaten the young. They will not listen. It will survive as the dominant insight into the reality of love and happiness, or it will not survive at all. That does not mean that all persons will live under the convention of marriage. As a matter of fact in civilized ages all persons never have. It means that the convention of marriage, when it is clarified by insight into reality, is likely to be the hypothesis upon which men and women will ordinarily proceed. There will be no compulsion behind it except the compulsion in each man and woman to reach a true adjustment of his life.

It is in this necessity of clarifying their love for those who are closest to them that the moral problems of the new age come to a personal issue. It is in the realm of sexual relations that mankind is being schooled amidst pain and worry for the novel conditions which modernity imposes. It is there, rather than in politics, business, or even in religion, that the issues are urgent, vivid, and inescapable. It is there that they touch most poignantly and most radically the organic roots of human personality. And it is there, in the ordering of their personal attachments, that for most men the process of salvation must necessarily begin.

For disinterestedness in all things, as Dean Inge says, is a mountain track which the many are likely in the future as in the past to find cold, bleak, and bare: that is why "the road of ascent is by personal affection for man." By the happy ordering of their personal affections they may establish the type and the quality and the direction of their desires for all things. It is in the hidden issues between lovers, more than anywhere else, that modern men and women are compelled, by personal anguish rathei than by laws and preachments or even by the persuasions of abstract philosophy, to transcend naive desire and to reach out towards a mature and disinterested partnership with their world.

CHAPTER XV

THE MORALIST IN AN UNBELIEVING WORLD

1. *The Declaration of Ideals*

OF all the bewilderments of the present age none is greater than that of the conscientious and candid moralist himself. The very name of moralist seems to have become a term of disparagement and to suggest a somewhat pretentious and a somewhat stupid, perhaps even a somewhat hypocritical, meddler in other men's lives. In the minds of very many in the modern generation moralists are set down as persons who, in the words of Dean Inge, fancy themselves attracted by God when they are really only repelled by man.

The disesteem into which moralists have fallen is an historical accident. It so happens that those who administered the affairs of the established churches have, by and large, failed utterly to comprehend how deep and how inexorable was the dissolution of the ancestral order. They imagined either that this change in human affairs was a kind of temporary corruption, or that, like the eighty propositions listed in the Syllabus of Pope Pius IX, it could be regarded as due to "errors" of the human mind. There were, of course, churchmen who knew better, but on the whole those who prevailed in the great ecclesiastical establishments could not believe that the skepticism of mind and the freedom of action which modern men exercise were due to inexorable historic causes. They declined to acknowledge that modern freedom was not merely a wilful iconoclasm, but the liquidation of an older order of human life.

Because they could not comprehend the magnitude of the revolution in which they were involved, they set themselves the task of impeding its progress by chastising the rebels and refuting their rationalizations. This was described as a vindication of morals. The effect was to associate morality with the vindication of the habits and dispositions of those who were most thoroughly out of sympathy with the genuine needs of modern men.

The difficulties of the new age were much more urgent than those which the orthodox moralists were concerned with. The moralists insisted that conduct must conform to the established code; what really worried men was how to adjust their conduct to the novel circumstances which confronted them. When they discovered that those who professed to be moralists were continuing to deny that the novelty of modern things had any bearing upon human conduct, and that morality was a word signifying a return to usages which it was impossible to follow, even if it were desirable, there was a kind of tacit agreement to let the moralists be moral and to find other language in which to describe the difference between good and bad, right and wrong. Mr. Joad is not unrepresentative of this reaction into contempt when he speaks of "the dowagers, the aunts, the old maids, the parsons, the town councillors, the clerks, the members of vigilance committees and purity leagues, all those who are themselves too old to enjoy sex, too unattractive to obtain what they would wish to enjoy, or too respectable to prefer enjoyment to respectability." Thus for many the name of moralist came to be very nearly synonymous with antipathy to the genius and the vitality of the modern age.

But it is idle for moralists to ascribe the decline of their influence to the perversity of their fellow creatures. The phenomenon is world-wide. Moreover, it is most intensely present at precisely those points where the effect of science and the machine technology have been most thoroughly manifested. The moralists are not confronted with a scandal but with history. They have to come to terms with a process in the life of mankind which is working upon the inner springs of being and altering inevitably the premises of conduct. They need not suppose that their pews are empty and that their exhortations are ignored because modern men are really as wilful as the manners of the younger generation lead them to conclude. Much of what appears to be a tough self-sufficiency is protective: it is a brittle crust covering depths of uncertainty. If the advice of moralists is ignored, it is not because this generation is too proud to listen, or unaware that it has anything to learn. On the contrary there is such curiosity and questioning as never before engaged so large a number of men. The audience to which a genuine moralist might speak is there. If it is inattentive when the orthodox moralist speaks, it is because he seems to speak irrelevantly.

The trouble with the moralists is in the moralists themselves: they have failed to understand their times. They think they are dealing with a generation that refuses to believe in ancient authority. They are, in fact, dealing with a generation that cannot believe in it. They think they are confronted with men who have an irrational preference for immorality, whereas the men and women about them are ridden by doubts because they do not know what they prefer, nor why. The moralists fancy that they are standing upon the rock of eternal truth, surveying the chaos about them. They are greatly mistaken. Nothing in the modern world is more chaotic—not its politics, its business, or its sexual relations—than the minds of ortho-dox moralists who suppose that the problem of morals is somehow to find a way of reinforcing the sanctions which are dissolving. How can we, they say in effect, find for-mulas and rhetoric potent enough to make men behave? How can we revive in them that love and fear of God, that sense of the creature's dependence upon his creator, that obedience to the commands of a heavenly king, which once gave force and effect to the moral code?

They have misconceived the moral problem, and there-fore they misconceive the function of the moralist. An authoritative code of morals has force and effect when it expresses the settled customs of a stable society: the pharisee can impose upon the minority only such conven-tions as the majority find appropriate and necessary. But when customs are unsettled, as they are in the modern world, by continual change in the circumstances of life, the pharisee is helpless. He cannot command with authority because his commands no longer imply the usages of the community: they express the prejudices of the moralist rather than the practices of men. When that happens, it is presumptuous to issue moral commandments, for in fact nobody has authority to command. It is useless to command when nobody has the disposition to obey. It is futile when nobody really knows exactly what to command. In such societies, wherever they have appeared among civilized men, the moralist has ceased to be an administrator of usages and has had to become an interpreter of human needs. For ages when custom is unsettled are necessarily ages of prophecy. The moralist cannot teach what is revealed; he must reveal what can be taught. He has to seek insight rather than to preach.

The disesteem into which moralists have fallen is due at bottom to their failure to see that in an age like this one the function of the moralist is not to exhort men to be good but to elucidate what the good is. The problem of sanctions is secondary. For sanctions cannot be artificially constructed: they are a product of agreement and usage. Where no agreement exists, where no usages are established, where ideals are not clarified and where conventions are not followed comfortably by the mass of men, there are not, and cannot be, sanctions. It is possible to command where most men are already obedient. But even the greatest general cannot discipline a whole army at once. It is only when the greater part of his army is with him that he can quell the mutiny of a faction.

The acids of modernity are dissolving the usages and the sanctions to which men once habitually conformed. It is therefore impossible for the moralist to command. He can only persuade. To persuade he must show that the course of conduct he advocates is not an arbitrary pattern to which vitality must submit, but that which vitality itself would choose if it were clearly understood. He must be able to show that goodness is victorious vitality and badness defeated vitality; that sin is the denial and virtue the fulfilment of the promise inherent in the purposes of men. The good, said the Greek moralist, is "that which all things aim at"; we may perhaps take this to mean that the good is that which men would wish to do if they knew what they were doing.

If the morality of the naive hedonist who blindly seeks the gratification of his instincts is irrational in that he trusts immature desire, disregards intelligence and damns the consequences, the morality of the pharisee is no less irrational. It reduces itself to the wholly arbitrary proposition that the best life for man would be some other kind of life than that which satisfies his nature. The true function of the moralist in an age when usage is unsettled is what Aristotle who lived in such an age described it to be: to promote good conduct by discovering and explaining the mark at which things aim. The moralist is irrelevant, if not meddlesome and dangerous, unless in his teaching he strives to give a true account, imaginatively conceived, of that which experience would show is desirable among the choices that are possible and necessary. If he is to be listened to, and if he is to deserve a hearing among his fellows, he must set himself this task which is so much humbler than to command and so much more difficult than to exhort: he must seek to anticipate and to supplement the insight of his fellow men into the problems of their adjustment to reality. He must find ways to make clear and ordered and expressive those concerns which are latent but overlaid and confused by their preoccupations and misunderstandings.

Could he do that with perfect lucidity he would not need to summon the police nor evoke the fear of hell: hell would be what it really is, and what in all inspired moralities it has always been understood to be, the very quality of evil itself. Nor would he find himself in the absurd predicament of seeming to argue that virtue is highly desirable but intensely unpleasant. It would not be necessary to praise goodness, for it would be that which men most ardently desired. Were the nature of good and evil really made plain by moralists, their teachings would appear to the modern listener not like exhortations from without, but as Keats said of poetry: "a wording of his own highest thoughts and . . . almost a remembrance."

2. *The Choice of a Way*

What modernity requires of the moralist is that he should see with an innocent eye how men must reform their wants in a world which is not concerned to make them happy. The problem, as I have tried to show, is not a new one. It has been faced and solved by the masters of wisdom. What is new is the scale on which the problem is presented—in that so many must face it now—and its radical character in that the organic bonds of custom and belief are dissolving. There ensues a continual necessity of adjusting their lives to complex novelty. In such a world simple customs are unsuitable and authoritative commandments incredible. No prescription can now be written which men can naively and obediently follow. They have, therefore, to reëducate their wants by an understanding of their own relation to a world which is unconcerned with their hopes and fears. From the moralists they can get only hypotheses—distillations of experience carefully examined—probabilities, that is to say, upon which they may begin to act, but which they themselves must constantly correct by their own insight.

It is difficult for the orthodox moralists to believe that amidst the ruins of authority men will ever learn to do this. They can point to the urban crowds and ask whether anyone supposes that such persons are capable of ordering their lives by so subtle an instrument as the human understanding. They can insist with unanswerable force that this is absurd: that the great mass of men must be guided by rules and moved by the symbols of hope and fear. And they can ask what there is in the conception of the moralist as I have outlined it which takes the character of the populace into account.

What I take into account first of all is the fact, which it seems to me is indisputable, that for the modern populace the old rules are becoming progressively unsuitable and the old symbols of hope and fear progressively unreal. I ascribe that to the inherent character of the modern ways of living. I conclude from this that if the populace must be led, if it must have easily comprehended rules, if it must have common symbols of hope and fear, the question is how are its leaders to be developed, rules to be worked out, symbols created. The ultimate question is not how the populace is to be ruled, but what the teachers are to think. That is the question that has to be settled first: it is the preface to everything else.

For while moralists are at sixes and sevens in their own

souls, not much can be done about morality, however high or low may be our estimates of the popular intelligence and character. If it were necessary to assume that ideals are relevant only if they are universally attainable, it would be a waste of time to discuss them. For it is evident enough that many, if not most men, must fail to comprehend what modern morality implies. But to recognize this is not to prophesy that the world is doomed unless men perform the miracle of reverting to their ancestral tradition. This is not the first time in the history of mankind when a revolution in the affairs of men has produced chaos in the human spirit. The world can endure a good deal of chaos. It always has. The ideal inherent in any age is never realized completely: Greece, which we like to idealize as an oasis of rationality, was only in some respects Hellenic; the Ages of Faith were only somewhat Christian. The processes of nature and of society go on somehow none the less. Men are born and they live and die with some happiness and some sorrow though they neither envisage wholly nor nearly approximate the ideals they pursue.

But if civilization is to be coherent and confident it must be *known* in that civilization what its ideals are. There must exist in the form of clearly available ideas an understanding of what the fulfilment of the promise of that civilization might mean, an imaginative conception of the good at which it might, and, if it is to flourish, at which it must aim. That knowledge, though no one has it perfectly, and though relatively few have it at all, is the principle of all order and certainty in the life of that people. By it they can clarify the practical conduct of life in some measure, and add immeasurably to its dignity.

To elucidate the ideals with which the modern world is pregnant is the original business of the moralist. Insofar as he succeeds in disentangling that which men think they believe from that which it is appropriate for them to believe, he is opening his mind to a true vision of the good life. The vision itself we can discern only faintly, for we have as yet only the occasional and fragmentary testimony of sages and saints and heroes, dim anticipations here and there, a most imperfect science of human behavior, and our own obscure endeavor to make explicit and rational the stresses of the modern world within our own souls. But we can begin to see, I think, that the evidence converges upon the theory that what the sages have prophesied as high religion, what psychologists delineate as matured personality, and the disinterestedness which the Great Society requires for its practical fulfilment, are all of a piece, and are the basic elements of a modern morality. I think the truth lies in this theory.

If it does, experience will enrich and refine it, and what is now an abstract principle arrived at by intuition and dialectic will engender ideas that marshal, illuminate, and anticipate the subtle and intricate detail of our actual experience. That at least can be our belief. In the meantime, the modern moralist cannot expect soon to construct a systematic and harmonious moral edifice like that which St. Thomas Aquinas and Dante constructed to house the aspirations of the mediæval world. He is in a much earlier phase in the evolution of his world, in the phase of inquiry and prophecy rather than of ordering and harmonizing, and he is under the necessity of remaining close to the elements of experience in order to apprehend them freshly. He cannot, therefore, permit the old symbols of faith and the old formulations of right and wrong to prejudice his insight. Insofar as they contain wisdom for him or can become its vehicles, he will return to them. But he cannot return to them with honor or with sincerity until he has himself gone and drunk deeply at the sources of experience from which they originated.

Only when he has done that can he again in any honest sense take possession of the wisdom which he inherits. It requires wisdom to understand wisdom; the music is nothing if the audience is deaf. In the great moral systems and the great religions of mankind are embedded the record of how men have dealt with destiny, and only the thoughtless will argue that that record is obsolete and insignificant. But it is overlaid with much that is obsolete and for that reason it is undeciphered and inexpressive. The wisdom it contains has to be discovered anew before the old symbols will yield up their meaning. That is the only way in which Bacon's aphorism can be fulfilled, that "a little philosophy inclineth man's mind to atheism, but depth in philosophy bringeth men's minds about to religion." The depth in philosophy which can bring them about is a much deeper and more poignant experience than complacent churchmen suppose.

It can be no mere settling back into that from which men in the ardor of their youth escaped. This man and that may settle back, to be sure; he may cease to inquire though his questions are unanswered. But such conformity is sterile, and due to mere weariness of mind and body. The inquiry goes on because it has to go on, and while the vitality of our race is unimpaired, there will be men who feel with Mr. Whitehead that "to acquiesce in discrepancy is destructive of candor and of moral cleanliness," and that "it belongs to the self-respect of intellect to pursue every tangle of thought to its final unravelment." The crisis in the religious loyalties of mankind cannot be resolved by weariness and good nature, or by the invention of little intellectual devices for straightening out the dilemmas of biology and Genesis, history and the Gospels with which so many churchmen busy themselves. Beneath these little conflicts there is a real dilemma which modern men cannot successfully evade. "Where is the way where light dwelleth?" They are compelled to choose consciously, clearly, and with full realization of what the choice implies, between religion as a system of cosmic government and religion as insight into a cleansed and matured personality: between God conceived as the master of that fate, creator, providence, and king, and God conceived as the highest good at which they might aim. For God is the supreme symbol in which man expresses his destiny, and if that symbol is confused, his life is confused.

Men have not, hitherto, had to make that choice, for the historic churches have sheltered both kinds of religious experience, and the same mysteries have been the symbols of both. That confusion is no longer benign because men are no longer unconscious of it. They are aware that it is a confusion, and they are stultified by it. Because the popular religion of supernatural governments is undermined, the symbols of religion do not provide clear channels for religious experience. They are choked with the debris of dead notions in which men are unable to believe and unwilling to disbelieve. The result is a frustration in the inner life which will persist as long as the leaders of thought speak of God in more senses than one, and thus render all faith invalid, insincere, and faltering.

3. *The Religion of the Spirit*

The choice is at last a personal one. The decision is rendered not by argument but by feeling. Those who believe that their salvation lies in obedience to, and communion with, the King of Creation can know how whole-hearted their faith is by the confidence of their own hearts. If they are at peace, they need inquire no further. There are, however, those who do not find a principle of order in the belief that they are related to a supernatural power. They cannot be argued into the ancient belief, for it has been dissolved by the circumstances of their lives. They are deeply perplexed. They have learned that the absence of belief is vacancy; they know, from disillusionment and anxiety, that there is no freedom in mere freedom. They must find, then, some other principle which will give coherence and direction to their lives.

If the argument in these pages is sound, they need not look for and, in fact, cannot hope for, some new and unexpected revelation. Since they are unable to find a principle of order in the authority of a will outside themselves, there is no place they can find it except in an ideal of the human personality. But they do not have to invent such an ideal out of hand. The ideal way of life for men who must make their own terms with experience and find their own happiness has been stated again and again. It is that only the regenerate, the disinterested, the mature, can make use of freedom. This is the central insight of the teachers of wisdom. We can see now, I think, that it is also the mark at which the modern study of human nature points. We can see, too, that it is the pattern of successful conduct in the most advanced phases of the development of modern civilization. The ideal, then, is an old one, but its confirmation and its practical pertinence are new. The world is able at last to take seriously what its greatest teachers have said. And since all things need a name, if they are to be talked about, devotion to this ideal may properly be called by the name which these greatest teachers gave it; it may be called the religion of the spirit. At the heart of it is the knowledge that the goal of human effort is to be able, in the words I have so often quoted from Confucius, to follow what the heart desires without transgressing what is right.

In an age when custom is dissolved and authority is broken, the religion of the spirit is not merely a possible way of life. In principle it is the only way which transcends the difficulties. It alone is perfectly neutral about the constitution of the universe, in that it has no expectation that the universe will justify naive desire. Therefore, the progress of science cannot upset it. Its indifference to what the facts may be is indeed the very spirit of scientific inquiry. A religion which rests upon particular conclusions in astronomy, biology, and history may be fatally injured by the discovery of new truths. But the religion of the spirit does not depend upon creeds and cosmologies; it has no vested interest in any particular truth. It is concerned not with the organization of matter, but with the quality of human desire.

It alone can endure the variety and complexity of things, for the religion of the spirit has no thesis to defend. It seeks excellence wherever it may appear, and finds it in anything which is inwardly understood; its motive is not acquisition but sympathy. Whatever is completely understood with sympathy for its own logic and purposes ceases to be external and stubborn and is wholly tamed. To understand is not only to pardon, but in the end to love. There is no itch in the religion of the spirit to make men good by bearing down upon them with righteousness and making them conform to a pattern. Its social principle is to live and let live. It has the only tolerable code of manners for a society in which men and women have become freely-moving individuals, no longer held in the grooves of custom by their ancestral ways. It is the only disposition of the soul which meets the moral difficulties of an anarchical age, for its principle is to civilize the passions, not by regulating them imperiously, but by transforming them with a mature understanding of their place in an adult environment. It is the only possible hygiene of the soul for men whose selves have become disjointed by the loss of their central certainties, because it counsels them to draw the sting of possessiveness out of their passions, and thus by removing anxiety to render them harmonious and serene.

The philosophy of the spirit is an almost exact reversal of the worldling's philosophy. The ordinary man believes that he will be blessed if he is virtuous, and therefore virtue seems to him a price he pays now for a blessedness he will some day enjoy. While he is waiting for his reward, therefore, virtue seems to him drab, arbitrary, and meaningless. For the reward is deferred, and there is really no instant proof that virtue really leads to the happiness he has been promised. Because the reward is deferred, it too becomes vague and dubious, for that which we never experience, we cannot truly understand. In the realm of the spirit, blessedness is not deferred: there is no future which is more auspicious than the present; there are no compensations later for evils now. Evil is to be overcome now and happiness is to be achieved now, for the kingdom of God is within you. The life of the spirit is not a commercial transaction in which the profit has to be anticipated; it is a kind of experience which is inherently profitable.

And so the mature man would take the world as it comes, and within himself remain quite unperturbed. When he acted, he would know that he was only testing an hypothesis, and if he failed, he would know that he had made a mistake. He would be quite prepared for the discovery that he might make mistakes, for his intelligence would be disentangled from his hopes. The failure of his experiment could not, therefore, involve the failure of his life. For the aspect of life which implicated his soul would be his understanding of life, and, to the understanding, defeat is no less interesting than victory. It would be no effort, therefore, for him to be tolerant, and no annoyance to be skeptical. He would face pain with fortitude, for he would have put it away from the inner chambers of his soul. Fear would not haunt him, for he would be without compulsion to seize anything and without anxiety as to its fate. He would be strong, not with the strength of hard resolves, but because he was free of that tension which vain expectations beget. Would his life be uninteresting because he was disinterested? He would have the whole universe, rather than the prison of his own hopes and fears, for his habitation, and in imagination all possible forms of being. How could that be dull unless he brought the dullness with him? He might dwell with all beauty and all knowledge, and they are inexhaustible. Would he, then, dream idle dreams? Only if he chose to. For he might go quite simply about the business of the world, a good deal more effec ively perhaps than the worldling, in that he did not pl   absolute value upon it, and deceive himself. Would   hopeful? Not if to be hopeful was to expect the   submit rather soon to his vanity. Would he be hop   s? Hope is an expectation of favors to come, and he would take his delights here and now. Since nothing gnawed at his vitals, neither doubt nor ambition, nor frustration, nor fear, he would move easily through life. And so whether he saw the thing as comedy, or high tragedy, or plain farce, he would affirm that it is what it is, and that the wise man can enjoy it.

APPENDIX

ACKNOWLEDGMENTS

AT the suggestion of the publishers, the references which follow have been segregated in an appendix instead of being scattered as footnotes through the text. They felt, rightly enough, I think, that in a book of this character the purpose of the notes was to acknowledge indebtedness for the material cited rather than to support the argument, and that the reader would prefer not to have the text encumbered by the apparatus of a kind of scholarship to which the author makes no pretensions.

While these notes, except in a few instances, refer only to matter actually used in the text, they are also an approximate bibliography of the works which I have consulted. I wish I could adequately acknowledge the obligation I owe to my teachers, William James, George Santayana, and Graham Wallas, though that perhaps is self-evident. I should like to thank Miss Jane Mather and Miss Orrie Lashin for help in the preparation of the manuscript. I am under special obligation to my wife, Faye Lippmann, without whose assistance I could not have completed the book.

W. L.

New York City, January, 1929.

[331]

NOTES

PAGE LINE

4   32   Quoted in Irving Babbitt, *Rousseau and Romanticism*, p. 181.

5   4   John Herman Randall Jr., *The Making of the Modern Mind*, p. 118.

5   21   From *The City of Dreadful Night*, cited, Babbitt, op. cit., p. 332.

5   24   For discussion of this theme, cf. Babbitt, op. cit. passim.

5   29   Shelley, *Prometheus Unbound*, Act III, Scene IV.

6   12   From Byron, *The Island*, cited, Babbitt, op. cit., p. 186.

6   16   From T. H. Huxley, *Address on University Education*, delivered, 1876, at the formal opening of Johns Hopkins University. I am indebted to Mr. Henry Hazlitt for the quotation.

7   11   Cited, Babbitt, op. cit., p. 341.

7   20   Nietzsche, *Thus Spake Zarathustra*, LXIX, cited, Babbitt, op. cit., p. 261.

11 12   Cf. W. R. Inge, *The Platonic Tradition in English Religious Thought*.

11 19   W. C. Greene, Introduction to Selection from the *Dialogues of Plato*, p. xxiv.

13 27   Calvin, *Institutes*, Book IV, Chapter X, Paragraph 7, cited A. C. M'Giffert, *Protestant Thought Before Kant*, p. 90.

21 32   Harry Emerson Fosdick, *Adventurous Religion*, p. 59.

24 8   W. C. Brownell, Scribner's Magazine, Vol. XXX, p. 112, cited in footnote, William James, *The Varieties of Religious Experience*, p. 115.

24 25   William James, *The Varieties of Religious Experience*, p. 518.

25 12   James, op. cit., p. 519.

26 7   Alfred North Whitehead, *Science and the Modern World*, pp. 249-250.

27 12   Bettrand Russell, *A Free Man's Worship*, in *Mysticism and Logic*, p. 54.

27 27   Kirsopp Lake, *The Religion of Yesterday and Tomorrow*.

30 2   W. R. Inge, *Science, Religion and Reality*, p. 388.

NOTES

PAGE LINE

31   3   Cf. W. B. Riley, *The Faith of the Fundamentalists,* Times Current History, June, 1927.

34   18   *Fundamentalism and the Faith,* Commonweal, Aug. 19, 1925.

35   25   George Santayana, *Reason in Religion,* p. 97.

37   22   The material in this section is taken from Harry Emerson Fosdick, *The Modern Use of the Bible.*

40   2   Fosdick, op. cit., p. 83.

42   5   Fosdick, *The Desire for Immortality,* in *Adventurous Religion.*

44   10   W. R. Inge, *The Philosophy of Plotinus,* Vol. II, p. 166.

44   23   W. R. Inge, *The Platonic Tradition in English Religious Thought.*

47   30   Fosdick, *The Modern Use of the Bible.*

51   22   Cf. Rudolf Otto, *Chrysostom on the Inconceivable in God,* in *The Idea of the Holy.* Appendix I; cf. also the *Catholic Encyclopedia,* Vol. VIII, p. 452; cf. also William James, *The Varieties of Religious Experience,* Lecture III.

56   21   Lord Acton, inaugural *Lecture on the Study of History,* in *Lectures on Modern History.*

70   29   Otto Gierke, *Political Theories of the Middle Ages*—Translated by F. W. Maitland, p. 7.

71   14   From the Song of Roland, cited, Henry Adams, *Mont-Saint-Michel and Chartres,* p. 29.

72   18   For an analysis of the texts on which this claim was based, cf. James T. Shotwell and Louise Ropes Loomis, *The See of Peter.*

73   18   Cited in A. C. M'Giffert, *Protestant Thought Before Kant,* p. 44.

74   7   For a comprehensive condemnation by the Holy See of modern opinions which undermine the authority of the Roman Catholic Church, see the Syllabus of Pius IX (1864) and the Syllabus of Pius X (1907). The Syllabus of 1864 lists and condemns eighty principal errors of our time, and is described by the Catholic Encyclopedia (Vol. XIV, p. 369) as opposition "to the high tide of that intellectual movement of the Nineteenth Century which strove to sweep away the foundations of all human and Divine order." The Syllabus of 1907 condemns sixty-five propositions of the Modernists which would "destroy the foundations of all natural and supernatural knowledge." (Catholic Encyclopedia, Vol. XIV,

NOTES

[334]

NOTES

PAGE	LINE	
119	28	Cf. *Catholic Encyclopedia*, Vol. X, p. 342.
123	17	Whitehead, *Science and the Modern World*, p. 257.
127	2	A. S. Eddington, *Stars and Atoms*, p. 121.
128	1	John Herman Randall Jr., *The Making of the Modern Mind*, p. 100.
128	9	*Epist. ad Can Grand*, cited in footnote to *Paradiso* in the Temple Classics.
129	3	Cf. P. W. Bridgman, *The Logic of Modern Physics*, p. 45.
129	23	C. S. Peirce, *How to Make Our Ideas Clear in Chance, Love and Logic*, edited by Morris R. Cohen.
130	4	Bridgman, op. cit., p. 38.
135	2	Cited L. R. Farnell, *The Attributes of God*, p. 275.
137	31	Cf. M. C. Otto, *Natural Laws and Human Hopes*, pp. 32 et seq.
146	29	The *Catholic Encyclopedia*, Vol. XII, p. 345.
147	29	Cf. B. L. Manning, *The People's Faith in the Time of Wyclif*.
148	3	Fosdick, *Adventurous Religion*, p. 85 et seq.
148	9	Santayana, *Reason in Religion*, p. 43.
148	17	L. R. Farnell, *The Attributes of God*, p. 15.
149	14	Manning, op. cit.
159	2	Herbert Asbury, *A Methodist Saint, The Life of Bishop Asbury*, p. 265.
160	20	Cf. *Encyclopedia Britannica*, "Asceticism."
161	17	Cf. *Catholic Encyclopedia*, Vol. I, p. 768.
162	5	Quoted in Irving Babbitt, *Rousseau and Romanticism*, p. 45.
162	19	*Rabelais*, Book II, Chapter 34.
163	6	Cited Henry Osborn Taylor, *Thought and Expression in the Sixteenth Century*, Vol. I, p. 330.
163	25	Babbitt, op. cit., p. 161.
163	28	Cf. Dora Russell, *The Right to be Happy*.
164	5	Cf. Bertrand Russell, *Political Ideals*.
165	17	T. W. Rhys Davids, *Buddhism*, p. 111.
166	22	*Ethics*, Book II, Chapter 9.
177	3	S. Freud, *Formulierung über die zwei Prinzipien des psychischen Geschehens*, 1911, Jahrb, Bd., I, s. 411.
177	10	S. Ferenczi, *Stages in the Development of the Sense of Reality*, 1913. In *Contributions to Psychoanalysis*, translated by Dr. Ernest Jones.
192	13	Spinoza, *Ethics*, Part V, Prop. XLII.
192	23	Cf. T. W. Rhys Davids, *Buddhism*, p. 110.
192	31	*Confucian Analects*, Book II, Chapter 4.
195	25	A. N. Whitehead, *Religion in the Making*, pp. 15-16.

NOTES

NOTES

PAGE LINE

288   6   Genesis XXXVIII; cf. Harold Cox, *The Problem of Population*, pp. 208-211, for an interpretation of the story of Onan in the light of Deut. XXV, which shows that the crime of Onan was not the spilling of his seed, but a breach of Jewish tribal law in refusing "to perform the duty of a husband's brother" with his brother's widow.

289   1   Psalm 127, cf. Cox, op. cit.

289   9   The historical data are from A. M. Carr-Saunders, *The Population Problem*, Chapter I.

295   6   Havelock Ellis, *Love as an Art*, in Count Hermann Keyserling's *The Book of Marriage*, p. 388.

295   21   Santayana, *The Life of Reason*, Vol. II, p. 10.

297   3   C. E. M. Joad, *Thrasymachus, or The Future of Morals*, pp. 54-55.

297   15   Havelock Ellis, *The Family*, in *Whither Mankind*, p. 216.

299   4   Quoted in Judge Ben B. Lindsey and Wainwright Evans, *The Companionate Marriage*, p. 210.

302   18   Cf. Alfred Weber, *History of Philosophy*, p. 72.

304   24   *Love—Or the Life and Death of a Value*, Atlantic Monthly, August, 1928.

310   14   *Reason in Society*, p. 22.

313   6   W. R. Inge, *The Philosophy of Plotinus*, Vol. II, p. 161.

320   15   John Keats, Letters to John Taylor, Feb. 27, 1818—in *Oxford Book of English Prose*, No. 379.

INDEX

INDEX

INDEX

[342]

INDEX

INDEX

Lindsey, Judge, 298, 307
Locke, 266
Love, art of, 293, 295, 301, 303, 305, 308-309; value of, 302-304, 306, 310
Lowell Lectures, 25
Loyalty, 261-263, 268-269, 272, 325
Lucretius, 218
Luther, 13, 14-15, 39, 53-54, 73-74, 79, 196
Lutheran Church, 13
Lutherans, 77

Machen, Prof. J. Gresham, 32, 33-34
Machine process, 246, 253-254, 274
Machine technology, 242-243, 247, 251, 252, 254, 257, 258-259, 274, 284, 316
Mâle, 100, 101
Malthus, 289
Manichæans, 52
Man, nature of, 152, 243
Manner of life, 235
Markets, 246-247
Marriage, 89, 286, 288, 289, 291, 309, 310-311, 312; companionate, 298, 307
Marxianism, 16
Mary, St. *See* Virgin Mary.
Masses, 148-149, 278
Matriarchal societies, 91
Maturity, 174-175, 176-177, 179-180, 183-184, 185, 186, 189, 190, 191-192, 204, 209, 225, 230, 237, 239, 313, 323, 325, 327, 328-329
Maxwell, 240
Mazzini, 18
Meaning of things, 183
Mechanism, 125, 128, 130-131
Medical progress, 218
Melanchthon, 79
Mencken, H. L., 13, 16
Mendel's law, 231
Messianic Kingdom, 11
Methodism, 6; American, 158
Mexico, 253, 265

Middle Ages, 70-72, 73, 94, 129, 131, 161, 265, 266
Mill, James, 289
Milton, 74, 266
Minority, recalcitrant, 279
Miracles, 118, 119-120
Mississippi flood, 273-274
Modernism, 18, 32, 33, 59, 77, 117, 217
Modernists, 27, 28, 29, 31, 32, 35, 42, 51
Modernity, 5, 8, 14, 15, 19, 56, 68, 96, 105, 110, 112, 143, 158, 196-197, 208, 229, 251, 284, 316, 318, 320, 321
Modern man, 4, 8-10, 12, 19, 21, 24, 40, 41, 51, 54, 57, 59, 94, 111, 112, 113, 114, 152, 153, 158, 161, 194, 203, 227-228, 315, 316
Modern men. *See* Modern man.
Modern Movement in Art, The, 104
Modern spirit, 36, 110, 143
Modern state, 260, 262-263, 267, 272-273, 275, 279, 311
Modern world, 14, 19, 20, 268-269, 270, 300, 311, 322-324
Mohammed, 145
Mohammedanism, 199
Monasticism, 204-206
Montaigne, 48, 175, 196
Moral certainty, 9-10, 15, 115
Moral codes, 3, 49, 135, 167, 170, 171, 201, 208-209, 226, 228, 272, 317, 319
Moral confusion, 155, 228, 230
Moral effect, 179-180
Moral effort, 175
Moral guidance, 14, 205
Moral insight, 227-228, 229
Moralists, 164, 165, 166, 167, 170, 172, 173, 208-209, 225, 244, 300, 314-315, 316-319, 320-321, 323
Morality, 114-115, 117, 136, 137-139, 145; divine, 49-50; sanctions of, 78, 166, 176, 228; theistic, 138. *See also* Morals.
Moral law, 46, 48, 191, 233

INDEX

Plot, John, 149
Plotinus, 155
Political conduct, 264-265, 284
Political machine, 264
Politician, the, 279-282
Pope, the, 13, 15, 72, 79, 81, 85, 265, 270-271
Pope Innocent IV, 85
Pope Paul V, 81
Pope Pius IX, 75
Population, growth of, 289-291
Post-Darwinians, 18
Pragmatism, 119
Prayer, 146-149
Pre-machine age, 253
Presbyterians, 79
Priesthood, 73
Primitive peoples, 159
Procreation, 166
Progress, religion of, 18
Prohibition, 31, 277
Propaganda, 281
Prophet, artist as, 101-102, 103, 104
Prophets, 12
Protestantism, 15, 30, 32, 34, 52, 77, 86
Protestants, 34-35
Pseudo-religions, 125
Psychiatry, 158, 159
Psychoanalysis, 6, 125, 174, 177, 179, 220
Psychology, 143, 171, 172, 173, 174, 220; abnormal, 171; folk, 171; popular, 114; scientific, 173, 176
Public interest, 257-258
Public opinion, 167
Public schools, 76-77
Public utilities, regulation of, 254-255
Purgatory, 146
Puritanism, 154, 302
Purpose, cosmic, 9
Pythagoras, 204-205

Rabelais, 161, 162-163
Randall, Dr., 127-128
Rationalists, 24-25
Rationalization, 39

Reality, 177, 179, 180, 193, 216, 272, 312, 319
Reason and faith, 51, 121
Rebellion, 16-17, 19, 190
Rebels, 15-18, 19
Reconstruction, essays in, 14
Redemption, 11, 115
Reformation, 13, 72-73, 94, 154
Reformers, Eighteenth-Century, 15; Protestant, 34, 39, 40, 73, 96
Relative motion, 124
Religion, 8, 10, 17, 18-19, 23, 112, 123, 131, 284, 324; aristocracy in, 197, 200, 202, 203; need of, 123; of the spirit, 44, 46, 196-197, 203, 205-206, 327-328; popular, 14, 32-33, 47, 50, 69, 91, 94, 127, 131-132, 143, 145, 176, 194, 195-196, 201, 202, 208, 216, 227, 232, 244, 325 (*See also* Theology, popular); traditional, 122, 124, 203
Religious experience, 33, 90-91, 125, 325-326
Religious synthesis, 111, 124
Religious thought, 96
Religious wars, 74
Religious writing, 97
Renaissance, 94-95, 161; High, 154
Renan, 7
Renunciation, 45, 156, 157, 191, 192, 206
Republic, 159-160
Revelation, 124, 126, 127, 133, 134, 135, 136, 137, 143, 318, 326; logic of, 121; sense of, 13
Revivals, 14
Revolution, French, 289; industrial, 210, 248; mechanical, 19, 234, 236, 241, 248, 289; Russian, 250-251; spiritual, 133-134
Rewards and punishments, 201, 202, 213
Riggs, Father, 34
Righteousness, sense of, 16
Right of revolution, 82
Right to believe, 25
Rights of men, 242, 267
Roland, 71

[346]

INDEX